Organization and Insignia of the American Expeditionary Force 1917-1923

TO HELL WITH THE KAISER

Organization and Insignia of the American Expeditionary Force 1917-1923

Robert J. Dalessandro and Michael G. Knapp

Insignia photography by William Keller and Kurt Keller

Schiffer Military History
Atglen, PA

Acknowledgments

This project could never have been possible without the resources of the Army Heritage and Education Center at Carlisle Barracks, Pennsylvania. The matchless collections of both the Military History Institute and the Army Heritage Museum provided the authors endless opportunities to understand the complexities of the American Expeditionary Force and the American Army in general. Three-time Pulitzer Prize winning author, Rick Atkinson best characterized this collection as, "a national treasure beyond value." We certainly agree. The staff of the Army Heritage and Education Center was ever helpful – our particular thanks go out to the Patron Services Division of Military History Institute, Dr. Con Crane's fine organization, particularly Dr. Richard "Dick" Sommers, Art Bergeron, Rich Baker, the professionals of Historical Services Division, Louise Arnold-Friend, and Randy Hackenberg. Roger Durham, Jay Graybeal, Chris Semancik and Ryan Meyer from the Army Heritage Museum were of immeasurable help to the project always willing to go the extra mile. A special thanks to Courtney Peter, the Publications Coordinator for the Daughters of the American Revolution Magazine, for helping us sort out the use of the Army Air Service Squadron insignia. Numerous collectors provided advice and made their personal collections available to us for our research into the insignia of the AEF. Gus Radle, Dave Johnson, Steve Johnson, and Dan Griffin have been particularly helpful. We are appreciative of the typing support we were given by Teresa Highlands; grateful thanks to our wives Rebecca Dalessandro and Amy Knapp for the exquisite proofreading support and to Captain Ginger Shaw for her superior Power Point chart making expertise. A special thanks to Lieutenant Colonel Jerry Torrence for his support to this project and his outstanding leadership, organizational abilities and friendship. People like Jerry really make our world a better place by making a difference every day. Finally thanks to our Editor, Bob Biondi for his help and advice.

Dedication

To those who inspire future generations of Americans and to the men and women of the Armed Services who have put their lives on the line for over 230 years so that the American people might enjoy their freedom.

• • •

"Those who long enjoyed such priviledges as we enjoy forget in time that men have died to win them."
— Franklin D. Roosevelt.

Book design by Robert Biondi.

Library of Congress Catalog Number: 2007942664.

Printed in China.
ISBN: 978-0-7643-2937-1

We are always looking for people to write books on new and related subjects. If you have an idea for a book, please contact us at the address below.

Published by Schiffer Publishing Ltd.
4880 Lower Valley Road
Atglen, PA 19310
Phone: (610) 593-1777
FAX: (610) 593-2002
E-mail: Info@schifferbooks.com.
Visit our web site at: www.schifferbooks.com
Please write for a free catalog.
This book may be purchased from the publisher.
Please include $3.95 postage.
Try your bookstore first.

In Europe, Schiffer books are distributed by:
Bushwood Books
6 Marksbury Ave.
Kew Gardens, Surrey TW9 4JF
England
Phone: 44 (0)20 8392-8585
FAX: 44 (0)20 8392-9876
E-mail: info@bushwoodbooks.co.uk
www.bushwoodbooks.co.uk
Free postage in the UK. Europe: air mail at cost.
Try your bookstore first.

CONTENTS

INTRODUCTION

For Americans accustomed to a large standing military, it is hard to believe that on the eve of American entry into World War One the United States Army was still operating under the mid-nineteenth century concept of organization. The storied divisions imprinted forever in the pages of the American military history had yet to come into being. The names of units that would become household words later in the twentieth century were still unknown – the Big Red One, 1st Infantry Division, the Screaming Eagles, 101st Infantry Division or the Rainbow Division, 42nd Infantry Division, were all in the distant future.

By the late nineteenth century, the Army was still patterned on the Civil War organizational model, which ran from the company level and rose in strength up to Army level. During this period, the company functioned as the basic building block for all organizations. A company had just over 100 soldiers assigned with a captain in command; ten companies formed the regiment under the charge of a colonel.

Above the regimental level there was some degree of flexibility – normally, three to five regiments formed the brigade commanded by a more senior colonel or in some cases a Brigadier General. Three to five brigades comprised a division commanded by a Major General and three to five divisions produced a corps. Above the corps level, the pattern changed with no set number of corps forming an Army.

As an example, on the eve of the battle of Chickamauga, the Army of the Cumberland, the principal Federal operating army in the Western Theater of the Civil War, had four infantry and a cavalry corps; while at the battle of Gettysburg, the Army of the Potomac had seven infantry and one cavalry corps.

This structure would change as a result of the lessons of the War with Spain in 1898. The Army drew heavy criticism on its inflexible structure and lackluster execution of mobilization. As a result, then Secretary of War Elihu Root directed a series of studies that would transform both staff procedures and organization of the Army.

The National Defense Act of 1916, the Baker Board and decisions of the War Department and General Pershing, recast the Army on the eve of deployment to Europe. These decisions brought the fledgling United States Army into the Twentieth Century.

By late 1917, the Army of the United States and consequently its fighting arm, the American Expeditionary Force, was composed of three major components: the Regular Army, the National Guard and the National Army. The Regular Army was to incorporate those longstanding regiments; the full time soldiers of the Army, the National Guard would incorporate the state regiments and the divisions formed for the emergency on the Mexican Border, and a new arm, the National Army was created to accommodate the huge number of conscripts resultant of the Selective Service Act. [A detailed discussion of the planning, fielding and development of the divisional structure of the period can be found in John B. Wilson, *Maneuver and Firepower, The Evolution of Divisions and Separate Brigades*. Washington, DC: Center of Military History, 1998]

In the end, this envisioned structure never fully materialized. Shortages in personnel and equipment and pressure to field an army in Europe quickly by the Allies, forced the deployment of a field army largely composed of mixed units at all levels with less regard for uniformity.

This compilation will act as a resource for better understanding the organization, structure, operations and assignment of the forces that comprised the American Expeditionary Force and the Occupation Forces from 1917-1923.

In this work we have assembled a compendium of information from numerous, diverse, scarce and out of print primary sources. The division combat and service narratives are from a typescript publication *Brief Histories of Divisions, U.S. Army 1917-1918*. This study prepared in the Historical Branch of the War Plans Division of the Army General Staff in June of 1921, was never intended for commercial publication, and as such extant copies are extremely difficult to find. We made the decision to publish the summary of division operations from this pamphlet without any changes to the text aside from correcting errors in spelling. We felt these capsule histories best represented the War Department position on the contributions of the combat divisions in the period immediately following the Armistice. Likewise, the combat summaries used for the Air Service squadrons come from a contemporary source. The War Department prepared a concise summary of operations for each of the American squadrons assigned to the AEF. This work appears in the Daughters of the American Revolution Magazine Volume LIV, Number 3, March 1920. Once again, these appear in our work largely unedited. Other information is extracted from the pertinent authority publications. As an example, the description of Camp Pontanezen is extracted directly from *The Medical Department of the United States in the World War*, 1923.

In many instances, we chose to use the spellings of places and individuals as they would have been in the period 1917-1923. While this generally should not present any problems to the researcher, some smaller towns may, over time, have been subsumed into larger communities.

In addition to great changes in structure, this period also saw the birth of the storied divisional shoulder sleeve insignia so readily recognizable today. Insignia used to distinguish soldiers on the battlefield was not new in the American tradition. Upon assuming command of the Army of the Potomac, Major General Joseph Hooker devised a series of corps and division insignia that he felt would be useful in identifying stragglers on the battlefield and returning them to their proper unit. The system used a series of simple geometric designs for the corps, color coded to designate subordinate divisions. As an example, the First Corps, Army of the Potomac, wore a disc as the corps emblem. This disc was coded red for 1st division, 1st Corps, white for 2nd division, blue for 3rd division and had there been a 4th division assigned to the corps it would have worn a green badge.

These insignia quickly became a treasured part of unit identity adding to the organizational esprit de corps. So important were these insignias to the veteran soldier by the end of the war that every corps badge appears on the obverse of the Grand Army of the Republic membership medal.

After the Civil War, massive reductions in Army strength saw the corps and division of the Civil War period dissolve - with them went the use of their insignia. In 1898, the brief War with Spain saw a temporal revival of the corps badge system, however the limited duration of the war never allowed for the codification and enduring use.

When the American Expeditionary Force arrived in Europe, they saw the British Army using a plethora of insignia to distinguish units and special troops on the battlefield. First used with the massive volunteer armies of the Kitchner Battalions of 1915, these had evolved from simple geometric shapes and color combinations, to elaborate embroidered highly symbolic patches.

It was only natural that unit level insignia would appear in the American Expeditionary Force. By some accounts, it was the 81st Division that started the trend when they showed up for embarkation with the "Wildcat" patch on their shoulders. Whoever was responsible, by the end of the war, shoulder sleeve insignia was universal with hundreds of separate and distinct designs. This book will not attempt to catalog every example, but will serve to illuminate most of the common patterns, including the rationale, symbolism, and design.

Lastly, we included an extensive bibliography of known sources on the individual regiments as an aid to researchers. We hope that this body of material will serve as a ready source and starting point for future study of the American Expeditionary Force.

Robert J. Dalessandro & Michael G. Knapp,
Carlisle, Pennsylvania 2007

Abbreviations

BHD	*Brief Histories of Divisions, U.S. Army 1917-1918,* 1921.
GO34	Headquarters, First Army, AEF, General Order Number 34, 1918.
AABE	*American Armies and Battlefields in Europe*, 1938.
Campbell	*Aviation Badges and Insignia of the United States Army 1913-1946,* 1977.
OB	*Order of Battle of the United States Land Forces in the World War,* 1931.
Castelbled	*History of the AEF,* 1937.
Farrow	*A Dictionary of Military Terms,* 1918.
Keller and Keller	*United States Shoulder Patches and Related Insignia World War I to Korea, 1st to 40th Division,* 2001.
Keller and Keller	*United States Shoulder Patches and Related Insignia World War I to Korea, 41st to 106th Division,* 2002.
Morgan	*Shoulder Sleeve Insignia of the A.E.F. 1917-1919,* 1986.
OAEF	*United States Army in the World War, 1917-1919, Organization of the American Expeditionary Forces,* 1988.
BPOAEF	*Battle Participation of Organizations of the American Expeditionary Forces in France, Belgium and Italy 1917-1918,* 1920.
Wilson	*Armies, Corps, Divisions, and Separate Brigades,* 1993.
JBW	*Maneuver and Firepower The Evolution of Divisions and Separate Brigades,* 1998.
National Geographic	*National Geographic Magazine,* volume XXXVI.
CP	*Cloth Patch of the U.S. Armed Forces: Divisions,* 1968.
Military Images	*Military Images*, volume XXVII.

THE GENERAL HEADQUARTERS, AMERICAN EXPEDITIONARY FORCE, AND SERVICES OF SUPPLY

American and French sentries on duty at the gates to AEF GHQ, Chaumont, France, 1918. Courtesy National Archives

Opposite
Top left: French Prime Minister, Georges Clemenceau, and General John J. Pershing review the Guard of Honor at AEF GHQ, Chaumont, France, June 23rd, 1918. Courtesy National Archives

Top right: "Hello Girls" American Signal Corps telephone operators L. Provost, Minerva Nadeau, Marie Gagnon, and Rose Langlier enter the gates to AEF GHQ, Chaumont, France, April, 1918. Courtesy National Archives

Bottom: AEF General Headquarters, Chaumont, France. Courtesy National Archives

General Headquarters, American Expeditionary Force[1]

The American Expeditionary Force Headquarters or the General Headquarters (GHQ) was General John J. Pershing's principal headquarters in France. Organized July 5, 1917, the headquarters managed a myriad of staff activities in support of the combat forces including administration, policy, intelligence, operations, training, logistics, and coordination with Allied forces.

The General Headquarters did not exercise direct command of tactical operations. Instead they limited their activities to organization and development of the GHQ staff itself, plans for employment of troops, and organization of the AEF, thus delegating authority for execution of tactical operations to the subordinate command.

As the general staff concept was new to the United States Army, General Pershing relied chiefly on the recommendations of Colonel Chauncey Baker and the group that he led which came to be known as the Baker Board. Baker's studies in Europe prior to the arrival of the AEF laid the foundation for both divisional organization and staff structure.

The headquarters staff was divided in three major branches: the Commanding General's personal staff consisting of the Chief of Staff, Secretary of the General Staff, and other personal advisors, i.e. chaplain. The General Staff proper was divided into five sections; Administrative and Policy Section, Intelligence Section, Operations Section, Training Policy Section and Coordination Section. These sections were reorganized in 1918 into First through Fifth Section: First Section, Assistant Chief of Staff (Administration) G-1, Second Section, Assistant Chief of Staff (Intelligence) G-2, Third Section, Assistant Chief of Staff (Operations) G-3, Fourth Section, Assistant Chief of Staff (Supply) G-4, Fifth Section, and Assistant Chief of Staff (Training) G-5.

The Administrative and Technical Staff was organized functionally under the following sections: Headquarters Commandant, responsible for the command and administration of the staff, Adjutant General, the principal administrative advisor, Inspector General, responsible for oversight of standards and compliance with regulation, Judge Advocate General, the commanding general's legal advisor, Chief Quartermaster, the staff principal logistical advisor, Chief Surgeon, senior Medical advisor, Chief Engineer Officer, the staff authority on engineering missions, Chief Ordnance Officer, advisor on weapons systems and ordnance, Chief Signal Officer, the staff communications advisor, Chief of Air Service, staff authority on readiness and employed of the air arm, General Purchasing Agent, staff contracting advisor, Chief of Gas Service, responsible for advice concerning the employment of and defense against chemical weapons, Director General of Transportation, the staff advisor on movement control and employment of transportation assets, Commanding General – Lines of Communication, overall commander of the rear areas of operation, Chief of the Red Cross, and Provost Marshal General, who was the principal law enforcement officer with duties including enemy prisoner of war and deserter control.

159644

ORGANIZATION OF GENERAL HEADQUARTERS, AEF

July 5, 1917

GO No 8, 1917

(Corrected Copy [1])

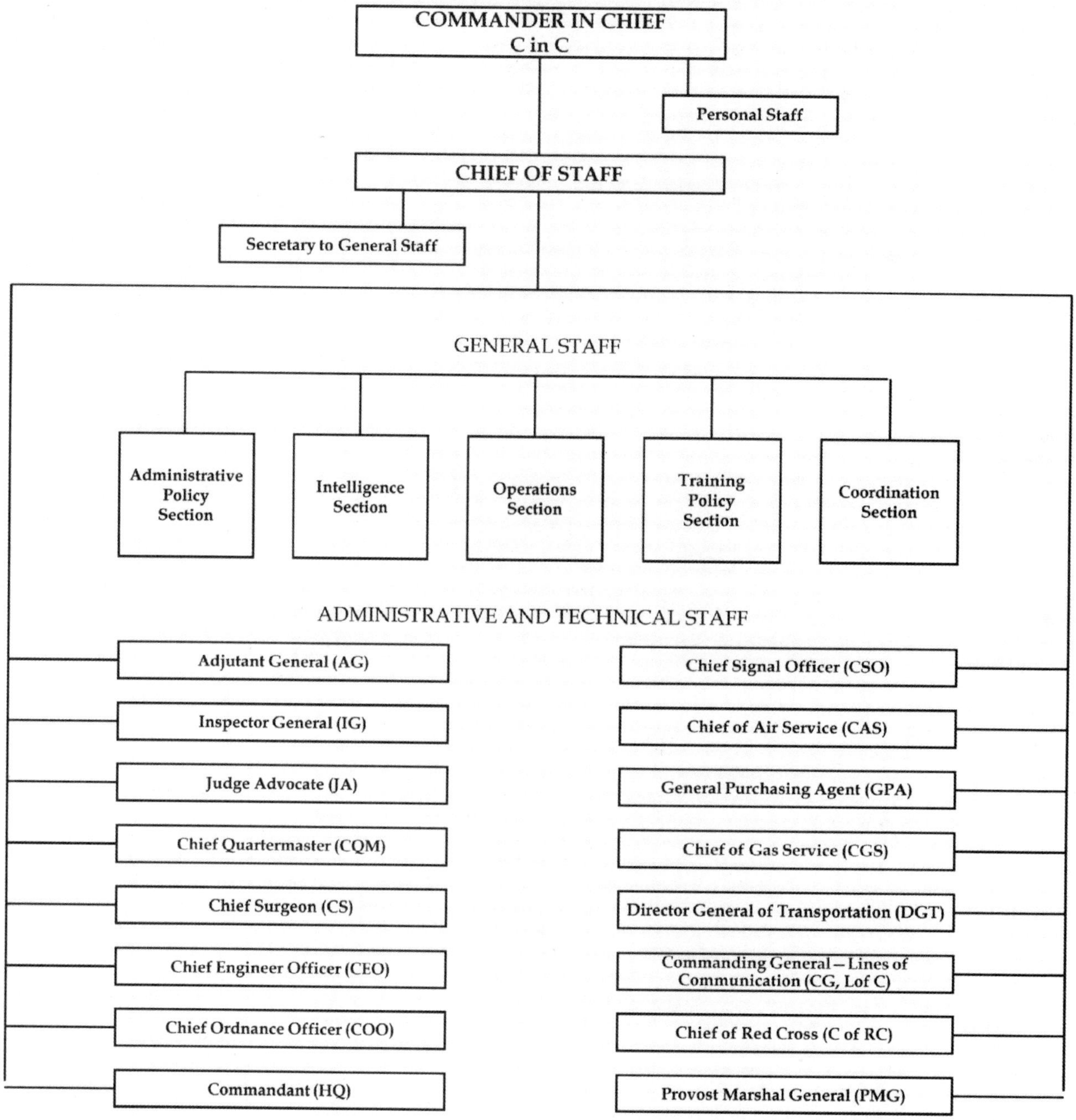

[1] General Order No 8 was originally issued on July 5, 1917, and provided for a General Staff of three sections–Administration, Intelligence, and Operations; and an administrative staff comprising Adjutant General, Judge Advocate General, Inspector General, Quartermaster, Engineer, Ordnance, Medical, Signal and Aviation Services. Further reorganization was made Aug 11, 1917, by issuance of corrected order shown above. (See Record of Events, GHQ)

Organization of AEF Headquarters, July, 1917.

ORGANIZATION OF GENERAL HEADQUARTERS, AEF

FEBRUARY 16, 1918

GO No 31, 1918

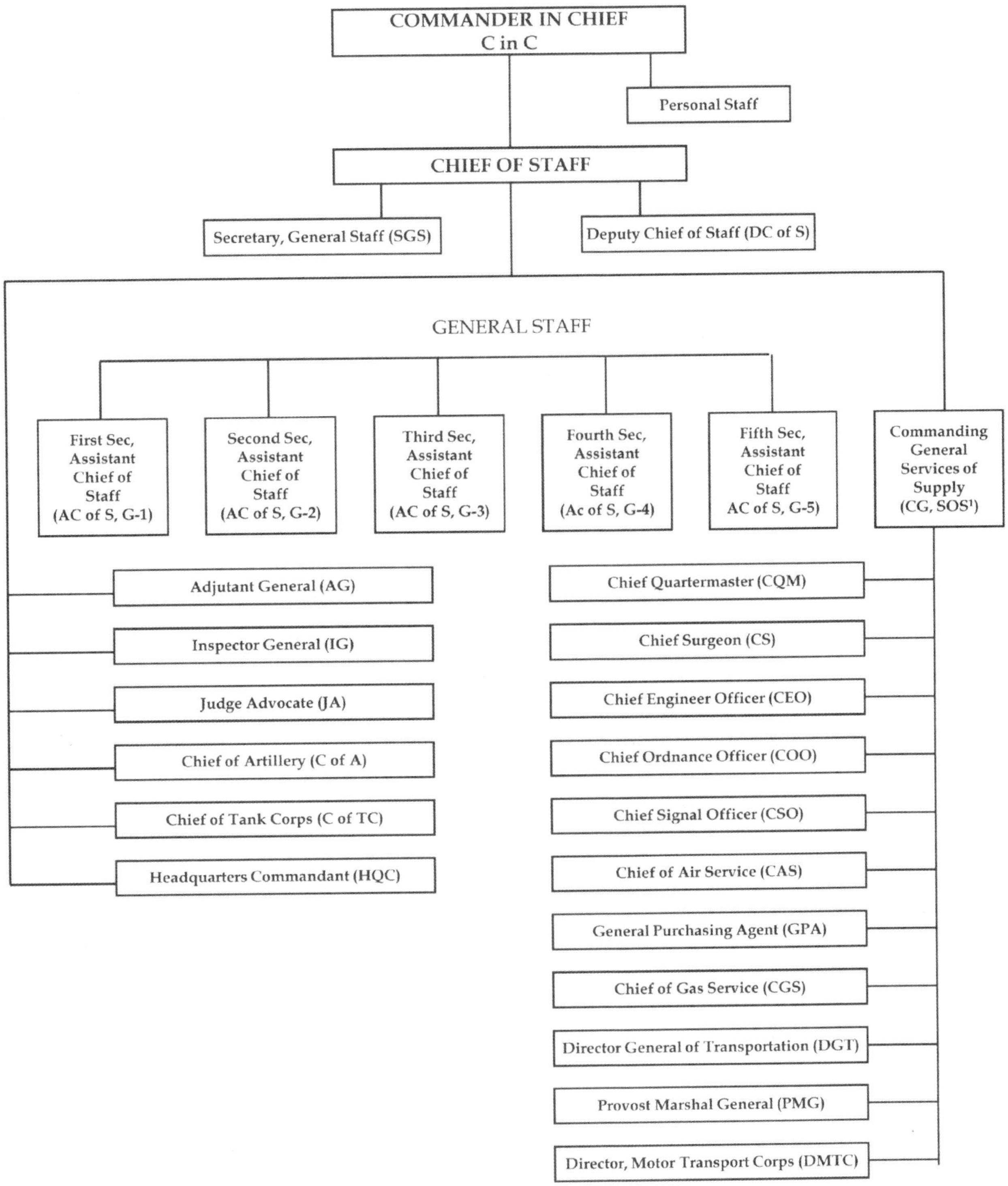

[1] Technical staff and supply services shown in the above table as subject to the orders of the Commanding General, SOS, maintain representatives with the General Starff at GHQ, AEF, to assure prompt service in The Zone of Operations.

Organization of the AEF Headquarters, February, 1918.

ORGANIZATION OF GENERAL HEADQUARTERS, AEF

NOVEMBER 11, 1918

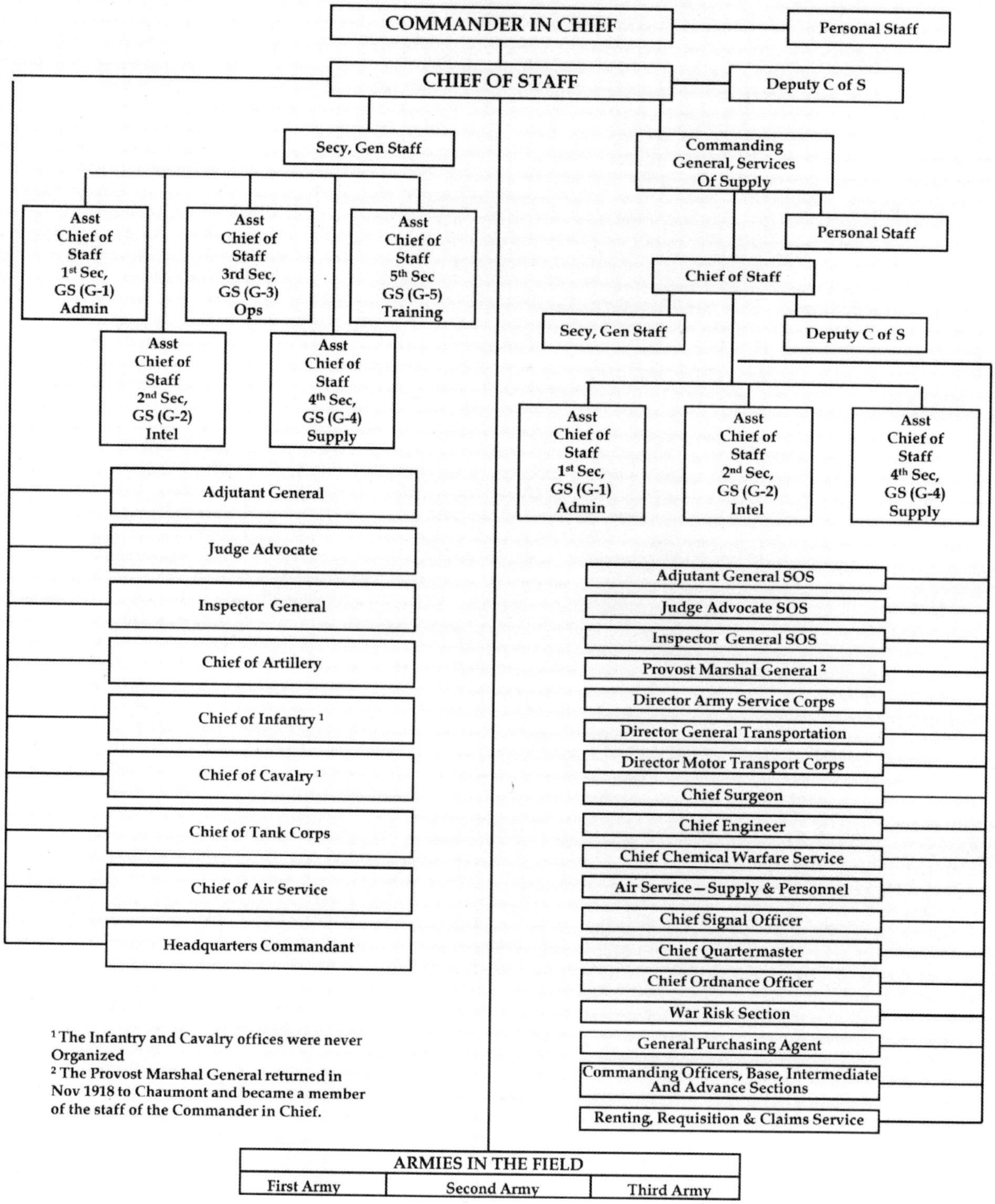

[1] The Infantry and Cavalry offices were never Organized

[2] The Provost Marshal General returned in Nov 1918 to Chaumont and became a member of the staff of the Commander in Chief.

Organization of the AEF Headquarters, November 11, 1918.

Insignia

General Headquarters

General Pershing personally selected the insignia of the GHQ. The insignia, which consisted of a disc divided horizontally into three equal red, white and blue fields, alluding to the colors of the United States. The insignia is normally found with the colored field of printed construction sewn within an olive drab wool outer frame. Examples also exist with felt on felt construction.

Liaison Service

The insignia of the Liaison Service was based upon that of the French General Staff with some modification.[2] It consisted of a winged torch with lightning bolts upon a dark blue triangular shield with a rounded top. Their mission was to effect staff coordination and as such functioned as the principal link between the American forces command and staff in theater and forces and staffs of our Allies.

Central Records Office

The Central Records Office was the clearing house for the personnel records of the AEF. The insignia was a gold eagle holding in its talons a union shield, upper portion blue with three stars and remainder divided into three red, white and blue fields; all upon a five sided shield in dark blue.

Postal Service and Courier Express

The postal service selected an emblem of the white greyhound at full speed upon a blue rectangle. The Courier Express made use of the same insignia substituting a silver greyhound as their emblem. The postal service was responsible for mail delivery to the AEF and as such, the image of the full speed greyhound drew some sarcasm from soldiers.[3] The function of the Courier Express was to connect the General Headquarters in France with the War Department in Washington, DC. In England, silver greyhounds were used as a symbol of messengers from the time of the medieval kings.

Wool General Headquarters insignia with printed center.

Embroidered General Headquarters insignia.

General Headquarters insignia with the Third Army insignia inset used during the Occupation Period.

Bullion Liaison Service insignia.

Bullion Central Records Office insignia.

Variant of the bullion Central Records Office insignia.

A wool with bullion version of the Central Records Office insignia.

Wool Postal Express insignia.

Silver bullion insignia denoting the Courier Service.

Major General Francis J. Kernan, Commanding General of the Services of Supply. Courtesy National Archives

Services of Supply[4]

The Services of Supply was created by the Army Field Service Regulation. The primary mission was to relieve the combat forces, "from every consideration except that of defeating the enemy." As such, it was responsible for running the Lines of Communication and most all of the activities in support of the AEF combat forces in the field. Geographically it included all of France and Great Britain. It was divided into seven Base Sections, an Intermediate Section, an Advanced Section, and two independent Districts, Paris and Tours. In October 1918, an additional base section was organized to administer to troops in Italy and in 1919 a base section was established to support the Army of Occupation. The headquarters was at Tours.[5]

The staff organization of the Services of Supply was formalized on August 29, 1917. Initially, it was composed of a Commanding General Line of Communications, a chief of staff and four major staff branch chiefs responsible for the administration of Base Sections 1-3 respectively and the Intermediate section. In addition, there were administrative and technical staffs responsible for specialty functions. In March of 1918, the title of the Commanding Officer changed to Commander, Services of Supply and the staff was realigned into four sections; G-1 though G-4 to mirror the organization of the AEF General Headquarters. In addition to this realignment, the administrative and technical staff sections were expanded. The staff was further refined in July of 1918 with the removal of the G-3 section; a result of the organizational focus on logistical matters. By the Armistice the staff underwent a final reorganization further defining the roles of the subordinate staff chiefs.

Commanding Generals

Colonel David S. Stanley (Ad interim), Major General Richard S. Blanchard, Brigadier General Mason M. Patrick (Ad interim), and Major General Francis J. Kernan.

Major General Francis J. Kernan, Commander of the Services of Supply leaves his office at S.O.S. Headquarters, Tours, France, January, 1919. Of note are the U.S. Marine Corps detachment troops. Courtesy National Archives

Above: Chateau Beaulieu, Major General Kernan's residence in Tours, France, July, 1918. Major General Kernan is standing in the foreground. Courtesy National Archives

Right: Major General James G. Harbord and Major General Charles Dawes AEF HQ chiefs. Courtesy National Archives

Crude felt on felt SOS insignia.

Standard die cut felt on felt version of the SOS insignia.

The version features unusual reversed colors.

Insignia

Advance Section

Services of Supply

The Service of Supply selected a monogram of "SOS" of red on a blue background. Variations are known where the colors are reversed. Many of the subordinate activities of the Service of Supply created individual patches. Examples are known to exist for units down to detachment level. We chose to list some of the more commonly encountered examples.

Ambulance Service

The Ambulance Service selected the Gallic Rooster upon a red disc which had been used by the American Ambulance Service Volunteers in France prior to American's entry into the war as tribute to the original members of the ambulance service.

American Embarkation Centers

This insignia was worn by the personnel operating the embarkation centers in France.

Army Service Corps

Units of the Army Service Corps whose mission was to supply transport the Army under the auspices of the Quartermaster General. Their insignia was a stylized wheel in red with a golden center all on a shield of black with the letter "A" "S" and "C" for Army Service Corps at each angle of the shield.

Motor Transport Corps

The motor transport corps insignia was never officially adopted by the AEF. Many variants exist but they fall into two general categories: those which incorporate the "MTC" monogram alone, and those using the insignia of the Transportation Corps, the winged helmet of Mercury upon a moving wheel, with the addition of the monogram "MTC" for Motor Transport Corps.

Reserve Mallet (Motor Transport Corps)

Before America entered the war, there were volunteers serving in the French Motor Transport Corps. Although many left the French Army to serve with the AEF upon America's entry, a number stayed with the French and constituted the Reserve Mallet, named for their commander Captain Mallet of the French Army. They selected as their insignia a gold hunting horn upon a green shield.[6]

Ports of Embarkation (POE)

Although not a formal part of the AEF, the principal ports of embarkation at New York and Hoboken, New Jersey were where most members of the AEF and the bulk of the supplies passed. The POE adopted an insignia of a staggered monogram "PE" for Port of Embarkation above two letter abbreviation of the state "NY" or "NJ."

Right: Embroidered on felt SOS monogram.

Far right: Embroidered on felt Ambulance Service insignia.

The advance section, located in the north and northeastern part of France, embraced in a general way the territory north of Paris, and Dijon. Its geographical limits, as prescribed by General Orders, No. 75, Headquarters, A. E. F., December 14, 1917, included the Departments of Nord, Pas du Calais, Somme, Oise, Aisne, Ardennes, Marne, Merthe et Moselle, Meuse, Haute Marne, Cote d'Or, Vosges, Haute Saone, and Doubs. These limits were somewhat changed from time to time.

This section, which was that immediately behind the front, contained twenty-two training areas where tactical divisions were billeted, either on their way to the front or for rest, replacement, or refitting. In addition to these were the training areas where troops were trained, the staff and line schools of all branches of the service, the supply depots, and other installations of the technical services. Despite the fact that practically all of these areas and formations were under direct control of either general headquarters of the American Expeditionary Forces, or Headquarters, Services of Supply, the number of troops under the jurisdiction of the section commander sometimes amounted to more than 200,000. The section had been organized to extend the jurisdiction of the commanding officer, Services of Supply, up to the points where supplies would be delivered to the field transportation of combat forces, but in practice distribution was made from regulating stations which were under the direct control of the general staff, general headquarters. Headquarters of the advance section were located at Neufchateau, opened on November 1, 1917.

Commanders of the Advance Section were Lieutenant Colonel John F. Madden, Colonel Harry Burgess, Colonel Johnson Hagood, Brigadier General William R. Sample, and Colonel John S. Switzer.

Highly detailed die cut felt on felt example.

Embroidered insignia of the American Embarkation Center.

Motor Transport Corps insignia using felt on felt construction with chain stitched details.

Variation of a fully embroidered Ambulance Service insignia.

Lovely bullion on velvet Ambulance Service insignia.

A variation of the American Embarkation Center insignia done entirely with French soutache.

A bullion with embroidered detailing example of the Army Service Corps insignia.

Embroidered Motor Transport Corps insignia.

Highly unusual example of the Motor Transport Corps insignia.

Felt on felt monogram "MTC" used by a Motor Transport soldier.

Another version of the "MTC" monogram insignia.

Embroidered on felt example of the "MTC" design.

Embroidered on felt example of the Reserve Mallet insignia.

Beautiful bullion on velvet example.

Port of Embarkation New York insignia embroidered chain stitching on wool.

Opposite
Top: Interior view of one of the thousands of warehouses in the Advanced Section, S.O.S. Author's Collection

Bottom: French Army trucks and ambulances parked in the Place Garriere, Neufchateau, France, Headquarters of the Advance Section, Services of Supply. Drawn by Captain W.J. Duncan. Courtesy National Archives

Advanced Section Services of Supply of embroidered on wool construction.

This example is embroidered in only one color.

Die cut with chain stitched "AS" monogram.

Insignia

Advanced Section

The insignia of the Advanced Section consisted of a red Cross of Lorraine upon a blue bordered grey or olive drab disc flanked by the letter "A" and "S" in red.

Advanced Section (Ordnance)

Ordnance soldiers assigned to the Advanced Section of the SOS selected an insignia with the letters "A" and "S" for Advanced Section in a wheel with an ordnance bomb in the center all in red on a dark blue background.

Railhead Regulating Stations

The railhead was defined by Farrow as, "a locality on the railway where ammunition and supplies are transferred to ammunition parks and supply columns."[7] This was normally the point where the standard gauge rail ended and supplies had to be trans-loaded onto narrow gauge rail, division trucks and/or wagons. Farrow defined Regulating Stations as, "a place where railway trains are marshaled, and whence are dispatched to the divisions."[8] At this point supplies inbound from the ports and depots were broken out to the divisions and trans-shipped forward to the railhead. The Railhead and Regulating Stations wore the basic same insignia; that of a white "R" centered upon a diamond of dark blue or black. Railheads were distinguished by a yellow border and Regulating Stations by a red border.[9] Twelve variations are extant which feature changes in the color of the "R" or border. It has been long believed that this color coding distinguishes individual stations; however, documentary confirmation of this theory has yet to surface.

Reversed construction Advanced Section insignia.

Advanced Section Ordnance personnel insignia featuring embroidered construction.

Right: Railhead and Regulating Station insignia with yellow letter "R"; it is believed that the color variations signified different stations.

Far right: This example features a red "R" with a white border.

This insignia employs a green "R" with a bullion border.

Embroidered insignia with both red "R" and border.

A version of the insignia with red border and a white "R".

Principal Stations and Depots

Name	Established	Activities
Dijon (Côte-d'Or)	July 26, 1917	QM Depot
Jonchery(Haute-Marne)	Oct. 25, 1917	Ordnance Depot
Is-sur-Tille (Côte-d'Or)	Sept 20, 1917	Regulating Station
Neufchâteau (Vosges)	Nov. 2, 1917	HQ, Advance Section
Bourbonne-les-Bains (Haute-Marne)	Nov. 8, 1917	Remount
Colombey-les-Belles (Meurthe-et-Moselle)	Nov. 13, 1917	Air Service Depot
Eclaron (Haute-Marne)	Dec. 22, 1917	Forestry
Vittel (Vosges)	Jan. 27, 1918	Hospital Center
Langres (Haute-Marne)	Feb 4, 1918	Motor Transport
Bricon (Haute-Marne)	Apr. 3, 1918	Forestry
Poincon (Seine-Inférieure)	May 10, 1918	Chemical Warfare Service Depot
Bazoilles (Vosges)	July 2, 1918	Hospital Center
Doulaincourt (Haute-Marne)	July 12, 1918	Ordnance Repair Shop
Beaune (Côte-d'Or)	July 31, 1918	Hospital Center
Lux (Côte-d'Or)	July 1918	Remount
Toul (Meurthe-et-Moselle)	Aug. 27, 1918	Hospital Center
St-Dizier (Haute-Marne)	Sept. 2, 1918	Regulating Station
Rimaucourt (Haute-Marne)	Sept. 14, 1918	Hospital Center
Liffol-le-Grand (Vosges)	Oct. 12, 1918	Regulating Station

Felt on felt variation with gold bullion "R".

Organization

Air Service: Squadrons: 13 service; 11 aero; 4 supply; 1 replacement; 4 construction; 3 repair. Depots: 1 spare parts; 1 advance supply; 2 air parks; 1 casual detachment; 3 photo sections; 1 repair shop; 1 balloon company; 1st Battalion, British Royal Dragoons; 2 mechanics companies.

Army Service Corps: 4 rest camp detachments; 10 administrative labor companies; 1 cement mill company; 2 depot labor companies; 11 prisoner of war escort companies; 2 labor companies; 1 provisional casual company; 1 women's detachment.
Army Transport Corps: 3 Railway Transportation Officer detachments.
Cavalry: 1 Regiment.
Chemical Warfare Service: 1 detachment.
Engineers: elements of 19 regiments and 20 battalions, including railway, forestry, highway, quarry, construction, shop and supply, searchlight, camouflage, sappers and train, service, and corps.
Infantry: 2 companies 1st Army Headquarters Regiment; 2 pioneer regiments.
Medical: Hospitals: 4 American Red Cross; 33 base; 18 camp; 1 contagious; 4 evacuation; 1 mobile; 1 advance veterinary; 7 veterinary; 2 laboratories; 4 convalescent camps; 6 Hospital centers; 7 Hospital units; 1 detachment; 1 laboratory unit; 1 advance supply depot; 2 supply depots; 2 mobile surgical units; 1 mobile veterinary section; 1 provisional casual company; 32 sanitary squadrons.
US Ambulance Service: 1 section; 1 provisional casual company.
Motor Transport Corps: 4 overhaul parks; 1 service park; 1 supply depot; 1 spare parts depot; 2 chauffeurs companies; 2 general repair shops; 6 machine shop truck units; 4 mechanics companies; 2 motorcycle companies; 1 motor transport repair shop unit; 18 motor supply train companies; 11 motor truck companies; 1 motor transport repair unit.
Ordnance: 2 advance ordnance depots; 9 mobile ordnance repair shops; 2 detachments; 1 repair shop.
Quartermaster: 2 advance remount depots; 3 animal transport depots; 33 bakery companies; 1 mechanical bakeries advance depot; 15 butchery companies; 6 clothing units; 10 field remount squadrons; 1 fire hose and truck company; 1 forestry detachment; 1 garden service detachment; 2 gas and oil branches; 5 graves registration units; 18 labor battalions; 9 laundry companies; 5 mobile laundry companies; 1 laundry depot; 15 pack trains; 16 detachments; 3 Quartermaster depots; 27 sales commissaries; 4 salvage squadrons; 2 salvage units; 7 supply companies; 3 wagon companies.

Below: Artillery Repair Shop at Mehun sur Yevres, France. Author's Collection

Signal Corps: 1 meteorological section; 1 service company; 1 advance supply depot; 1 supply depot; 4 telegraph battalions.
Tank Corps: 2 companies.
Miscellaneous: 1 convoy detachment; 1 electric compressor group; 1 motor compressor group.

Intermediate Section

This was the largest of the SOS sections situated between the Advanced and Base sections as a clearinghouse to accommodate traffic between the base ports and the front. The commanders of the Intermediate Section were: Lieutenant Colonel John F. Madden, Major William Elliott, Brigadier General Arthur Johnson, Brigadier General Charles Gerhardt, Major General William H. Hay, Colonel Samuel Reber, and Colonel Howard G. Davids.

Ordnance Sergeant Henry A. McCune (left) and an unidentified soldier at the Ordnance Repair Shops, Mehune sur Yevres, France. Author's Collection

Christmas Card given to hospital staff members from the nurses of Base Hospital No. 1. Author's Collection

Corporal Pasquale D'Alessandro was assigned to Base Hospital No. 1 and later Convalescent Camp No. 7 both activities were located at Vichy, France Author's Collection

Entrance to Camp Pontanezen, France. Note the insignia for the camp as well as the representations of the 8th Division patches, and the ubiquitous duckboard sidewalk. Courtesy Military History Institute

Above: Some troops heading to the de-lousing station, the first stop on the trip home. Camp Pontenazen, Brest, France. Courtesy Military History Institute

Right: Old stone barracks used to house some of the troops at Camp Pontenazen. Courtesy Military History Institute

Below: Camp Headquarters, Camp Pontenazen, Brest, France. Note the duckboard construction of the arch bearing the camp insignia. Courtesy Military History Institute

Insignia

Intermediate Section

The insignia of the Intermediate Section is rarely encountered. Examples do exist of a modified Advanced Section insignia of a red Cross of Lorraine upon a blue bordered, gray or olive drab disc flanked by the letter "I" and "S" in red in lieu of the "A" and "S" of Advance Section.

Artillery Repair Shop

The Artillery Repair Shop was a subordinate unit of the Ordnance Repair Shops and was responsible for the repair and overhaul of both damaged Allied and captured German Artillery.

Base Hospitals

A base hospital was a unit that used fixed facilities such as hotels and pre-existing hospitals for the treatment of the wounded. Many base hospitals adopted insignia – none were authorized. Two examples are illustrated: Base Hospital 50 – which uses the colors of the medical corps crimson red and yellow and incorporates the letter "W" for the University of Washington and the state of Washington where the unit was mobilized. The second example is of Base Hospital 53 – this unit was organized at Camp Greenleaf, Georgia, served in the advance section arrived at Langres, where later it formed a part of that hospital center. Its insignia is a simple monogram of the number "53."

Camp Pontanezen

This was the debarkation camp and point of return to America for much of the AEF. Although a subset organization to Base Section #5, members of the camp adopted their own unique insignia. They adopted a red disk upon which was placed a string of duckboards. Personnel serving at Camp Potanezen used the duckboards to cross the mud which was omnipresent in the camp. The camp itself is discussed in detail under the Base Section #5 listing.

Ordnance Repair Shops

The ordnance repair shops were composed of six departments: military, administration, shops, supply, inspection, and salvage. The major support activities were accomplished in the shops department and supply department. The shops department was divided into six divisions: artillery repair, small arms and machine gun, woodworking, optical repair, construction and maintenance and electrical; supply department was responsible for recordkeeping and functioned as one of the general ordnance supply depots for the AEF. The Ordnance Repair Shops selected an insignia of a black Flaming Bomb with red flames, long the symbol of the Ordnance Corps, with the red monogram "ORS" superimposed.[10]

General Intermediate Supply Depot

The supply depots assigned to the Intermediate Section selected as their insignia a monogram of the letters "G" "I" "S" "D" for General Intermediate Supply Depot all upon a black lozenge.

Very unusual hand embroidered on wool Intermediate Section insignia.

Scarce Intermediate Section Base Section 1 insignia.

Bottom
Left: Beautiful example of an Effects Depot, St. Nazaire insignia.

Center: Artillery Repair Shop insignia embroidered on felt construction.

Right: Embroidered Base Hospital 50 insignia.

This unique Base Hospital 50 Receiving Station insignia is of felt on felt construction.

Felt on felt construction insignia of Base Hospital 53.

Insignia of Base Hospital 65 of felt on felt construction with chain stitched numeral "65."

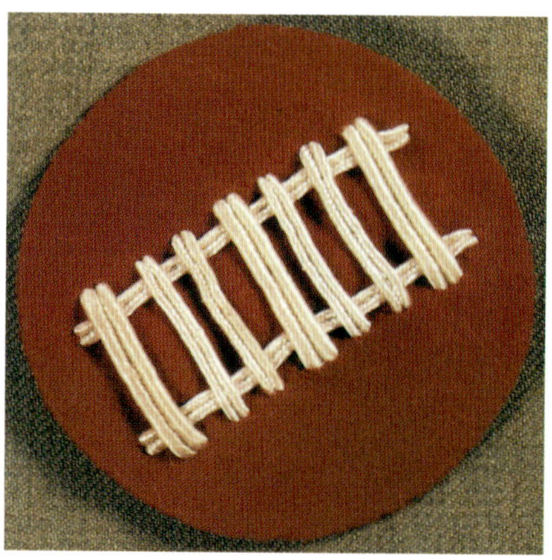

Above
Left: Duckboard insignia of Camp Pontanezan executed in French soutache.

Center: Ordnance Repair Shop insignia of felt on felt construction using embroidered highlights.

Right: An embroidered on felt version of the insignia.

Right: Bullion embroidered insignia of the General Intermediate Supply Depot.

Principal Stations and Depots

Name	Established	Activities
Nevers (Nièvre)	July 10, 1917	Quartermaster Depot
Gièvres (Loir-et-Cher)	Aug 1917	General Storage Depot
Châteauroux (Indre)	Sept 1917	Base Hospital
Issoudun (Indre)	Sept 1, 1917	Quartermaster Depot
Clermont-Ferrand (Puy-de-Dôme)	Nov 1917	Aviation Instruction Center
Romorantin (Loir-et-Cher)	Jan 17, 1918	Air Service Production Center
Blois (Loir-et-Cher)	Jan 20, 1918	Casual Officers Depot
Mehun-sur-Yèvre (Cher)	Jan 28, 1918	Ordnance Depot and Repair Shops
St-Aignan (Loir-et-Cher)	Jan 1918	Replacement Depot
Montierchaume (Indre)	Apr 1918	General Storage Depot
Orléans (Loiret)	June 1918	Base Hospital
Mesves-sur-Loire (Nièvre)	June 15, 1918	Hospital Center
Allerey (Saône-et-Loire)	June 23, 1918	Hospital Center
Verneuil (Nièvre)	July 14, 1918	Motor Reconstruction
Mars-sur-Allier (Nièvre)	July 19, 1918	Hospital Center
Sougy (Nièvre)	Aug 1, 1918	Veterinary Hospital
Le Mans (Sarthe)	Aug 1, 1918	Replacement Depot
Vichy (Allier)	Aug 12, 1918	Hospital Center
Lyon (Rhone)	Aug 19, 1918	Salvage Depot
Chenevières (Meurthe-et-Moselle)	Sept 9, 1918	Ordnance Depot
Le Mans (Sarthe)	Dec 15, 1918	Embarkation Center

Organization

Air Service: 1 supply depot; aero squadrons; 1 service; 10 construction; 5 supply; 4 repair; 1 replacement; 3 balloon companies; 2 armorers detachments; 31 companies mechanics.

Army Service Corps: 7 Prisoner of War Escort companies; 34 administrative labor companies; 4 depot labor companies; 2 guard companies; 1 battalion native labor regiment.

Army Transport Corps: 4 Railway Transportation Officer detachments.

Artillery: 6 battalions Coast Artillery Corps.

Cavalry: 7 troops.

Chemical Warfare Service: 1 Gas Defense Section; 1 Gas Depot.

Engineers: Elements 7 regiments and 21 battalions, including railway, forestry, construction, crane, and supply troops.

Infantry: 2 companies 1st Army Headquarters Regiment; 1 Pioneer Regiment (less 1 battalion).

Marines: 1 regiment (less 2 companies).

Medical: 2 American Red Cross convalescent homes; 29 base Hospitals; 19 camp Hospitals; 1 central laboratory; 3 convalescent camps; 2 evacuation Hospitals; 1 field Hospital; 2 Medical supply depots; 6 sanitary squadrons ; 3 veterinary Hospitals.

Motor Transport Corps: 2 Motor Transport Corps detachments; 1 spare parts depot; 1 motor transport repair shop; 3 mechanical repair shops; 2 motor car companies; 9 motor supply train companies; 1 motor truck company.

Ordnance: 4 detachments, including depot and design; 2 intermediate depots; 1 repair shop.

Quartermaster: 1 Army garden service; 1 base animal transport depot; 13 bakery companies; 18 butchery companies; 1 clothing unit; 6 field remount squadrons; 2 fire hose and truck units; 1 gas and oil branch; 1 ice plant company; elements of 12 labor battalions; 5 laundry companies; 5 mobile laundry companies; 9 pack trains; 4 Quartermaster depots; 13 Quartermaster detachments; 1 refrigerator plant; 2 remount depots; 3 sales commissaries; 4 salvage depots; 1 stevedore company; 1 civilian contract company; 14 supply companies; 2 wagon companies.

Signal Corps: 1 depot battalion; 2 intermediate signal corps depots; 4 telegraph battalion companies; 2 service companies.

Tank Corps: 1 tank battalion.

Miscellaneous: 3 leave centers; 1 central records office; 1 General Headquarters and Headquarters Battalion Company; 2 military prisons; 2 postal express services; 1 military police provisional company; 2 provisional convalescent companies.

Base Section #1

Principal Stations and Depots

Name	**Established**	**Activities**
St-Nazaire (Loire-Inférieure)	June 22, 1917	Base Port
Nantes (Loire-Inférieure)	July 11, 1917	Base Port
Savenay (Loire-Inférieure)	Aug 21, 1917	Base Hospital
Les Sables d'Olonne (Vendée)	Aug 31, 1917	Base Port
Saumur (Maine-et-Loire)	Sept 6, 1917	Artillery School
Cotquidan (Morbihan)	Sept 27, 1917	Artillery Camp/Aerial Observation School
Angers (Maine-et-Loir)	Oct 19, 1917	Engineers Training Base
Paimboeuf (Loire-Inférieure)	Nov 30, 1917	Naval Air Station
St-Maxient (Deux-Sèvres)	Dec 9, 1918	Air Service Replacement
Fromentine (Vendée)	Feb 4, 1918	Naval Air Station
La Trinité-Porhot (Morbihan)	Mar 14, 1918	Naval Air Station
Meucon (Morbihan)	Apr 14, 1918	Artillery Camp
St-Jean-de-Monts (Vendée)	May 7, 1918	Air Gunnery School

Organization

Army Service Corps: 24 administration labor companies; 3 depot labor companies; 1 labor company; 17 prisoner of war escort companies.

Army Transport Service: Railway Transportation Officer detachments.

Cavalry: 1 squadron.

Engineers: 2 regiments (construction); 1 regiment (railway operating); 1 regiment (depot div); 3 regiments; 5 service battalions; 1 engineer depot.

Infantry: 1 battalion less 2 companies; Army Headquarters Regiment; 2 pioneer regiments less detachments.

Marines: 1 regiment less 1 battalion.

Medical: 1 ambulance company; 8 camp Hospitals; 6 evacuation ambulance companies; 1 field Hospital; 8 base Hospitals; 4 sanitary squads; 2 veterinary Hospitals; 1 medical supply depot; 1 medical base storage depot.

Motor Transport Corps: 21 motor trucks companies; 1 motorcycle company; 4 engineer Motor Transport Service; 9 repair unit companies.

Navy: air service detachments.

Ordnance: 2 ordnance depots; 5 ordnance detachments; 1 railway ordnance detachment.

Quartermaster: 4 bakery companies; 4 butchery companies; 8 field remount squadrons; 4 labor battalions; 6 stevedore battalions; 8 supply companies; laundry and fire protection units.

Signal Corps: 4 detachments.

Trains: 1 supply train; 1 ammunition train company; 2 supply train companies.

Base Section #2

Principal Stations and Depots

Name	**Established**	**Activities**
Talence (Gironde)	July 28, 1917	Base Hospital
Bordeaux (Gironde)	Aug 30, 1917	Base Port
Grange-Neuve (Gironde)	Sept 1, 1917	Rest and Embarkation
Génicart (Gironde)	Sept 1, 1917	Rest and Embarkation
Bassens Dock (Gironde)	Nov 2, 1917	Freight debarkation
Camp de Souge (Gironde)	Nov 11, 1917	Artillery training

Merignac (Gironde)	Nov 1917	Remount depot
Dax (Landes)	Dec 22, 1917	Forestry Hospital
Limoges (Haute Vienne)	Jan 1, 1918	Hospitals/artillery training
Mimizan (Landes)	Jan 19, 1918	Forestry
Libourne (Gironde)	Feb 9, 1918	O & T Center
Cazaux (Ariège)	Feb 9, 1918	Air Instruction Center
Le Courneau (Gironde) Camp Hunt	Feb 19, 1918	Artillery training
La Courtine (Creuse)	Feb 1918	Artillery training
Montpont (Saône-et-Loire)	Mar 3, 1918	Base Hospital
Carbon Blanc (Gironde)	Apr 18, 1918	Remount
St-Supplylice (Gironde)	Apr 21, 1918	Storage Depot
Beau Desert (Gironde)	June 22, 1918	Hospital Center
Bayonne (Basses Pyrénées)	Aug 15, 1918	Remount
Perigueux (Dordogne)	Sept 5, 1918	Hospitals
St-Loubes (Gironde)	Sept 12, 1918	Ammunition depot
Angouléme (Charente)	Sept 1918	O & T Center

Organization

Army Service Corps: 3 labor companies; 4 depot labor companies; 9 Prisoner of War Escort companies; 27 administrative labor companies; 11 native labor units.

Army Transport Service: Army Transport Service Engineers (Checkers).

Cavalry: 1 regiment.

Chemical Warfare Service: 3 detachments.

Engineers: 1 regiment (railway construction); 1 regiment (forestry); 1 regiment (highway); elements of 15 regiments, including railway shop and crane operator units, 2 service battalions, 2 depots.

Infantry: 2 companies First Army Headquarters Regiment; 1 battalion pioneer infantry.

Marines: 1 battalion.

Medical: 3 American Red Cross convalescent homes; 3 American Red Cross Hospitals; 8 base Hospitals; 9 camp Hospitals; 1 evacuation ambulance company; 1 medical supply depot; 1 medical base storage depot; 1 mobile field laboratory; 1 sanitary squad; 1 veterinary Hospital.

Motor Transport Corps: 1 machine shop truck unit; 5 motor car companies; 2 motor supply trains; 8 motor truck companies; 1 engineer motor truck company.

Ordnance: 2 ordnance depots; 7 ordnance detachments.

Quartermaster: 1 advance animal transport; 6 bakery companies; 3 butchery companies; 6 Quartermaster detachments; 3 Quartermaster depots; 4 field remount squadrons; 2 fire hose and truck companies; 4 labor battalions; 1 meat handling section; 1 mobile laundry company; 1 refrigerator plant; 1 remount depot; 1 salvage depot; 5 stevedore battalions; 5 supply companies; 8 civilian construction companies.

Signal Corps: 3 service company detachments.

Trains: 2 ammunition train companies; 2 supply train companies.

Base Section #3

Principal Stations and Depots

Name	Established	Activities
Southampton, England	Sept 1, 1917	Rest Camp
Winchester, England	Nov 7, 1917	Rest Camp
Romsey, England	Dec 26, 1917	Rest Camp
London Depot, England	Dec 1917	Transit Depot
Paignton, England	Jan 1, 1918	Hospital
Liverpool, England	Jan 10, 1918	Hospital
Hursley Park, England	Apr 20, 1918	Hospital
Knotty Ash, England	Apr 24, 1918	Rest Camp
Flower Down, England	July 26, 1918	Air Service Camp

Swansea Depot, Wales	June 1918	Storage Depot
Dartford, England	July 18, 1918	Hospital
Portsmouth, England	July 28, 1918	Hospital
Tottenham, England	Aug 1, 1918	Hospital
Codford, England	Sept 23, 1918	Air Service Camp
Sarisbury Court	Sept 27, 1918	Hospital

Organization

Air Service: 32 aero service squadrons; 31 aero squadrons; 8 aero construction squadrons; 13 aero repair squadrons; 19 aero construction companies; 2 aero replacement squadrons; 2 aircraft acceptance parks.
Engineers: 1 detachment.
Infantry: 1 battalion; 1 pioneer battalion.
Medical: 3 American Red Cross units; 5 base Hospitals; 4 camp Hospitals; 1 medical supply depot; 1 base laboratory.
Motor Transport Corps: 1 Motor Transport Corps detachment; 1 truck company.
Quartermaster: 1 butchery company; 3 Quartermaster depots; 1 stevedore detachment.
Signal Corps: 1 service company.
Tank Corps: 1 salvage & repair company.

Base Section #4

Principal Stations and Depots

Name	Established	Activities
Rouen (Seine-Inférieure)	May 25, 1917	Sub-Base
Boulogne (Pas-de-Calais)	May 30, 1917	Hospital
Etretat (Seine-Inférieure)	May 31, 1917	Hospital
Dannes-Camiers (Pas-de-Calais)	June 11, 1917	Hospital
Le Tréport (Seine-Inférieure)	June 12, 1917	Hospital
Le Havre (Seine-Inférieure)	Aug 2, 1917	Base Port
Calais (Pas-de-Calais)	June 28, 1918	Sub-Base
Caen (Calvados)	Sept 15, 1918	Hospital
Dunkirk (Nord)	Dec 10, 1918	Hospital

Organization

Army Service Corps: 1 Prisoner of War Escort company.
Artillery: 1 battalion Coast Artillery Corps.
Engineers: 1 company (inland waterway); 1 engineer train; 2 service battalion companies.
Infantry: 3 First Army regiment detachments; 1 provisional company; 1 detachment.
Marines: 1 company.
Medical: 3 detachments.
Motor Transport Corps: 11 motor truck companies.
Quartermaster: 1 bakery company; 1 mobile laundry company; 1 detachment; 1 stevedore company; 1 supply company; 1 salvage detachment.
Signal Corps: 1 service company.
Miscellaneous: 4 casual detachments; 4 military police detachments; 1 ammunition train company.

Base Section #5

Principal Stations and Depots

Name	Established	Activities
Rennes (Ille-et-Vilaine)	Sept 7, 1917	Railroad operation
Brest (Finistère)	Nov 10, 1917	Base Port
Pontanezen (Finistère)	Jan 1918	Rest and Embarkation

Landerneau (Finistère)	June 1, 1918	Hospital
Cherbourg (Manche)	June 25, 1918	Port
St-Malo (Ill-et-Vilaine)	Aug 18, 1918	Leave area
Kerhornou (Finistère)	Sept 16, 1918	Hospital center
Granville (Manche)	Oct 12, 1918	Coal Port

Organization
Army Service Corps: 2 Army Service Corps detachments; 3 Prisoner of War Escort companies.
Army Transport Service: Transportation Department (Army Transportation Service).
Artillery: 1 battery Coast Artillery Corps; 1 ammunition train (less 2 companies).
Cavalry: 1 troop.
Chemical Warfare Service: 1 port detachment.
Engineers: elements of 10 regiments and 3 service battalions, including forestry and railway shop troops.
Infantry: 2 companies; First Army Headquarters Regiment; 1 pioneer battalion (less 2 companies).
Marines: 3 guard companies.
Medical: 1 base Hospital; 2 camp Hospitals; 2 ambulance companies; 1 base laboratory.
Motor Transport Corps: 1 machine shop truck unit; 1 motorcycle company; 19 motor truck companies; 1 reception park.
Ordnance: 1 detachment; 1 ordnance depot.
Quartermaster: 1 bakery company; 3 butchery companies; 3 depot labor companies; 1 Quartermaster depot; 1 labor battalion; 2 mobile laundry companies; 1 salvage corps; 2 stevedore battalions; 1 supply company.
Signal Corps: 1 service company; 1 telegraph battalion.
Miscellaneous: 1 ammunition train company; 2 supply trains (less 4 companies).

Camp Pontanezen
One of the most notable activities of the SOS fell under Base Section #5, Camp Pontanezen. According to the final report of the Medical Department published in *The Medical Department of the United States Army in the World War*:

> From January to December, 1918, Camp Pontanezen functioned as a debarkation and rest camp, with a small permanent garrison. From (and including) December 1918, it operated as an embarkation camp. The permanent strength of this camp rose to about 15,000.
>
> In the spring of 1918 a board of officers examined Camp Pontanezen and found it fairly satisfactory for about 10,000 men, provided certain improvements were made. Some of the improvements recommended by the board were effected, but during the summer and fall of 1918 the small permanent garrison was straining every nerve to keep the tide of men and supplies moving toward the front, and had but little time or resources wherewith to accomplish much in the way of improvement.
>
> The camp consisted of an interior and an exterior area. The interior area, covering approximately 15 acres, was enclosed by a wall and contained six old and very large stone barracks and several other smaller buildings. This area, known as Pontanezen Barracks, had long been used by the French as a military garrison. The exterior area, comprising farmland surrounding the enclosure, was gradually extended by requisitioning land from the French as it was needed. It expanded from about 90 to approximately 1,000 acres when the camp reached its maximum capacity in the spring of 1919.
>
> The final dimensions of the camp were approximately 1 mile wide by 1½ miles long. It lay on a hillside, sloping toward the south, about a mile and a half from the harbor. Though the slope afforded drainage, there was neither good roads, walks, sewers, nor drainage ditches, and was cut up into small rectangles by dykes and hedges. Consequently, conditions at first were very unsatisfactory, for not only was it necessary to utilize the camp before it was ready, but also the weather was cold and inclement and the soil such that it formed a deep and tenacious mud. The last mentioned fact greatly interfered with

> both construction and service. Other defects were insufficient kitchens, lack of mess halls, inadequate means of sterilizing mess kits, poor latrines, limited bathing and disinfecting facilities, limited means for washing hands, shortage of fuel, and an inadequate water supply, which was polluted. These unsatisfactory conditions were intensified by the relative lack of trained camp personnel and the great numbers of troops which arrived.
>
> At first there were only two roads, which ran north and south; however, two east and west roads soon were built, and a number of good thoroughfares had been completed by April, 1919. Also by that time footways, largely "duckboard," were provided.

In addition to Pontanezen Barracks, the only other shelter at first available consisted of several temporary barracks, which had been erected in November, 1918, and pyramidal tents for 5,000 men. Prior to this time, a number of the troops had to occupy shelter tents. In the latter part of December, 1918, only 44 per cent of the pyramidal tents were floored; however, by April, 1919, barracks and floored tents were adequate. At that time 450 barracks each accommodating 110 men, and 5,000 floored tents, each accommodating 6 men, were available.

Base Section #6

Principal Stations and Depots

Name	**Established**	**Activities**
Marseille (Bouches-du-Rhône)	May 30, 1918	Base Port
Marseille (Bouches-du-Rhône)	June 21, 1918	Motor Reception Park
Miramas (Bouches-du-Rhône	July 9, 1918	Storage Depot
"Riviera" (Alpes-Maritimes)	July 1918	Hospital Center
Toulon (Var)	Aug 25, 1918	Port

Organization

Army Service Corps: 2 Prisoner of War Escort companies; 3 cement mills companies.
Army Transport Corps: 2 Army Transport Corps detachments.
Artillery: 2 batteries Coast Artillery Corps.
Cavalry: 1 troop.
Chemical Warfare Service: 1 repair detachment.
Engineers: elements of 7 regiments and 2 service battalions.
Infantry: 1 company First Army Headquarters Regiment; 1 pioneer regiment (less 1 battalion and 2 companies); 1 pioneer company.
Marines: 1 company.
Medical: 3 ambulance companies; 1 American Red Cross convalescent home; 1 base laboratory; 1 camp Hospital; 1 field Hospital; 2 US military Hospitals.
Motor Transport Corps: 1 motor car company; 3 motor supply train; 8 motor truck companies.
Quartermaster: 1 bakery company detachment; 2 butchery companies; 2 labor battalions (less 2 companies); 2 Quartermaster detachments; 1 stevedore battalion (less 2 companies).
Signal Corps: 1 service company.
Trains: 1 supply train company.

Base Section #7

Principal Stations and Depots

Name	**Established**	**Activities**
La Pallice (Charente-Inférieure)	Nov 7, 1917	Base Port
La Rochelle (Charente-Inférieure)	Jan 17, 1918	Camp Pullman
Rochefort-sur-Mer (Charente-Inférieure)	Jan 26, 1918	Port
Pèrigny (Charente-Inférieure)	Mar 1, 1918	Hospital
Tonnay-Charente (Charente-Inférieure)	June 20, 1918	Coal Port

Mortagne-sur-Gironde (Charente-Inférieure)	July 17, 1918	Cement Mill
Marans (Charente-Inférieure)	Aug 13, 1918	Port
Aytre (Charente-Inférieure)	Oct 1, 1918	Car Erecting Plant
Aigrefeuille-d'Aunis (Charente-Inférieure)	Oct 11, 1918	Hospital

Organization
Air Service: 1 supply depot.
Army Service Corps: 1 administrative labor company; 1 cement mills company; 2 Prisoner of War Escort companies; 1 depot labor company.
Army Transport Service: elements of 2 stevedore battalions.
Cavalry: 4 troops.
Engineers: elements of 5 regiments and 1 service battalion; including forestry, railway construction, and railroad shop troops.
Infantry: 1 detachment First Army Headquarters Regiment.
Marines: 1 company.
Medical: 2 camp Hospitals.
Motor Transport Corps: 1 detachment; 1 mechanics air service company; 2 motor car companies; 1 motor supply train; 2 motor truck companies.
Ordnance: 2 detachments.
Quartermaster: 1 bakery company; 3 butchery companies; 3 Quartermaster depots; 4 field remount squadrons; 1 fire hose truck company; 1 ice plant company; 1 labor battalion company; 1 labor battalion (less 2 companies); 1 refining company; 1 remount depot; 1 salvage detachment.
Signal Corps: 1 service company; 1 telegraph battalion.

Base Section #8

Principal Stations and Depots

Name	Established	Activities
Foggia, Italy	Sept 28, 1917	Aerial Training
Furbara, Italy	May 13, 1918	Aerial Gunnery
Genoa, Italy	June 14, 1918	Port
Mantua, Italy	July 19, 1918	Motor Transport Corps Shop
Villafranca di Verona, Italy	July 26, 1918	Infantry Camp
Castelfranco, Italy	Sept 7, 1918	Motor Transport Corps Shop
Vicenza, Italy	Sept 7, 1918	Hospital
Padua, Italy	Oct 28, 1918	American Red Cross Hospital
Alessandria, Italy	Oct 31, 1918	Supply Dept

Organization
Air Service: 2 aviation detachments.
Ambulance Service: ambulance service repair shop unit; 15 ambulance sections.
Infantry: 1 regiment.
Motor Transport Service: 2 machine shop truck units.
Medical: 1 base Hospital; 1 field Hospital.
Quartermaster: 1 detachment; 1 sales commissary; 1 supply depot.

Base Section #9

Principal Stations and Depots

Name	Established	Activities
Rotterdam (Holland)	Mar 1, 1919	Sub-Base
Antwerp (Belgium)	Mar 22, 1919	Base Port

General Intermediate Supply Depot insignia of embroidered construction.

A combination insignia of bullion and embroidered construction.

Far left: The insignia of Motor Truck Company Number 1; a black swan embroidered upon a white rectangle. Truck Company Number Two replaced the swan with a coiled black rattlesnake.

Left: Motor Truck Company Number 3 was represented by a black hand embroidered camel.

A scarecrow surrounded by four crop plantings was the insignia of Truck Company Number 4; this insignia is again embroidered.

Opposite
Top: Military Police Company of Paris pose in the Jardin des Tuileries, April, 1918. These troops are the 30th Company, 5th Regiment, United States Marine Corps. Courtesy National Archives

Bottom: American and allied soldiers enjoy themselves in the Y.M.C.A. tea garden at 31 Avenue Montaigne, Paris. Courtesy National Archives

Organization

Army Service Corps: 3 guard companies.
Engineers: 1 engineer train.
Infantry: a detachment of pioneer infantry.
Medical: 1 Camp Hospital; 1 evacuation ambulance company.
Military Police Corps: 2 criminal investigation detachments.
Motor Transport Corps: 1 Headquarters motor command; 1 motorcycle company; 1 service park unit.
Quartermaster: 2 sales commissaries; 1 supply train.

District of Paris

The District of Paris was responsible for activities within the environs of the city of Paris.

Insignia

The unit chose an insignia of the Fleur-de-Lis of Bourbon Kings in white upon an inverted black or navy blue triangle. The insignia is not frequently encountered as according to the *Stars and Stripes*, the French people were often hostile or rude to the troops wearing the patch and as a result many soldiers refused to wear it.[11]

Principal Stations and Depots

Name	Established	Activities
Neuilly-sur-Seine (Seine)	July 23, 1917	Hospital
Paris (Seine)	Nov 1, 1917	Hospital
Paris (Seine)	Nov 15, 1917	Hospital

Right: Bullion flour de lis insignia of the District of Paris.

Far right: Embroidered example of the District of Paris insignia.

Joinville-le-Pont (Seine)	Apr 26, 1918	Hospital
Auteuil (Seine-et-Oise)	May 27, 1918	Hospital
Paris (Seine)	June 6, 1918	Engineer Depot
Aubervilliers (Seine)	June 13, 1918	Medical Supply Depot
Paris (Seine)	June 27, 1918	Overhaul Park
Paris (Seine)	July 20, 1918	Hospital
St Denis (Seine)	July 25, 1918	Hospital
Sèvres (Seine-et-Oise)	Aug 6, 1918	Hospital
St Cloud (Seine-et-Oise)	Sept 14, 1918	Convalescent Home
Paris (Seine)	Sept 16, 1918	Hospital
Paris (Seine)	Sept 26, 1918	Hospital
Nogent-sur-Marne (Seine)	Nov 1, 1918	Convalescent Camp

Organization

Air Service: aero squadrons: 4 supply, 3 service, 2 construction, 1 replacement. 15 mechanics companies; 2 detachments.

Army Service Corps: 5 administrative labor companies.

Artillery: anti-aircraft: 4 battalions; 11 batteries.

Chemical Warfare Service: 1 laboratory.

Engineers: elements of 4 regiments and 1 battalion, including railway shop, forestry, searchlight, surveying and printing, and inland waterway troops.

Medical: American Red Cross: 2 convalescent homes; 10 Hospitals. 3 base Hospitals; 1 camp Hospital; 1 evacuation Hospital; 1 repair shop; 1 supply depot; 3 mobile Hospitals; 1 mobile operating unit; 1 mobile optical unit.

Motor Transport Corps: 1 overhaul park; 2 machine shop truck units; 1 limousine company; 1 motorcycle company; 1 touring car company; 1 supply train truck company.

Quartermaster Corps: 1 butchery company; 1 laundry company; 1 salvage depot; 1 labor company.

Signal Corps: 2 service companies; 2 telegraph battalions.

ARMIES AND CORPS

First Army

Organized August 10, 1918 in the Regular Army at Le Ferte-sous-Jouarre, France and demobilized at Marseille April 20, 1919.[1]

Insignia:
The black letter "A" signifies Army and alludes to the first letter of the alphabet, hence First Army. This insignia was approved in November of 1918. The First Army insignia often incorporates branch within the legs of the letter "A." Almost immediately, the Corps Headquarters began the first of several attempts to inculcate basic designs to distinguish various subordinate elements of the corps. Primarily these designs were geometric patterns in red and white or in the basic branch color of the organization. These efforts culminated with Memorandum 45, dated 14 December 1918, which formally established a system for each major assigned branch. Despite this proactive measure, literally scores of variations of First Army patches are extant that do not follow the guidelines set forth in Memorandum 45. Oddly enough, varieties outside of regulation are far more common than those following the instructions of the memorandum.[2] A final variation of the insignia exists for the personnel working at First Army Headquarters. This insignia appears in two forms; both of which incorporate a monogram of a red "A" and "R" to the left and right of a gold or yellow letter "H" upon which is superimposed a white number "1." This monogram is representative of headquarters First Army. One form appears on a dark blue circular background with a second form superimposed upon a red-bordered diamond. Doubtless, more varieties of the World War I First Army Patch exist than of any other army, corps or division insignia. Keller & Keller's publication, *United States Army Shoulder Patches and Related Insignia from World War I to Korea, Army Groups, Armies and Corps*, provides the best catalog of these variations.

Campaigns:
St. Mihiel Operation, Meuse-Argonne, Lorraine 1918.[3]

Organization:[4]
August 30 – September 16, 1918:

Corps: I, IV, V, French II (Colonial).
Divisions: 1st, 2nd, 3rd, 4th, 5th, 26th, 33rd, 35th, 42nd, 78th, 80th, 82nd, 89th, 90th, French: 2nd Dismounted Cavalry, 15th (Colonial).
Air Service:
American: Headquarters, Air Service First Army, 1st Pursuit Wing, 1st Pursuit Group, 2nd Pursuit Group, 3rd Pursuit Group, 1st Day Bombardment Group, Night Bombardment Group,

Lieutenant General Hunter Liggett commanded First Army from October 1918 to April 1919; this portrait predates his tenure as commander. Courtesy National Archives

Brigadier General Hugh A. Drum, Chief of Staff of the First Army, France, 1918. Courtesy National Archives.

Lieutenant George Bishop and Sergeant Edwin H. Janzer of the Field Ammunition Office, Ordnance Department, First Army prepare detonators, Stenay, France, January, 1919. Courtesy National Archives.

Headquarters for the First Army "La Marie" in Souilly, France, 1918. Courtesy National Archives.

American Army officers attending a conference at First Army Headquarters, Tonnerre, France, January, 1919. Courtesy National Archives.

Army Observation Group, Army Artillery Observation Group, Army Air Service Troops.
French: 1st Air Division, 1st Air Brigade, Pursuit Wing Number 1, Pursuit Group 15, Pursuit Group 18, Pursuit Group 19, Park Group 6, Bombardment Group 9, 2nd Air Brigade, Pursuit Wing 2, Pursuit Group 13, Pursuit Group 117, Pursuit Group 20, Bombardment Wing 13, Bombardment Group 4, Pursuit Group 14, Park 103, Pursuit Squadron 46.
Balloon Companies:
American: 9th, 10th, 11th, 12th, 42nd, 43rd, 69th.
French: 39th, 41st, 93rd
Artillery:
American: Headquarters, Army Artillery, Coast Artillery Regiments: 42nd, 43rd, 44th, 51st, 52nd, 53rd, 57th, 59th, 60th, 65th, Anti-Aircraft Artillery: 1st AA Machine Gun Battalion, Company A, 2nd AA Machine Gun Battalion, Battery B, 1st AA Battalion (CAC), 2nd AA Battalion (CAC), 7th AA Battery (CA), 66th Field Artillery Brigade, First Army Artillery Park, 2nd Corps Artillery Park, First Army Artillery and Ammunition Park, Headquarters Railway Artillery, First Army Sound Ranging Sections 2 & 4, Flash Ranging Sections 1 & 2.
French:
24th Field Artillery, 71st, 73rd, 74th, 76th 77th, 78th, 82nd, 211th Artillery, 1st, 9th, 13th Naval Batteries, 19th, 23rd Anti-Aircraft Artillery Group, 9th Searchlight Company, Mobile Repair Unit 202.
Cavalry: 2nd Cavalry Regiment.
Chemical Warfare: 1st Gas Regiment.
Engineers: 11th, 12th, 15th, 21st, 24th Engineer Regiment (Railway), 22nd Engineer Regiment (Forestry), 23rd Engineer Regiment (Highway), 26th Engineers Regiment (Water Supply), 27th Engineers Regiment (Mining), 28th Engineer Regiment (Quarry), 37th Engineers Regiment (Electrical & Mechanical), 56th Engineer Regiment (Searchlight), 464th Engineer Regiment (Pontoon), 602nd Engineer Regiment, 51st, 52nd, 53rd Infantry Regiment (Pioneer).
Medical Corps: 45th, 51st Base Hospital, 1, 3, 6, 7, 8, 9, 13, 14th Evacuation Hospital, 114th Army Red Cross Hospital, 1st, 2nd, 3rd, 4th, 39th Mobile Hospital, 41st, 117th, 171st Field Hospital, First Army Mobile Veterinary Hospital, 5th Veterinary Hospital.
Signal Corps: 319th Field Signal Battalion, 401st, 411th Telegraph Battalion, Army Radio Section Signal Center Number 1, Radio Intelligence Section, Meteorological Division and Section, Photo Detachment, Pigeon Companies and Lofts, Detachment of Telephone Operators (Female).
Tank Corps: 344th, 354th Tank Battalion.

This is the basic First Army insignia; the embroidered letter "A" designates the First Army all executed upon an olive drab background.

Many variations of the First Army insignia exist that designate subordinate units. The upper and lower sections of the "A" are often used to distinguish these units. In this example, the First Corps insignia is added to the upper section of the "A." As such, this is the insignia of the First Army, First Corps.

This example uses both the upper and lower sections to designate the unit. The lower propeller being pierced by the arrow indicates Anti-Aircraft Machine Gun Battalions. When coupled with the "1" located in the upper block, this identifies the unit as the 1st Anti-Aircraft Machine Gun Battalion.

The 3rd Pioneer Infantry Regiment adopted this embroidered First Army insignia along with a red shell below the legs of the "A."

Examples of First Army insignia also exist with both Corps and Divisional insignias added to the basic design. In this fully embroidered example of a First Army, 5th Corps, 37th Division insignia, the divisional insignia occupies the upper section while the corps insignia serves as fill for the space between the legs of the "A."

This First Army, 59th Ammunition Train insignia uses crimson red, the color used by the ordnance branch as a background along with the letter "T" bisecting the "A." The insignia forms the monogram "AT" for ammunition train.

Miscellaneous: Ordnance Detachment First Army, Army Traffic Police, Army Motor Transport Park, Graves Registration Unit 301, Field Remount Squadron 304th, 108th, 303rd Mobile Ordnance Repair Shop, Provisional Water Trains.

September 26, 1918 – November 11, 1918:

Corps:
American: I, III, IV, V, VI, VII.
French: II (Colonial), XVII, XXXIII.
Divisions:
American: 1st, 2nd, 3rd, 4th, 5th, 6th, 7th, 26th, 28th, 29th, 32nd, 33rd, 35th, 36th, 37th, 40th, 42nd, 77th, 78th, 79th, 80th, 81st, 82nd, 88th, 89th, 90th, 91st, 92nd.
French: 2nd Dismounted Cavalry, 5th Cavalry, 10th, 15th (Colonial), 18th, 39th, 73rd.
Air Service:
American: Headquarters, Air Service First Army, 1st Pursuit Wing, 1st Pursuit Group, 2nd Pursuit Group, 3rd Pursuit Group, 1st Day Bombardment Group, Night Bombardment Group, Army Observation Group, Army Artillery Observation Group, Army Air Service Troops.
French: 16th Pursuit Group.
Artillery:
American: Headquarters, Army Artillery, 31st, 32nd, 39th Coast Artillery Brigade, 44th, 51st, 55th, 56th, 57th, 58th, 59th, 60th, 65th Coast Artillery Regiment, First Army Artillery Park, First Army Provisional Park, 51st, 52nd, 53rd Ammunition Train, Tractor Artillery Replacement Battalion, 2nd Section Range Finders, 30th Coast Artillery Brigade (Railway Artillery), 42nd, 43rd, 52nd, 53rd Coast Artillery Regiment, 1st, 2nd, 3rd, 4th, 5th Naval Batteries.
French:73rd, 81st, 82nd, 86th, 87th, 282nd, 317th, 420th Heavy Artillery, 6th, 10th, 11th, 12th, 16th, 17th, 18th Naval Batteries, 151st Foot Artillery.
Anti-Aircraft Artillery: 1st, 2nd AA Artillery Battalion, 1st, 2nd AA Machine Gun Battalion. II Corps Artillery Park, Special Meteorological Section for Long Range, Artillery Repair Shop, Ammunition Reclamation Depot 1, Ammunition Depot Consolidated, French Searchlight Company Number 3.
Chemical Warfare:
American:
1st Gas Regiment. Army Gas Depots A, C, D, and E.
British: Royal Engineers, Special Companies D, E, P, R, Z, & J.
Engineers: 11th, 12th, 14th, 15th, 16th, 21st, 22nd, 24th Engineer Regiment (Railway), 23rd Engineer Regiment (Road), 24th Engineer Regiment (Shop), 25th Engineer Regiment (Construction), 26th Engineers Regiment (Water Supply), 27th Engineers Regiment (Mining), 28th Engineer Regiment (Quarry), 35th Engineer Regiment (Railway Shop), 37th Engineers Regiment (Electrical & Mechanical), 40th Engineer Regiment (Camouflage), 56th Engineer Regiment (Searchlight), 2nd, 3rd, 5th, 6th, 54th, 56th, 59th, 801st, 802nd, 804th, 805th, 806th, 807th, 808th , 815th 816th Infantry Regiment (Pioneer) 505th, 508th, 522nd, 524th, 527th, 528th, 530th, 535th, 537th, 542nd, 544th, 545th 546th, 603rd, 604th Service Battalions, 17th, 18th, 303rd, 330th, 339th, 344th Labor Battalions, 114th Engineer Regiment.
Medical Corps: 45th , 51st , 83rd, Base Hospital, 1st, 3rd, 4th, 5th, 6th, 7th, 8th, 9th, 10th, 11th, 12th, 13th, 14th , 15th, 16th, 20th, 21st, 22nd, 23rd, 59th, 114th Evacuation Hospital, 1st, 2nd, 4th, 5th, 6th, 7th 8th, 9th, 39th Mobile Hospital, 14th, 39th, 41st, 42nd, 44th, 116th, 117th, 162nd, 163rd, 332nd Field Hospital, 14th, 110th, 114th Army Red Cross Hospital, Army Mobile Veterinary Hospital.
Military Police: First Army Military Police Battalion, Army Traffic Police.
Quartermaster Corps: First Army Graves Registration Service
Signal Corps: 317th, 319th, 322nd Field Signal Battalion, 52nd, 55th, 401st, 411th Telegraph Battalion, Army Radio Section Signal Center Number 1, Radio Intelligence Section, Meteorological Section, Photo Section, Mobile Pigeon Lofts, Stationary Pigeon Lofts, Detachment of Telephone Operators (Female).
Tank Corps: 1st Brigade Tank Corps: 344th, 345th, 3rd Brigade Tank Corps: 504th, 505th French Tank Regiment, , French 1st & 4th Tank Group.

Commanding Generals:
General John J. Pershing, Lieutenant General Hunter Liggett.

Bibliography:

Lanza, Conrad H. *The Army Artillery, First Army*. 2 vols. Typescript, no date.

Liggett, Hunter. *Commanding an American Army: Recollections of the World War*. Boston, MA: Houghton Mifflin, 1925.

Ray, Max A. *The History of the First United States Army From 1918-1980*. Ft. Meade, MD: First Army Field Print, 1980.

U.S. Army. *First Army. Report of the Commanding General, First Army, American Expeditionary Forces: Organization and Operations*. Mimeo. np, nd.

—. *Report of the First Army, American Expeditionary Forces, Organization and Operations*. Fort Leavenworth, KS: General Service Schools Press, 1923.

—. *Summaries of Intelligence, First Army, American Expeditionary Forces: Complete in Two Parts*. np, 1918.

—. *Summary of Operations, First Army, American Expeditionary Forces, Aug. 9 to Nov. 11, 1918*. France, 1919.

U.S. Army. War College. Historical Section. *The Genesis of the American First Army*. Washington, DC: GPO, 1938.

—. *Order of Battle of the United States Land Forces in the World War: American Expeditionary Forces: General Headquarters, Armies, Army Corps, Services of Supply, and Separate Forces*. Washington, DC: GPO, 1937.

The addition of a felt red horse head at the base of the "A" signifies the 305th Field Remount Squadron. Red is used as the remount mission fell under the purview of the ordnance department.

Left: Another example of First Army Anti-Aircraft Machine Gun Battalions; this example does not designate the specific battalion.

Above: This example of Aircraft Machine Gun Battalions adds a blue background behind the propeller and arrow perhaps indicating a specific battalion.

Left: The standard American Aircraft roundel of the AEF was (from the outside) red, blue, and white; when this roundel is coupled with the First Army "A", the insignia indicates First Army Air Service. This unusual variant example locates the roundel between the legs of the "A" but omits the color blue.

This more commonly encountered, fully embroidered example, of the First Army Air Service insignia follows the conventional use of the roundel.

Another example of the First Army Air Service insignia locates the roundel in the center of the "A."

This First Army Anti-Aircraft Artillery insignia uses scarlet red, representative of the branch color of Artillery, and locates two additional "A"s at the base of the First Army "A" forming a monogram for "AAA" or Anti-Aircraft Artillery.

On December 14, 1918, General Hunter Liggett attempted to formalize First Army insignia. Memorandum 45 used a series of red and white shapes to distinguish between subordinate units. First Army Artillery was designated by red and white divided horizontal fill between the lower legs of the "A."

Left: The red and white "A" insignia was in use by First Army Artillery prior to the adoption of Memorandum 45; this example of a First Army Artillery Park precedes the memorandum adding a white bear in the top section of the "A."

Prior to Memorandum 45, the First Army Band added the bullion lyre, long used in the Army to distinguish band members, to the "A" to denote their insignia.

Memorandum 45 specified a red and white divided rectangle placed between the legs of the "A" vertically to designate First Army Band.

Left: The shield and colors of the American Chemical Society are added behind the "A" of the First Army to designate the First Army Chemical Warfare section or 1st Gas Regiment.

The red castle, the symbol of the Corps of Engineers, placed between the legs of the "A" indicates First Army Engineers. This example features die cut "A" and castle.

Another First Army Engineer insignia; fully embroidered "A" and castle.

This insignia follows memorandum 45 and designates First Army Headquarters Battalion and unassigned personnel.

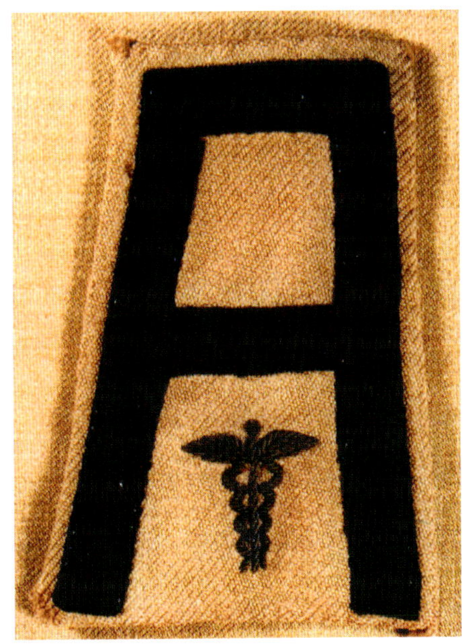

Above
Left: This First Army Medical insignia also follows the approved pattern specified in Memorandum 45.

Center: A First Army Medical insignia using the caduceus of the Medical Corps as the designating feature of the design.

Right: A variant First Army Medical insignia with bullion caduceus.

Far left: First Army Military Police patterned after the Memorandum 45 design.

Left: Per Memorandum 45, this insignia was to designate, "All other enlisted personnel, miscellaneous and special services, Army field clerks."

This is the First Army Motor Transport insignia specified in the memorandum.

A variant of the First Army Motor Transport insignia predates the memorandum and incorporates the Army Motor Transport Corps insignia as its distinguishing feature.

This insignia designates the wearer as an officer of the Headquarters First Army not assigned or attached to organizations or services; this example follows Memorandum 45.

Above

Left: First Army Ordnance uses the red flaming bomb of the Ordnance Corps between the legs of the "A"; this pattern was approved by Memorandum 45.

Center: A fully embroidered variant of the First Army Ordnance insignia.

Right: An unusual example of the First Army Pioneer insignia; this specimen uses the letter "P" to indicate pioneers.

Left: A fully embroidered example of the First Army Quartermaster insignia; this is the approved design under Memorandum 45.

A variant example using the quartermaster emblem between the legs of the "A" to designate First Army Quartermaster.

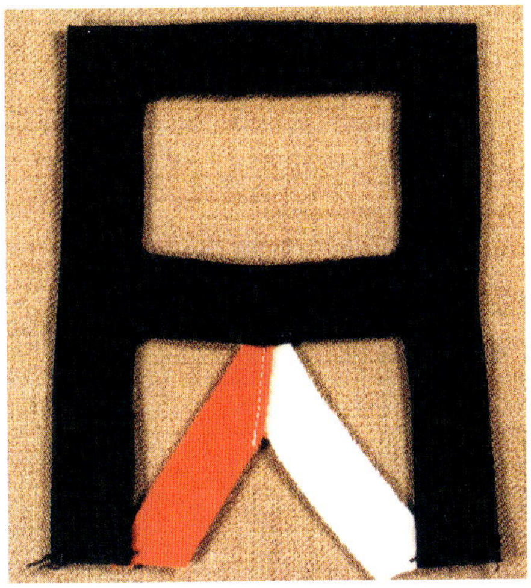

This First Army Service Battalions insignia follows the Memorandum 45 guidance.

An orange diamond placed between the legs of the "A" indicate First Army Signal units under the guidance of Memorandum 45.

This variant uses the crossed semaphore flags, the branch insignia of the Signal Corps, between the legs of the "A' to designate First Army Signal units.

The addition of the tank corps triangle indicates First Army Tank Corps units on this fully embroidered example.

This insignia worn by the First Army Headquarters staff personnel was never authorized under Memorandum 45; the fully embroidered example incorporates a monogram indicative of First Army Headquarters.

Lieutenant General Robert Lee Bullard, commander Second Army. Courtesy National Archives.

Army insignia originally used "A" for First Army, "B" for Second Army and "C" for Third Army, however, the Second Army insignia quickly changed to a "2" in lieu of the "B." This is the standard felt on felt insignia.

Second Army

Second Army was organized September 20, 1918 at Toul, Meurthe-et-Moselle. The unit was demobilized April 15, 1919 in France.[5]

Insignia:
On a green background the numeral "2" with the top red and the bottom white suggesting the unit designation and the red and white representative of the colors found on the army standard. The insignia was approved on December 11, 1918. An alternate version exists bearing a block figure "B". This design was originally prepared based on the idea that if First Army was an "A", Second should wear a "B". This style was never officially sanctioned.

Campaigns:
Lorraine 1918[6]

Organization:[7]
October 12, 1918 – November 11, 1918

Corps: IV, VI, VII for supply, French II (Colonial) and French XVII.
Divisions: 4th, 7th, 28th, 33rd, 35th, 37th, 79th, 88th (175th Infantry Brigade), 92nd, French 39th, French 2nd Dismounted Cavalry.
Air Service:
American: Headquarters, Chief of Air Service, Second Army. 4th Pursuit Group: Headquarters; 17th, 25th, 141st, and 148th Squadrons; 6th Air Park. 5th Pursuit Group: Headquarters; 41st, 138th, and 648th (Park) Squadrons. 2nd Day Bombardment Group: Headquarters; 100th and 163rd Squadrons; Photo Section 9, miscellaneous units: Squadrons: 14, 138, 278, 354, and 484. Photo Section 11.
French: Aero Squadrons: 28th, 47th, 277th; Balloon Companies: 20, 52. 92nd Balloon Company (Anti-Aircraft).
Artillery:
American: 39th and 40th Coast Artillery Brigade Headquarters. Detachments of 42nd, 43rd, 51st, and 57th Coast Artillery Regiments. Army Artillery Repair Park 201. First Army Ammunition and Artillery Park. 1st Battalion Trench Artillery. Advance Unit Army Ordnance Park 10.
French: Repair Section 282nd Heavy Artillery. Units of 5th Foot Artillery (120 mm, 155 mm), 39th Foot Artillery (75mm), 103rd Foot Artillery (155 mm), 120th Foot Artillery (155 mm), 155th Foot Artillery (155 mm), 182nd Foot Artillery (155 mm), 273rd Foot Artillery (75 mm), 1st Tractor Company, 82nd Heavy Artillery (Tractor). Flash Ranging Section 67, 73, Sound Ranging Section 16. Anti-aircraft Artillery: Battery C 1st Anti-Aircraft Battalion. 2nd Anti-Aircraft Battalion less Battery A. 1st Anti-Aircraft Machine Gun Battalion less Company A. Group of 75 mm semi-fixed sections Numbers: 27, 46, 48, 55, 57, 70, 119, 123, 125, 162, 163, 164, 195, 197, 208, and 213.
Chemical Warfare Service: British Royal Engineers: Headquarters Company and Special Companies C, E, F, O, and 3.
Engineers: Detachments of the following engineer regiments: 11th (Railway), 12th (Railway), 15th (Railway), 20th (Forestry), 21st (Railway and Shop), 22nd (Railway Construction), 23rd (Highway), 24th (Shop), 26th (Water Supply), 27th (Mining), 28th (Quarry), 29th (Topographical), 37th (Electrical and Mechanical), 40th (Camouflage), 41st (Forestry), 56th (Searchlight), 114th (Divisional), 301st (Divisional). Service battalions, complete or part: 505th, 508th, 522nd, 524th, 528th, 530th, 535th, 542nd, 543rd, 546th. Pioneer Infantry Regiments, complete or part: 51st, 59th, 803rd, 804th, 806th, 808th, 813th. Miscellaneous units: 465th Pontoon Train. 802nd Water Tank Train, Detachment of 1st Provisional Water Train, 2nd Provisional Water Train, 805th Labor Battalion, 324th Labor Battalion, Mobile Water Purification Unit. Administrative Labor Company 101, French Labor Company 22.
Graves Registration Service: 308th, 309th, and 310th Graves Registration Units.
Medical Corps: Hospitals: Evacuation: 1st, 2nd, 12th, 13th, and 18th. Field: 4th, 44th, and 117th.

A fully embroidered variant of the Second Army insignia.

Another variant of the fully embroidered "2."

Veterinary: 2nd, 3rd, 5th, and 102nd. Neurological: 3rd. Base: 3rd, 55th, 61st, 78th, 82nd, and 87th. Mobile: 3rd, 4th, 7th, 39th. Justice Hospital Group. Ambulance Companies: Evacuation: 1st, 3rd, 4th, 7th, 8th, 10th, 12th, and Provisional Company 1. Field: 41st, 44th, and 161st. US Ambulance Sections: 520th, 570th, 571st, 600th, and 603rd. Miscellaneous Units: Mobile Surgical Units 10 and 11. Veterinary Sections: 7 and 8. Mobile Veterinary Unit 303. Sanitary Squads 310 and 316. Orthopedic Train Battalion: 3 companies Toul Hospital Center.

Military Police: Second Army MP Battalion (after Oct 24); before that date the following companies: Co A, 5th MP (5th Div), Co B, 7th MP (7th Div), Co B, 310th MP (35th Div), Co A, 314th MP (89th Div).

Signal Corps: Headquarters Detachment Signal Corps. 115th Field Signal Battalion. Detachment of 310th Field Signal Battalion. 405th, 409th, and 419th Telegraph Battalions. Army Photo Section 2. Army Radio Section 2. Photo Section 37. Mobile (Signal) Machine Shop. Pigeon Lofts: Stationary: 1, 5, 7, 9, 15, 16, 18, 23, 25, 30, 31, and 33; Mobile: 14, 17, 19, 21, 22, 23, and 33.

Miscellaneous: Second Army Headquarters and Headquarters Troop. 2nd Heavy Mobile Ordnance Repair Shop. Machine Shop Truck Units 8, 314, 338, 398, and 399. Motor Transport Corps Overhaul Park. Motor Truck Co 480. Quartermaster Corps Supply Companies 305 and 419. Advance Services Supply Park (Army Service Park 1). Air Service Park 2. Field Remount Squadron 304. Sales Commissary Units: 3, 5, 12, 31, 304, 312, and 313. Laundry Companies: 503, 504, and 510. Mobile Laundry Company 307. Butchery Companies: 310, 343, and 351. Mobile Ordnance Repair Shop 308. First Army Supply Train (later 439th Supply Train). Detachments of 305th and 324th Labor Battalions. VI Corps Replacement Battalion. Mobile Water Purification Unit. Second Army Postal Depot.

During Post Armistice Activities, November 12, 1918 – April 15, 1919:

Corps: IV, VI, IX, French XVII.

Divisions: 3rd, 4th, 5th, 7th, 28th, 33rd, 35th, 79th, 88th, 92nd.

Air Service:

American: Headquarters Air Service Second Army, 4th Pursuit Group: Headquarters; 17th, 25th, 141st, and 148th Squadrons; 6th Air Park. 5th Pursuit Group: Headquarters; 41st, 138th, and 648th (Park) Squadrons, 2nd Day Bombardment Group: Headquarters; 73rd (Park), 100th, and 163rd Squadrons; Photo Sections: 9, 11, 16. 2nd Day Observation Group: Headquarters; 85th, 135th, 168th, 258th, 278th, and 354th Squadrons; Photo Section 3. Miscellaneous units: 56th, 86th (Park), 199th, 223rd, 281st, 484th.

French: 47th and 277th Squadrons, Photo Section 13. 3rd Air Park (Air Service Casual Company 4). Detachment of Air Service 1st Motor Mechanic Regiment.

Balloons: IX Corps Balloon Group Headquarters.

American: Balloon Companies: 10, 13, 14, 15, 16, 24, 25, 26, 44, and 69.

French: Balloon Companies: 20, 52.

Artillery:

American: 39th Artillery Brigade (Coast Artillery Corps) Headquarters, 40th Artillery Brigade (Coast Artillery Corps) Headquarters, 44th Coast Artillery. Detachment 51st Coast Artillery. 53rd Coast Artillery: 2 batteries (340mm), 2 batteries (190 mm), 1 battery (400 mm). 58th Coast Artillery. Detachment of 65th Coast Artillery. Anti-Aircraft Artillery: Battery C, 1st AA Artillery. 2nd AA Artillery Battalion less Battery A. 1st AA Machine Gun Battalion less Company A. AA Batteries 5, 11, 12.

French: 74th Heavy Artillery (190 mm); 5th Foot Artillery (120 mm, 155 mm) 50th Battery, 7th Foot Artillery, 182nd Foot Artillery (155 mm), 117th Heavy Artillery, 142nd Heavy Artillery, 1 battery 47th Railroad Artillery, Repair Section 282nd Tractor Heavy Artillery. Group 75mm semi-fixed sections, Numbers: 27, 46, 48, 55, 57, 70, 119, 123, 125, 162, 163, 164, 195, 208, 213.

Cavalry: Detachments of the 2nd Cavalry Regiment.

Chemical Warfare Service: British Royal Engineers: Headquarters Company and Special Companies C, E, F, O, and S.

Engineers: Detachments of the following Engineer regiments: 11th (Railway), 12th (Railway), 14th (Railway), 21st (Railway and Shop), 22nd (Railway Construction), 23rd (Highway), 24th

Right: This fully embroidered Second Army insignia uses the "B" coupled with an inset 4th Corps insignia to designate the wearer as Second Army, 4th Corps.

Far right: The addition of the Engineer Castle at the base of the "2" is used in this example for Second Army Engineers.

Below: A rarely encountered Second Army Remount Depot includes a monogram "RD" below the Second Army insignia.

(Shop), 26th (Water Supply), 28th (Quarry), 29th (Topographical), 40th (Camouflage), 47th (Railway Maintenance), 56th (Searchlight), 63rd (Transportation), and 313th (Divisional). Service battalions, complete or part: 505th, 508th, 515th, 522nd, 524th, 526th, 527th, 528th, 530th, 535th, 537th, 540th, 542nd, 543rd, 545th, 546th. Pioneer Infantry Regiments, complete or part: 3rd, 59th, 803rd, 804th, 805th, 806th, 807th, 813th, 815th, 816th. Labor Battalions: 305th, 313th, 318th, 319th, 322nd, 324th, 328th, 329th, 330th, 332nd, 339th, 341st, 343rd, 344th, 347th. Depot Labor (Service) Companies: 22nd, 34th, 36th, 38th, 39th, 40th. Miscellaneous units: Railroad and Construction Companies 41 and 42. 1st Railroad Artillery Construction Battalion. Various Engineer depots. Group of French 9th Searchlight Company. French Flash Ranging Sections 67 and 73. French Sound Ranging Section 16. 465th Pontoon Train. 302nd Water Tank Train.

Graves Registration Service: 308th, 309th, 312th, and 313th Graves Registration Units.

Medical Corps: Hospitals: Evacuation: 1st, 2nd, 12th, 13th, 15th, 18th, and 37th; Mobile: 3rd, 7th, and 39th; Field: 39th, 41st, 117th, 157th, 158th, and 159th; Veterinary: 2nd, 3rd, 5th, 7th, 8th, 9th, 12th, 13th, 17th; Neurological: 3rd; Base: 83rd, 90th, 91st; Center: Commercy. Ambulance Companies: 32, 33, 39, 41, 157, 158, 159. Evacuation Companies: 1, 3, 4, 7, 12, 32, 33, 68, 69, 70, 71, and Provisional Company 1. US Ambulance Sections: 560, 570, 571, and 600.

Miscellaneous Units: Surgical Unit 11. Veterinary Sections: 7, 8, 103, and 301. Convalescent Depot 1. Advance Medical Supply Depot 2. Provisional Sanitary Squad 1. Units of the 115th Sanitary Train.

Military Police: Second Army MP Battalion, 2nd Provisional MP Battalion (144th MP Battalion).

Signal Corps: Headquarters Detachment Signal Corps. 115th Field Signal Battalion. 409th and 419th Telegraph Battalions. Army Signal Park "A". Second Army Photo Section. Army Radio Section 2. Pigeon Lofts: Stationary: 1, 5, 7, 9, 15, 16, 18, 23, 25, 26, 30, and 31; Mobile: 17, 19, 22, and 33.

Miscellaneous Units: Second Army Headquarters and Headquarters Troop. Headquarters Detachment, 2nd and 4th Heavy Mobile Ordnance Repair Shops. Mobile Ordnance Repair Shop 308. Machine Shop Truck Units 311, 338, 378, and 388. Motor Transport Corps Overhaul Park. Motor Truck Company 480. Supply Company 419. Air Service Park 784. Advance Services Supply Park. Service Parks 1 and 2. Service Parks Units: 311, 320, 338, 378, 388, 407, 417, and 420. Motor Supply Train 439. Prisoner of War Companies: 22, 61, 64, 65, 77, 78, 85, 94, 104, 226, 252, and 258. Salvage units: 4, 5, 7, 13, 14, 19, 21, 22, 24, 25, 301, 303, 304, 307, 315, and 319. Mobile Laundry Companies: 301, 307, 308. Laundry Companies: 503, 504, 508, 510, 512, 515, and 516. Clothing and Bathing Unit 336. Bakery Company 309. Depot Labor

Companies: 38, 39, and 40. Railroad and Construction Companies 43 and 44. Second Army Postal Depot. Sales Commissary Units: 58, 61, and 313. Mobile Laboratory. Field Remounts Squadron 304 and 305. Army Supply Train, Second Army. IV and VI Corps Replacement Battalions. Second Army Machine Gun and Small Arms Center.

Commanding Generals:
General John J. Pershing, Lieutenant General Robert L. Bullard.

Bibliography:

Adams, James Greenleaf. *Review of American Forces in Germany*. Coblenz, Germany: James G. Adams, 1921.
American Battle Monuments Commission. *American Armies and Battlefield in Europe*. Washington: Government Printing Office, 1938.
Harbord, James G. *The American Army in France, 1917-1919*. Boston: Little, Brown and Company, 1936.
Millett, Allan Reed. *The General Robert L. Bullard, An Officership in the United States Army, 1881-1925*. Westport, CT: Greenwood Press, 1975.
Pershing, John J. *My Experiences in the World War*. New York: Frederick A. Stokes Co., 1931.
39th Anniversary, Second United States Army, 1918-1957. Arlington: Cooper-Trent of Virginia, 1957.
Thomas, Shipley. *The History of the A.E.F.* New York: George H. Doran Co., 1920.

Major General Joseph T. Dickman, the first commander of the Third Army, Germany, 1919. Courtesy National Archives.

Third Army

The Third Army was organized at Ligny-en-Barrois, France between 7 and 15 November 1918 and was demobilized on July 2, 1919 in Germany.[8]

Insignia:
The insignia consisted of a blue disc with a white letter "A" within a red circle forming the monogram "A O O" emblematic of Army of Occupation, the principal duty of the Army following the 1918 Armistice. The disc with two borders alludes to the numerical designation (3) of the unit. There is a variant insignia with the letter "C" following the "A" as First Army, "B" as Second Army and "C" as Third Army. This insignia was never authorized.

Campaigns:
None.

Organization:[9]

This building was the Headquarters of the Third Army in Coblenz, Germany, 1919. Courtesy National Archives.

Corps: III, IV, VI, VII.
Divisions: 1st, 2nd, 3rd, 4th, 5th, 32nd, 33rd, 42nd, 89th, 90th.
Air Service: 17th, 27th, 41st, 94th, 103rd, 138th, 141st, 638th Squadrons (Pursuit). 96th, 166th Squadrons (Day Bombardment). 9th, 24th, 85th, 88th, 91st, 168th, 186th, 258th, 278th, 354th Squadrons (Observation). 462nd and 463rd Construction Squadrons. 1st, 2nd, 3rd, 4th, and 6th Air Parks. 2nd 3rd, 5th, 9th, 10th, 11th, 12th, 13th, 16th, and 104th Photo Sections. 14th Company 1st Air Service Mechanics Regiment.
Balloon Companies: 2nd, 13th, 14th, 15th, 16th, 25th, 26th, and 44th.
Artillery: 66th Field Artillery Brigade (146th, 148th FA) (155 mm). 1st Battalion 10th Field Artillery (75 mm).
Cavalry: 2nd Cavalry Regiment less 2nd and 3rd Squadrons. Troop K 3rd Cavalry. French 2nd Cavalry Division.
Chemical Warfare Service: Demonstrations Parties Numbers 1, 2, and 3.
Engineers: 24th Engineers: Companies C and E. 26th Engineers: Companies C and F. 29th Engineers: Company M. 37th Engineers, 115th Engineers. Companies A, E, and D, 301st Engineers. Pioneer Infantry: 1st, 51st, 54th, and 56th. 3rd Battalion, 3rd Pioneer Infantry Headquarters Provisional Engineers. 301st Water Train.

As with the other armies, Third Army's original insignia was to be a "C." Given the Armistice and the Armies' principal mission of the occupation of Germany, the insignia changed to a monogram for Army of Occupation. Here is a standard fully embroidered example.

A variant of the Third Army insignia.

Another example of the Third Army insignia of much higher quality.

Infantry: 4th, 7th, 30th, 38th Infantry Regiments (3rd Division); 39th, 47th, 58th, 59th Infantry Regiments, 11th Machine Gun Battalion (4th Division). Third Army Composite Regiment.
Medical Corps: Third Army Sanitary Train: US Ambulance Service Sections 542, 590, 601, and 603; Evacuation Ambulance Companies: 5, 26, 29, 30, 31, and 33. Evacuation Hospitals: 2nd, 3rd, 4th, 6th, 7th, 8th, 9th, 12th, 13th, 14th, 16th, 18th, 19th, 22nd, 26th, 27th, 29th, 30th, and 49th. Field Hospital 343. Third Army Mobile Laboratory. Army Mobile Laboratory. Medical Supply Depot. Medical Supply Depots 1 and 2. Advance Medical Supply Depot 2. Mobile Surgical Units 1 and 12. Mobile Field Laboratory 315.
Military Police: Third Army MP Battalion. 139th and 141st MP Battalions. 1st General Headquarters MP Battalion. IV Corps MP Company. VI Corps MP Company. VII Corps MP Company. MP Companies: 216, 286, and 299.
Signal Corps: 322nd Field Signal Battalion. Telegraph Battalions: 51, 417. Third Army Radio Section. Meteorological Section. Post Signal Office.
Miscellaneous: Mobile Veterinary Section: 110, 117, 301, and 308. Corps Mobile Veterinary Hospitals: 1 and 7. Third Army Veterinary Evacuation Sections: 1, 2, and 3. Veterinary Unit 12. VII Corps Field Veterinary Unit. Field Remount Squadrons: 301, 302, 303, 304, 306, 309, 310, 311, 312, 314, 322, and 344. Mobile Veterinary Hospitals 308 and 315. I and VI Corps Artillery Parks. Graves Registration Provisional Unit "B" Group 1. Salvage Squadrons: 1, 3, 12, 16, 301, 303, 309 and 310. 4th Ammunition Train (4th Div). 501st Mobile Ordnance Repair Shop. Mobile Ordnance Repair Shop. 1st Heavy Artillery Mobile Ordnance Repair Shop. Ordnance Depot 303. Third Army Machine Gun and Small Arms Center. Ammunition Depots 351 and 400. Third Army Quartermaster Depot. Third Army Quartermaster Depot Detachment, Port Commander Detachment, Third Army Water Transport Service. Transportation Corps Detachment (later Headquarters 24th Grand Division Transportation Corps). Advance Embarkation Section. Third Army Provisional Supply Train; Motor Truck Companies: 431, 432, 433, 434, 435, 436, 441, 450, 463, 464, 466, 467, 468, 469, 517, 831, "A", "B", "C" 314th Supply Train, "F" 315th Supply Train. Service Park Units: 302, 305, 307, 361, 390, 391, 394, 396, 397, 398, 399, and 696. 19th Provisional Motor Command (Companies A, B, C, D, E, F). Motor Transport Companies: 428, 814, 815, 816, 817, 818, and 819. Third Army Park Detachment Motor Transport Corps Repair Units 310 and 320. Headquarters Garage Detachment Supply Co 334. Bakery Companies: 1, 7, 10, 11, 302, 307, 310, 339, 349, and 365. Butchery Companies 306, 316, and 351. Sales Commissary Units 12, 19, 39, 47, 49, 59, and 311. Third Army Leave Area Sales Commissary. Mobile Bathing Units 11, 13, and 14. Clothing and Bathing Units 320, 322, 324, 325, 326, 327, 330. Laundry Companies 503, 516, 523, 525, 526, and 528. Third Army Regional Replacement Depot. Army Post Office 927. Inter-Allied Railway and Inland Waterway Commission Detachment. Motor Dispatch Service Detachment, Graves Registration Unit 309. Headquarters Third Army. Headquarters Troop Third Army.

This beautiful example uses bullion and fine embroidery.

The "C" pattern Third Army insignia with roundel indicating Third Army Air Service.

Commanding Generals:
Major General Joseph T. Dickman, Major General Edward F. McGlachlin, Jr., Lieutenant General Hunter Liggett.

Bibliography:
History of the Third U.S. Army, November 14, 1918 to July 2, 1919. Washington, Second Section, General Staff, 1919.
Metheny, E.A. *History of the Third United States Army, 1918-1962.* Fort McPherson, GA: Third United States Army, 1967.
Review of American Forces in Germany. Coblenz, Germany: James G. Adams, 1921.

Major General William M. Wright, succeeded Major General Dickman as the third Commander of I Corps in November of 1918. Courtesy National Archives.

I Corps

The First Corps was organized at Neufchateau, France 15-20 January 1918. It was demobilized in France on March 25, 1919.[10]

Insignia:
The Corps chose a black disc with a white border. The disk was the insignia of the First Corps, during the Civil War and was one of the hardest fighting corps in the Army of the Potomac. Under the command of Major General John F. Reynolds, this corps was largely credited with saving the Federal Army on the first day of the battle of Gettysburg. This most certainly was a factor in the decision to retain the insignia.

Campaigns:
Champagne-Marne, Aisne-Marne, St. Michiel, Meuse-Argonne, Ile de France 1918, Champagne 1918. Lorraine 1918.[11]

Organization:[12]

Headquarters of I Corps for the Champagne offensive, at Rarecourt, France, August, 1918. Courtesy National Archives.

On Front West of Château-Thierry, July 4-17, 1918:

Divisions: 1st, 2nd, 3rd, 4th, 26th, 28th, French 167th.
Air Service: Corps Observation Group: Headquarters; 1st, 12th, and 88th, Aero Squadrons; Flight B 648th Aero Squadron; Photo Section 1. 183rd Aero Squadron. First Pursuit Group: Headquarters; 27th, 94th, 95th, and 147th, Aero Squadrons; Flight C 648th Aero Squadron.
Balloon Wing I Corps: Balloon Wing Company A; 1st and 2nd Balloon Companies.
Artillery:
American: Headquarters 66th Field Artillery Brigade; Headquarters, 1st and 3rd Battalions 146th FA (155); 1st Battalion Trench Artillery Coast Artillery Corps; 1st Anti-Aircraft Battalion (75); Headquarters Corps Artillery; I Corps Artillery Park; 1st and 2d Battalions.
French: 103rd Artillery (105mm); 1st Battalion, 334th Artillery (155mm); 1st and 3rd Battalions 333rd Artillery (155mm); Flash Ranging Section 83.
Engineers: Companies B and D 30th Engineers (later 1st Gas Regiment units); detachment of 40th Engineers (camouflage unit); Sound Ranging Section 2 (detachment of Company B 29th Engineers).
Infantry: I Corps Replacement Battalion; 2 Battalions French 161st Territorial.
Medical Corps: Mobile Veterinary Hospitals 1 and 103.
Signal Corps: 332nd Field Signal Battalion; 406th Telegraph Battalion.
Miscellaneous: Corps Headquarters; Headquarters Troop; Corps Remount Depot.

DURING THE AISNE-MARNE OPERATION, JULY 18-AUG 6, 1918:

Divisions: 3rd, 4th, 26th, 28th, 32nd, 42nd, French. 62nd, 167th.
Air Service: Corps Observation Group: Headquarters 1st, 12th, and 88th, Aero Squadrons; Flight B 648th Aero Squadron; Photo Section 1. 183d Aero Squadron (later 1st Park Company). First Pursuit Group: Headquarters; 27th, 94th, 95th, and 147th, Aero Squadrons; Flight 3 648th Aero Squadron.

Fully embroidered I Corps insignia.

A felt on felt version of the I Corps insignia.

Balloon Wing I Corps: Balloon Wing Company A; 1st and 2nd Balloon Companies.
Artillery:
American: 66th Field Artillery Brigade; 1st Battalion Trench Artillery, Coast Artillery Corps; 1st Anti-Aircraft Battalion (75mm); Headquarters Corps Artillery; I Corps Artillery Park; II Corps Artillery Park; Flash Ranging Section 1.
French: 3rd Battalion 90th Artillery (155mm); 1st Battalion 102nd Artillery (105mm); 2nd Battalion 107th Artillery (120mm); 1st Battalion 131st Artillery (105mm); 2nd and 4th Battalions 281st Artillery (220mm); 5th Battalion 285th Artillery (280mm); 1st Battalion 288th Artillery (220mm); 1st Battalion 307th Artillery (155mm); 1st Battalion 318th Artillery (155mm); 1st Battalion 333rd Artillery (155mm); 3rd Battalion 333rd Artillery, subsequently 8th Battalion 109th Artillery (155mm); 1st Battalion 334th Artillery (155mm); 2nd and 3rd Battalions 407th Artillery (155mm); Flash Ranging Section 83.
Cavalry:
American: Troops A and C, 2nd Cavalry; detachment of Troop K, 3rd Cavalry.
French: 2nd, 38th, and 164th Cavalry Division.
Engineers: 1st Pioneer Infantry; detachments of 14th, 23rd, 26th, 37th, and 40th, Engineers; Companies B and C, 27th Engineers; Headquarters 1st Battalion and Companies B and D, 30th Engineers (later 1st Gas Regiment units); 101st Engineers and Train (26th Div); 308th Engineers and Train (83rd Div); Sound Ranging Section 2 (detachment of Company B, 29th Engineers).
Infantry: I Corps Replacement Battalion; 2 battalions French 67th Territorial.
Medical Corps: Mobile Veterinary Hospitals 1 and 103; Field Hospitals 162 and 163; Ambulance Company 163.
Signal Corps: 322nd Field Signal Battalion; 406th Telegraph Battalion.
Tank Corps: French 319th and 326th Tank Companies.
Miscellaneous: Corps Headquarters and Headquarters Troop; Corps Remount Depot; Provisional Corps Supply Train; Motor Supply Train 414; 2nd Replacement Battalion USMC.

ON THE VESLE FRONT, AUG 7-13, 1918:

Divisions: 4th, 26th, 42nd, 77th, French 62nd.
Air Service: Corps Observation Group: Headquarters; 1st, 12th, and French 237th, Aero Squadrons; Flight B 648th Aero Squadron; Photo Sec. 1. 183rd Aero Squadron (later 1st Park Company). First Pursuit Group: Headquarters; 27th, 94th, 95th, and 147th, Aero Squadrons; Flight 3 648th Aero Squadron; 218th Aero Squadron (later 4th Park Company).
Balloon Wing I Corps: Balloon Wing Company A; 1st and 2nd Balloon Companies.
French: 59th Balloon Company.
Artillery:
American: 66th Field Artillery Brigade (155mm); 1st Battalion Trench Artillery, Coast Artillery Corps; 1st Anti-Aircraft Battalion (75mm); Headquarters Corps Artillery; I Corps Artillery Park; II Corps Artillery Park; Flash Ranging Section 1.
French: 67th Artillery Brigade; 29th Battery, 68th Foot Artillery; 25th Battery, 69th Foot Artillery; 3rd Battalion, 90th Artillery; 1st Battalion, 102nd Artillery (105mm); 1st Battalion, 286th Artillery (220mm); 7th and 8th Battalions, 307th Artillery (155mm); 2nd Battalion, 407th Artillery (155mm).
Cavalry: Troops A and C, 2nd Cavalry; detachment of Troop K, 3rd Cavalry.
Engineers: 1st Pioneer Infantry; detachments of 14th, 23rd, and 26th Engineers; Companies B and C, 27th Engineers; Companies B and D, 30th Engineers (later 1st Gas Regiment units); 308th Engineers and Train (83rd Div); Sound Ranging Section 2 (detachment of Company B, 29th Engineers).
Infantry: I Corps Replacement Battalion; I Corps Replacement Battalion USMC; 2 battalions French 67th Territorial.
Medical Corps: Mobile Veterinary Hospital 1; Field Hospitals 161, 162, and 163; Ambulance Company 163.
Signal Corps: 322nd Field Signal Battalion; 406th Telegraph Battalion.
Miscellaneous: Corps Headquarters; Headquarters Troop; Corps Remount Depot; Motor Supply Train 414.

DURING THE ST-MIHIEL OPERATION AUG 22-SEPT 17, 1918:

Divisions: 1st, 2nd, 5th, 35th, 78th, 82nd, 90th.
Air Service:
American: Corps Observation Group: Headquarters; 1st, 12th, and 50th Aero Squadrons; Flight B, 648th Aero Squadron; Photo Section 1.
Balloon Wing I Corps: Balloon Wing Company A; 1st, 2nd, 5th, and 42nd Balloon Companies.
French: 208th, 211th, and 214th Aero Squadrons, 6th, 7th, and 69th Balloon Companies.
Artillery:
American: 59th Coast Artillery (8" howitzers); 60th Coast Artillery (155mm); 164th Field Artillery (89th Div); 1st Battalion Trench Artillery (240mm); 1st Anti-Aircraft Machine Gun Battalion; I Corps Provisional Artillery Park; Flash Ranging Section 1.
French: 46th Artillery Ammunition Section (105mm); 49th Field Artillery-Portée (75mm); 35th, and one-half of 40th Batteries 176th Trench Mortar (150mm); 37th and 38th Batteries 176th Trench Mortar (240mm); one-half of 40th Battery 176th Trench Mortar (240mm); one-half of 2nd Battalion 182nd Foot Artillery (155mm); one-half of 3rd Battalion 183rd Foot Artillery (155); 219th Field Artillery-Portée (75); 3rd Battalion 282nd Artillery (220mm); 238th Field Artillery - Portée (75mm); 247th Field Artillery - Portée (75mm); 2nd Battalion 342nd Artillery (155mm); 317th Artillery (155mm); 1st and 3rd Battalions 413th Artillery (155mm); 451st Artillery (105mm). French Sector Artillery: 2nd, 3rd, and 23rd Batteries 6th Foot Artillery (120mm); 2nd Battery 6th Foot Artillery (145); 13th Battery 6th Foot Artillery (155mm); 1st and 3rd Battalions 182nd Foot Artillery (120mm); 1st and 2nd Battalions 183rd Foot Artillery (120mm).
Cavalry: Headquarters 1st Squadron and Troops A, C, and D, 2nd Cavalry.
Chemical Warfare: Headquarters 1st Battalion and Companies A, C, E, and F, 1st Gas Regiment.
Engineers: Detachments of 26th, 27th, and 30th Engineers; 2nd and 3rd Battalions 53rd Pioneer Infantry; 111th Engineers and Train (36th Div); Sound Ranging Section 2A (detachment of 29th Engineers).
Medical Corps: I Corps Sanitary Train: Headquarters; Evacuation Ambulance Company 12; Ambulance Company 163; Ambulance Sections 520, 570, and 603; Field Hospitals 161, 162, and 163. Mobile Veterinary Hospital 1.
Signal Corps: 322nd Field Signal Battalion; 406th Telegraph Battalion.
Tank Corps: 13th, 14th, and 15th Battalions of French 505th Mobile Artillery (209 light tanks); 34th and 35th Battalions of 11th Groupment of Mobile Artillery (28 medium tanks).
Miscellaneous: Corps Headquarters; Headquarters Troop; Corps Remount Depot; Motor Supply Train 414; I Corps Replacement Battalion; 302nd Supply Company; Company A 307th Military Police.

DURING THE MEUSE-ARGONNE OPERATION, SEPT 21-NOV 10, 1918:

Divisions: 1st, 6th, 28th, 35th, 36th, 42nd, 77th, 78th, 80th, 82nd, 91st, 92nd, French 5th Cavalry.
Air Service:
American: Corps Observation Group: Headquarters; 1st, 12th, and 50th Aero Squadrons; Flight B, 648th Aero Squadron; Photo Section 1.
Balloon Wing I Corps; Balloon Wing Company A; 1st, 2nd, and 5th Balloon Companies.
French: 211th Aero Squadron, 93rd Balloon Company.
Artillery:
American: 59th Coast Artillery (8" howitzers); 65th Coast Artillery (9.2"); I Corps Provisional Artillery Park; III Corps Artillery Park: Headquarters and 2 Batteries, 1st Battalion Trench Artillery (240mm); one Company 52nd Ammunition Train; the motorized section 103rd Ammunition Train (28th Div); Companies A and C, 315th Ammunition Train (90th Division); Company A, 316th Ammunition Train (91st Division); 1st, 2nd, 9th, 10th, 37th, 38th, and 39th Batteries, Flash Ranging Section 1 and 2A (detachments of 29th Engineers).

French: 176th Trench Mortar (58mm); 3rd, 4th, 12th, 23rd, and one-half of 40th Batteries, 176th Trench Mortar (240mm); 11th and one-half of 40th Batteries, 176th Trench Mortar (150mm); 219th Field Artillery - Portée (75mm); 238th Field Artillery- Portée (75mm); 247th Field Artillery Portée (75mm); 4th and 5th Battalions, 282nd Artillery (220mm); 5th Battalion and 29th Battery 289th Artillery (280mm); 2nd and 3rd Battalions, 317th Artillery (155mm); 2nd Battalion, 342nd Artillery; 413th Heavy Artillery; 416th Heavy Artillery; 451st Heavy Artillery and 46th Ammunition Section (105mm); 12th, 17th and 85th Sound Ranging Sections; 14th, 37th, 57th, 73rd, 74th, and 79th Flash Ranging Sections. 39th Battery, 5th Foot Artillery (155mm); 6th Foot Artillery; 37th, 38th, 41st, and 42nd Batteries, 8th Foot Artillery; 39th Battery, 8th Foot Artillery (155mm); 43rd Battery, 8th Foot Artillery (95mm); 1st Battalion, 183rd Artillery (120mm).

Cavalry: Regimental Headquarters, 1st Squadron, and Troops F and H, 2nd Cavalry.

Chemical Warfare: Headquarters, 1st Battalion and Companies C and E, 1st Gas Regiment.

Engineers: 111th Engineers and Train (36th Division); 114th Engineers and Train (39th Division); 307th Engineers and Train (82nd Division); 317th Engineers and Train (92nd Division); 53rd Pioneer Infantry; 339th Labor Battalion.

Medical Corps:

American: I Corps Sanitary Train: Headquarters; Evacuation Ambulance Company 11; Ambulance Companies 41, 161, and 163; Ambulance Sections 506, 520, 569 and 570, Mobile Veterinary Hospitals 1, 103, and 117.

French: Ambulance Sections 5, 131, 145, 505, 506, and 524, Sanitary Sections 50, 145.

Signal Corps: 322nd Field Signal Battalion; 406th Telegraph Battalion.

Tank Corps:

American: 1st Brigade Tank Corps: 344th Tank Battalion (57 tanks); 345th Tank Battalion (62 tanks); 321st Tank Company. 9th Company, 2nd Motor Mechanic Regiment.

French: 14th Company of Heavy Tanks (22 tanks); 17th Company of Heavy Tanks (22 tanks).

Miscellaneous: Corps Headquarters; Headquarters Troop; Corps Remount Depot; 303rd Remount Squadron; Motor Supply Train 414; I Corps Replacement Battalion; 302nd Supply Company; Service Park Unit 368; Company A, 317th Military Police Company (I Corps Military Police Company).

Commanding Generals:

Major General Hunter Liggett, Major General Joseph T. Dickman, Major General William M. Wright, Major General Samuel D. Sturgis.

Bibliography:

U.S. Army, I Corps. Field Orders Numbers 2-95, 5 Jul-9 Nov 1918. Mimeo,1918.

—, G-2. *Summary History of the First American Army Corps From Its Creation, January 15,1918, to the Cessation of Hostilities, November 11, 1918.* Mimeo, 1918.

U.S. Army War College, Historical Section. *Order of Battle of the United States Land Forces in the World War: American Expeditionary Forces: General Headquarters, Armies, Army Corps, Services of Supply, and Separate Forces.* Washington, DC:GPO, 1937.

Wright, W.M. *General Mission on 1st Army Corps in St. Mihiel Operation, with a Review of Its Activities From August 10th to September 16th, 1918.* Mimeo, France, 1919.

Major General George W. Read, Commander of II Corps, France, 1918. Courtesy National Archives.

II Corps

The corps was organized February 24, 1918 at Montreuil, France and demobilized February 1, 1919 at LeMans, France.[13]

Insignia:

This corps incorporated the traditional colors of blue and white, which stem from the use of these colors on the standard of a field corps. The insignia consists of a blue rectangle, bordered white, with the Roman numeral II flanked by a rampant Lion (sinister) and rising Eagle (dexter) facing each other. The Lion and Eagle are representative of the combined nature of this corps. The II Corps was composed of troops from Britain and the United States; the Lion symbolizes Britain and the Eagle symbolizes the United States.

Campaigns:
Somme Offensive.[14]

Organization:[15]

ON THE BRITISH FRONT, INCLUDING THE SOMME OFFENSIVE OPERATION, JUNE 15-NOV 18, 1918:

Divisions: 27th, 30th, 33rd, 37th, 78th, 82nd, 91st; British 1st & 6th; Australian 2nd, 3rd and 5th.
Air Service:
American: 17th, 148th Aero Squadrons; 193rd Observation Flight detachment.
Australian: 3rd Aero Squadron.
British: 5th Balloon Wing.
Artillery:
Australian units: 2nd, 3rd, 4th, 5th Divisional Artillery (4.5" howitzers); 6th & 12th Army Brigades Field Artillery (4.5" howitzers).
British units: Headquarters, VII Corps Royal Artillery; Headquarters, VII Corps Heavy Artillery; 9th , 41st Mobile Brigades, Royal Garrison Artillery (6" howitzers); 51st, 93rd Mixed Brigades, Royal Garrison Artillery (6", 8" & 9.2" howitzers); 68th, 71st Brigades, Royal Garrison Artillery (8" howitzers); 18th Brigade Royal Garrison Artillery (9.2" howitzers); 73rd Army Brigade Royal Garrison Artillery Headquarters; 222nd, 449th, 504th Siege Batteries, Royal Garrison Artillery (6" howitzers); 49th Siege Battery, Royal Garrison Artillery (12" howitzers).
Cavalry: British 20th Hussars.
Engineers:
Australian: First Army Troops Company; 1st & 2nd Tunneling Companies; 3rd & 5th Battalions of Pioneer Infantry; one section Electrical and Mechanical Company, Australian Corps Troops, Mechanical Transport Company.
British: 144th, 146th, 216th, 238th, 288th Army Troops Companies, Royal Engineers; Number 1 Siege Company Royal Anglesey Engineers; 182nd Tunneling Company, Royal Engineers, one section 353rd Electrical and Mechanical Company, Royal Engineers.
Medical Corps:
American: Corps Mobile Veterinary Hospital.
British: Motor Ambulance Company 37, Casualty Clearing Station Numbers 12, 41, 48, 50, 53, 58.
Signal Corps: 318th Field Signal Battalion; 412th Telegraph Battalion.
Tanks Corps:
American: 301st Tank Battalions; 6th Tank Battalion less one company.
British: 2nd Tank Brigade Headquarters; 4th Tank Brigade: 1st, 4th Battalion.
Miscellaneous: Corps Headquarters; Headquarters Troop; Corps Replacement Battalion; Corps, Military Police Company; Corps Salvage Repair Company; Bakery Company 10; 74th Labor Company; Company D, 345th Labor Battalion; Graves Registration Service Unit 302; 159th Infantry Replacement Regiment; 143rd Machine Gun Replacement Battalion.

DURING POST-ARMISTICE ACTIVITIES, NOV 19, 1918-JAN 31, 1919:

Divisions: 27th, 30th, 37th, 91st, 92nd.
Medical Corps: Corps Mobile Veterinary Hospital; Mobile Veterinary Section 108; 106th Sanitary Train.
Signal Corps: 318th Field Signal Battalion; 412th Telegraph Battalion.
Miscellaneous: Corps Headquarters; Headquarters Troop; Corps Replacement Battalion; Corps Military Police Company; Corps Salvage Repair Company; 822nd Labor Company; Company D, 345th Labor Battalion; Graves Registration Service Unit 307; 159th Infantry Replacement Regiment; 143rd Machine Gun Replacement Battalion; Sales Commissary Unit 61.

Performer Elsie Janis visits the American II Corps. She is escorted by Colonel G.S. Simonds, II Corps Chief of Staff, and General Sir Henry Horne, Commander of the British First Army, Bruges, France, July, 1918. Courtesy National Archives.

This fully embroidered insignia of the II Corps features the Eagle representing the United States along with the Lion representing England. The II Corps was a combined US/UK Corps.

A high quality bullion example of the II Corps insignia.

Commanding General:
Major General George W. Read.

Bibliography:

U.S. Army, II Corps. *Monograph, II Corps*, 1918.

—, *Records of the World War: Field Orders, 2nd Army Corps*. Washington, DC: GPO, 1921.

U.S. Army War College, Historical Section. *Order of Battle of the United States Land Forces in the World War: American Expeditionary Forces: General Headquarters, Armies, Army Corps, Services of Supply, and Separate Forces*. Washington, DC: GPO, 1937.

War Department, General Staff, Historical Branch, War Plans Division. *Operations of the 2nd American Corps in the Somme Offensive, August 8 to November 11, 1918*. Washington, DC:GPO, 1920.

III Corps

Third Corps was organized May 16, 1918 at Mussy-sur-Seine, France and demobilized on August 9, 1919 at Camp Sherman, Ohio.[16]

Insignia:
The insignia of the Third Corps incorporates the field corps blue and white color scheme. The insignia is in the shape of a caltrop: a defensive device which when dropped always lands with one of its pointed spikes pointing upward. This device was used against mounted and dismounted troops since antiquity. The profile shows three of the points in blue alluding to the corps number with a triangular center in white.

Campaigns:
Aisne-Marne, Oise-Aisne, Meuse-Argonne, Champagne 1918, Lorraine 1918.[17]

Secretary of the Navy, Josephus Daniels (fourth from left, front row) visits with Major General John L. Hines, Commander of III Corps (front row with no hat) at his home at Neuweid on the Rhine, Neuweid, Germany, 1919. Courtesy National Archives.

Headquarters Commandant, Captain J.C. Thompson, III Corps and his staff at Echternach, Luxemburg, December, 1918. Courtesy National Archives.

Organization:[18]

DURING THE AISNE-MARNE OPERATION, AUG 4-6, 1918

Divisions: 3rd, 28th, 32nd , French 4th.
Air Service:
American: 88th Aero Squadron; Photo Section 48; 4th Balloon Company.
French: 4th, 39th, 58th, 273rd & 380th Aero Squadrons; 44th, 47th, 54th & 90th Balloon Companies.
Artillery:
American: 31st Heavy Artillery Brigade: 55th and 56th Regiments Coast Artillery.
French: Headquarters III Corps Artillery; III and XXXVIII Corps Artillery Parks; III Corps Ammunition Train; 11th Field Artillery (75mm); 13th Artillery Train; 1st and 2nd Battalions 89th Artillery (155mm); 1st Battalion 103rd Artillery (105mm); 1st Battalion 138th Artillery and Ammunition Train (105mm); 214th Field Artillery (75mm); 307th Anti-aircraft Machine Gun, B Co; 3rd Battalion 316th Artillery (155mm); 2nd Battalion 338th Artillery (155mm).
Cavalry:
American: Troop I, 2nd Cavalry.
French: 2nd Squadron and 2 Machine Gun Sections, 7th Chasseurs; 2 Squadrons and 2 Machine Gun Sections, 10th Chasseurs.
Engineers:
American: 1st Battalion, 14th Engineers; 2nd Battalion, 1st Pioneer Infantry.
French: Engineer Companies 3/3 & 3/4; Bridge Companies 3/16 & 6/17, III Corps Engineer Train.
Medical Corps:
French: Ambulance Companies 5/2, 7/3 & 13/3. III Corps Collecting detachment.
Signal Corps:
American: 308th Field Signal Battalion; 52nd Telegraph Battalion.
French: III Corps Telegraph Company; XXXVIII Corps Radio Section.
Miscellaneous:
American: Corps Headquarters; Headquarters Troop; Corps Replacement Battalion.
French: III Corps Supply Train; 203rd Supply Train; 1st and 3rd Battalions 26th Territorial Infantry; III Corps Slaughtering Section.

The III Corps chose the three pointed caltrop as their insignia; this is the standard die cut variety.

A fully embroidered example of the III Corps insignia.

WHILE ON THE VESLE FRONT, AUG 7-17, 1918:

Divisions: 3rd, 28th, 32nd, 77th, French 4th, 164th.
Air Service:
American: Headquarters Air Service III Corps; 88th Aero Squadron; Photo Section 6; 4th Balloon Company.
French: Corps Aviation Staff; 4th, 39th, 58th, 280th & 380th Aero Squadrons; Photo Section 48; 44th & 54th Balloon Companies.
Artillery:
American: 31st Heavy Artillery Brigade: 55th & 56th Regiments Coast Artillery; 121st Field Artillery (155mm); I & II Corps Artillery Parks.
French: 11th Field Artillery (75mm); 1st and 2nd Battalions 89th Artillery (155mm); 1st Battalion, 103rd Artillery (105mm); 6th Battalion, 112th Artillery (155mm); 1st and 2nd Battalions 138th Artillery (105mm); 214th Field Artillery (75mm); 1st and 3rd Battalions 221st Field Artillery (75mm); 307th Anti-Aircraft Machine Gun Company, 3rd Battalion 316th Artillery (155mm); 1st Battalion, 320th Artillery (155mm); 2nd Battalion, 338th Artillery (155mm).
Cavalry:
American: Troop I, 2nd Cavalry; Troop K, 3rd Cavalry.
French: 2nd Squadron and 2 Machine Gun Sections, 7th Chasseurs; 2 Squadrons and 2 Machine Gun Sections, 10th Chasseurs.
Chemical Warfare: Company B, 1st Gas Regiment.
Engineers:
American: 14th Engineers; Company A, 23rd Engineers; Company D, 26th Engineers; Company C, 27th Engineers; detachment of 40th Engineers (camouflage), 308th Engineers and Train; 1st Pioneer Infantry.
French: Engineer Companies 3/3 & 3/4; Bridge Companies 3/16 & 6/17.
Medical Corps:
American: 41st Ambulance Company; 41st Field Hospital Company; Corps Mobile Veterinary Hospital 1.
French: Ambulance Companies 5/2, 7/3 & 13/3; III Corps Collecting detachment.
Signal Corps:
American: 308th Field Signal Battalion; 52nd Telegraph Battalion; Pigeon detachment (4 cotes).
French: III Corps Telegraph Company; XXXVIII Corps Radio Section. 1st and 3rd Battalions 26th Territorial Infantry; Sec 13 Aux Supply Train; 203rd Supply Train; III Corps Slaughtering Section.
Miscellaneous: Corps Headquarters; Headquarters Troop; Corps Replacement Battalion; Truck Co 10.

DURING THE OISE-AISNE OPERATION, AUG 18-SEPT 9, 1918:

Divisions: 28th, 32nd, 77th, French 62nd.
Air Service:
American: Headquarters Air Service III Corps; Corps Observation Group: 88th Aero Squadron; Photo Section 6.
French: 239th, 280th & 284th Aero Squadrons. 4th Balloon Company. 47th and 54th Balloon Companies.
Artillery:
American: 31st Heavy Artillery Brigade: 55th and 56th Regiments Coast Artillery (155mm); 121st Field Artillery (155mm); I Corps Artillery Park.
French: 29th Anti-Aircraft Battalion (less Companies 15, 16 & 207, Machine Gun); 307th Anti-Aircraft Machine Gun Company.
Cavalry:
American: Troop I, 2nd Cavalry; Troop K, 3rd Cavalry.
French: 1st and 2nd Squadrons, 10th Chasseurs.
Chemical Warfare: Company B, 1st Gas Regiment.

Engineers:
American: 14th Engineers; Company A, 23rd Engineers; Company D, 26th Engineers; Company C, 27th Engineers; detachment of 40th Engineers (camouflage), 308th Engineers and Train; 1st Pioneer Infantry.
French: Bridge Companies 3/6, 14/18, and 14/19; Engineer Company 24/4.
Medical Corps: 322nd Ambulance Company; 332nd Field Hospital Company; Corps Mobile Veterinary Hospital 1; Corps Veterinary Hospital 103.
Signal Corps: 308th Field Signal Battalion; 52nd Telegraph Battalion; 4 pigeon lofts.
Miscellaneous: Corps Headquarters; Headquarters Troop; Corps Replacement Battalion; 501st Mobile Ordnance Repair Shop; Remount Squadron 302, Sales Commissary Unit 33.

WHILE ON MEUSE-ARGONNE FRONT, INCLUDING OPERATIONS, SEPT 14-NOV 11, 1918:

Divisions: 1st, 3rd, 4th, 5th, 28th, 32nd, 33rd, 35th, 79th, 80th, 89th, 90th, 91st, French 157th.
Air Service:
American: Headquarters Air Service III Corps: Corps Observation Group: 88th and 90th Aero Squadrons; 199th Park Squadron; Photo Section 6.
French: 204th, 205th, 208th, and 284th Aero Squadrons. III Corps Balloon Group: 3rd, 4th, 9th, 11th, and 42nd Balloon Companies.
Artillery:
American: 57th Field Artillery Brigade (32nd Division); 66th Field Artillery Brigade (less 147th Field Artillery and 116th Trench Mortar Battery); 13th Field Artillery (4th Division); 16th Field Artillery (4th Division); 3rd Battalion, 51st Coast Artillery (8" Howitzer); 56th Coast Artillery (155mm); 57th Coast Artillery (155mm); 60th Coast Artillery (155mm); 77th Field Artillery (4th Division); Company, C, 2nd Anti-Aircraft Machine Gun Battalion; I Corps Artillery Park, 305th Trench Mortar Battery.
French: 2 battalions, 81st Artillery (145mm); 228th Field Artillery (75mm); 250th Field Artillery-Portée (75mm); 29th Battery and 6th Battalion, 289th Artillery; 2 battalions, 289th Artillery (220mm); 308th Artillery (155mm CS/17); 407th Artillery (155mm LS/17); 413th Artillery (155mm LS/17); 456th Artillery (105mm); Flash Ranging Sections 56 and 73; Sound Ranging Section 27.
Cavalry: Troop I, 2nd Cavalry; Troop K, 3rd Cavalry.
Chemical Warfare: 1st Battalion (Companies A and B); Provisional Battalion (Companies A, C and F).
Engineers:
American: 5th Engineers & Train (7th Division); 6th Engineers & Train (3rd Division); 7th Engineers & Train (5th Division); 305th Engineers & Train (80th Division); 308th Engineers & Train; 315th Engineers & Train (90th Division); 1st Pioneer Infantry; one battalion 808th Pioneer Infantry; 464th Pontoon Company.
French: 17/16, 15/18, 9/19 Bridge Companies.
Medical Corps:
American: Headquarters III Corps Sanitary Train: Ambulance Sections 560, 571, 599, 602; Ambulance Company 332; Headquarters Field Hospital Section; Field Hospital 332; Mobile Hospital 1. Evacuation Ambulance Company No 1. Corps Mobile Veterinary Hospital 1; Corps Mobile Veterinary Sec 103.
French: Mobile Ambulance Sections 63, 84, 85.
Signal Corps:
American: Mobile Pigeon Lofts 9 & 11; 308th Field Signal Battalion; 52nd Telegraph Battalion.
French: Mobile Pigeon Lofts 45, 47, 63, & 222.
Miscellaneous: Corps Headquarters; Headquarters Troop; III Corps Military Police Company; MSTU 405: 415th Motor Supply Train; 501st Mobile Ordnance Repair Shop; Mobile Laundry 301; Remount Squadron 302; Sales Commissary Unit 33.

MARCH TO THE RHINE AND OCCUPATION OF COBLENZ BRIDGEHEAD, NOV 17, 1918-JULY 1, 1919:

Divisions: 1st, 2nd, 3rd, 4th, 32nd 42nd, French 2nd Cavalry.
Air Service: Headquarters Air Service, III Corps: Corps Observation Group: 1st, 24th, 88th, 90th, 168th, 186th, 199th (Park), and 258th Aero Squadrons; Photo Sections 5, 6, 16, 101, 104.
III Corps Balloon Group: Balloon Wing Company B; 1st, 3d, 4th, 9th, 14th, 24th, and 44th Balloon Companies.
Artillery: 66th Field Artillery Brigade (less 147th Field Artillery and 116th Trench Mortar Battery); FRS 1; I Corps Artillery Park.
Cavalry: 1st Squadron & Troop I, 2nd Cavalry; Troop K, 3rd Cavalry.
Engineers: 4th Engineers (less one battalion) & Train; Company F 26th Engineers; Co B 37th Engineers; Detachment of 40th Engineers (camouflage); 308th Engineers & Train; 464th Pontoon Company; 1st Pioneer Infantry; 56th Pioneer Infantry.
Medical Corps: Corps Sanitary Train: Headquarters; Headquarters Ambulance Section; Ambulance Companies 162, 163, 329, 331, 332. Headquarters Field Hospital Section; Field Hospital 162, 163, 329, 332, 343, Mobile Veterinary Hospital 1.
Military Police: 139th MP Battalion; III Corps MP Company; 286th MP Company; 299th MP Company.
Signal Corps: 308th Field Signal Battalion; 52nd Telegraph Battalion.
Miscellaneous: Corps Headquarters; Headquarters Troop; III Corps Educational Center; III Corps Reinforced Brigade; APO 754; Baking Companies 7 & 365; 501st Mobile Ordnance Repair Shop; 415th Motor Supply Train; Service Park Units 390 & 405; Remount Squadrons 302 & 306; Sales Commissary Unit 33.

Commanding Generals:
Major General William M. Wright, Major General John E. McMahon, Major General Robert L. Bullard, Major General John L. Hines, Major General Edward F. McGlachlin, Jr.

Bibliography:
U.S. Army War College, Historical Section. *Order of Battle of the United States Land Forces in the World War: American Expeditionary Forces: General Headquarters, Armies, Army Corps, Services of Supply, and Separate Forces*. Washington, DC: GPO, 1937.

Major General Charles H. Muir, Commander, IV Corps, at Boucq, France, October, 1918. Courtesy National Archives.

IV Corps

The corps was organized June 20, 1918 at Neufchateau, France and demobilized on May 11, 1919.[19]

Insignia:
The insignia of the IV Corps also incorporates the field corps blue and white color scheme. Their insignia is a disc divided into four equal parts of alternating blue and white fields alluding to the corps number

Campaigns:
St. Mihiel, Lorraine 1918.[20]

Organization:[21]

ON THE ST-MIHIEL FRONT, INCLUDING THE OPERATION, AUG 20-SEPT 16, 1918:

Division: 1st, 2nd, 3rd, 6th, 36th, 37th, 42nd, 78th, 79th, 82nd, 89th, 90th, 91st, 92nd.
Air Service:
American: Corps Observation Group: Headquarters; 8th, 24th, 50th, 90th, and 135th Aero Squadrons; Flight C, 255th Aero Squadron (later 3rd Air Park); Photo Sections 4 and 6.

Corps Balloon Group: Balloon Wing Companies B and C; 2nd and 4th Balloon Companies.
French: 218th Observation Squadron
Artillery:
American: 1st and 2nd Battalions, 44th Coast Artillery (8" howitzers); 2nd Battalion, 57th Coast Artillery (155mm); 55th Field Artillery Brigade and Ammunition Train; 58th Field Artillery Brigade and Ammunition Train; 67th Field Artillery Brigade and Ammunition Train; 148th Field Artillery (155mm); II Corps Artillery Park; 108th Mobile Ordnance Repair Shop; Sound Ranging Section 4; Flash Ranging Section 2.
French: 6th Artillery (2 batteries 95mm, 3 batteries 120mm, 1/2 battery 145mm, and 1/2 battery 155mm); also affûts-trucs (railway mounting) (4 batteries of 4 pieces 120mm, 1 battery of 2 pieces 155mm); 4th Battalion 73rd Artillery (270mm); 10 batteries 120th Artillery; 39th Battery 176th Trench Mortar (58mm); 160th Artillery (8 batteries 120mm, 6 batteries 155mm, and 2 batteries 220mm); 212th Field Artillery (75mm); 228th Field Artillery (75mm); 250th Field Artillery (75mm); 1st Battalion 308th Artillery (155mm); 317th Artillery (155mm); 1 Battalion 320th Artillery (155mm); 330th Artillery (155mm); 2nd Battalion 342nd Artillery (155mm); 454th Artillery (105mm); 456th Artillery (105mm); 2 batteries (95mm); sector Artillery.
Cavalry: Troops B, D, F, H, and M, 2nd Cavalry.
Chemical Warfare: Headquarters; Companies A and F, 1st Gas Regiment.
Engineers: 6th Engineers and Train (3rd Division); 51st Pioneer Infantry; 301st Engineers and Train; 2nd Battalion 310th Engineers.
Medical Corps:
American: Corps Sanitary Train: Headquarters; Ambulance Sections 560, 571, and 603; Evacuation Ambulance Company 11. Detachment of Mobile Veterinary Hospital 5.
French: Ambulance Section 131.
Signal Corps: 310th Field Signal Battalion; 401st and 405th Telegraph Battalions.
Tanks Corps:
American: 1st Tank Brigade: Headquarters; 326th and 327th Tank Battalions. 3rd Tank Brigade.
French: 14th and 17th Companies of 4th Heavy Battalion.
Miscellaneous: Corps Headquarters; Headquarters Troop; Motor Supply Train 413; Corps Replacement Battalion; Machine Shop Truck Unit 369; Sales Commissary Unit 31; Company A 303rd Train Headquarters and Military Police (78th Division).

Top: Major General Muir and the IV Corps Staff, France, October, 1918. Courtesy National Archives.

Above: Lieutenant M. O'Brien of the IV Corps poses showing his Corps insignia. Courtesy Military History Institute

WHILE IN TOUL SECTOR AND THIAUCOURT ZONE, SEPT 17-NOV 16, 1918:

Divisions: 1st, 2nd, 4th, 5th, 7th, 28th, 33rd, 35th, 37th, 42nd, 77th, 78th, 79th, 82nd, 88th (1 brigade), 89th, 90th, 92nd, French 69th.

This is a standard example of a felt on felt IV Corps insignia.

A fully embroidered example.

Air Service:
American: Corps Observation Group: Headquarters: 8th, 85th, 90th, 135th, 168th, 218th, and 258th Aero Squadrons; Flight C, 3rd Air Park (formerly 255th Aero Squadron); Photo Section. 4.
Corps Balloon Group: Balloon Wing Company C; 3rd, 9th, 10th, 13th, 15th, 16th, 43rd, and 69th Balloon Companies.
French: 208th, 214th, and 218th Aero Squadrons.
Artillery:
American: 21st Field Artillery (155mm); Headquarters, 39th Artillery Brigade Coast Artillery; 44th Coast Artillery (8" howitzers); 51st Coast Artillery (less 3rd Battalion) (240mm and 270mm); 58th Coast Artillery (8" howitzers); 3rd Battalion, 65th Coast Artillery (9.2" howitzers); 134th Field Artillery (75mm); 135th Field Artillery (75mm); 136th Field Artillery (155mm); 150th Field Artillery (155); 3rd Battalion, 303rd Field Artillery (155); 309th Field Artillery (155mm); 328th Field Artillery (75mm); 329th Field Artillery (75mm); 351st Field Artillery (155mm); 165th Field Artillery Brigade; 2nd Battalion Trench Artillery (95mm); 2 batteries 1st Battalion Trench Artillery (95mm and 240mm); II Corps Artillery Park; IV Corps Artillery Park; Flash Ranging Sections 1A, 2A, and 3A; Sound Ranging Sections 1A, 2A, and 3.
French: Groups of 6th Artillery; 3rd and 4th Groups 155th Artillery (formerly 6th Artillery) consisting of 4th, 9th, 10th, 11th, 12th, 13th, 14th, 15th, and 16th Batteries (105mm, 120mm, 145mm, and 155mm); detachment of 132nd Artillery (95mm); 1st and 4th Battalions 160th Artillery (120mm); 35th Battery 176th Trench Mortar (58mm); 182nd Artillery (120mm, 155mm and 220mm); 183rd Artillery (85mm, 120mm, 155mm, and 220mm); 268th Artillery (75mm and 90mm); 1st Battalion 342nd Artillery (155mm); 1st, 3rd, and 9th Caterpillar Companies.
Cavalry: Troop M, 2nd Cavalry.
Engineers: 5th Engineers and Train (7th Division); 7th Engineers and Train (5th Division); 51st Pioneer Infantry; 301st Engineers and Train.
Infantry: 7th Infantry Brigade (4th Division); 175th Infantry Brigade (88th Division).
Medical Corps: Corps Sanitary Train (301st Sanitary Train): Headquarters; Ambulance Companies 301, 302, and 303; Field Hospitals 301, 302, and 303, Evacuation Ambulance Company 3. Mobile Hospitals 3, 39. Corps Mobile Veterinary Hospital, Mobile Veterinary Section 301, Evacuation Hospitals 1, 2, 12, 13.
Signal Corps: 310th Field Signal Battalion; 405th Telegraph Battalion.
Miscellaneous: Corps Headquarters; Headquarters Troop; Motor Supply Train 431 (Motor Supply Train 413): Truck Companies 431, 432, 433, 434, 435, and 436. IV Corps Provisional Replacement Battalion; Machine Shop Truck Unit 369; 306th Remount Squadron; Company B, 1st Train Headquarters and Military Police (1st Division); Company B, 7th Train Headquarters and Military Police (7th Division); Company A, 303rd Train Headquarters and Military Police

Major General Charles P. Summerall, the last commander of the V Corps, at Pouilly, France, November, 1918. Courtesy National Archives.

(78th Division); Company A, 315th Train Headquarters and Military Police (90th Division); IV Corps Military Police Company; Laundry Units 303, 304, and 308.

DURING MARCH FROM THIAUCOURT ZONE TO THE RHINE AND WHILE OCCUPYING TERRITORY WEST OF THE COBLENZ BRIDGEHEAD NOV 17, 1918-MAY 11, 1919:

Divisions: 1st, 3rd, 4th, part of 6th, 42nd.
Air Service: Headquarters; 12th, 85th, 278th, 354th, 462nd (Construction), and 463rd (Construction), Aero Squadrons. Photo Sections 3, 4, 9, and 13.
Corps Balloon Group: Headquarters; 2nd, 13th, 15th, and 16th Balloon Companies.
Artillery: IV Corps Artillery Park; Flash Ranging Section 2; Mobile Ordnance Repair Shop.
Cavalry: Troop M, 2nd Cavalry.
Engineers: 301st Engineers and Train; Headquarters 1st Battalion and Company A, 37th Engineers; 51st Pioneer Infantry.
Medical Corps: Corps Sanitary Train (301st Sanitary Train): Headquarters; Ambulance Companies 301, 302, and 303; Field Hospitals 301, 302, and 303; Corps Mobile Veterinary Hospital; Mobile Veterinary Section 301.
Signal Corps: 310th Field Signal Battalion; 405th and 417th Telegraph Battalions.
Miscellaneous: Corps Headquarters; Headquarters Troop; Motor Supply Train 413: Headquarters; Motor Truck Companies 431 to 436 including; Machine Shop Truck Unit 369; 306th Remount Squadron; Sales Commissary Unit 31; Bakery Companies 7 and 365; Corps Military Police Company; 2nd Provisional Military Police Company; 141st Military Police Battalion.

2nd Lieutenant George E. Stone, Signal Corps, Officer in Charge of 4th Corps Photo Unit. Cochem, Germany, January 9, 1919. Courtesy National Archives

Commanding Generals:
Major General Joseph T. Dickman, Major General Charles H. Muir, Major General Robert L. Howze, Major General Charles P. Summerall.

Bibliography:
U.S. Army War College, Historical Section. Order of Battle of the United States Land Forces in the World War: American Expeditionary Forces: General Headquarters, Armies, Army Corps, Services of Supply, and Separate Forces. Washington, DC: GPO, 1937.

V Corps

The corps was organized between July 7-12, 1918 at Remiremont, France and was demobilized May 2, 1919 at Camp Funston, Kansas.[22]

Insignia:
The insignia of V Corps generally incorporates the blue and white colors of a field corps. The insignia is the five-sided blue pentagon bordered in white and divided into five wedges. Variations exist using different colored wedges to designate subordinate units within the corps. Some of the known examples of this practice include V Corps Artillery which replaced the bottom blue wedge of the pentagon with a red wedge, or replaced all the blue wedges with red wedges, V Corps Cavalry which replaced all the blue wedges with yellow wedges, V Corps Infantry which substitutes a light blue wedge for the bottom wedge, and V Corps Signal which replaces the white background with orange.

This is the standard V Corps insignia; a fully embroidered pentagon in white filled with blue wedges.

Campaigns:
St. Mihiel, Meuse-Argonne, Lorraine 1918.[23]

Organization:[24]

ON THE ST-MIHIEL FRONT, INCLUDING THE OPERATION, AUG 29-SEPT 16, 1918.

Colonel A.W. Foreman (left) of the V Corps and Colonel W.C. Sweeney of GHQ, pose beside the monument erected by the V Corps to show their location on November 11, 1918 at Bouzancy, France, in April, 1919. Courtesy National Archives.

The V Corps had a penchant for using color variations in the wedges of the pentagon to designate subordinate units; in this example red is used as fill for all the wedges indicative of V Corps Artillery.

A second example of the V Corps Artillery insignia.

This example of the V Corps Artillery insignia replaces only the bottom wedge with artillery red retaining the remaining wedges in blue.

Divisions: 3rd, 4th, 26th, 33rd, 80th, French Units: 2nd Dismounted Cavalry, French 15th Colonial Infanty.
Air Service:
American: Corps Observation Group: 88th, 99th and 104th, Aero Squadrons; Photo Section 5.
Balloon Wing V Corps: Balloon Wing Company B; 6th, 7th, 8th and 12th, Balloon Companies.
French: 42nd Division Aero Squadron; 223rd Aero Squadron, 9th Balloon Company.
Artillery:
American: 66th Field Artillery Brigade less 148th Field Artillery (155).
French: 2 batteries 20th Field Artillery (75mm); 22nd Field Artillery, 3rd and 6th Battalions, 71st Artillery (240mm); 1st & 4th Battalions, 73rd Artillery (270mm); 4 groups of 155mm, 2 groups of 145mm, both 81st Artillery; 3rd Battalion, 86th Artillery (155mm); 6th Battalion, 142nd Artillery (155mm); 203rd Field Artillery (75mm); 211th Field Artillery - Portée (75mm); 238th Artillery (75mm); 246th Artillery (75mm); 5th Battalion, 282nd Artillery (280mm); 4 battalions of 220mm, and 2 battalions of 280mm, both 286th Artillery; 330th Artillery (155mm); 342nd Artillery; 3 battalions 417th Artillery (155mm); 2 battalions 420th Artillery (155mm); 20th, 28th, 32nd, Batteries 176th Artillery Trench Mortar (240mm); 11th and 16th Batteries of Naval guns (four 16" pieces); 2nd Ammunition Section. French sector Artillery: 15th & 16th Batteries, 5th Foot Artillery (155mm); 22nd Battery, 5th Foot Artillery (220mm); 26th & 28th Batteries, 5th Foot Artillery (120mm); 3 batteries (220mm) & 2 batteries (155mm).
Chemical Warfare: 2nd Battalion, 1st Gas Regiment.
Engineers: 43rd Pioneer Infantry; Headquarters and 2nd Battalion 310th Engineers; 527th Engineers; Headquarters and 1st Battalion 602nd Engineers.
Medical Corps:
American: Ambulance Sections 542 and 604.
French: Ambulance Sections 63, 85 and 131.
Signal Corps: 317th Field Signal Battalion; 55th Telegraph Battalion.
Tank Corps: 1st Brigade Tank Corps.
Miscellaneous: Corps Headquarters; Headquarters Troop; 415th Motor Supply Train (V Corps Provisional Artillery Park); V Corps Provisional Motor Supply Train (also known as 418th & 432nd Motor Supply Train); Corps Replacement Battalion; Companies B and D, 116th Supply Train; Machine Shop Truck Units 308 & 316; Corps Remount Depot (Field Remount Squadron 301); Company B, 4th Military Police (4th Division); Company B 108th Military Police.

DURING THE MEUSE-ARGONNE OPERATION, SEPT 21-NOV 11, 1918.

Divisions: 1st, 2nd, 3rd, 6th, 29th, 32nd, 37th, 42nd, 77th, 79th, 80th, 89th, 91st, French 73rd.
Air Service:
American: Headquarters Air Service, V Corps; Corps Observation Group: 99th, 104th and 183rd (1st Park Company), Aero Squadrons; Photo Section. 5.
V Corps Balloon Group: Headquarters Balloon Group, (Balloon Wing Company B until Oct); 6th, 7th, 8th, 12th & 43rd, Balloon Companies.
French: 214th and 215th Aero Squadrons, 39th Balloon Company.
Artillery:
American: 31st Brigade Coast Artillery (55th, 56th & 57th, Regiments, Coast Artillery, and 52nd Ammunition Train) (155mm); 59th Coast Artillery (8" howitzers); 65th Coast Artillery (9.2" howitzers) less 1 battalion; 66th Field Artillery Brigade (155) less 148th Field Artillery; II Corps Artillery Park.
French: 15th, 16th, 22nd & 28th Batteries, 5th Foot Artillery; 34th, 35th & 36th Batteries, 8th Foot Artillery; 5th, 6th, 7th, 8th, 17th, 18th, 19th, 20th, 24th, 28th & 32nd Batteries, 176th Artillery Trench Mortar. 203rd Field Artillery (75mm); 211th Field Artillery (75mm); 212th Field Artillery - Portée (75mm); 219th Artillery (75mm); 5th Battalion, 282nd Artillery (280mm); 6th Battalion 289th Artillery (280mm); 301st Artillery (155mm); 330th Artillery (155mm); 342nd Artillery; 420th Artillery (155mm); 454th Artillery (105mm); 494th Artillery; Flash Ranging Section 57, Sound Ranging Section 17.
Cavalry: Troops B, D, F & H, 2nd Cavalry.
Chemical Warfare: Headquarters, 2nd Battalion and Companies B and D, 1st Gas Regiment.
Engineers: 1st, 2nd, 6th, 104th & 112th Regiments of Engineers; Headquarters and 2nd Battalion, 310th Engineers; Headquarters and 1st Battalion 602nd Engineers; 52nd Pioneer Infantry.
Medical Corps:
American: Ambulance Sections 542, 590, 602, 603 & 604; Field Hospitals 338 and 339; Army Mobile Veterinary Section 103.
French: Sanitary Sections 63, 84, 85, 131.
Signal Corps: 317th Field Signal Battalion; 55th Telegraph Battalion.
Tank Corps:
American: 1st Brigade Tanks: 325th and 326th Tank Battalions. Headquarters, 3rd Tank Corps (later Headquarters 306th Tank Brigade); 331st and 345th Tank Battalions; 316th Repair and Salvage Company (later 321st Repair and Salvage Company).
French: 504th Regiment Tanks (less 1 battalion); 505th Regiment Tanks.
Miscellaneous: Corps Headquarters; Headquarters Troop; 415th Motor Supply Train (V Corps Provisional Artillery Park); V Corps Provisional Motor Supply Train (also known as 418th and 432nd Motor Supply Train) Motor Shop Truck Unit 308 (Service Park Unit 308); Corps Remount Depot (312th Remount Squadron); Companies B and D 116th Supply Train; Sales Commissary Unit 317; Corps Replacement Battalion; Company A, 4th Military Police (4th Division); Company B, 101st Military Police (26th Division).

A variant of the V Corps Artillery insignia of embroidered construction removing all the blue wedges and replacing the bottom wedge with an artillery red wedge.

Green and black were the branch colors of the Air Service. This V Corps Air Service insignia substitutes the bottom blue wedge with a green and black wedge.

The V Corps Cavalry insignia substitutes the bottom wedge with yellow, the traditional branch color of the cavalry.

Far left: This V Corps Engineer insignia replaces the left and right bottom wedges with Engineer Red wedges of felt on felt construction.

Left: A variant V Corps Engineer insignia of embroidered construction with soutasch.

The V Corps Infantry units highlighted their specialty using an embroidered Infantry Blue lower wedge.

This V Corps Ordnance insignia example features a black and scarlet bottom wedge; these colors were specified between 1902 and 1921 as the enlisted hat cord colors of the Ordnance Corps.

A V Corps insignia outlined in Signal Corps orange, identifies this insignia as V Corps Signal.

DURING POST-ARMISTICE ACTIVITIES, NOV 12, 1918-FEB 11, 1919.

Divisions: 2nd, 5th, 26th, 29th, 42nd, 77th, 80th, 82nd, 89th, 90th.
Air Service:
American: Headquarters Air Service, V Corps; Corps Observation Group: 99th, 104th & 183rd (1st Park Company), Aero Squadron; Photo Section 5.
V Corps Balloon Group: Headquarters; 6th, 7th, 8th & 12th Balloon Companies.
French: 214th and 215th Aero Squadrons.
Artillery:
American: 58th Field Artillery Brigade less 123rd Field Artillery (33rd Division); 59th Coast Artillery; II Corps Artillery Park.
French: 57th Flash Ranging Section, Sound Ranging Section 17.
Cavalry: Troops D and F, 2nd Cavalry.
Engineers:
American: Company I, 2nd Pioneer Infantry; 52nd Pioneer Infantry; Company C, 101st Engineers (26th Division); Headquarters and 2nd Battalion, 310th Engineers; Headquarters and 1st Battalion, 602nd Engineers; 603rd Engineers; 604th Engineers.
French: Pontoon Companies 9/19 and 15/18.
Medical Corps: Ambulance Company 335; Ambulance Sections 542, 590, 603 & 604; Field Hospital 335, 338 & 339; Army Mobile Veterinary Section 103.
Signal Corps: 317th Field Signal Battalion; 55th and 406th Telegraph Battalions.
Tank Corps: 306th Brigade Tank Corps; Headquarters; 331st and 345th Tank Battalions; 316th Repair and Salvage Company.
Miscellaneous: Corps Headquarters; Headquarters Troop; 432nd Motor Supply Train (formerly 418th Motor Supply Train); Service Park Unit 308; 312th Remount Squadron; V Corps Military Police; Sales Commissary Unit 317.

Major W.H. Halslip, Secretary of the General Staff, 5th Army Corps, Cheppy, Meuse, France. Courtesy National Archives

Commanding Generals:
Major General William M. Wright, Major General George H. Cameron, Major General Charles P. Summerall.

Bibliography:

Burtt, W.B., "Explanation and Execution of Plans of Operation-5th Army Corps-Argonne-Meuse Operation." Lecture, 27 Jan 1919.

U.S. Army War College, Historical Section. *Order of Battle of the United States Land Forces in the World War: American Expeditionary Forces: General Headquarters, Armies, Army Corps, Services of Supply, and Separate Forces.* Washington, DC: GPO, 1937.

VI Corps

The Sixth Corps was organized between July 23 and August 1, 1918 at Neufchateau, France and demobilized at Camp Devens, Massachusetts in May 1919.[25]

Insignia:
The VI Corps insignia is that of a blue disc with a white numeral "6" superimposed; representing the corps number.

Campaigns:
Lorraine 1918.[26]

Organization:[27]

DURING OCCUPATION OF THE MARBACHE SECTOR (LORRAINE), OCT 23-NOV 13, 1918.

Divisions: 7th, 88th, 92nd.
Air Service: Corps Observation Group: Headquarters; 8th and 354th Aero Squadrons; Photo Section 11. Corps Balloon Group: 10th and 12th Balloon Companies.
Artillery: 160th Field Artillery Brigade Headquarters (85th Division); 2 battalions of 328th Field Artillery (85th Division); 310th Trench Mortar Battery (85th Division); 3rd Battalion, 58th Coast Artillery (8" howitzers); 3rd Battalion, 65th Coast Artillery (9.2" howitzers); Battery B, 1st Battalion Trench Artillery; Corps munitions detachments; Provisional Supply Company.
Engineers: 115th Engineers and Train (40th Division); 2nd Battalion, 301st Engineers (76th Division); 51st Pioneer Infantry; 804th Pioneer Infantry.
Medical Corps: 115th Sanitary Train (40th Division); Field Hospitals 157, 158 & 159; Corps Mobile Veterinary Hospital.
Signal Corps: 301st Field Signal Battalion (76 Division); 417th Telegraph Battalion.
Miscellaneous: Corps Headquarters; Headquarters Troop; Detachment of 306th Remount Squadron; Corps Replacement Battalion; Corps Military Police Company; Sales Commissary Unit 315; Mobile Laundry Unit 307; Machine Shop Truck Unit 399; Salvage Company 21.

DURING POST-ARMISTICE ACTIVITIES, NOV 13, 1918-APR 10, 1919.

Divisions: 5th, 7th, 28th, 33rd, 88th, 92nd.
Air Service: Corps Observation Group: Headquarters; 8th and 354th Aero Squadrons; Photo Section 11.
Corps Balloon Group: Headquarters; 10th, 13th, 14th, 15th, 16th & 44th Balloon Companies.
Artillery: 160th Field Artillery Brigade Headquarters (85th Division); 328th, 329th & 330th Regiments Field Artillery (85th Division); 310th Trench Mortar Battery (85th Division); 39th Brigade Coast Artillery; 44th Coast Artillery, and units of 51st and 58th Coast Artillery; 3rd Battalion, 65th Coast Artillery; 2nd Trench Mortar Battalion; Corps Munitions Detachment.
Engineers: 115th Engineers and Train (40th Division); 804th Pioneer Infantry.
Medical Corps: 115th Sanitary Train: (40th Division): Field Hospitals 157, 158 & 159; US Ambulance Service section 570; Evacuation Ambulance Company 68; Corps Mobile Veterinary Hospital (Mobile Veterinary Section 301).
Signal Corps: 301st Field Signal Battalion (76th Division); 417th Telegraph Battalion.
Miscellaneous: Corps Headquarters; Headquarters Troop; Corps Military Police Company; Sales Commissary Unit 315; Clothing and Bath Unit 334; Service Park Unit 399; Corps Provisional Supply Company; Remount Squadron 304.

Major General Omar Bundy, commander of the VI Corps at Marbache, France, August, 1918. Courtesy National Archives.

Major General Adelbert Cronkhite, the last commander of the VI Corps, photographed at Villerupt, France, March, 1919. Courtesy National Archives.

Commanding Generals:
Major General Omar Bundy, Major General Charles C. Ballou, Major General Charles T. Menoher, Major General Charles H. Martin, Major General George Bell, Jr., Major General Robert L. Bullard, Major General Adelbert Cronkhite.

Bibliography:
U.S. Army War College, Historical Section. *Order of Battle of the United States Land Forces in the World War: American Expeditionary Forces: General Headquarters, Armies, Army Corps, Services of Supply, and Separate Forces*. Washington, DC: GPO, 1937.

This example of the VI Corps insignia is embroidered on felt.

A variant of the VI Corps insignia embroidered on twill.

VII Corps

The corps was formed at Remiremont, France on August 19, 1918 and demobilized at Camp Upton, New York from July 9-11, 1919.[28]

Insignia:
The insignia of the VII Corps is a shield in blue with a white numeral 7 representative of the corps designation.

Campaigns:
Streamer with Inscription.[29]

Organization:[30]

DURING POST-ARMISTICE ACTIVITIES, NOV 21, 1918-MAY 11, 1919.

Divisions: 5th, 6th, 26th 29th, 33rd, 35th, 36th, 78th, 79th, 80th, 81st, 88th, 89th, 90th, 92nd.
Air Service: Corps Air Service Headquarters; 9th, 88th, 186th & 258th, Aero Squadrons; Photo Section 10, 11, & 12.
Corps Balloon Group: Headquarters and Balloon Companies 2, 3, 25 & 26.
Artillery: 166th Field Artillery Brigade: 347th & 348th Regiments Field Artillery (91st Division).
Engineers: 310th & 602nd Engineers; 310th Engineer Train; 603rd & 604th Engineers; 54th Pioneer Infantry.

Right: Major General William H. Haan, Commander of the VII Corps inspects troops of the 90th Division, Wittlich, Germany, February, 1919. Courtesy National Archives.

Below: An unidentified soldier models the VII Corps insignia. Wittlich, Germany, December, 1918. Courtesy National Archives.

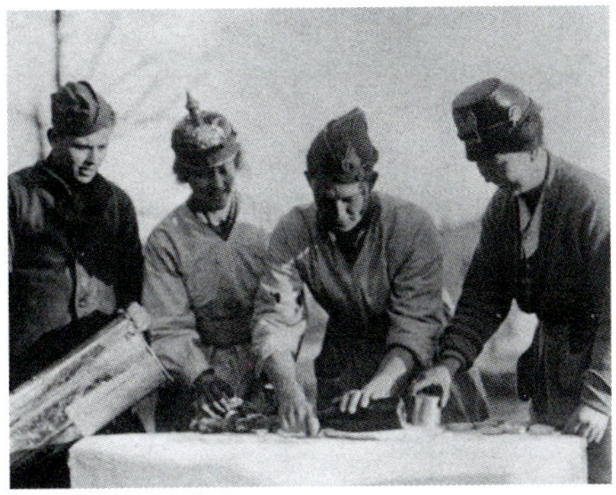

Far left: The General Headquarters building, VII Corps, in Trier, Germany, 1919. Courtesy National Archives.

Left: Private D.L. Greer, Miss H.C. Perry, Private V. Ratman, and Miss P.F. Parkman make doughnuts for the boys of the VII Corps, Dun sur Meuse, France, November, 1918. Courtesy National Archives.

Medical Corps: 114th Sanitary Train: (Later VII Corps Sanitary Train); Ambulance Companies 153, 154 & 155; Field Hospitals 153, 154, 155 & 156. VII Corps Field Veterinary Unit; Corps Mobile Veterinary Hospital 7; 308th Mobile Veterinary Section, Evacuation Ambulance Companies 5, 6 & 8.

Signal Corps: 326th Field Signal Battalion; 51st and 55th Telegraph Battalions.

Miscellaneous: Corps Headquarters; Headquarters Troop; VI and VII Corps Military Police Companies; 418th Motor Supply Train: Motor Truck Company 469, 471, 472 & 473; 414th Motor Supply Train: Motor Truck Companies 439 & 442. Provisional Motor Supply Company No 1 (formerly Company C, 5th Division Motor Supply Train); Service Park Unit 396 (369th Machine Shop Truck Unit); 312th Remount Squadron; Company F, 315th Motor Supply Train; Troops F and G, 2nd Cavalry; 304th Remount Squadron; Corps Sales Commissary; Detachment of 302nd Bakery Company; APO 792.

Commanding Generals:

Major General William M. Wright, Major General Omar Bundy, Major General William G. Haan, Major General Charles H. Martin, Major General Henry T. Allen.

Bibliography:

U.S. Army War College, Historical Section. *Order of Battle of the United States Land Forces in the World War: American Expeditionary Forces: General Headquarters, Armies, Army Corps, Services of Supply, and Separate Forces*. Washington, DC: GPO, 1937.

The standard VII Corps insignia design embroidered on felt.

A beautifully executed example of the VII Corps insignia embroidered on velvet.

VIII Corps

Eighth Corps was formed between November 26-29, 1918 at Montigny-sur-Aube (Cote-D'Or), France and was demobilized April 20, 1919 in France.[31]

Insignia:

A blue octagon bordered in white alluding to the number of the corps, with the white numeral "8" superimposed which is also representative of the numerical designation.

Campaigns:

None.

Organization:[32]

DURING POST-ARMISTICE ACTIVITIES, NOV 30, 1918-APR 20, 1919.

Divisions: 6th, 29th, 36th, 77th, 78th, 81st.

Air Service: 168th & 186th Aero Squadrons.

Engineers: Headquarters and 1st Battalion, 605th Engineers; Company L, 808th Pioneer Infantry.

Medical Corps: Corps Medical detachment.

Major General Henry T. Allen, Commander of the VIII Corps at Montigny-sur-Aube, France, January, 1919. Courtesy National Archives.

Top right: Major General Allen and his staff on the steps of the chateau used as the Corps Headquarters, Montigny-sur-Aube, France, January, 1919. Courtesy National Archives.

This standard VIII Corps insignia is embroidered on wool felt.

Margaret Wilson (standing) eldest daughter of President Wilson, poses with Major General Allen in the VIII Corps "Octagon Club", France, 1919. Courtesy National Archives.

A variation of the VIII Corps insignia also embroidered on felt.

Miscellaneous: Corps Headquarters; Headquarters Troop; Corps Military Police Company; 414th Motor Supply Train: Headquarters; Motor Truck Companies 412, 413, 437, 438, 439, 440, 441, 442 & 470. 411th Service Park Unit (Machine Shop Truck Unit 411); Sales Commissary Unit 52.

Commanding Generals:

Major General Henry T. Allen, Major General Walter H. Gordon.

Bibliography:

U.S. Army War College, Historical Section. *Order of Battle of the United States Land Forces in the World War: American Expeditionary Forces: General Headquarters, Armies, Army Corps, Services of Supply, and Separate Forces*. Washington, DC: GPO, 1937.

IX Corps

The corps was formed November 25-29, 1918 at Ligny-en-Barrois, France and demobilized May 5, 1919 in France.[33]

Insignia:
Ninth corps did not follow the blue and white color scheme normally used by corps level units. They chose a blue disk bordered in red with the red Roman Numeral IX representative of the corps numerical designation.

Campaigns:
None.

Organization:[34]

DURING POST-ARMISTICE ACTIVITIES, NOV 30, 1918-MAY 5, 1919.

Divisions: 6th, 7th, 28th, 33rd, 35th, 79th, 81st, 88th.
Air Service: Corps Balloon Group: Headquarters; 24th, 25th & 26th Balloon Companies.
Artillery: 62nd Field Artillery Brigade and 112th Ammunition Train (37th Division); 151st Field Artillery Brigade less the 301st Field Artillery (76th Division).
Engineers: 313th Engineers and Train (88th Division); 1st Battalion, 115th Engineers (40th Division); 803rd Pioneer Infantry.
Medical Corps: Evacuation Ambulance Company 69.
Signal Corps: 317th Field Signal Battalion.
Miscellaneous: Corps Headquarters; Headquarters Troop; Corps Military Police Company; 290th Military Police Company; 274th Military Police Company; 2nd Provisional Military Police Company, Sales Commissary Unit 51; Clothing and Bathing Unit 335; Mobile Laundry Unit 518; Service Park Unit 419.

Commanding Generals:
Major General Adelbert Cronkhite, Lieutenant Robert L. Bullard, Major General Joseph E. Kuhn, Major General William Weigel, Major General Charles P. Summerall, Major General Henry T. Allen, Major General Charles J. Bailey.

Bibliography:
U.S. Army War College, Historical Section. *Order of Battle of the United States Land Forces in the World War: American Expeditionary Forces: General Headquarters, Armies, Army Corps, Service of Supply, and Separate Forces*. Washington, DC: GPO, 1937.

Captain J. Hastie, Jr, commander of the Headquarters Detachment and his men pose in front of the Corps Headquarters, St. Mihiel, France, February, 1919. Courtesy National Archives.

Major General Charles P. Summerall, Commanding General of the IX Corps, at a Corps review at Beisles, France, April, 1919. Courtesy National Archives.

The typical IX Corps insignia embroidered upon wool felt background.

A die cut; felt on felt construction IX Corps insignia.

Brigadier General William D. Connor (left) Commander of the American Forces in France, visits a unit in Montoir, France, November, 1918. Courtesy National Archives.

American Forces in France

Insignia:
None.

Campaigns:
None.

Organization:
September 30, 1919.

Air Service: First Air Park.
Army Service Corps: Headquarters, Army Service Corps and Labor Bureau. Various detachments at Paris, Brest, Marseille, and St-Nazaire. Headquarters, Rent, Requistion and Claims Service at Paris, with other sections at St-Nazaire, Brest, Is-sur-Tille, and Bordeaux. Polish Typhus Expedition. Peace Commission. Prisoners of War Escort Companies: 1, 2, 9, 33, 60, 61, 63, 64, 65, 66, 68, 71, 72, 73, 75, 76, 77, 78, 79, 81, 82, 85, 87, 96, 122, 202, 203, 205, 206, 207, 208, 209, 210, 211, 213, 214, 218, 219, 220, 221, 224, 230, 233, 234, 235, 237, 238, 239, 240, 241, 242, 243, 245, 246, 247, 248, 249, 250, 251, 253, 256, 257, 262, 268, 269, 272, 273, 274. Administrative Service Companies: 4, 13, 26, and 145. Guard Companies: 139, 140, 141, 142, 143, 144, 145, 149, and 150. Provisional Guard Companies: 1 to 10 inclusive. Prisoner of War Enclosure 7. Bureau of Prisoner of War Enclosures.
Medical Corps: Camp Hospitals 33 and 121. Detachments at Is-sur-Tille, St-Nazaire, Brest, and Bordeaux. 308th Mobile Veterinary Section.
Military Police: Provost Marshal Base Section 5. Headquarters Detachment, District of Paris. 123rd Battalion: Companies 246 and 285. Military Police Companies: 222, 265, 302, 303, 306.
Motor Transport Corps: Detachments at Paris, St-Nazaire, and Brest. Motorcycle Company 306. Motor Transport Companies: 617, 618, 683, 698, 699, 700. Service Park Units: 420, 535, 536, 714.
Ordnance Corps: Ordnance Depots at St-Nazaire and Ordnance detachments at Paris and St-Nazaire.
Quartermaster Corps: Quartermaster Depots at Brest and Bordeaux. Quartermaster detachments at Brest and Bordeaux. Quartermaster detachments at Paris, Is-sur-Tille. Quartermaster detachments 500 and 501 at Brest. Graves Registration Service units at Amiens and Soissons. Remount Squadrons: 301, 302, 306, 310, 312. Mechanical Bakery Company, Motor Truck Companies: 3, 422, 485, 534, Motor Supply Train 428.
Signal Corps: 35th Service Company. Detachment at Brest.
Transportation Corps: Headquarters 1st, 2nd, and 5th Grand Divisions. Miscellaneous detachments.
Miscellaneous: Base Sections 1 and 5. Advance Section. Provisional District of Great Britain. Headquarters, Postal Express Service and Companies A and I, 15th Separate Battalion USMC. Marine Detachment Base Section No 2. Headquarters American Forces in France.

Commanding General:
Brigadier General William D. Connor

Major General Edward F. McGlachlin, Jr. commander of the American Forces in Germany. (photo taken in the 1920s) Courtesy National Archives.

American Forces in Germany

Insignia:
None.

Campaigns:
None.

Organization:

Troops in Area of American Forces in Germany, July 5, 1919.

Divisions: 1st, 2nd, 3rd, 4th, and 5th.
Air Service: 1st Air Park. III Corps Air Service Headquarters. Aero Squadrons 1, 24, 138, 186, and 258; 462 (Construction). Photo Sections 5, 16, 101, and 104.
III Corps Balloon Group Headquarters. Balloon Companies 14, 24, and 44.
Engineers: Company M, 29th Engineers.
Infantry: Composite Regiment 39th Infantry.
Medical Corps: Evacuation Hospitals: 16, 27, 49. Field Hospitals 329, 332, and 343. Ambulance Companies 329, 331, 332. Evacuation Ambulance Companies 5 and 29. Evacuation Hospitals 19, 26, and 30. 308th Mobile Veterinary Section. Corps Mobile Veterinary Hospitals: 1 and 7. VII Corps Field Veterinary Unit. Third Army Laboratory. Medical Supply Depot No 2. Advance Medical Supply Depot No 2. Army Veterinary Evacuation Sections 1, 2, and 3. III Corps Sanitary Train.
Military Police: Third Army Military Police Battalion. III Corps Military Police Company. IV Corps Military Police Company. VI Corps Military Police Company. VII Corps Military Police Company. Military Police Companies 144, 281, 282, 286, and 299.
Ordnance: Ammunition Depots 351 and 400. 1st Heavy Artillery Mobile Ordnance Repair Shop. 501st Mobile Ordnance Repair Shop.
Quartermaster: Third Army Quartermaster Depot. 334th Supply Company. Sales Commissaries 12, 33, 39, 49, 56, and 312. Third Army Area Sales Commissary. Salvage Squadrons 1, 12, 16, and 309. Bakery Companies 1, 7, 302 and 321. Laundry Companies 312, 33, 315, 318, 323, 326, 328, 503, 523, and 525. Clothing and Bath Units 322, 324, and 327. Butchery Companies 306 and 316. Post Quartermaster Detachment.
Signal Corps: 308th and 322nd Field Signal Battalions. 51st, 52nd, and 417th Telegraph Battalions. Third Army Radio Net.
Miscellaneous: Third Army Headquarters. III Corps Headquarters and Headquarters Troop. Third Army Machine Gun Detachment. Third Army Provisional Supply Train: Motor Truck Companies 428 and 817. 19th Provisional Motor Command: Motor Transport Companies 814, 815, 816, and 818. Motor Supply Trains 415 and 417. Service Park Units 302, 305, 361, 390, 394, 397, 399, 405, and 696. Motor Truck Companies 450, 463, 464, 465, 466, 467, 468, and 517. Motor Transport Companies 818 (detachment), 819, and 831. Third Army Remount Depot. Wengerohr Remount Depot. Remount Squadrons 301, 302, 303, 304, 306, 311, 312, 314, 322, and 344. Advance Ordnance Depot 303. Provisional Unit "B", Graves Registration Service. Motor Transport Corps Repair Unit 310. 14th Company, 1st Air Service Motor Mechanics Regiment. Port Commanders Detachment: Headquarters, 24th Grand Division Transportation Corps. Regulating Station. Advance Embarkation Section. Inter-Allied Railway and Inland Waterway Commission Detachment. Motor Dispatch Service Unit. Army Center of Artillery Studies. Third Army Machine Gun and Small Arms Center. I Corps Artillery Park. APO 754 and 927. 55th Pioneer Infantry Battalion. Regional Replacement Depot.

Headquarters building of the American Forces in Germany. This building occupied an entire block in Coblenz, Germany. Photo taken circa 1919. Courtesy Military History Institute

Troops in Area of American Forces in Germany, October 31, 1919

American forces in Germany on Oct 31, 1919, numbered 381 officers, 8,333 enlisted men; with personnel attached, but not part of the forces assigned to Germany, approximately 1,000.

Organization:
Headquarters, Headquarters Troop, Mounted Detachment, 8th Infantry, 7th Machine Gun Battalion, 2nd Battalion, 6th Field Artillery, Company A, 1st Engineers, 1st Field Signal Battalion, Motor Command Number 41, Base Hospital and agencies, Medical Supply Depot, Ordnance Detachment, Quartermaster Detachment, Replacement Depot, Provisional Military Police Company, Port of Antwerp Detachment, Railway Transportation Detachment.

Military Police on duty during the first snowstorm of the season in Cochem, Germany. The sergeant not on duty but enjoying the bracing air is James Collers, Motor Transportation Corps, January 23, 1919. Courtesy National Archives

Troops in Area of American Forces in Germany, December 31, 1920

Organization:
1st Engineers (Companies A, B, and D), Finance Detachment, Air Service Detachment, Motor Commands 34 and 41, 1st Field Signal Battalion, Station Hospital Coblenz, Provisional Sanitary Train, Medical Supply Depot, Quartermaster Coblenz-LŸtzel, Quartermaster Depot Bendorf, Post Quartermaster Coblenz, Quartermaster Andernach, Quartermaster Mayen, Ordnance Detachment, and Port of Antwerp Under Headquarters Commandant: Headquarters Troop, Provisional Guard Battalion, Headquarters Company, Casual Depot, Provost Marshal and Detachment, Provost Military Prison Company, Military Prison, Disciplinary Barracks, and Postal Detachment. Under 1st Brigade Headquarters, 8th Infantry, Mounted Detachment, 2nd Battalion 6th Field Artillery, 7th Machine Gun Battalion. Under 2nd Brigade: Brigade Headquarters, 5th Infantry, 50th Infantry, and Machine Gun Battalion.

Commanding Generals:
Major General Edward F. McGlachlin, Jr., Major General Henry T. Allen.

Colonel George E. Stewart, first commander of the American Expeditionary Force, North Russia, October, 1918. Courtesy National Archives.

American Expeditionary Forces, North Russia

In July 17, 1918, President Wilson agreed to send three battalions of infantry and one battalion of engineers to support the Allied expedition to North Russia. In late July, General Pershing ordered the 85th Division to form the "Murmansk Expedition" with Colonel George Evans Stewart as commander. The expedition sailed from England on August 27, 1918 and arrived at Archangel, Russia on September 4, 1918. Details of their combat operations can be found under the 85th Division summary of operations. In February 1919, two companies of Railway Troops joined a contingent, forming the North Russia Transportation Corps Expeditionary Force. The Expedition was discontinued on August 5, 1919.[35]

Colonel Stewart and his staff in front of their headquarters in Archangel, Russia, November, 1918. Courtesy National Archives

Insignia:
The expedition selected a light blue shield representing the cold of artic North Russia with a white polar bear, a resident of these climes, standing on an iceberg. Variations exist with the letters "N" "R" for North Russia upon a black diamond.

Standard felt on felt North Russia Expeditionary Force insignia with white polar bear upon a blue field.

Organization:

Infantry: 339th Infantry Regiment.
Engineers: 310th Engineer Regiment.
Medical: 337th Field Hospital, 337th Ambulance Company.
Miscellaneous: North Russia Transportation Corps Expeditionary Force: 167th (Operations) & 168th (Maintenance) Companies Transportation Corps.

Commanders:
Colonel George E. Stewart, Brigadier General Wilds P. Richardson.

Embroidered on felt monogram "NR" representative of North Russia.

Bibliography:

Bozich, Stanley J. & Bozich, Jon R. *"Detroit's Own" Polar Bears: The American North Russia Expeditionary Force1918-1919*. Frankenmuth, Michigan: Polar Bear Publishing Company, 1985

Carey, Donald E [Neil G. Carey Ed.]. *Fighting the Bolsheviks: the Russian War Memoir of Private First Class Donald E. Carey, U.S. Army 1918-1919*. Novato, California: Presidio Press, 1997.

Doolen, Richard M. *Michigan's Polar Bears: The American Expedition to North Russia, 1918-1919*. Ann Arbor, MI: University of Michigan, 1965.

Goldhurst, Richard. *The Midnight War: The American Intervention in Russia, 1918-1920*. New York, McGraw-Hill: 1978.

Gordon, Dennis. *Quartered in Hell: the Story of the American North Russia Expeditionary Force1918-1919*. Missoula, Montana: The Doughboy Historical Society: 1982.

Johnson, Robert C. "Mapping Northern Russia for the Archangel Expedition." *Military Engineer* 12 (1920): pp. 437-46.

Moore, Joel R. *"M" Company, 339th Infantry, in North Russia*. n.p. 1920.

—. et. al. *The History of the American Expedition Fighting the Bolsheviki: Campaigning in North Russia 1918-1919*. Detroit: Polar Bear, 1920.

York, Dorothea. *The Romance of Company "A", 339th Infantry, A.N.R.E.F. (American North Russia Expeditionary Force)*. Detroit: McIntyre, 1923.

American Expeditionary Forces, Siberia

In summer 1918, the United States decided to join the military action in Siberia with an expedition to Vladivstok. The War Department selected the 27th and 31st Infantry Regiments, then on duty in the Philippines, to form the core of the expedition. They then tasked Major General William S. Graves to select 500 "sturdy" infantrymen from the 8th Division to bring the regiments to full strength. The expedition sailed from Manila and San Francisco in August, 1918 and arrived at Vladivostok, Russia the same month. Details of their combat operations can be found under the 8th Division summary of operations. The Expedition was discontinued in December, 1919.[36]

Major General William S. Graves, Commander of the Siberian expedition. Vladivostok, Russia, 1918. Courtesy National Archives.

Insignia:
The expedition selected a dark blue artillery shell shaped field bordered in white with the superimposed figure of a polar bear on its haunches; the letter "S" representing Siberia placed upon the chest of the bear.

Colonel H.D. Styer, commander of the 27th Infantry Regiment, with his staff in Khabarovsk, Russia, 1918. Courtesy National Archives.

The standard insignia of the AEF Siberia; a felt on felt rearing polar bear with monogram "S" for Siberia upon a dark blue shell shaped field.

Variant Siberian Expeditionary Force insignia ; a monogram "S" over monogram "AEF" upon a black diamond.

Organization:

Infantry: 27th & 31st Infantry Regiments.
Engineers: 310th Engineer Regiment.
Medical: Evacuation Hospital 17, Medical Supply Depot 7, Veterinary Field Unit.
Miscellaneous: Headquarters, Headquarters Detachment, two sections, Bakery Company 391.

Commanders:
Colonel Henry D. Styer, Major General William S. Graves, Colonel Frederic H. Sargent.

Bibliography:

Goldhurst, Richard. *The Midnight War: The American Intervention in Russia, 1918-1920.* New York: McGraw-Hill, 1978.

Johnson, Robert C. "Mapping Northern Russia for the Archangel Expedition." *Military Engineer* 12 (1920): pp. 437-46.

Kindall, Sylvain G. *American Soldiers in Siberia*. New York: R.R. Smith, 1945.

Miller, Russell S. & Betty K. *The Forgotten Heroes of Siberia (Polar Bear Division)*. n.p., 1990.

Paul, Frank A. *Regimental History, Thirty-First US Infantry, July 1916-July 1920*. Manila: 1920

Smith, Erik A. *Partisans and Polar Bears: The Story of the 31st United States Infantry Regiment in Siberia, 1918-1920*. Thesis, San Jose State University, 1993.

U.S. Army. *History of the Twenty-Seventh US Infantry*. Schofield Barracks, HI: 1922.

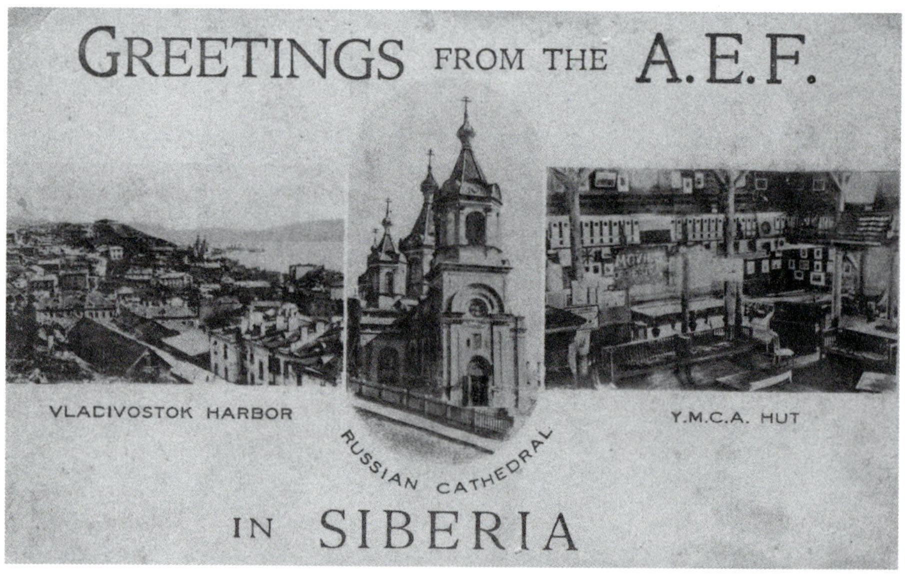

A Post card from the AEF in Siberia, 1918. Courtesy Military History Institute

Opposite
Top: Two Military Policemen pose with a Siberian and his Bactrian camel near Vladivostok, 1919. Courtesy Military History Institute

Bottom: An unidentified American soldier poses with his Russian counterpart in front of a captured Red Army armored train near Lake Baikal, Russia, January 1920. Courtesy Military History Institute

ИРИТЕЛЬ

CHAPTER THREE

THE REGULAR ARMY DIVISIONS

Opposite
Top: Infantry Division, 1917.
Bottom: Infantry Division, May 1917.

AEF Infantry Division Organization

Infantry Divisions were formed from new Tables of Organization in May, 1917. The division numbering scheme was developed by the War College Division of the Army General Staff and the Adjutant General; with the Regular Army Division numerical designations successively from 1 through 25, National Guard Divisions 26 through 75, and National Army Divisions 76 through 100. Additionally, Regular Army Cavalry Divisions were to be numbered starting at 15. Infantry, cavalry, field artillery and brigades were to be numbered 1 through 50 for the Regular Army, 51 through 150 for the National Guard and 151 and above for the National Army. Regiments were also aligned with their parent component. The Regular Army regiments numbered within the bock from 1 through 100, the National Guard 101 through 300, and the National Army 301 through 400.

The 1917 Infantry Division was organized with a total strength of 18,919 men. The principal maneuver elements of the division were two infantry brigades, a field artillery brigade, a trench mortar battery, and an air squadron.

Each of the two infantry brigades were further divided into a headquarters, two infantry regiments, a supply company, medical section and chaplain. Each of the assigned regiments had three battalions. The battalion had a headquarters, three infantry companies and a machine gun company with six machine guns.

The field artillery brigade was composed of a headquarters, two field artillery regiments of three-inch guns and one regiment of six-inch guns, a supply company, medical section and chaplain. The three-inch regiment had a headquarters battery and two battalions assigned. Each battalion had a headquarters and three firing batteries of four guns. The six inch regiment had a headquarters battery and three battalions assigned. Each battalion had a headquarters and two batteries of four guns.

Trench mortar batteries were organized into a headquarters, three platoons of two sections with two mortars in each section for a total of twelve six-inch Newton-Stokes Mortars.

The air squadron was composed of headquarters, twelve aero sections, an engineering section, and supply section. It had twelve aircraft assigned.

Each division had a significant command and support element including the division headquarters company, an engineer battalion, field signal battalion and trains.

The division headquarters consisted of the division commander's staff and planners. The engineer battalion was composed of a headquarters and three engineer companies which oversaw the division needs in the basic Engineer Corps mission areas of mobility, counter-mobility, survivability (including construction of defensive works), general engineering missions, and topography.

Infantry Division, 1917

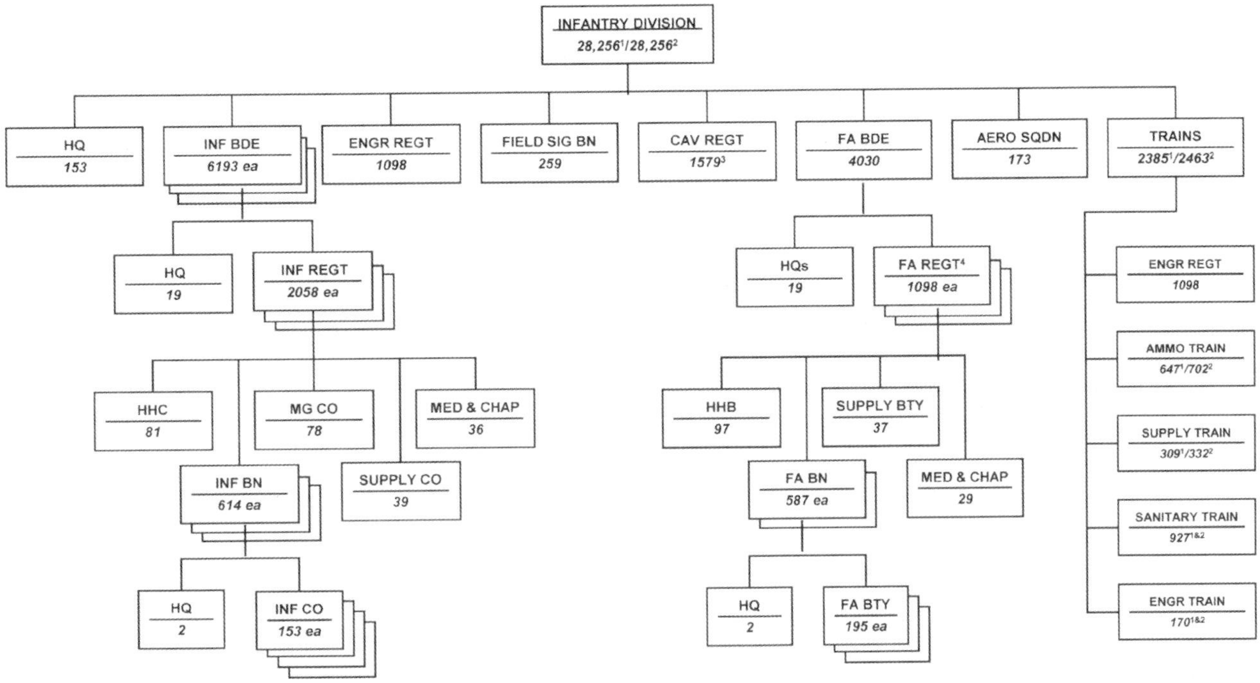

[1] Division trains equipped with wagons
[2] Division trains equipped with motorized vehicles
[3] Chart 2, Cavalry Division, 1917, depicts the structure of the Cavalry Regiment
[4] Contains two 3" gun regiments and one 3.8" howitzer regiment

Infantry Division, 24 May 1917

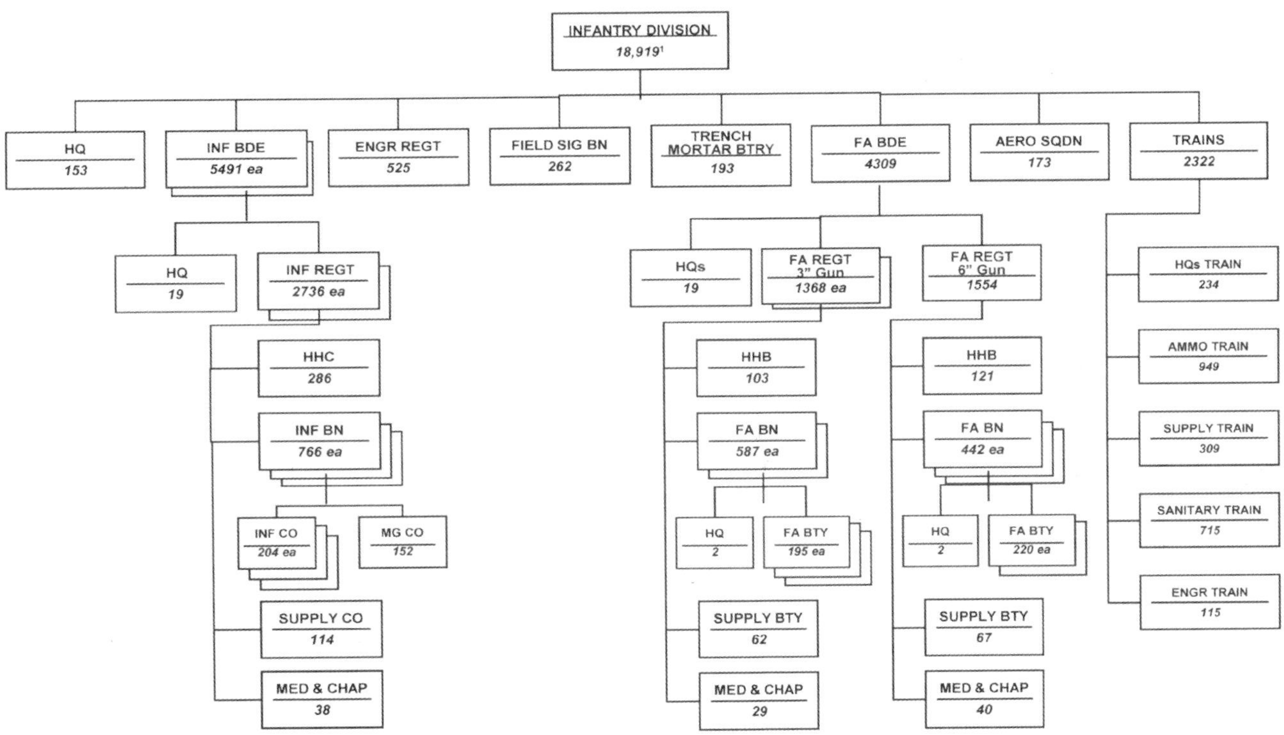

[1] Memo, WCD for CofS, 21 May 1917, sub: Plans for a Possible expeditionary force to France, indicates that the division would total 19,922, but a check of the math indicates that the total was 18,919.

Infantry Division, 8 August 1917

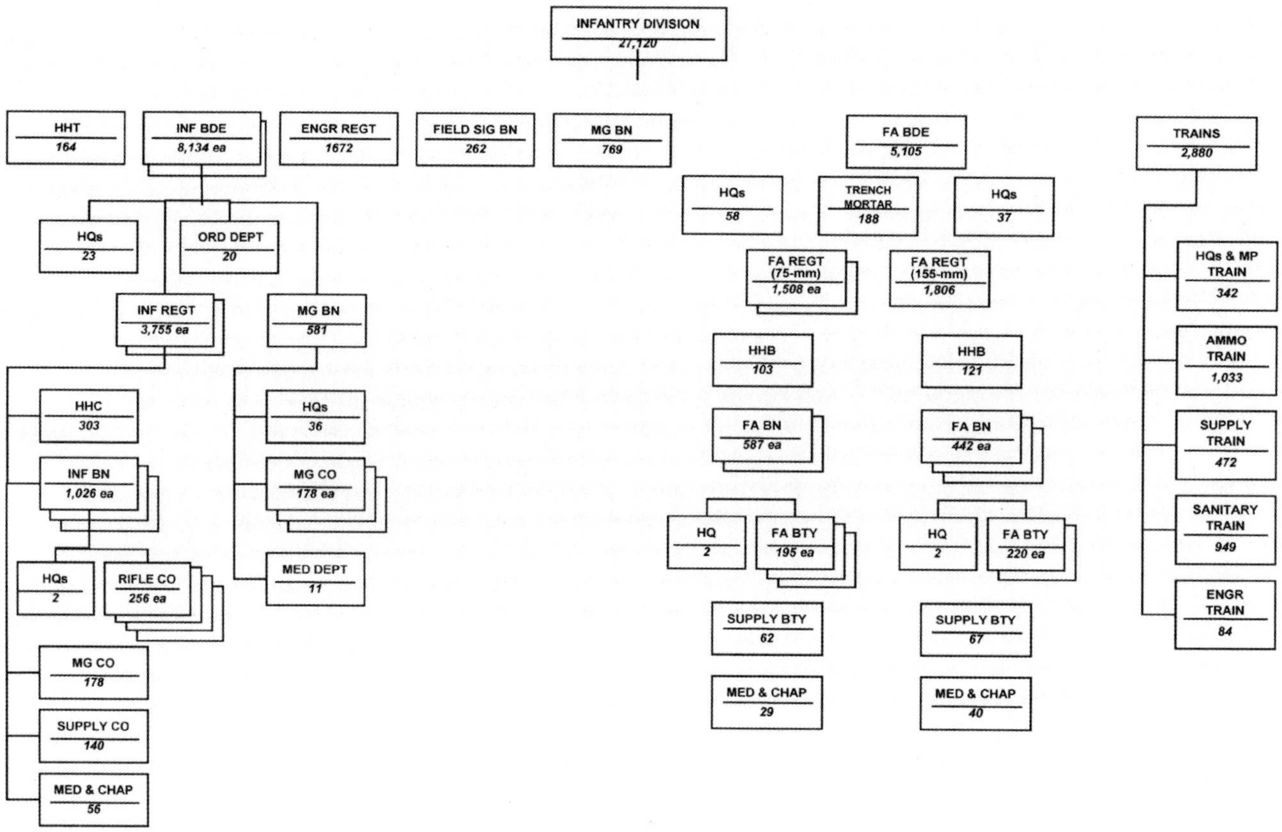

Cavalry Division, 1917

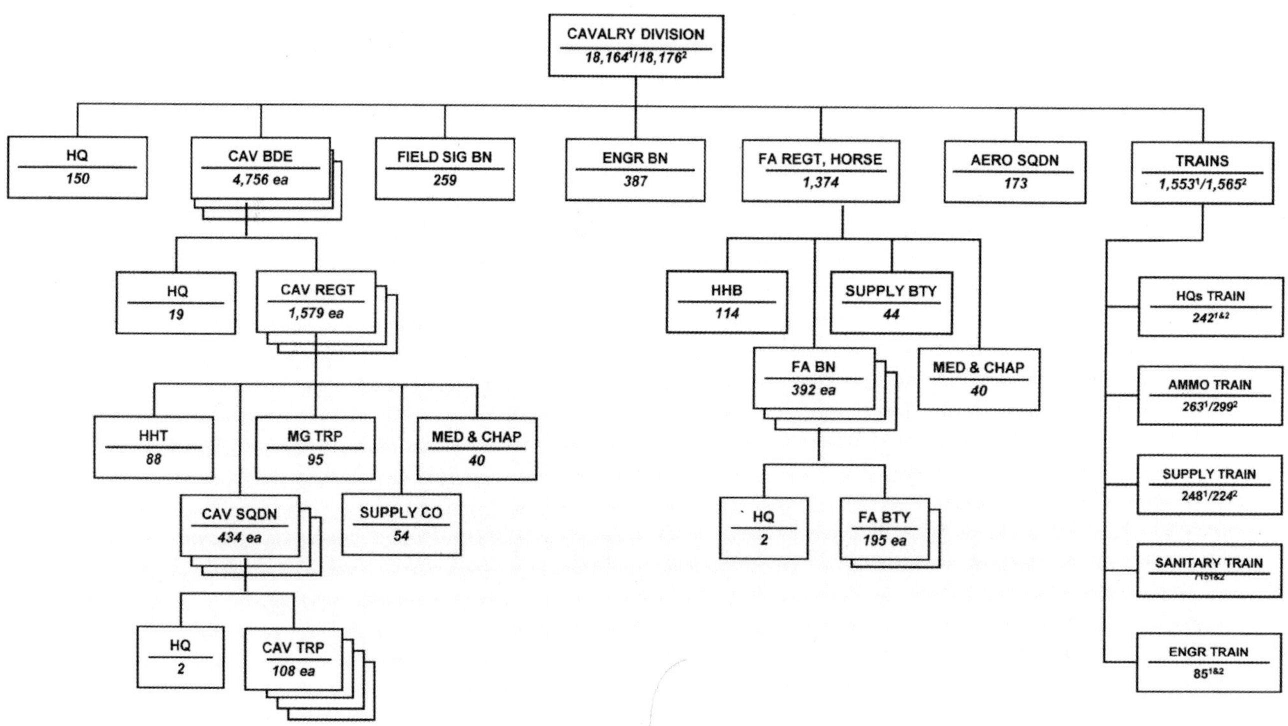

[1] Division trains equipped with wagons
[2] Division trains equipped with motorized vehicles

Opposite
Top: Infantry Division, August 1917.
Bottom: Cavalry Division, 1917.

Divisional field signal battalions consisted of a headquarters, supply section, wire company, radio company and an outpost company equipped with field telephones and switchboards.

The division's chief logistical element was the division trains. The trains consisted of a headquarters train, ammunition train, supply, sanitary train, and engineer train. The headquarters train included a headquarters and two companies and controlled the operations of the divisional train, and ammunition train, whose mission was "transporting the divisional artillery and infantry ammunition reserve, or in bringing up the same from the refilling point to the combat trains of organizations"[1] consisted of a headquarters and three companies with each company having a headquarters and two sections:

> "The sanitary train is composed of ambulance companies [two motor driven and two animal drawn], field hospital companies [two motor driven and two animal drawn], and camp infirmaries [four]. The sanitary train is commanded by the division surgeon, or in his absence, by the senior medical officer of the attached elements, who, upon its release from the control of the commander of trains, operates it in accordance with orders or instructions received from division headquarters."[2]

The Engineer train consisted of a headquarters and supply section, searchlight section with six searchlight units and three trench-light wagons with batteries and flares, and pontoon section capable of bridging 225 feet.

The 1917 changes to the Army also created two types of Cavalry Divisions.[3] The difference between the two came from the composition of the trains. The division equipped with wagons had a strength of 18,164 and the division equipped with motorized trains had 18,176 assigned.

The principal maneuver elements of the division were three cavalry brigades, a field artillery regiment (horse drawn), and an air squadron.

Each of the three cavalry brigades were further divided into a headquarters and three cavalry regiments. Each of the assigned regiments had a headquarters troop, three squadrons, machine gun troop, supply troop, and medical and chaplain section. The squadron had a headquarters and four cavalry troops.

The horse drawn field artillery regiment was composed of a headquarters, 3 field artillery battalions, a supply battery, medical section and chaplain. Each battalion had a headquarters and two firing batteries of four 3-inch guns. This gave the regiment a total of twenty-four guns.

The air squadron was composed of headquarters, twelve aero sections, an engineering section, and supply section. It had twelve assigned aircraft.

The division had a command and support element including the division headquarters company, an engineer battalion, field signal battalion and trains.

On August 8, 1917, given the final report of the Baker Commission, the War College Division changed the organization of the division.

The modified Infantry Division was enlarged to a total strength of 27,120 men. The principal maneuver elements of the division were two infantry brigades, a field artillery brigade, and a machine gun battalion.

Each of the two infantry brigades were further divided into a headquarters, two infantry regiments, a machine gun battalion, and an ordnance department. The machine gun battalion had a headquarters, three machine gun companies with sixteen heavy machine guns in each company and a medical department. Each of the assigned regiments had a headquarters, three battalions, a machine gun company with sixteen heavy machine guns, supply company and a medical and chaplain detachment. The battalion had a headquarters and four infantry companies. This organization of four company battalions gave rise to the nickname of the "Square Division."

The infantry company consisted of a headquarters and four platoons, each platoon had a platoon headquarters and four sections: first section (hand bombers), second section (rifle grenadiers), third section (riflemen), fourth section (automatic riflemen). The first section had three bomber squads each consisting of one leader, one thrower, one carrier and one scout. Second section had six rifle grenadiers and three carriers. The third section had seventeen riflemen and fourth section had four automatic rifle teams each consisting of one gunner and two carriers with one corporal in charge of every two guns.

The field artillery brigade was composed of a headquarters, two field artillery regiments of 75mm guns and one regiment of 155mm guns, a trench mortar battery, and an ordnance department. The 75mm regiment had a headquarters battery, two firing battalions, a supply battery, and a medical and chaplain detachment assigned. Each battalion had a headquarters and three firing batteries of four guns. The 155mm regiment had a headquarters battery, three firing battalions, a supply battery, and medical and chaplain detachment assigned. Each battalion had a headquarters and two batteries of four guns.

The trench mortar battery was organized into a headquarters, three platoons of two sections with two mortars in each section for a total of twelve six-inch Newton-Stokes Mortars.

Each division machine gun battalion was divided into a headquarters, four machine gun companies with sixteen heavy machine guns each, and a medical and chaplain section.

Divisions retained a significant command and support element including the division headquarters troop, an engineer regiment, a field signal battalion and trains.

The field signal battalion remained unchanged as did the function of the headquarters troop. Engineer elements were drastically increased from a single battalion to a regiment of a headquarters and two battalions.

The division trains remained largely unchanged, excepting the addition to the headquarters train of a detachment of military police.

Major General E.F. McGlachlin confers with Brigadier General Frank Parker on the outskirts of Treves, Germany, December, 1918. Courtesy National Archives.

Below: Major General Robert L. Bullard and his entire staff of the 1st Division, France, January, 1918. Standing immediately to General Bullard's right is his Chief of Staff, Lieutenant Colonel George C. Marshall. Courtesy National Archives.

1st Infantry Division

The War Department constituted the division on May 24, 1917 naming it Headquarters, First Expeditionary Division; it was re-designated the 1st Infantry Division on July 6, 1917. It was composed chiefly of troops in service near the Mexican Border at Brownsville, El Paso, San Benito, Fort Bliss, Ringgold, and Sam Houston.[4]

Insignia:

The division selected a red Arabic numeral "1" on an olive drab shield "about five inches high"[5] symbolizing the division's designation. Red was used for the color of the "1" as the

original patch was reportedly cut from the red cloth of a captured German Field Mutz (Cap). This patch was approved for official wear on October 31, 1918.[6]

Campaigns:
Montdidier-Noyon Defense, Aisne-Marne Offensive, St. Mihiel Offensive, Meuse-Argonne Offensive, Ansauville Sector, Cantigny Sector, Saizerais Sector, Sommerviller Sector.[7]

Division Organization (1917-1919):[8]

1st Infantry Brigade:

16th Infantry Regiment
18th Infantry Regiment
2nd Machine Gun Battalion

2nd Infantry Brigade:

26th Infantry Regiment
28th Infantry Regiment
3rd Machine Gun Battalion

Division Troops:

1st Machine Gun Battalion
1st Field Artillery Brigade:
5th Field Artillery Regiment
6th Field Artillery Regiment
7th Field Artillery Regiment
1st Trench Mortar Battery

Division Support:

1st Engineer Regiment
2nd Field Signal Battalion
1st Train Headquarters and Military Police
1st Ammunition Train
1st Supply Train
1st Engineer Train
1st Sanitary Train (Ambulance Companies & Field Hospitals 2nd, 3rd, 12th, and 13th)

Division Combat Narrative:[9]
The first troops sailed from Hoboken June 13, 1917, and disembarked at St. Nazaire, June 26, 1917. Division Headquarters landed June 27, 1917. The remainder of the troops followed in rapid succession except the Supply Train which did not arrive in France until May 6, 1918. The Division (less artillery) was sent to the Gondrecourt area for training. For a similar purpose the artillery brigade went to Valdahon. En route from St. Nazaire to Gondrecourt, the 2nd Battalion, 16th Infantry, participated in the July 4th parade in Paris, the first public appearance of American troops in France.

The Division entered the line October 21, 1917, in the Luneville sector, near Nancy, each unit being attached to a corresponding French unit. At 6:05 A. M., October 23, 1917, Battery C, of the 6th Field Artillery, in position 400 meters east of Bathlemont, fired the first American shot of the war. In this sector the First Division took the first German prisoner to be captured in the war by the Americans, and suffered the first losses, three men of the 16th Infantry being killed, November 3, 1917.

On the night of November 20, 1917, the Division was withdrawn from the line to the Gondrecourt Area to continue its training. It again entered the line in the Ansauville sector, near Toul, on the night of January 15-16, 1918. This sector became a more or less active one. On

This division poster on the side of a railway car leaves no doubt as to the future destination of the division, nor to where it's been. Courtesy Military History Institute.

Colonel Stephen O. Fuqua, Chief of Staff for the 1st Division poses for the camera. Courtesy National Archives.

A felt on felt example of a 1st Division insignia. Legend has it that the red fabric used for the "1" on the pattern patch was cut from a captured German Feld Mutze (Fatigue Cap). The use of red harkens back to the Civil War division color designations; red was the color used by first division in the Federal Army of the Civil War.

1st Division patch with an embroidered "1" on an olive drab wool background.

March 28, 1918, while the Division was still occupying this sector, General Pershing placed it at the disposal of the Allied High Command.

In accordance with orders received from the Allied Command, the Division was withdrawn to Toul on April 3, 1918, and was immediately sent by rail to Picardy, where on April 25, 1918, it took over the active Cantigny sector, near Montdidier.

Cantigny marked a salient in one of the most advanced parts of the German lines. It was desirable to straighten this line, especially in view of an Allied offensive movement, which was contemplated. This offensive had to be given up owing to the development of a new German thrust toward the Marne. The plans for the capture of Cantigny, however, were carried out, partly for the local advantage, but chiefly for the moral effect, both on friend and enemy, of showing American troops in an independent offensive operation.

The operation was well planned and well executed. The attack was made on the morning of May 28, 1918. All objectives were taken and held against strong counter attacks, constantly repeated for the next two days.

The Division remained in the Cantigny sector until July 7, 1918, when it was withdrawn to Dammartin-en-Goele. The lines along the Marne salient had meanwhile become stabilized. On July 15, 1918, the Germans launched another short-lived offensive in Champagne, and on the 18th, the Allies took the offensive, never to lose it again.

The first operation of the Allies was to straighten out the Marne salient, driving one attack eastward near Soissons, while another one came northward from the line of the Marne. The First Division with the Second American Division, and the First Moroccan Division, made the attack from the west. For four days the Division advanced against determined resistance, finally crossing the Soissons-Château-Thierry road and bringing Soissons itself under the American guns. The First Division was relieved by the 15th (Scottish) Division, on the night of July 23-24, 1918. This completed this phase of operations. The First Division had lost 8,365 men, including 60% of its Infantry officers. It had advanced 11 kilometers and captured 3,500 prisoners, 68 guns and quantities of other material.

The Division after its relief from the Soissons offensive, was again moved eastward. On August 7, 1918, it took over the quiet Saizerais sector, near Toul. Here it remained until August 24th, when it was withdrawn to Vaucouleurs, in preparation for a new offensive.

The First American Army was at last fully organized, and was about to undertake its first independent operation, the forcing of the St. Mihiel salient. The plan called for a double attack, one from the west and one from the south, the line between being lightly held by French troops. The southern attack consisted of a right wheel by a long line, with its right on the Moselle River. The First Division formed the left, or marching flank, of this line, thus being required to make the greatest advance. The attack began at 5:00 A. M., September 12, 1918. The next morning the First Division established connection with the 26th Division at Vigneulles, which had come in from the western face, and the St. Mihiel salient had ceased to exist. The First Division was relieved by the 42nd Division, and withdrawn to the Nonsard Wood as reserve of the 4th Corps. During the advance the Division captured 1,195 prisoners, 30 field guns and howitzers, 50 machine guns and quantities of ammunition and stores. Its casualties amounted to 585.

This operation was not pushed further. On September 20th, the First Division was shifted west for the Meuse-Argonne offensive. The Division moved on September 27, 1918, to Nixeville, thence to Neuvilly, and on the night of September 30th relieved the 35th Division near Very.

The next eleven days the Division fought continuously in an advance east of the Aire Valley against the most stubborn resistance of the best German troops. Fleville, Exermont, and the rugged wooded country beyond were taken, and on the night of October 11, 1918, the line ran east and west one-half a kilometer north of Sommerance. The First Division was relieved by the 42nd Division on the night of October 11-12, 1918. The Division had lost 9,194 men, but it had advanced 7 kilometers at a critical point of the line, and captured 1,400 prisoners, 13 field guns and many other stores. After relief from this offensive, the Division was moved to the vicinity of Bar-le-Duc for a brief rest.

On October 31, 1918, the Division was in reserve of the 5th Corps. On the night of November 5-6, 1918, it entered the line north of the Stonne-Beaumont road, and by noon November 6, 1918, had reached the Meuse, at Mouzon. It now turned to the left, and paralleling the river, advanced, until, on the afternoon of the 7th, it was occupying the heights of Sedan, with the city at its mercy. The French, for reasons of sentiment, wished to be the first to enter, so the Division was withdrawn to La Pesane, and on the 11th, the Armistice found it near Buzancy. From here it marched to Eix, a few miles from Verdun. Its losses since October 1, 1918, had been 10,116, more than those of any other Division in the Meuse-Argonne operations.

During operations the division took 6,661 prisoners. Its casualties totaled 26,332.

The Division was now assigned to the Third Army, the Army of Occupation, and started for Germany on November 17, 1918. It crossed the Moselle River at Wormeldingen and entered the enemy's country on December 1, 1918. The Rhine was crossed on December 13, 1918, and the Division established itself in the Coblenz Bridgehead. Here it remained until August 16, 1919, when the movement home was begun.

Division Headquarters embarked at Brest on August 25, 1919, and arrived at New York, September 5, 1919.

The Division commanders were: Major General William L. Sibert, Major General Robert L. Bullard, Brigadier General Charles P. Summerall, Brigadier General Frank E. Bamford, Brigadier General Frank Parker, and Major General Edward F. McGlachlin.

Days in the Front Line: 47 (training) 148 (sector) 28 (battle) for a total of 223. During operations the division took 6,469 prisoners and its casualties totaled 4,996 soldiers killed in action or died of wounds, 17,324 wounded in action.[10]

This variation of the 1st Division insignia uses an embroidered "1" on wool.

Reference Bibliography:

General Division Histories:

"Aisne-Marne Offensive: Documents Pertaining to the Attack of the 1st U.S. Division Southwest of Soissons, July 18-22, 1918". Typescript, 1927.

American Battle Monuments Commission. *1st Division Summary of Operations in the World War.* Washington, DC: Government Printing Office, 1944.

Bogert, George D. *"Let's Go!" 10 Years' Retrospect of the World War.* San Francisco: Crocker, 1927.

Butler, Alban B. *"Happy Days!": A Humorous Narrative in Drawings of the Progress of American Arms, 1917-1919.* Washington, DC: Society of the First Division, 1928.

Commendations of First Division, American Expeditionary Forces, 1917-1919, France, Germany. n.p., 1919.

Coutler, Charles S. and O'Connor, Harry J. *The Bridgehead Sentinel: A Souvenir of the Coblenz Bridgehead.* n.p., 1919.

DuPuis, Antoine A., [comp.] *1st Infantry Division: "Cantigny," April-July 1918.* Mimeo, 1972.

Eddy, M.S. "Critical Analysis or the Operations of the German Forces Opposed to the American

1st Division From 1-11 October 1918; Original Military Study." *Review of Military Literature* (Sep 1935): pp. 5-38.

The Fighting First: First to Land – Last to Leave. Mimeo, New York: Ad Press, 1920.

Johnston, Edward S. "Employment of Chemical Troops in the Attack of the American 1st Division, During the Second Phase of the Meuse Argonne Offensive, 1918." *Chemical Warfare* (Oct 1932): p. 1185.

"In Memory of Seventeen Years Ago: Famous Fighting First Division Will Celebrate Initial Entry of American Troops Into Allied Front Lines, October 17, 1917." *USA Recruiting News* (15 Oct 1934): p. 9.

Miller, Henry R. *The First Division.* Pittsburgh, Pennsylvania: Crescent Press, 1920.

Smith, Richard N. *The Colonel: The Life and Legend of Robert R. McCormick, 1880-1955.* NY: Houghton Mifflin, 1997.

Society of the First Division. *History of the First Division During the World War 1917-1919.* Philadelphia: Winston, 1922.

—. *Memorial Album: Pictorial History of the 1st Division.* San Diego, California: By the Society, 1950.

Stewart, Redmond C. *Experiences of a Non-Combatant Soldier of A.E.F.*. n.p., 1921.

Ouilla Polker of the 1st Engineers wearing a Boche leather helmet taken from a prisoner. Seicheprey, Meurthe-et-Moselle, France. September 12, 1918. Courtesy National Archives

U.S. Army, 1st Infantry Division. *World War Records: First Division, A.E.F., Regular*. Washington, DC: 1928-30. [25 vols, each in 2 parts]

—. *World War Records, First Division, A.E.F. German Documents*. Washington, DC, 1930. [4 vols, each in 3 parts]

U.S. War Dept. *Victory Parades of the First Division, United States Army: Official Souvenir Program*. Washington, DC: Sep 10-17, 1919.

16th Infantry Regiment

The Daring Regiments: Adventures of the AEF in World War I. New York: Dodd, Mead, 1967.

McHenry, Herbert L. *As a Private Saw It: My Memories of the First Division, World War I*. Indiana, Pennsylvania: Halldin, 1988.

The Story of the Sixteenth Infantry in France. Montabaur-Frankfurt: Flock, 1919.

18th Infantry Regiment

Allen, Oliver. "The 18th Infantry (U.S.) in the St. Mihiel Offensive." *Monographs of the World War*. Ft. Benning, Georgia: Infantry School, 1923.

26th Infantry Regiment

Frasier, Lyman S. "Operations of the Third Battalion, 26th Infantry, First Division in the Second and Third Phases of the Meuse Argonne Offensive." Ft Benning, Georgia: Infantry School, 1926.

U.S. Army. 26th Infantry Regiment. *The Twenty-Sixth Infantry in France*. Montabaur-Frankfurt: Flock, 1919.

28th Infantry Regiment

U.S. Army, 28th Infantry Regiment. *The Story of the Twenty-Eighth Infantry in the Great War*. Coblenz, Germany: n.p., 1919.

—, Headquarters Co. *Complete History of Headquarters Company of the Twenty-Eighth United States Infantry*. Montabaur: Flock, 1919.

1st Engineer Regiment

"Division Maneuvers in the A.F. in G." *Military Engineer* 15 (Jan/Feb 1923): pp. 30-34.

Farrell, Thomas F. "Bridging the Rhine in Record Time." *Military Engineer* 14 (May/Jun 1922): pp. 147-48 & 176.

—. "The Capture and Defense of Hill 269 by the 1st Engineers." *Military Engineer* 13 (Jan/Feb 1921): pp. 51-57.

—. "Memories of the Battle of Soissons." *Military Engineer* 15 (Jul/Aug 1923): pp. 327-31.

—. "Operations of a Divisional Engineer." *Military Engineer* 14 (Mar/Apr 1922): pp. 99-101.

—. ed. *A History of the First US Engineers, 1st US Division*. Coblenz, Germany: n.p., 1919.

Schley, J.L., & Noce, Daniel. "Engineer Operations Fifth Army Corps." *Military Engineer* 15 (Sep/Oct 1923): pp. 425-34.

Suchocki, Boleslaw. "The Battle of Cantigny." *Military Engineer* (Sep/Oct 1921): pp. 393-96.

Weaver, Theron D. "The 163rd Division Crosses the Meuse." *Military Engineer* 21 (Nov/Dec 1919).

5th Field Artillery Regiment

Bowley, F.W. "Decoration of the Colors of the Fifth and Seventeenth Regiments of Field Artillery. *Field Artillery Journal* 12 (1922): p. 39.

Craig, L.A. "The First Field Artillery Brigade at Soissons." *Field Artillery Journal* (Jul 1924): pp. 317-36.

U.S. Army, 5th Artillery Regiment. *Brief History of the Fifth Field Artillery, 1st Division, American Expeditionary Forces, 1917-1918*. n.p.,1919.

6th Field Artillery Regiment

Craig, L.A. "The First Field Artillery Brigade at Soissons." *Field Artillery Journal* (Jul 1924): pp. 317-36.

Heard, Ralph T. *A History of the Sixth Regiment Field Artillery, First Division, United States Army*. n.p.,1919.

7th Field Artillery Regiment

Craig, L.A. "The First Field Artillery Brigade at Soissons." *Field Artillery Journal* (Jul 1924): pp. 317-36.

Holbrook, Lucius R. "The Seventh (Field Artillery)." *Field Artillery Journal* (1923): pp. 246.

Summerall, Charles P. "Notes on the 1st Division in the Battle of Soissons. *Field Artillery Journal* (Jul/Aug 1920): pp. 331-64.

U.S. Army,7th Artillery Regiment. History of the Seventh Field Artillery (First Division, A.E.F.): World War I, 1917-1919. n.p., 1929.

This old wagon wheel makes a solid revolving base for the Hotchkiss anti-aircraft gun; squad of Battery E, 6th Field Artillery, 1st Division. Menil La Tour, France. Courtesy National Archives

2nd Infantry Division

The War Department directed the organization of the 2nd Division on September 21, 1917 from units of the Regular Army stationed at various posts in the United States, en route to Europe or already in Europe constituting the division on October 26, 1917.[11]

Insignia:

The division selected as its insignia a red Indianhead upon a white star placed upon a black shield. Adopted November 6, 1918, and initially used by Division Headquarters; the design was originally painted on a truck, having been submitted by Sergeant L.D. Lundey, Company A, 2nd Supply Train, in response to a division-wide contest to select a division insignia. Sergeant Lundy's design was approved by the division commander, Major General Bundy, and his staff in April 1918.[12] The Indian represented the most American of symbols. The shape and color of the background designated many of the division's subordinate elements. The chart below shows the basic shapes. The color of the shape further defined the element. Black represented the headquarters company, red, the 1st battalion, yellow, the 2nd battalion, blue, the third battalion, purple, the machine gun company, and green for the supply company. The color breakdown for division support elements was as follows: 4th Machine Gun Battalion, purple, 1st Signal Battalion, red, Transportation and Military Police, blue, and 2nd Supply Train, green.[13]

Campaigns:

Aisne Defensive, Aisne-Marne Offensive, St. Mihiel Offensive, Meuse-Argonne Offensive, Chateau-Thierry Sector, Marbache Sector, Toulon Sector, Toulon-Troyon Sectors, Troyon Sector.[14]

Above: Major General Hines, commander of the 3rd Corps awards the Distinguished Service Medal to Colonel Hugh B. Myers, Chief of Staff, 2nd Division in Engers, Germany, June, 1919. Courtesy National Archives.

Left: Major General John A. Lejeune, U.S.M.C., 2nd Division commander confers with his primary staff, Lieutenant Colonel High Matthews, G-1, Colonel Preston Brown, Chief of Staff, Colonel James C. Rhea, G-3, and Lieutenant Colonel G.A. Herbst, G-2, at his headquarters in Marbache, France in August, 1918. Courtesy National Archives.

Right: A group of Marines serving in the Army of Occupation, all are members of the 3rd Platoon, 45th Company, 3rd Battalion, 5th Regiment, U.S.M.C. From left to right; Corporal Terry, Private McDonald, Private Malbin, Corporal Dollens, Private Adams, and Private Smith. Courtesy Military History Institute.

Below: Lieutenant Colonel F.C. Miller, 2nd Division Quartermaster poses with his staff in La Cheppe, France, October, 1918. Of note is the division insignia used on the sign outside the building. Courtesy National Archives.

Right: The pattern patch of the 2nd Division. This rare example from the War Department files has the notation, "Emblem of the 2nd Division, Regular, A.E.F. Designed by Sgt L. D. Lundey, Co A Supply Train. Passed on and approved by Major General Bundy and staff in the month of April, 1918." Army Heritage Museum.

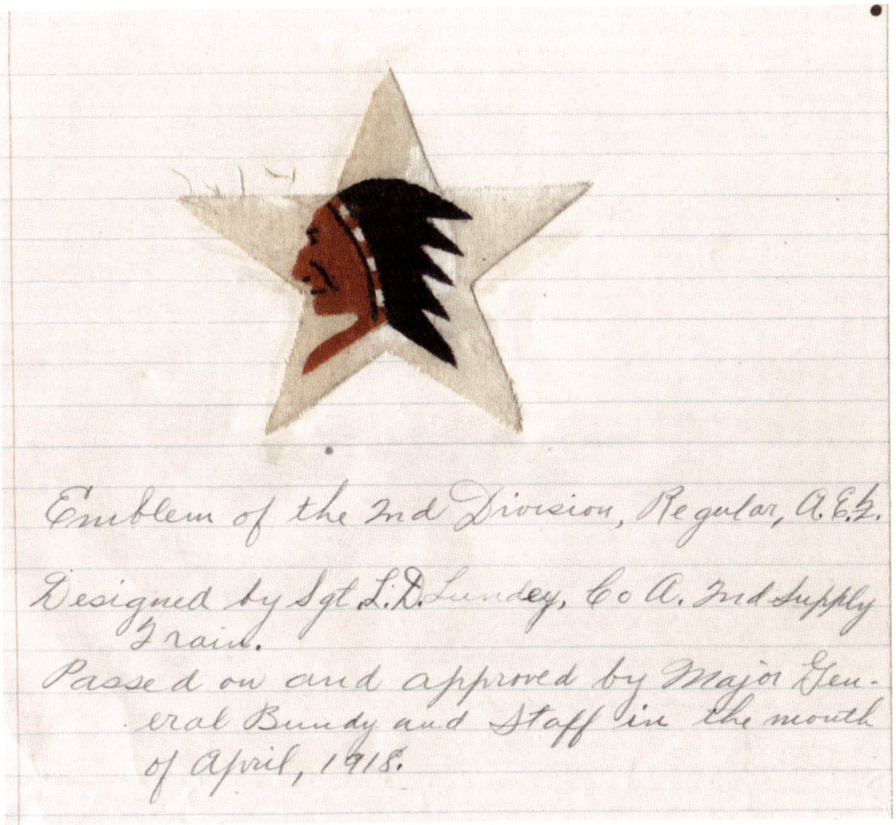

Below: This chart illustrates the general shapes used to identify subordinate unit insignia within the 2nd Division. The color of the shape further delineated the unit: headquarters - black; 1st battalion - red; 2nd battalion - yellow; 3rd battalion - blue; machine gun company - purple; supply company - green.

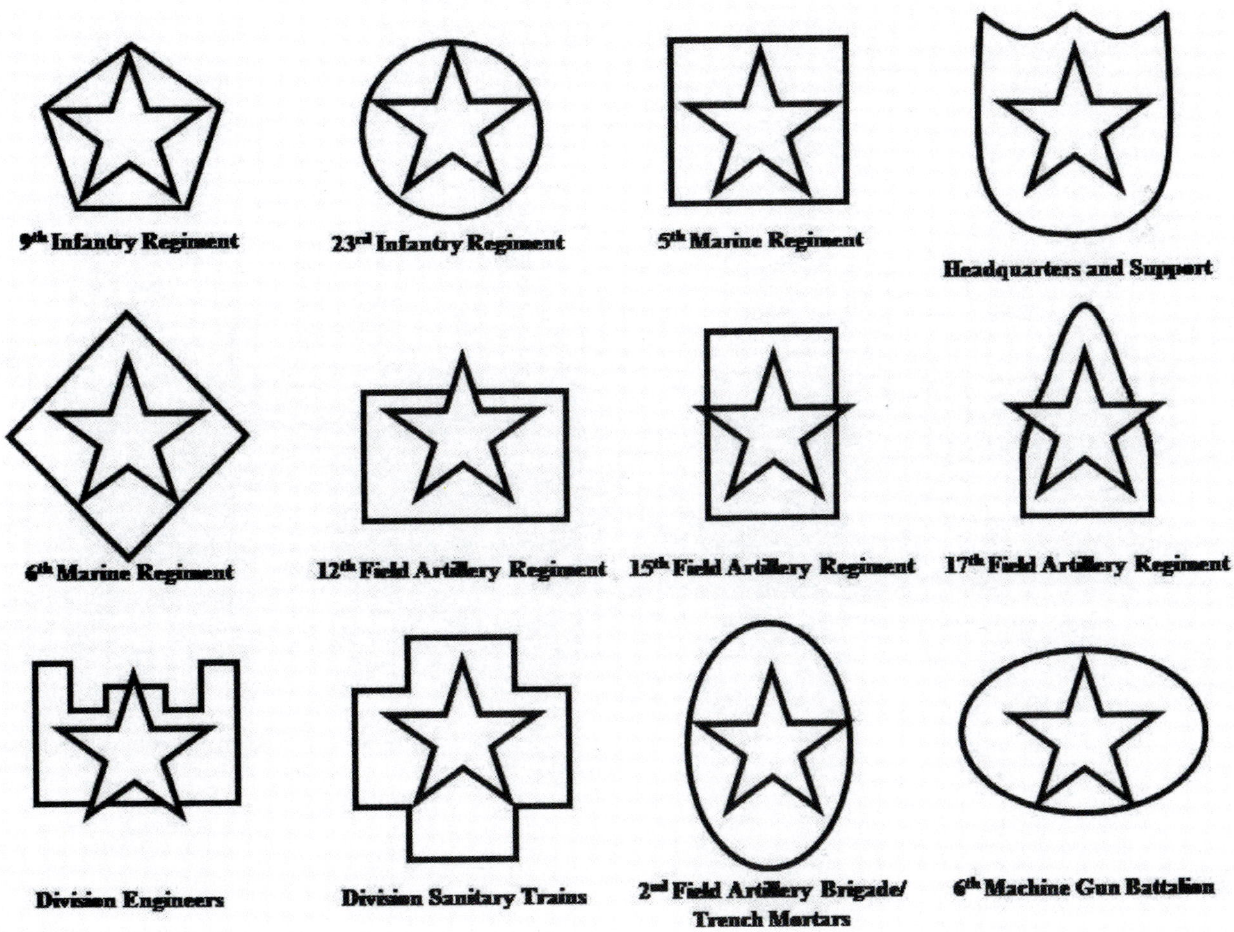

The 2nd Division modified their shoulder sleeve insignia to identify many of their units; the red rectangle oriented horizontally identifies this as the insignia of the 1st Battalion, 12th Field Artillery Regiment. This insignia uses a hand painted Indian head.

Division support elements used the shield shape as a means of identification with the color of the shield designating the specific unit. A red shield identifies this insignia as the 1st Battalion, 2nd Signal Regiment.

The 2nd Battalion, 2nd Engineer Regiment uses the standard 2nd Division color coding, in this case yellow to designate the second battalion, coupled with the Engineer Castle design used for the 2nd Engineer Regiment.

Division Organization (1917-1919):[15]

3rd Infantry Brigade:

9th Infantry Regiment
23rd Infantry Regiment
5th Machine Gun Battalion

4th Marine (Infantry) Brigade:

5th Marine Regiment
6th Marine Regiment
6th Machine Gun Battalion (Marines)

Division Troops:

4th Machine Gun Battalion

2nd Field Artillery Brigade:

12th Field Artillery Regiment
15th Field Artillery Regiment
17th Field Artillery Regiment
2nd Trench Mortar Battery

Division Support:

2nd Engineer Regiment
1st Field Signal Battalion
2nd Train Headquarters and Military Police
2nd Ammunition Train
2nd Supply Train
2nd Engineer Train
2nd Sanitary Train (Ambulance Companies & Field Hospitals 1st, 15th, 16th, 23rd)

Division Combat Narrative:[16]

The first unit of the division arrived in France June 27, 1917; the last element March 15, 1918.

For training purposes the infantry elements were sent to the department of Haute Marne and division headquarters were established at Bourmont. Upon arrival of the artillery in December and January, it was sent to Valdahon for instruction. During the latter month all elements of the division were assembled in the vicinity of Bourmont for final training.

On March 16th the division went into a quiet portion of the line between Verdun and St. Mihiel – the Toulon – Troyon sectors. Here the troops were mingled with the French, and took part in numerous minor operations; and on the night of April 13th-14th the 9th Infantry repulsed an unusually strong raid with complete success. The division remained in this sector until May 13th when it moved to the vicinity of Chaumonten-Vexin (Oise) for further training preparatory to relieving the 1st Division near Montdidier.

But on May 27th the Germans began their offensive between the Aisne and the Marne and the division was placed at the disposal of the French. From June 1st to 3rd it relieved exhausted French troops near Montreuil-aux-Lions on a twelve kilometer front blocking the direct highway to Paris. The German advance, however, soon spent its force, and no serious effort was made to penetrate the extended divisional front. But the moral effect upon both friends and enemies of this intervention of Americans at this precise time and place was very great. On June 4th the division commenced a series of vigorous attacks. In spite of desperate resistance the village of Bouresches was taken. Belleau Wood was occupied and on July 1st Vaux and the Bois de la Roche were captured. On July 9th after having spent 40 days in action which cost losses of 9,000 men the division was relieved and moved to a reserve position along the line Montreuil-St. Aulde.

On July 18th the Allies began the operation known as the Aisne-Marne offensive, its immediate purpose being the reduction of the Chateau-Thierry salient. The 2nd Division with the 1st American and 1st Moroccan Divisions made the main attack from the west, south of Soissons. There was no artillery preparation and the attack was in the nature of a surprise. The division advanced eight kilometers in 26 hours, capturing the powerfully-organized positions of Beaurepaire Farm, Vaucastille and Vierzy, and by the end of the second day it was facing Tigny, having lost 5,000 men, but having captured 3,000 prisoners and 75 guns. The division, except the artillery, was relieved by a French division on the night of July 19th-20th, and assembled near Pierrefonds. The artillery remained in support of the French until July 25th.

The division was in training in the Ormoy-Villers area until July 28th when it moved to the vicinity of Nancy and on August 6th it relieved a French unit in the Marbache Sector, where it remained until relieved by the 82nd Division on August 16th.

It then moved to the Colombey-les-Belles area, where active preparation for the impending St. Mihiel offensive was taken up. In this operation it formed the left flank of the American 1st Corps on the south face of the salient north of Limey. Advancing through Remenauville it occupied Thiaucourt and captured Jaulny on September 12th. During the next three days it extended and consolidated its gains; on the night of the 15th-16th it was relieved by the 78th Division and withdrew to the Toul area.

The American Meuse-Argonne operation started on September 26th. As a part of the same strategic combination, the French 4th Army attacked in the Champagne, its right connecting with the left of the American 1st Army. For this operation the 2nd Division was placed at the disposal of the French and moved to Chalons-sur-Marne and thence to Suippes. On the night of October 1st-2nd it entered the line northwest of Somme-Py, and attacked the morning of the 3rd. During the next four days against intense resistance, it advanced steadily, and took Medeah Farm and Blanc Mont ridge and the ground up to the St. Etienne-Orfeuil Road suffering a loss of 5,400 men and capturing 2,300 prisoners. On the night of October 6th-7th the 36th American division arrived to relieve it. The relief was completed October 10th except for the artillery and engineers who remained in action with the 36th Division. The division moved eastward to join the American 1st Army.

Passing through the Argonne Forest, the division concentrated in and around Exermont where it was in reserve of the 5th Army Corps. Its artillery and engineers rejoined the night of October 31st and on the same night it relieved the 42nd Division in line south of St. Georges. On November 1st a general attack was made, preceded by an intense artillery bombardment and accompanied by a powerful barrage. The division overran the towns of St. Georges and Landres-et-St. Georges with little difficulty, disposed of stubborn resistance in Bois des Hazois without loss of time, and captured Landreville, Chennery and Bayonville. Opposition stiffened at the south edge of the Bois de la Folie. However, by a series of audacious and skillfully executed night maneuvers the division rapidly pushed forward through these woods, Fossé, Nouart, and the Bois de Belval, and by November 6th had reached Létanno on the Meuse. From the 6th to the 10th was spent in reconnoitering the river and preparing for a crossing. On the night of the 10th-11th a crossing was effected at Létanne. Another attempt made at the same time to cross the Meuse at Mouzon was unsuccessful.

After the armistice the division was assigned to the Army of Occupation, and began its march on November 17th. It entered Germany at Bollendorf on December 1st, crossed the Rhine at Remagen, on the 13th, and established itself in the Coblenz bridgehead with headquarters at Heddesdorf. Here it remained until the movement home was begun, division headquarters sailing from Brest July 25th and arriving at New York August 3rd.

The division commanders were: Brigadier General Charles. A. Doyen, Major General Omar Bundy, Major General James G. Harbord , Major General John A. LeJeune U.S.M.C., and Colonel Harry A. Eaton.

Days in the Front Line: 58 (training) 48 (sector) 33 (battle) for a total of 139. During operations the division took 12,026 prisoners and its casualties totaled 5,155 soldiers killed in action or died of wounds, 18,080 wounded in action.[17]

The elongated oval with black background belonged to the 2nd Field Artillery Brigade.

The 4th Machine Gun Battalion uses the shield reserved for Division support elements in purple as their insignia.

A beautifully executed 1st Battalion, 5th Marine Regiment shoulder sleeve insignia. The 5th Marines were identified through the use of square background; battalions use the standard division color scheme with red designating the first battalion.

The standard color coding called for yellow in the second battalion. Although time faded, this insignia belongs to the 2nd Battalion, 5th Marine Regiment.

Blue was used to designate the third battalion as in this 3rd Battalion, 5th Marine Regiment insignia.

The black velvet background identifies this example as the Headquarters, 5th Marine Regiment.

Reference Bibliography:

General Division Histories:

American Battle Monuments Commission. *2nd Division, Summary of Operations in the World War.* Washington, DC: Government Printing Office, 1944.

Andriot, R. *Belleau Wood and the American Army: The 2nd and 26th Divisions (June and July 1918).* Washington, DC: Belleau Wood Memorial Assn., 192-.

Bruce, Andrew D. *Operations of the Second Division (U.S.) During Third Phase of Meuse-Argonne.* Ft. Benning, Georgia: The Infantry School, 1924.

Hillman, Rolfe L. "Second to None: The Indianheads." US Naval Institute Proceedings (Nov 1987): pp. 56-62.

Joyce, Dan. "Insignia of the Second Division, AEF." Military Collector & Historian (Summer1988): pp. 66-72.

"Mann Gegen Masse." Militar-Wochenblatt (18 Jan 1931): p. 1039.

Spaulding, Oliver L. and Wright, John W. *The Second Division American Expeditionary Force in France, 1917-1919.* Nashville, Tennessee: Battery Press, 1989.

The Trail's Pictorial Review, Second Division. n.p., 1922.

U.S. Army, General Staff, War Plans Division. Historical Branch. *Blanc Mont (Meuse-Argonne-Champagne), April 1920.* Washington, DC: 1920.

—. *Blanc Mont (Meuse-Argonne-Champagne), June 1921.* Washington, DC: Government Printing Office, 1922.

U.S. Army, 2nd Infantry Division. *Commendations of Second Division, American Expeditionary Forces, 1917-1919.* Cologne, Germany: 2nd Division Association, 1919.

—. General Order, No. 64, 25 Jun 1919.

—. 2nd Infantry Division. *Records of the Second Division (Regular).* [10 vols].

—. Historical Section. *Translations, War Diaries of German Units Opposed to the Second Division (Regular), 1918.* [9 vols].

—. *The Second Division, American Expeditionary Forces, 1917-1919.* Neuwied am Rhein, Germany: 2nd Division Association, 1919.

—. *The Second Division: Syllabi of the Histories of Regiments and Separate Organizations.* Coblenz, Germany: Coblenzer Volkszeitung, 1919.

—. Historical Section. *Translations, War Diaries of German Units Opposed to the Second Division (Regular), 1918.* [9 vols.] Washington, DC: Army War College, 1930.

9th Infantry Regiment

MacNider, Hanford. *The A.E.F. of a Conscientious Subaltern.* Mason City, Iowa: Klipto, 1923.

9th Infantry, 1917-1919, "Syracuse to the Rhine": A Synopsis. n.p., ca. 1919-30.

The Ninth US Infantry in the World War. Neuweid-am-Rhine: Heusersche Buchdrückerei, 1919.

Welborn, Elizabeth B. *Ira Clinton Welborn, 1874-1956, Colonel, United States Army.* n.p., 1994.

Williamson, S.T. *The Night March: An Untold War Story.* New York: *New York Times Magazine*, 1928.

Wood, Lambert A. *His Job: Letters Written by a 22-Year Old Lieutenant in the World War to his Parents and Others in Oregon.* Portland, Oregon: Metropolitan Press, 1936.

23rd Infantry Regiment

McCrossen, Bernard J. *Diary of the Machine Gun Company, 23rd Infantry, Second Division,1917-1919.* n.p., 1919.

5th Marine Regiment

Boyd, Thomas Alexander. *Through the Wheat.* NY.: Scribner's, 1923.

Hemrick, Levi E. *Once A Marine.* New York: Carlton Press, 1968.

Mackin, Elton E. *Suddenly we didn't want to die: Memoirs of a World War I Marine.* Novato, California: Presidio Press, 1993.

Thomason, John W., Jr. *Fix Bayonets!* New York: Blue Ribbon Books, 1926.

6th Marine Regiment

Morgan, Daniel. *When the World Went Mad*. Christopher Publishing House,1931.

Scanlon, William T. *God Have Mercy On Us: A Story of 1918*. Boston, Houghton Mifflin, 1929.

12th Field Artillery Regiment

Binns, John J. "Second Field Artillery Brigade on the March." *Field Artillery Journal* (Mar 1926): pp. 180-83.

Foster, Pell W. *A Short History of Battery "B", 12th Field Artillery, Second Division, in the World War*. n.p., 1921.

Wahl, George D. "Battery 'B' of the Twelfth Field Artillery During the Late War." *Field Artillery Journal* (1924): pp. 15-30, 131-43 & 221-36.

15th Field Artillery Regiment

Cone, Anthony. *E Battery Goes to War: Being the Extracts From the Wartime Diary of First Sergeant*. n.p., 1929.

17th Field Artillery Regiment

Smith, Herbert E. "Masters of the Big Guns: Seventeenth Field Artillery Enjoys an Excellent War Record and History." US Army Recruiting News (Jun 1, 1931): p. 6.

Vencill, Ralph K. *From Robinson to the Rhine: Battery "A" 17th Field Artillery, 1917-1918-1919*. n.p., 1919.

2nd Engineer Regiment

Anderson, William T. "Devil Dogs in Olive Drab: The 2nd Engineers at Belleau Wood." Army History (Spring 2003): pp. 20-29.

Peek, E.D. "Army Engineer Operations: In the St. Mihiel and Meuse-Argonne Offensives." *Military Engineer* (Sep/Oct 1922): pp. 287-90.

U.S. Army. Corps of Engineers. 2nd Regt. *A History of the Second Regiment of Engineers, United States Army, From Its Organization in Mexico, 1916, to Its Watch on the Rhine, 1919*. n.p., 1919.

—. *The Official History of the Second Regiment of Engineers and Second Engineer Train, United States Army, in the World War*. San Antonio, Texas: San Antonio Printing, 1920.

Another Headquarters, 5th Marine Regiment insignia using felt on felt construction.

The diamond shaped background was selected to designate the 6th Marine Regiment. The standard color of red is used to designate this example as 1st Battalion, 6th Marine Regiment.

Yellow background coupled with the diamond indicate this as a 2nd Battalion, 6th Marine Regiment insignia. This example uses the standard embroidered Indian Head and star.

Another example of 2nd Battalion, 6th Marine Regiment using a painted Indian Head.

Blue was reserved for the third battalion. This 3rd Battalion, 6th Marine Regiment insignia uses the embroidered Indian Head and star.

A quality insignia with painted Indian Head and velvet background. The purple horizontally elongated oval used identifies the unit as the 6th Machine Gun Battalion. Purple was the division's standard color for machine gun units.

Blue felt with a felt construction Indian Head with chain-stitched features comprise the elements of this 3rd Battalion, 9th Infantry Regiment insignia.

A conidial shape was selected for the 17th Field Artillery Regiment. This insignia for the Supply Company, 17th Field Artillery Regiment used the division's standard green background with denoted supply organizations.

The pentagon shaped background was allocated to the 9th Infantry Regiment. Red is used for first battalion. This embroidered example is from the 1st Battalion, 9th Infantry Regiment.

A yellow rectangle oriented horizontally indicates this example is from the 2nd Battalion, 12th Field Artillery Regiment.

A circular background was reserved for the 23rd Infantry regiment. As with the other division organizations, red represented the first battalion. Shown here is a typical 1st Battalion, 23rd Infantry Regiment insignia using the embroidered Indian Head on wool felt background.

A 2nd Battalion, 9th Infantry Regiment example uses yellow cut out felt with the standard Indian Head and Star as an inset.

A vertical rectangle in yellow denotes the 15th Field Artillery Regiment. As this was the second numbered Field Artillery regiment in the Division, yellow was used as a background.

3rd Battalion, 23rd Infantry Regiment is distinguished by the blue background. Note the use of the standard Indian Head as an inset to the felt background.

The Headquarters, 23rd Infantry Regiment uses a black felt background with the painted Indian Head.

The Machine Gun Company, 23rd Infantry Regiment employs the division standard purple as a designation for machine gun units.

The green background marks this insignia as that of the Supply Company, 23rd Infantry Regiment.

A nicely manufactured 2nd Division Headquarters insignia. The shield represents division support elements and black background denotes the headquarters. This was the pattern worn by the division staff.

The cross shaped background was used to designate the division sanitary train; this example of a 2nd Division Sanitary Train insignia has a fully embroidered Indian Head inset into the felt background.

The division supply train used the shield shape as background which was reserved for support organizations along with the color green designating the supply function; this example of the 2nd Division Supply Train insignia is fully embroidered on felt.

3rd Infantry Division

The War Department organized the 3rd Division at Camp Greene, North Carolina on November 21, 1917. It was composed of troops stationed at Camps Greene, Forrest, Shelby, Stanley, Stuart, Travis, and Forts Bliss, Clark, Douglas, Leavenworth and Washington Barracks.[18]

Insignia:
The division selected as its insignia a blue square with three parallel white stripes, running diagonally from lower left to upper right, representing the three major operations in which the division participated. The blue symbolizes the loyalty of the troops of the division.[19] The insignia was granted AEF approval on October 24, 1918.[20]

Campaigns:
Somme Defense, Aisne Defensive, Champagne-Marne Defensive, Aisne-Marne Offensive, St. Mihiel Offensive, Meuse-Argonne Offensive, Amiens Sector, Chateau-Thierry Sector, Vesle Sector.[21]

A group of General Officers from left to right; Major General Hunter Liggett, 1st Corps; Major General Omar Bundy, 2nd Division Commander; Major General Joseph T. Dickman, 3rd Division Commander, and Brigadier General Sladen, commander of the 5th Brigade of the 3rd Division. Chateau Thierry, France, June, 1918. Courtesy National Archives.

An unidentified soldier of the 3rd Division poses for a portrait. Courtesy Military History Institute.

Soldiers of the 3rd Division Surgeon's office in Andernach, Germany, January, 1919. Courtesy National Archives.

Division Organization (1917-1919):[22]

5th Infantry Brigade:

4th Infantry Regiment
7th Infantry Regiment
8th Machine Gun Battalion

6th Infantry Brigade:

30th Infantry Regiment
38th Infantry Regiment
9th Machine Gun Battalion

Division Troops:

7th Machine Gun Battalion

3rd Field Artillery Brigade:

10th Field Artillery Regiment
18th Field Artillery Regiment
76th Field Artillery Regiment
3rd Trench Mortar Battery

This unusual 3rd Division insignia is embroidered on an olive drab felt background.

A more typical 3rd Division insignia; felt on felt with white stripes against a blue background.

A high quality 3rd Division insignia velvet background with silver cording.

Private A.O. Donough, from Company A, 7th Machine Gun Battalion, 3rd Division drives an unidentified soldier in his sidecar, Germany, 1919. Courtesy Military History Institute.

A fully embroidered 3rd Division insignia with the Third Army insignia inset used during the Occupation period.

The pennant shaped alternate version of the 3rd Division insignia. This insignia was never officially adopted by the division.

Division Support:

6th Engineer Regiment
5th Field Signal Battalion
3rd Train Headquarters and Military Police
3rd Ammunition Train
3rd Supply Train
6th Engineer Train
3rd Sanitary Train (Ambulance Companies & Field Hospitals 5th, 7th, 26th, 27th)

Division Combat Narrative:[23]

The first unit to go overseas was the 6th Engineers which was designated for early duty in France. It arrived December 20, 1917. A detachment of the regiment serving with the British occupied active sectors and took part in the operation known as the Somme Defensive. Division Headquarters arrived in France on April 4th, and the last unit May 12, 1918.

For training purposes the division (less artillery and engineers) was sent to the Châteauvillain area, the artillery going to Coetquidan for the same purpose. The artillery rejoined the division July 6, 1918, and was present with it in the Marne Defensive, and the Aisne-Marne Offensive, remaining with the division until September 7, 1918, when it was detached for participation in the St. Mihiel Offensive with the 4th Corps. The artillery brigade rejoined the division September 15, 1918, and from this time until the armistice, served as division artillery either with the 3rd or some other division.

On May 27th, the Germans began their offensive between the Aisne and the Marne, and the 3rd Division was placed at the disposal of the French. The first unit to enter the line was the 7th Machine Gun Battalion, which, on May 31st, and June 1st, 1918, distinguished itself by its stubborn defense against the crossing of the Marne at Château-Thierry.

In June, the entire division went into line in the Château-Thierry sector. Operating under the 38th Army Corps (French), it took an active part in the Aisne Defensive June 1st to June 5th. On June 15th, the 7th Infantry was detached and placed at the disposal of the 2nd Division in Belleau Woods where it relieved the 5th and 6th Marines (4th Brigade). It was withdrawn from the line on the night of June 23-24, and rejoined the division. In the Champagne-Marne Defensive, July 15th to 18th, holding the south bank of the Marne River for twelve kilometers east from Château-Thierry, the division earned for itself the highest commendation for gallantry in an action which marked the turning point of the war. Its entire front was subjected to an intense artillery bombardment. Then came the infantry attack, its greatest strength being between Fossoy and Moulins. The 6th Brigade (30th and 38th Inf.), defending the right flank, effectually frustrated the enemy's contemplated advance to the south through the valley of the Surmelin River. Holding the extreme right in the defensive line, the 38th Infantry bears the proud distinction of being the only regimental organization particularly mentioned in General Pershing's report on the operations in the A.E.F.

On July 18th, the Allies began the operation known as the Aisne-Marne Offensive; its immediate purpose being the reduction of the Château-Thierry salient. In this operation the division attacked across the Marne east of Château-Thierry and advanced northeast to the Ourcq. Jaulgonne was entered on July 22nd; le Charmel offered stubborn resistance, and was only captured on July 25th after four days' bitter fighting. The Ourcq was reached on the 26th and Ronchéres was taken on the 28th. The division was relieved on July 30th by the 32nd Division, and assembled south of Château-Thierry. On August 2nd the 6th Brigade was dispatched to support of the 3rd French Army Corps operating toward the Vesle. It was relieved from this duty on August 10th and rejoined the division which had gone into rest area near Gondrecourt.

On September 4, the division proceeded to the Vaucouleurs area preparatory to taking part in the St. Mihiel Offensive. In this operation it was in the reserve of the 4th Army Corps.

The Meuse-Argonne Offensive started on September 26. The division passed into the 5th Army Corps on September 29, and on September 30 relieved the 79th Division in the front line. On October 12, it passed into the 3rd Army Corps. For twenty-seven days the division was continuously in the front line during which period it advanced seven kilometers against organized defenses, encountering particularly strong resistance in the taking of Bois de Cunel and Hill 299. The division was relieved on October 27 by the 5th Division, and proceeded to the Tannois rest area.

After the armistice the division was assigned to the Army of Occupation and began its march on November 17. It entered Germany via the Remich and Schengen bridges, on December 1. On December 15, it started the march along the Rhine River road and established itself on December 17 in the Coblenz bridgehead with headquarters at Andernach. Here it remained until the movement home begun. Division Headquarters sailed from Brest on August 14, and arrived at New York on August 23, 1919.

The division commanders were: Major General Joseph T. Dickman, Brigadier General James A. Irons, Colonel Alexander Ovenshine, Brigadier General Sladen, Major General Beaumont B. Buck, Brigadier General Preston Brown, and Major General Robert L. Howze.

Days in the Front Line: 0 (training) 39 (sector) 50 (battle) for a total of 89. During operations the division took 2,240 prisoners and its casualties totaled 3,401 soldiers killed in action or died of wounds, 12,000 wounded in action.[24]

Reference Bibliography:

General Division Histories:

American Battle Monuments Commission *3rd Division, Summary of Operations in the World War.* Washington, DC: Government Printing Office, 1944.

Cochrane, Rexmond C. *The 3rd Division at Chateau Thierry, July 1918*. Army Chemical Center, Maryland: USA Chemical Corps Historical Office, 1959.

Dickman, Joseph T. *The Great Crusade: A Narrative of the World War*. New York: Appleton, 1927.

Hemenway, Frederic V. *History of the Third Division, United States Army in the World War for the Period December 1, 1917 to January 1, 1919*. Cologne, Germany: Schauberg, 1919.

U.S. Army, 3rd Infantry Division. *Third Division Citations*. Germany: Reinhartz, 1919.

30th Infantry Regiment

Butts, Edmond L. *The Keypoint of the Marne and Its Defense by the 30th Infantry*. Mesasha, WI: Banta, 1930.

Heavey, W.F. "German Crossing of the Marne River." *Military Engineer* (May/Jun 1926): pp. 175-79.

U.S. Army, 30th Infantry Regiment. HQ Co. *Headquarters Company, 30th Inf., July 15th, 1919*. Mayen, Germany: Louis Schreder, 1919.

38th Infantry Regiment

Fretwell, Frank M. *The Rock of the Marne: A Narration of the Military Exploits of Gen. Ulysses Grant McAlexander at the Second Battle of the Marne*. Seattle, Washington: n.p., 1923.

Lovejoy, Clarence E. *The Story of the Thirty-Eighth*. Coblenz: Gorres-Druckerei, 1919.

Woodridge, Jesse W. *The Giants of the Marne: A Story of McAlexander and His Regiment*. Salt Lake City: Seagull Press, 1923.

—. *The Rock of the Marne: A Chronological Story of the 38th Regiment, US Infantry*. NY: Columbia, 1919.

10th Field Artillery Regiment

Anderson, Jonathan W. "With the Tenth Field Artillery at the Second Battle of the Marne." *Field Artillery Journal* (Sep 1923): pp. 375-83.

Hesse, Kurt. "Drama on the Marne (July 16, 1918) Truths from the Front." *Field Artillery Journal* (Mar 1921): pp. 140-52.

Hayes, Cassey. "Operations in the 2nd Battalion, 10th Field Artillery in the Second Battle of the Marne." *Field Artillery Journal* (Sep 1923): pp. 443-50.

Shepard, nfn. "The Employment of the Artillery Fifth Army Corps, Argonne-Meuse Operations." *Field Artillery Journal* (Apr/Jun 1919): pp. 148-82.

18th Field Artillery Regiment

Hesse, Kurt. "The Drama of the Marne (July 15, 1918): Truths from the Front." *Field Artillery Journal* (Mar 1921): pp. 140-52.

76th Field Artillery Regiment

Black, P.G. "With a Regiment of 75's in the Champagne-Marne Defensive." *Field Artillery Journal* (Nov 1919): pp. 556-74.

Hesse, Kurt. "Drama on the Marne (July 16, 1918) Truths from the Front." *Field Artillery Journal* (Mar 1921): pp. 140-52.

6th Engineer Regiment

Adams, Donald G., & Crane, Albert E. "For and Aft of the Infantry: The 6th Engineers in the American Offensives of 1918." *Military Engineer* (Nov/Dec 1921): pp. 470-73.

Crane, A.E. "The Sixth Engineers in the Meuse-Argonne." *Military Engineer* (Jan/Feb 1931): pp. 124-28.

U.S. Army, Corps of Engineers. 6th Regiment. *History of the Sixth Engineers, by Its Men.* NY: Knickerbocker, 1920.

American soldier of Company E, 39th Infantry Regiment, 4th Division looking over an old monument on the Rhine erected in honor of the Prussian victory in 1871 over the French. Coblenz, Rhenish Prussia, Germany, December 10, 1918. Courtesy National Archives

4th Infantry Division

The War Department organized the 4th Division at Fort Ethan Allen, Vermont on December 16, 1917. It was composed of regular army troops stationed at Camps Greene, Monterey, and Vancouver Barracks.[25]

Insignia:

The division selected as its insignia four green ivy leaves arranged in a cross with a small open circle in the center inside a light khaki square with each leaf pointing to one corner of the square. The four leaves represent the numerical designation of the division and the word "Ivy" suggests the Roman numeral "IV" for 4th Division. Ivy leaves are symbolic of fidelity and tenacity.[26] Approved October 30, 1918.[27]

Campaigns:

Aisne-Marne Offensive, St. Mihiel Offensive, Meuse-Argonne Offensive, Toulon Sector, Vesle Sector.[28]

Division Organization (1917-1919):[29]

7th Infantry Brigade:

39th Infantry Regiment
47th Infantry Regiment
11th Machine Gun Battalion

8th Infantry Brigade:

58th Infantry Regiment
59th Infantry Regiment
12th Machine Gun Battalion

Division Troops:

10th Machine Gun Battalion

4th Field Artillery Brigade:

Opposite
Top: Major General John L. Hines and his staff at Haudainville, France, September, 1918. Courtesy National Archives.

Middle: The Regimental Band of the 58th Infantry enjoys the sun in Nice, France, May, 1919. Courtesy Military History Institute.

Bottom: Infantrymen of the 4th Division escort German prisoners to the rear. Near Montreuil aux Lyons, France, July 1918. Courtesy National Archives.

U.S. OFFICIAL

A beautifully embroidered 4th Division insignia. This example follows the standard division pattern.

This felt on felt example is of the most common variety.

13th Field Artillery Regiment
16th Field Artillery Regiment
77th Field Artillery Regiment
4th Trench Mortar Battery

Division Support:

4th Engineer Regiment
8th Field Signal Battalion
4th Train Headquarters and Military Police
4th Ammunition Train
4th Supply Train
4th Engineer Train
4th Sanitary Train (Ambulance Companies & Field Hospitals 19th, 21st, 28th, 33rd)

Division Combat Narrative:[30]

The first unit to go overseas arrived in France May 10, 1917; the last element arrived June 8, 1918. The transport "Moldavia" carrying Companies "A" and "B", of the 58th Infantry, was torpedoed and sunk on May 23rd; 56 men of the two companies were lost.

The division (less artillery) was assigned to the 2nd American Army Corps, serving with the British, and was concentrated at Samer (Pas de Calais) for training. The artillery brigade went to Camp de Souge near Bordeaux for the same purpose, and did not rejoin the division until the first week in August. Early in June the division was placed at the disposal of the French and moved to Meaux (Seine et Marne) where training was continued nearer the front. During the German offensive of July 15th it was in reserve divided between the 2nd and 7th French Corps between Soissons and Château-Thierry. Here it suffered its first battle casualties.

The division participated in the Aisne-Marne offensive under the 2nd, 7th and 11th French Corps from July 18th to July 28th, when it became the reserve of the 1st American Army Corps then a part of the 6th French Army. It was concentrated in the Bois du Châtelet, and the Bois de Beuvardelle supporting the 42nd Division which was heavily engaged with the enemy on the banks of the Ourcq River. Some of its units were engaged under the orders of that division and participated in the capture of Sergy on July 29th. The division relieved the 42nd Division on the night of August 2nd-3rd on a line through Les Bons Hommes Farm-Forêt de Nesles-Bois de la Porte d'Arcy. The enemy was retiring, and the division pressed the pursuit as far as the Vesle River where it encountered serious resistance. On the night of August 11th-12th it was relieved by the 77th Division, and withdrew to the Bois de Dôle, and the Forêt de Nesles, the artillery brigade remaining in action until August 17th.

After a period of rest, replacement of losses, and training the division relieved French troops in the Toulon Sector southeast of Verdun as part of the 5th Corps, 1st American Army.

Private Anthony Muto (front right) from the 16th Field Artillery poses with some friends. Courtesy Military History Institute.

In the St. Mihiel Offensive it was on the extreme left flank of the troops engaged and was the pivot for the movement against the west face of the salient. It was therefore called upon for only a slight advance. On September 20th the division was relieved from the line and moved to Lemmes, west of the Meuse, and thence north to join in the Meuse-Argonne Offensive which was to begin on September 26th.

On the night of September 25th-26th the division took over the line of the Ruisseau de Forges north of Esnes as the left unit of the 3rd Corps. From September 26th until October 19th it was continuously in front line, successively attacking and capturing strongly contested positions in the Bois de Brieulles, the Bois du Fays, the Bois de Malaumont, the Bois de Peut-de-Faux, and the Bios de Forêt.

When the relief by the 3rd Division on October 19th was completed, the division moved to Lucey north of Toul in reserve to the Second Army. On November 3rd it was re-assigned to the 1st Army as part of the III Corps preparatory to its re-entry into the Meuse--Argonne Offensive. Before the move involved was completed the order was revoked and the division returned to control of the 2nd Army to participate in the contemplated attack on the Lorraine front. The signing of the Armistice on November 11th curtailed further offensive operations, and the division was concentrated at Boucq, northwest of Toul.

When the division was relieved in line on October 19th, the units of the 4th Field Artillery Brigade remained in action until the night of October 23rd-24th, when they were withdrawn to the Forêt de Hesse for a five day rest. The brigade was returned to the line in support of the 3rd Corps and participated in the great attack of November 1st. The 16th F.A. was attached to the 90th Division, which it supported until November 7th, when the regiment's active operations terminated. The 13th and 77th Regiments served with the 3rd Field Artillery Brigade during the next ten days, attached to the 5th Division, covering its crossing of the Meuse and later supporting its advance in pursuit east of the Meuse.

The division was now assigned to the Army of Occupation and began the march toward Germany on November 20. Passing through Luxembourg it entered Germany on December 3 and completed the occupation of its area about Cochem on December 17. From this area it was subsequently moved to relieve the 42nd Division along the banks of the Rhine with headquarters at Nieder-Breisig.

The division returned to the United States in July, 1919; headquarters sailed from Brest July 24 and arrived in New York July 31.

The division commanders were: Major General George H. Cameron, Brigadier General A. Poore, Major General John L. Hines, and Major General Mark L. Hersey.

Days in the Front Line: 0 (training) 11 (sector) 36 (battle) for a total of 47. During operations the division took 2,756 prisoners and its casualties totaled 2,903 soldiers killed in action or died of wounds, 9,917 wounded in action.[31]

An embroidered example adding the numerical designation of the units. The unit nickname is also a play on these numerals; IV or Ivy Division.

A finely embroidered example of the Fourth Division insignia that includes the addition of the Third Army insignia in the center of the Ivy leaves. These date from the Occupation Period following the Armistice.

4th Division insignia on the tunic of Private Karl D. Eaton. This version is of felt on wool construction with chain stitched on felt 3rd Army insignia inset. Private Collection

Reference Bibliography:

General Division Histories:

American Battle Monuments Commission. *4th Division, Summary of Operations in the World War.* Washington, DC: Government Printing Office, 1944.

Bach, Christian A. & Hall, Henry Noble. *The Fourth Division: Its Services and Achievements in the World War, Gathered From the Records of the Division.* Garden City, New York: Country Life Press, 1920.

39th Infantry Regiment

Cole, Robert B. *The History of the 39th US Infantry During the World War.* New York: Mc-guire, 1919.

Smith, Walter B. "Operations of the 1st Battalion 39th Infantry (4th Division) in the Aisne-Marne Offensive, July 18-20, 1918." Mailing List (1931): pp. 137-54.

47th Infantry Regiment

Heavey, W.F. "German Crossing of the Marne River." *Military Engineer* (May/Jun 1926): pp. 175-79.

Pollard, James E. *The Forty-Seventh Infantry: A History, 1917-1918-1919.* Saginaw, Michigan: Seeman & Peters, 1919.

58th Infantry Regiment

Hartman, James A. *Following My Father's Footsteps in World War I, 1917-1919: A Remembrance*. Privately printed, 2003.

Morrow, George L. *The Fifty-Eighty Infantry in the World War, 1917-1918-1919*. n.p., 1919.

59th Infantry Regiment

History of the 59th Pioneer Infantry 1918-1919, American Expeditionary Forces. Toul, France: Lemaire, 1919.

13th Field Artillery Regiment

Sawbridge, Benjamin M. *A Brief History of the 13th Regiment Field Artillery of the United States Army 1917-1918-1919*. n.p., n.d.

77th Field Artillery Regiment

Tierney, Dudley R. *The Seventy Seventh Field Artillery in the World War*. n.p., 1919.

4th Engineer Regiment

U.S. Army, Corps of Engineers. 4th Regiment. *Columbia to the Rhine: Being a Brief History of the Fourth Engineers, and Their Trop from the Columbia River, in the State of Washington, U.S.A., to the Rhine River in Germany*. Wald, Germany: Westdeutsche Grossdruckerei, 1919.

5th Infantry Division

The War Department organized the 5th Division at Camp Logan, Texas on December 11, 1917. It was composed of regular army troops stationed at Camps Forrest, Greene, Johnston, Logan, Stanley, and Fort Leavenworth.[32]

Private Karl D. Eaton, Company K, 59th Infantry Regiment, 4th Division shows off his field equipment in his yard following the war. Private Collection

Major General Hanson E. Ely poses with his staff in Longuyon, France, November, 1918. Courtesy National Archives.

Insignia:

The division selected as its insignia a red diamond on a vertical axis. This insignia originated as a transportation marking on equipment and supplies. Red was selected as a compliment to the Commanding General who came from the artillery branch. The "ace of diamond" shape was selected from the trade name of a popular company of the time "Diamond Dye" whose motto was "Diamond Dye – it never runs." The diamond shape furthermore represents a well

known engineering problem; being composed of two adjacent isosceles triangles it makes for the greatest strength.[33] Approved October 20, 1918.[34]

Campaigns:
St. Mihiel Offensive, Meuse-Argonne Offensive, Anould Sector, Marbache Sector, St. Die Sector.[35]

Division Organization (1917-1919):[36]

9th Infantry Brigade:

60th Infantry Regiment
61st Infantry Regiment
14th Machine Gun Battalion

10th Infantry Brigade:

6th Infantry Regiment
11th Infantry Regiment
15th Machine Gun Battalion

Division Troops:

13th Machine Gun Battalion

Valentines Day postcard printed in Trier, Germany by Bob Klein, Company B, 6th Infantry Regiment. Courtesy Military History Institute.

Lieutenant A. McLeod, a medical officer with the 11th Infantry Regiment examines Gas patients at a dressing station behind the line. Madeleine Farm, Nantillois, France, October, 1918. Courtesy National Archives.

Fully embroidered 5th Division insignia on olive drab wool.

A fine wool felt version of the 5th Division insignia attached to a closely cut olive drab background.

5th Field Artillery Brigade:

19th Field Artillery Regiment
20th Field Artillery Regiment
21st Field Artillery Regiment
5th Trench Mortar Battery

Division Support:

7th Engineer Regiment
9th Field Signal Battalion
5th Train Headquarters and Military Police
5th Ammunition Train
5th Supply Train
7th Engineer Train
5th Sanitary Train (Ambulance Companies & Field Hospitals 17th, 25th, 29th, 30th)

Division Combat Narrative:[37]

The first unit of the division arrived in France, March 20, 1918, and the last June 19. Bar-sur-Aube was selected as the training area for the infantry, while the artillery was sent to Valdahon for a similar purpose.

On June 1st the division was placed at the disposal of the 33rd French Army Corps, then operating in the Vosgos. To this sector it was immediately moved. Here the troops were mingled with the French behind the lines for further training. June 14th the division entered the line with combat units, half French. The sector was quiet but the division suffered its first casualties June 14th.

On July 15th the division was transferred to the quiet St. Die sector and on July 19th the command of the sector passed to the Americans. The Artillery joined the division July 28th, after having completed its training at Valdahon. In a local engagement of Aug 17th, the town of Frapelle and Hill 451 were taken and held against counter attacks.

The division was relieved by the French August 26th and repaired to Arches, south of Epinal, for rest and training. From this point it moved to the vicinity of Luneville, August 28th.

The St. Mihiel operation was about to begin, and on Sept. 8th the division took its place on a line running from Remenauville to Regnieville, on the southern face of the salient. The division moved to the attack at five o'clock on the morning of Sept. 12th, and meeting little resistance, rapidly advanced its line to the north. When relieved on the night of Sept. 16th-17th, it occupied a line running from Rembercourt to La Souleuvre Farm. The enemy's counter attacks were repulsed with little difficulty.

From September 17th-27th the division, minus the artillery, was stationed at Domevre-en-Haye, near Toul, for rest and training. The artillery remained in the St. Mihiel sector until

Three pals from the 6th Infantry Regiment, (left to right) P. McCourdy, Sam Kreig, and Dennis Wright clown for the camera. Courtesy Military History Institute.

after the signing of the armistice, and formed a part of the 2nd Army. On Sept. 27th-28th, the division moved to Pagny-sur-Meuse, west of Toul, and there resumed training.

At this time the Meuse-Argonne offensive was in full swing to the north and on October 3rd, the 5th moved to the Souilly area preparatory to entering the battle. On the night of the 5th, another move was made; this time to the Foret de Hesse, where it became a reserve unit of the 5th Army Corps.

On the 10th, orders were received to relieve the 80th, and a part of the 4th Division on a line just east of Cunel. On the 11th division headquarters were established in the Bois de Tuilerie. The relief began on the morning of the 12th on the line of the Cunel-Brieulles road. Immediately, patrols were sent out and these succeeded in entering Cunel and Bois de la Pultiers. On the same afternoon, before the relief was completed, a withdrawal was ordered that the division might reform for an attack. During the relief and the withdrawal the division was under continuous fire from both sides of the Meuse, and as a result suffered severely.

The line was re-entered on the 13th at the same point from which the division had withdrawn. From this position, an attack was launched on the morning of the 14th and Cunel captured. Then followed seven days of the bitterest fighting the division had ever experienced. The Bois des Rappes, directly in the line of attack, offered resistance that was not overcome until the 21st, and then only after terrific fighting in which the 5th suffered heavy losses. Throughout, the harassing fire from the east bank of the river continued unabated.

The tired division was relieved by the 90th on October 22nd, and retired to the rest area around Montfaucon.

On October 27th the division again entered the line, this time relieving the 3rd on a line running from the northeast corner of the Bois des Rappes, along the edge of the Bois de Foret; thence south parallel to the Meuse, to the Bois de Brieulles. The towns of Aincreville and Brieulles were immediately occupied; and on November 1st Clery-le-Grand was taken in order to secure an advantageous place in which to cross the Meuse. Then followed a series of attacks which brought the entire line parallel to the Meuse and facing east.

On November 2nd, after overcoming numerous difficulties, the river was crossed at Brieulles, and two days later a second bridge was constructed at Dun-sur-Meuse. The entire division then crossed and pursued the rapidly fleeing enemy northeast as far as the Foret de Woevre. On November 11, its line ran from Jametz, through Louppy to the far edge of the Foret de Woevre.

On November 22nd-23rd, the division was moved to the Longuyon-Longwy area. Here it attached to the 3rd Army, which had been designated as the Army of Occupation. One regiment, the 6th Infantry, was assigned as the garrison of Treves, in Roenish Prussia, when the advanced section of American General Headquarters was established; the rest of the division occupied southern Luxembourg, with headquarters at Esch-sur-Alzette. Here the divisional artillery rejoined, after a long sojourn in the St. Mihiel sector.

The division was relieved May 10 for return to this country, but its departure was delayed until July. Headquarters sailed from Brest July 13 and arrived at New York July 21.

The division commanders were: Major General John E. McMahon, and Major General Hanson E. Ely.

Days in the Front Line: 33 (training) 39 (sector) 32 (battle) for a total of 104. During operations the division took 2,356 prisoners and its casualties totaled 2,120 soldiers killed in action or died of wounds, 6,996 wounded in action.[38]

A die cut example of the 5th Division insignia. This is the most commonly encountered version which was made to be sewn directly on the uniform.

This fully embroidered insignia has an "A" in the center for the Third Army, and was for use during the Occupation of Germany.

Reference Bibliography:

General Division Histories:

American Battle Monuments Commission. *5th Division Summary of Operations in the World War.* Washington, DC: Government Printing Office, 1944.

Cochrane, Rexmond C. *The 5th Division Captures Frapelle, August 1918.* Army Chemical Center, Maryland: USA Chemical Corps History Office, 1958.

History of the Fifth Division. Luxembourg: Origer, 1918.

Raines, Edgar F., Jr. "The American 5th Division and Gas Warfare, 1918." *Army History* (Spring, 1992): pp. 6-10.

Society of the Fifth Div. *The Official History of the Fifth Division, U.S.A.*. Washington, DC: The Society 1919.

U.S. Army, 5th Infantry Division. *Citations of the Fifth Division United States Army*. Luxembourg: Kummer, 1919.

—. *Monograph, 5th Division*. Reports & documents, 1918.

—. *Report of the Part Taken by the Fifth Division in the St. Mihiel Operation, September 11th to September 15th (inclusive) 1918*. n.p., 1919.

U.S. War Dept. *Records of the World War: Field Orders, 1918, 5th Division*. Washington, DC: GPO, 1921.

60th Infantry Regiment

Army Times. *The Daring Regiments: Adventures of the AEF in World War I*. New York: Dodd, Mead, 1967.

Diary of the Machine Gun Co., 60th Infantry, Fifth Division, World War One. n.p., 1919.

Heldreth, Clyde, et. al. *History of Company "D" 60th Infantry, U.S. Army*. Esch, Luxemburg: n.p., 1919.

Noble, Carl. *Jugheads Behind the Lines*. Caldwell, Idaho: n.p., 1938.

61st Infantry Regiment

Roster of Company "I", 61st Infantry, 5th Division. n.p., 1919.

19th Field Artillery Regiment

U.S. Army, 19th Artillery Regiment. Battery A. *1918 Year book of "A" Battery, 19th Field Artillery, United States Regular Army*. n.p., 1918.

21st Field Artillery Regiment

Dowing, G.J. "War Experiences with the 155-mm. Howitzer." *Field Artillery Journal* (Jul 1926): pp 407-12.

7th Engineer Regiment

Hoge, W.M. "The 7th Engineers Bridge the Meuse." *Military Engineer* (Jan/Feb 1926): pp. 24-29.

U.S. Army, Corps of Engineers. 7th Regiment. *A Brief History of the Seventh Engineers, 5th Division*. n.p., 1919.

Major General Walter H. Gordon, 6th Division commander, Verdun, November, 1918. Courtesy National Archives.

6th Infantry Division

The War Department organized the 6th Division at Camp McClellan, Alabama on November 26, 1917. It was composed of regular army troops stationed at Camps Forrest and Logan and Forts Leavenworth, Riley, Sam Houston, and Vancouver Barracks.[39] This division was reported to have marched more than any other in the AEF and was known as the "Sight-Seeing Sixth."[40]

Insignia:
The division selected as its insignia a red six-pointed star whose points lie on an imaginary circle. This insignia is frequently embroidered with the figure "6" superimposed on the star; however, this was never authorized.

Campaigns:
Meuse-Argonne Offensive, Gerardmer Sector.[41]

Division Organization (1917-1919):[42]

11th Infantry Brigade:

51st Infantry Regiment
52nd Infantry Regiment
17th Machine Gun Battalion

Original drawings by Sergeant Charles W. Miller of Battery C, 3rd Field Artillery Regiment, 6th Division, who during the war contributed cartoons to Stars & Stripes and the Battery C Tattler. These were given to the Military History Institute in the 1970s along with his Veterans Survey. Courtesy Military History Institute.

12th Infantry Brigade:

53rd Infantry Regiment
54th Infantry Regiment
18th Machine Gun Battalion

Division Troops:

16th Machine Gun Battalion

6th Field Artillery Brigade:

3rd Field Artillery Regiment
11th Field Artillery Regiment
78th Field Artillery Regiment
6th Trench Mortar Battery

Division Support:

318th Engineer Regiment
6th Field Signal Battalion
6th Train Headquarters and Military Police
6th Ammunition Train
6th Supply Train
318th Engineer Train
6th Sanitary Train (Ambulance Companies & Field Hospitals 20th, 37th, 38th, 40th)

Portrait of Second Lieutenant Olaf W. Osnes, 52nd Infantry Regiment taken while attending the Sorbonne University in Paris, France, May, 1919. Courtesy Military History Institute.

Division Combat Narrative:[43]
The first unit of the division arrived in France July 10th; the last July 26th, 1918. Many units landed first in England and Scotland before crossing the Channel. While at Le Havre the artillery came under fire from an enemy aeroplane and suffered the first casualties inflicted upon the division.

A fully embroidered version of the 6th Division insignia on an olive drab background.

This variation uses black as a background replacing the standard olive drab.

After the training in the vicinity of Chateauvillain, the division, minus the artillery, departed Aug. 27th for Gerardmer, in the Vosges, which sector it occupied, under French command, until relieved October 11th. During this period the sector was quiet although enlivened with frequent raids and patrol combats. The division artillery at this time was in training at Valdahon.

The Meuse-Argonne Offensive being under way, the division, on October 27th, was sent north to take its place in the line. Detraining near St. Menehould, south of the Argonne, the long and trying march due north was begun. Lack of transportation facilities forced the troops to drag their machine guns and other equipment by hand through the forest and over roads that a retreating enemy had used every means at his command to make impassable. After a march of approximately fifty kilometers, divisional headquarters was established, Nov. 6th, at Stonne. At this time the division was a unit of the 1st Corps and in reserve.

On Nov. 6th the left of the 1st Corps rested in the vicinity of Stonne. Then began the turning movement eastward to the Meuse. As the left flank of the Corps swung to the northeast, liaison with the French on the left was temporarily lost. Into this gap units of the 6th were hurried, and what promised to be a dangerous situation was thus saved.

The enemy at this time was in full retreat and the necessity for its services no longer existing, the 6th was moved to the area northeast of Verdun. Before it could enter the line in this sector the signing of the armistice terms ended the fighting. The 11th Field Artillery went into action with the 89th Division during the Meuse-Argonne Offensive.

Division Headquarters were established at Aignay le Duc Nov. 30, 1918. On April 12, 1919, movement of the division to Germany was begun. Division Headquarters were established at Bad Bertrich on April 30th. On May 6th the movement of the division was stopped; about 60 per cent of the personnel having arrived in Germany. On May 20th, movement of troops to Brest was begun. Division Headquarters embarked June 3, 1919, and arrived at New York June 10th.

The Division commanders were: Brigadier General James B. Erwin, and Major General Walter H. Gordon.

Days in the Front Line: 6 (training) 37 (sector) 0 (battle) for a total of 43. During operations the division took 12 prisoners and its casualties totaled 68 soldiers killed in action or died of wounds, 318 wounded in action.[44]

Soldiers crowd around the Special Mascot of the 6th Division with his mount at the 8th Corps Horse and Motor Show, France, 1919. Courtesy National Archives.

An embroidered "6" is superimposed over the 6th Divisions' star on this finely embroidered example from the Occupation period.

Reference Bibliography:

General Division Histories:

A Short History of the Sixth Division. n.p., 1919.

"The Story of the Sixth, From December 1917 to April 1919." Typescript, 1919.

51st Infantry Regiment

U.S. Army, 51st Infantry Regiment. Co. L. *Roster of Company "L", 51st Infantry, 6th Division, American Expeditionary Forces*. n.p., ca 1914-18.

52nd Infantry Regiment

Farrell, Frank F. *52nd Pioneer Infantry, France, 1918-1919*. n.p., 1919.

U.S. Army. 52nd Infantry Regiment. *Greetings from the 52nd U.S. Infantry: Chickamauga Park, Georgia*. n.p., 1917.

53rd Infantry Regiment

The Gold Chevron: A History of the Fifty-Third US Infantry. n.p., 1919.

54th Infantry Regiment

Mabry, Gregory. *Recollections of a Recruit: An Official History of the Fifty-Fourth US Infantry*. New York: Schilling, 1919.

318th Engineer Regiment

Osborn, Charles M. *The Life of Co. D, 318 Engineers: June the Eighteenth, Nineteen Hundred and Nineteen*. n.p.,1919.

7th Infantry Division

The War Department organized the 7th Division at Camp Forrest, Georgia in March, 1918. It was composed of regular army troops stationed at Camps Travis and Wheeler, and Columbus Barracks.[45]

Insignia:

The division selected as its' insignia a red disc with a black "hourglass" of two pyramids point to point. The outline of the hourglass alludes to the numerical designation of the division showing two "7's", one inverted, one upright. The insignia originated as a divisional baggage mark-

7th Division commander, Brigadier General C.H. Barth and his staff, Ancy le Franc, France, September, 1918. Courtesy National Archives.

Left: Twins, Corporals Engward Nielsen and Louis Nielsen of the 7th Division pose in France, 1918 Above: In September, 1982, the Nielson brothers pose together again, Louis on the left and Engward on the right, at age ninety. Courtesy Military History Institute. Below: The Supply Company of the 34th Infantry Regiment prepare to leave Martincourt, France, en route to the front lines, October, 1918. Courtesy National Archives.

ing used before going overseas of two "7's" one upright and one upside down and backward painted upon a red disc.[46] The insignia was approved October 23, 1918.[47]

The standard 7th Division insignia employs felt on felt construction.

Campaigns:
Puvenelle Sector.[48]

Division Organization (1918-1919):[49]

13th Infantry Brigade:

55th Infantry Regiment
56th Infantry Regiment
20th Machine Gun Battalion

14th Infantry Brigade:

34th Infantry Regiment
64th Infantry Regiment
21st Machine Gun Battalion

Division Troops:

19th Machine Gun Battalion

A fully embroidered variation of the 7th Division insignia.

7th Field Artillery Brigade:

8th Field Artillery Regiment
79th Field Artillery Regiment
80th Field Artillery Regiment
7th Trench Mortar Battery

Division Support:

5th Engineer Regiment
10th Field Signal Battalion
7th Train Headquarters and Military Police
7th Ammunition Train
7th Supply Train
5th Engineer Train
7th Sanitary Train (Ambulance Companies & Field Hospitals 22nd, 34th, 35th, 36th)

Another fully embroidered example features finer embroidery work.

Division Combat Narrative:[50]
The first unit of the division to go overseas arrived in France August 6, 1918; the last arrived September 3, 1918.

For training purposes the division (less artillery) was sent to the 15th Training Area, with Headquarters at Ancy-le-Franc (Yonne). For a similar purpose the artillery brigade was sent to Camp Moucon (Morbihan). It never joined the division during operations.

The division, less artillery, departed on September 27 for the front detraining in the vicinity of Toul. It became reserve of the IV Corps, 1st Army. Headquarters was established successively at Gondreville, Villers-en-Haye and Euvezin. On October 10 it relieved the 90th Division in front line in the Puvenelle Sector from the Moselle River west to Jaulny, inclusive. The division passed to command of the 2nd Army upon its formation on October 13. From November 9 to November 11 it participated in the general attack made by the 2nd Army in the Meuse-Argonne Offensive. The division remained in the Puvenelle Sector until January 10, 1919, when it moved to the region north of Toul, with headquarters at Saizerais (Meurthe et Moselle), one regiment (34th Infantry) remaining in the devastated area for guard and police duty.

In April the division moved to the Colombey-les-Balles area, and then to the Le Mans Embarkation Center preparatory to returning to the United States.

Headquarters embarked June 12, 1919, and arrived in New York June 20, 1919.

The division commanders were: Brigadier General G.H. Barth, Brigadier General Lutz Wahl, Major General Edmund Wittenmeyer, Brigadier General G.H. Preston, and Major General E.F. McGlachlin, Jr.

Days in the Front Line: 0 (training) 33 (sector) 0 (battle) for a total of 33. During operations the division took 69 prisoners and its casualties totaled 287 soldiers killed in action or died of wounds, 1,422 wounded in action.[51]

Reference Bibliography:

General Division Histories:

American Battle Monuments Commission. *7th Division, Summary of Operations in the World War.* Washington, DC: Government Printing Office, 1944.

Fell, Edgar T., comp. *History of the Seventh Division, United States Army, 1917-1919.* Philadelphia, Pennsylvania: Moore, 1927.

5th Engineer Regiment

U.S. Army, Corps of Engineers. 5th Regiment. *Company C, Fifth Regiment Engineers, American Expeditionary Forces.* n.p., 1919.

A War History of Company "D" 5th Regiment of Engineers. Camp Humphreys, Virginia: n.p., 1919.

8th Infantry Division

The War Department organized the 8th Division at Camp Fremont, California on January 5, 1918. It was composed of regular army troops from the 8th, 12th, 13th and 62nd Infantry Regiments.[52]

Opposite
Top: General Pershing presents the Distinguished Service Cross to Private Alexander Truthko, Company A, 8th Infantry Regiment, Weisenthurm, Germany, September, 1921 as part of the Army of Occupation. Courtesy National Archives.

Bottom: A heavily armed group of gunslingers from Battery B, 81st Field Artillery Regiment, clown for the camera at Camp Doniphan, Fort Sill, Oklahoma, 1918. Courtesy Military History Institute.

Insignia:
The division selected as its' insignia a blue shield with a yellow arrow point up surmounted by an Arabic figure "8." The nickname of the division, "Pathfinder" is represented by the gold arrow with the figure "8" representing the numerical designation of the division.[53] The insignia was approved April 9, 1919.[54]

Campaigns:
None.

Division Organization (1918-1919):[55]

15th Infantry Brigade:

12th Infantry Regiment
62nd Infantry Regiment
23rd Machine Gun Battalion

16th Infantry Brigade:

8th Infantry Regiment
13th Infantry Regiment
24th Machine Gun Battalion

Division Troops:

22nd Machine Gun Battalion

5077

8th Field Artillery Brigade:

2nd Field Artillery Regiment
81st Field Artillery Regiment
83rd Field Artillery Regiment
8th Trench Mortar Battery

Division Support:

319th Engineer Regiment
320th Field Signal Battalion
8th Train Headquarters and Military Police
8th Ammunition Train
8th Supply Train
319th Engineer Train
8th Sanitary Train (Ambulance Companies & Field Hospitals 11th, 31st, 32nd, 43rd)

Division Service Narrative:[56]
The embarkation of the division began about October 30, 1918, at Hoboken, New Jersey, the first unit (319th Engineers and Train) arriving in France October 12, 1918, and the last (8th Field Artillery Brigade) November 9, 1918. The following were the only units of the division to go overseas: Division Headquarters; Headquarters Troop; 16th Infantry Brigade Headquarters, 8th Infantry; 8th Field Artillery Brigade Headquarters, the 2nd, 81st and 83rd Artillery, the 8th Trench Mortar Battery; 319th Engineer and Train.

The 15th Infantry Brigade Headquarters and 320th Field Signal Battalion embarked at Hoboken and after waiting on board for several days did not sail but debarked owing to the signing of the armistice.

The Pons area (Charente Inferieure) had been designated as the training area for the division. Soon after arrival in France the following units went to the Pons area: Division Headquarters and Headquarters Troop (both returning later to Pontanézen Barracks, Brest, for duty) 16th Infantry Brigade Headquarters (returning to Brest in February, 1919, for return to the United States) 8th Infantry (returning to Pontanézen Barracks, Brest, for duty.) The regiment left Brest July 11, 1919 for Coblenz, Germany, arriving there July 14th, since which time it has been on duty with the American Force in Germany). The 319th Engineers and Train arrived at Le Havre, October 12, 1918, leaving there for Pontanézen Barracks, Brest October 16, 1918, where it remained on duty until August 15, 1919 when the entire regiment and train sailed for the United States. The 8th Field Artillery Brigade Headquarters, 2nd, 81st and 83rd Field Artillery shortly after arrival at Brest proceeded to Plöërmel (Morbihan) where they remained until December 9th, on which date they proceeded to Brest from which port they sailed for the United States on January 4, 1919. The 8th Trench Mortar Battery a few days after arrival at Brest entrained for the Trench Artillery Training Center near Vitrey

Opposite
Top: An unidentified member of the 319th Engineer Regiment behind the wheel of a one ton locomotive. France, 1918. Courtesy Military History Institute.

Bottom: Officers of the 12th Infantry Regiment, Camp Hill, Newport News, Virginia, 1918. Courtesy National Archives.

A fully embroidered 8th Division insignia on a shield background. This variety is considered an early version of the division insignia.

This embroidered on felt insignia uses hand stitching to highlight the shield border.

Far left: An alternative insignia pattern for the 8th Division featured an embroidered Indian Head upon a yellow disc. This insignia was never officially adopted as it might be confused with the insignia of the 2nd Division.

Left: A felt on felt example of the alternative insignia using stitching to highlight the Indian's features.

(Haute Saône) where it arrived November 17, 1918, soon after returning to Brest from which place it sailed for the United States December 25, 1918. The Advance School Detachment upon arrival in Brest was absorbed for duty there by Headquarters Base Section No. 5 as was also the Billeting Detachment. None of the units of this division were in action.

The division commanders were: Colonel Elmer F. Taggart, Colonel George W. Van Dusen, Brigadier General Joseph D. Leitch, Major General John F. Morrison, Major General William S. Graves, and Major General Eli A. Holmick.

Reference Bibliography:

General Division Histories:
None.

Non-Commissioned officers of Headquarters Company, 46th Infantry Regiment at Camp Sheridan, Alabama. From left; Sergeant Weeks, First Sergeant Boyette, and Sergeant Hayes. Courtesy Military History Institute.

9th Infantry Division

The War Department organized the 9th Division at Camp Sheridan, Alabama on July 18, 1918. The cadre of the division came from regular units, however, all of the organizations were made up from draftees.[57]

Insignia:
The division selected as its insignia a red shield charged with a yellow numeral "9" on a blue disc. Another insignia variation was a blue square on end bordered yellow with a red "9" in the center pierced horizontally by a bayonet with a yellow star at top and bottom apex.[58]

An example of the 9th Division insignia embroidered on fine felt.

Campaigns:
None.

Division Organization (1918-1919):[59]

17th Infantry Brigade:

45th Infantry Regiment
67th Infantry Regiment
26th Machine Gun Battalion

18th Infantry Brigade:

46th Infantry Regiment
68th Infantry Regiment
27th Machine Gun Battalion

Division Troops:

25th Machine Gun Battalion

9th Field Artillery Brigade:

25th Field Artillery Regiment
26th Field Artillery Regiment
27th Field Artillery Regiment
9th Trench Mortar Battery

Division Support:

209th Engineer Regiment
209th Field Signal Battalion

Train Headquarters and Military Police
Ammunition Train
Supply Train
Engineer Train
Sanitary Train

Division Service Narrative:[60]
The division was in training until November, 1918, when it prepared for departure overseas. The signing of the armistice November 11 stopped all further troop movement, and the division began demobilization, which was completed in February, except for such units as belonged to the Regular Army.

The division had one commanding general: Major General Willard A. Holbrook.

Reference Bibliography:

General Division Histories:
None.

46th Infantry Regiment
Hill, Alfred G., & McGinness, J.K., eds. *The 46th Infantry, USA: A Record Since Its Organization, June 4, 1917.* Camp Sheridan, Alabama, 1919.

10th Infantry Division

The War Department organized the 10th Division at Camp Funston, Kansas in August, 1918. The cadre of the division came from regular units; however, all of the organizations were made up from draftees.[61]

Insignia:
The division selected as its insignia a gold Roman numeral "X" in a circle of gold on a marine blue square.

Campaigns:
None.

Division Organization (1918-1919):[62]

19th Infantry Brigade:

41st Infantry Regiment
69th Infantry Regiment
29th Machine Gun Battalion

A group of soldiers from Company A, 29th Machine Gun Battalion at Camp Funston, Kansas, 1918. Courtesy Military History Institute.

Barracks at Camp Funston under construction, September, 1917. Courtesy National Archives.

A 10th Division insignia embroidered on felt.

A felt on felt version of the 10th Division insignia.

20th Infantry Brigade:

20th Infantry Regiment
70th Infantry Regiment
30th Machine Gun Battalion

Division Troops:

28th Machine Gun Battalion

10th Field Artillery Brigade:

28th Field Artillery Regiment
29th Field Artillery Regiment
30th Field Artillery Regiment
10th Trench Mortar Battery

Division Support:

210th Engineer Regiment
210th Field Signal Battalion
Train Headquarters and Military Police
Ammunition Train
Supply Train
Engineer Train
Sanitary Train

Division Service Narrative:[63]
The division was in training until November, 1918, when it prepared for departure overseas. The signing of the armistice November 11 stopped all further troop movement, and the division remained at Camp Funston until demobilization which was completed February 18, 1919.

The division had one commanding general: Major General Leonard Wood.

Reference Bibliography:

General Division Histories:
None.

11th Infantry Division

The War Department organized the 11th Division at Camp Meade, Maryland in August, 1918. The 24th Field Artillery Brigade was organized and trained at West Point, Kentucky. The 17th and 63rd Infantry Regiments and the cadre of the division came from regular units; however, all of the organizations were made up from draftees.[64]

Insignia:
The division selected as its insignia a bust of Lafayette in blue superimposed on a red disc. It was selected to honor French aid to the American Colonies during the Revolutionary War. This insignia was never officially approved.[65]

Campaigns:
None.

Division Organization (1918-1919):[66]

Major General Jesse McI. Carter, and his staff at the review parade for the advance elements of the 11th Division as they prepare to ship overseas. Camp Meade, Maryland, October, 1918. Courtesy National Archives.

Headquarters building of the 11th Division. Camp Meade, Maryland, October, 1918. Courtesy National Archives.

Baking bread, Camp Meade, Maryland, 1918. Courtesy National Archives.

Fully embroidered example of an 11th Division insignia. The head of Lafayette is wonderfully executed.

A much more stylistic version of Lafayette's head appears in this 11th Division insignia.

21st Infantry Brigade:

17th Infantry Regiment
71st Infantry Regiment
32nd Machine Gun Battalion

22nd Infantry Brigade:

63rd Infantry Regiment
72nd Infantry Regiment
33rd Machine Gun Battalion

Division Troops:

31st Machine Gun Battalion

24th Field Artillery Brigade:

70th Field Artillery Regiment
71st Field Artillery Regiment
72nd Field Artillery Regiment
24th Trench Mortar Battery

Division Support:

211th Engineer Regiment
211th Field Signal Battalion
Train Headquarters and Military Police
Ammunition Train
Supply Train
Engineer Train
Sanitary Train

Division Service Narrative:[67]
The division was in training until November, 1918, when it prepared for departure overseas. The signing of the armistice November 11 stopped all further troop movement, and the division began demobilization which was completed in February, 1919, except for such units as belonged to the Regular Army.

The division had one commanding general: Major General Jesse McI. Carter.

Reference Bibliography:

General Divisional Histories:
None.

63rd Infantry Regiment
U.S. Army, 63rd Infantry Regiment. *A History of the Sixty-Third US Infantry, 1917-1919*. New York: By the Regiment, 1920.

12th Infantry Division

The War Department organized the 12th Division at Camp Devens, Massachusetts in July, 1918. The 12th Field Artillery Brigade was organized and trained at Camp McClellan, Alabama. The 36th and 42nd Infantry Regiments and the cadre of the division came from regular units; however, all of the organizations were made up from draftees.[68]

Above: Training on the Browning Automatic Rifle, Camp Devens, Massachusetts, 1918. Courtesy National Archives.

Right: Recruits drilling at Camp Devens, Massachusetts, 1918. Courtesy National Archives.

Insignia:

The division selected as its insignia a blue diamond upon which is superimposed the figure "12" pierced by a bayonet. It took the name "Plymouth Division" because it recruited from the New England States.[69]

A beautifully executed felt on felt 12th Division insignia.

Campaigns:

None.

Division Organization (1918-1919):[70]

23rd Infantry Brigade:

36th Infantry Regiment
73rd Infantry Regiment
35th Machine Gun Battalion

24th Infantry Brigade:

42nd Infantry Regiment
74th Infantry Regiment
36th Machine Gun Battalion

An embroidered example of the 12th Division insignia. This is the standard version of the shoulder sleeve insignia.

Division Troops:

34th Machine Gun Battalion

12th Field Artillery Brigade:

34th Field Artillery Regiment
35th Field Artillery Regiment
36th Field Artillery Regiment
12th Trench Mortar Battery

Division Support:

212th Engineer Regiment
212th Field Signal Battalion

Train Headquarters and Military Police
Ammunition Train
Supply Train
Engineer Train
Sanitary Train

Division Service Narrative:[71]
The division was in training until November, 1918, when it prepared for departure overseas. The signing of the armistice November 11 stopped all further troop movement, and the division began demobilization which was completed in January 31, 1919, except for such units as belonged to the Regular Army.

The division had one commander: Major General H. P. McCain.

Reference Bibliography:

General Divisional Histories:
U.S. Army, 12th Infantry Division. *Roster, Plymouth (12th) Division*. Camp Devens, Massachusetts, 1918.

74th Infantry Regiment
C'est La Guerre: A Musical Drama in Three Acts and Seven Scenes. Camp Devens, Massachusetts: n.p.,1919.

212th Engineer Regiment
Company C, 212th Engineers, Plymouth Division. Camp Devens, Massachuesetts: By the Company, 1918.
Slosser, Gaius J. *History of the 212th Engineers, 1918-1919*. n.p., 1919.

13th Infantry Division

The War Department organized the 13th Division at Camp Lewis, Washington in July, 1918. The 1st and 44th Infantry Regiments and the cadre of the division came from regular units; however, all of the organizations were made up from draftees.[72]

Insignia:
The division selected as its' insignia two proverbial "Bad Luck" symbols; the number "13" and a Black Cat surrounded by the "Good Luck" symbol of the Horse Shoe in red on a blue circle. This symbol was indicative of the Doughboy's confidence in his ability to overcome all "Hoo Doo's."[73]

"Preparing for War" soldiers of Company D, 76th Infantry Regiment in training at Camp Lewis, Washington, November, 1918 Courtesy Military History Institute.

Entrance Gate, Camp Lewis, Washington, 1918. Courtesy Military History Institute.

Unidentified 13th Division soldier relaxes on his truck's fender during a lull in training, Camp Lewis, Washington, 1918. Courtesy Military History Institute.

Campaigns:
None.

Division Organization (1918-1919):[74]

25th Infantry Brigade:

1st Infantry Regiment
75th Infantry Regiment
38th Machine Gun Battalion

26th Infantry Brigade:

44th Infantry Regiment
76th Infantry Regiment
39th Machine Gun Battalion

Division Troops:

37th Machine Gun Battalion

13th Field Artillery Brigade:

37th Field Artillery Regiment
38th Field Artillery Regiment
39th Field Artillery Regiment
13th Trench Mortar Battery

Division Support:

213th Engineer Regiment
213th Field Signal Battalion
Train Headquarters and Military Police
Ammunition Train
Supply Train
Engineer Train
Sanitary Train

Embroidered version of the 13th Division insignia; stitching is used to highlight the black cat and horseshoe.

The more common felt on felt 13th Division insignia.

A chain stitched variant of the 13th Division insignia on a fully embroidered background.

Division Service Narrative:[75]
The division was in training until November, 1918, at which time it was ready for overseas service. The signing of the armistice November 11 stopped all further troop movement, and the division began demobilization, which was completed in March, 1919, except for such units as belonged to the Regular Army.

The division had three commanders: Brigadier General Cornelius Vanderbilt, Brigadier General Frank B. Watson, and Major General Joseph D. Leitch.

Reference Bibliography:

General Divisional Histories:
Official History of the Thirteenth Division, 1918-1919. Tacoma, Washington: Hulbert, 1919.

213th Engineer Regiment
U.S. Army, 213th Engineer Regiment. *213th Engineers, Camp Lewis, Washington.* Seattle, Washington: Gateway, 1918.

14th Infantry Division

The War Department organized the 14th Division at Camp Custer, Michigan in July, 1918. The 10th and 40th Infantry Regiments and the cadre of the division came from regular units; however, all of the organizations were made up from draftees.[76]

Insignia:
The division selected as its insignia the head of a wolverine and the word "Wolverine" upon a yellow disc on a green shield; wolverines having been very common in Michigan in the early days.[77]

Two soldiers identified only as the tallest and shortest recruits at Camp Custer, Michigan, 1917. Courtesy Military History Institute.

Campaigns:
None.

Division Organization (1918-1919):[78]

27th Infantry Brigade:

10th Infantry Regiment
77th Infantry Regiment
41st Machine Gun Battalion

28th Infantry Brigade:

40th Infantry Regiment
78th Infantry Regiment
42nd Machine Gun Battalion

Division Troops:

40th Machine Gun Battalion

14th Field Artillery Brigade:

40th Field Artillery Regiment
41st Field Artillery Regiment
42nd Field Artillery Regiment
14th Trench Mortar Battery

Division Support:

214th Engineer Regiment
214th Field Signal Battalion
Train Headquarters and Military Police
Ammunition Train
Supply Train
Engineer Train
Sanitary Train

Division Service Narrative:[79]
The division was in training until January, 1919, when demobilization commenced. This was completed in February, except for such units as belonged to the Regular Army.

The division had two commanders: Brigadier General H.L. Laubach, and Major General Grote Hutcheson.

An embroidered on felt 14th Division insignia with intricate attention to the Wolverine; this is the more frequently encountered insignia for the division.

Reference Bibliography:

General Divisional Histories:
None.

40th Infantry Regiment
Dreyer, Richard H. *40th U.S. Infantry, Fort Snelling, Minn, 1917*. Iowa City, Iowa: Dreyer, 1917.

Below: Some of the officers and men of the 14th Sanitary Train stand in front of a Field Hospital and Dressing Station erected at Camp Custer, Michigan, 1918. Courtesy Military History Institute.

Right: Another embroidered 14th Division insignia; this one features a much stylized Wolverine.

15th Cavalry Division

The War Department organized the 15th Cavalry Division at Fort Bliss, Texas on December 10, 1917. The 1st, 2nd and 3rd Cavalry Brigades at Forts Sam Houston, Bliss and Douglas formed the cadre of the division.[80]

Insignia:
None.

Campaigns:
None.

Division Organization (1917-1918):

1st Cavalry Brigade

2nd Cavalry Brigade

3rd Cavalry Brigade

Division Service Narrative:
None

Reference Bibliography:
None.

15th Infantry Division

The War Department organized the 15th Division at Camp Logan, Texas on August 28, 1918. The Division Artillery was organized at Camp Stanley, Texas from National Army Cavalry. The Engineer Regiment and Train were organized at Camp Humphries, Virginia and joined the division at Camp Logan in November. The 43rd and 52nd Infantry Regiments and the cadre of the division came from regular units; however, all of the organizations were made up from draftees.[81]

Insignia:
A coiled Rattlesnake on a khaki background symbolizing the striking power of this deadly snake; a common resident of their mobilization camp.[82]

Campaigns:
None.

Division Organization (1918-1919):[83]

29th Infantry Brigade:

43rd Infantry Regiment
79th Infantry Regiment
44th Machine Gun Battalion

30th Infantry Brigade:

57th Infantry Regiment
80th Infantry Regiment
45th Machine Gun Battalion

Division Troops:

43rd Machine Gun Battalion
15th Headquarters Troop

15th Artillery Brigade:

43rd Field Artillery Regiment
44th Field Artillery Regiment
45th Field Artillery Regiment
15th Trench Mortar Battery

Division Support:

215th Engineer Regiment
215th Field Signal Battalion
15th Train Headquarters and Military Police
15th Ammunition Train
15th Supply Train
215th Engineer Train
15th Sanitary Train (Ambulance Companies & Field Hospitals 257th, 258th, 259th, 260th)

Division Service Narrative:[84]
In compliance with a letter from The Adjutant General of the Army dated July 31, 1918, the 15th Division was organized at Camp Logan, Texas, on August 28, 1918.

The 43rd and 57th Regular Army Infantry Regiments which were stationed at Camp Logan furnished the nucleus for the other infantry units of the Division.

The Divisional Artillery was organized at Camp Stanley, Texas, from National Army Cavalry and remained at that Camp for instruction.

The Engineer Regiment and Train was organized at Camp Humphries, Virginia, and joined the Division at Camp Logan in the early part of November. By the 1st of November the organization of the Division was about completed and all units were undergoing intensive training.

On December 4th the breaking up of the Division began, when one battalion of the 43rd Infantry was sent to Camp Bowie, Texas, and one battalion to Camp McArthur, Texas. On December 18th the 57th Infantry entrained for Camp Pike, Arkansas. By the middle of February, 1919, all organizations of the 15th Division not belonging to the Regular Army had been demobilized.

The Commanders of this Division were: Colonel D.J. Baker, and Brigadier General Guy V. Henry.

Reference Bibliography:

General Divisional Histories:
History of the Fifteenth Division, United States Army, World War 1918-1919. New York 1921.

57th Infantry Regiment
U.S.Army, 57th Infantry Regiment. *A History and Photographic Record of the 57th US Infantry*. San Antonio, Texas: San Antonio Printing, 1918.

79th Infantry Regiment
Fitzpatrick, Vincent DeP. *"Over Here": Affectionately Dedicated to the Officers and Men Preparing for "Over There", Camp Meade, Maryland*. Baltimore: Horn-Shafer, 1919.
Pekor, Richard B., & Davis, Harry P., eds. *A History and Photographic Record of the 79th US Infantry*. n.p., 1918.

80th Infantry Regiment

U.S. Army, 80th Infantry Regiment. *A History and Photographic Record of the 80th US Infantry*. n.p.,1918.

16th Infantry Division

The War Department organized the 16th Division at Camp Kearny, California in August, 1918. The 216th Engineer Regiment was organized at Camp Humphries, Virginia and joined the division in October. The 21st and 32nd Infantry Regiments and the cadre of the division came from regular units; however, all of the organizations were made up from draftees.[85]

Insignia:

This division selected a patch which was never approved of a Liberty Bell with the number "16" embroidered upon it.

Campaigns:

None.

Division Organization (1918-1919):[86]

31st Infantry Brigade:

21st Infantry Regiment
81st Infantry Regiment
47th Machine Gun Battalion

32nd Infantry Brigade:

32nd Infantry Regiment
82nd Infantry Regiment
48th Machine Gun Battalion

Division Troops:

46th Machine Gun Battalion

16th Field Artillery Brigade:

46th Field Artillery Regiment

Russian master violinist Mischa Elman entertains some soldiers at Camp Kearney, California, 1918. Courtesy National Archives.

Above left: Mess time in the field. A soldier enjoys a jelly sandwich at Camp Kearney, California, 1918. Courtesy National Archives.

Above right: Felt on felt 16th Division insignia using stitching to highlight the division numerical and Liberty Bell.

A view of training trenches at Camp Kearney, California, February, 1918. Courtesy National Archives.

47th Field Artillery Regiment
48th Field Artillery Regiment
16th Trench Mortar Battery

Division Support:

216th Engineer Regiment
216th Field Signal Battalion
16th Train Headquarters and Military Police
16th Ammunition Train
16th Supply Train
216th Engineer Train
16th Sanitary Train (Ambulance Companies & Field Hospitals 261st, 262nd, 263rd, and 264th)

Division Service Narrative:[87]
The division was in training until February, when demobilization commenced. This was completed in March, except for such units as belonged to the Regular Army.

The division commanders were: Major General David C. Shanks, Brigadier General Peter W. Davison, and Major General Guy Carleton.

Reference Bibliography:

General Divisional Histories:
History, Sixteenth Division, Camp Kearny, California: From July 31, 1918, (Date of Organization) To December 31, 1918. n.p., 1918.

21st Infantry Regiment
U.S. Army, 21st Infantry Regiment. *Roster and Historical Sketch of the Twenty-First Regiment of United States Infantry, January 1, 1915.* Vancouver Barracks, Washington: Weaver, 1915.

17th Infantry Division

The War Department organized the 17th Division at Camp Beauregard, Louisiana in August, 1918. The 17th Field Artillery Brigade was organized at Camp Bowie, Texas, and proceeded to Camp Doniphan, Fort Sill, Oklahoma on November 1st where it remained until demobilized. The 217th Engineer Regiment was organized at Camp Humphries, Virginia and joined the

Above: Private George C. Dobbs, 50th Machine Gun Battalion poses in front of newly constructed tent bases, Camp Beauregard, Louisiana, 1918. Courtesy Military History Institute.

Top right: A view of the YMCA hut at Camp Beauregard, Louisiana, 1918. Courtesy Military History Institute.

division in November. The 5th and 29th Infantry Regiments and the cadre of the division came from regular units; however, all of the organizations were made up from draftees.[88]

Insignia:
None.

Campaigns:
None.

Division Organization (1918-1919):[89]

33rd Infantry Brigade:

5th Infantry Regiment
83rd Infantry Regiment
50th Machine Gun Battalion

34th Infantry Brigade:

29th Infantry Regiment
84th Infantry Regiment
51st Machine Gun Battalion

Division Troops:

49th Machine Gun Battalion

17th Field Artillery Brigade:

49th Field Artillery Regiment
50th Field Artillery Regiment
51st Field Artillery Regiment
17th Trench Mortar Battery

Division Support:

217th Engineer Regiment
217th Field Signal Battalion
17th Train Headquarters and Military Police
17th Ammunition Train
17th Supply Train
217th Engineer Train
17th Sanitary Train (Ambulance Companies & Field Hospitals 265th, 266th, 267th, and 268th)

Division Service Narrative:[90]
The division was in training until January when demobilization commenced. This was completed in February, except for such units as belonged to the Regular Army.

The division had two commanding generals: Brigadier General Robert W. Mearns, and Major General Henry C. Hodges.

Reference Bibliography:

General Divisional Histories:
None.

18th Infantry Division

The War Department organized the 18th Division at Camp Travis, Texas in August, 1918. The 18th Field Artillery Brigade was organized at Camp Stanley, Texas, and joined the division in the end of August. The 218th Engineer Regiment was organized at Camp Humphries, Virginia and joined the division in November. The 19th and 35th Infantry Regiments and the cadre of the division came from regular units; however, all of the organizations were made up from draftees.[91]

Insignia:
The division selected as its insignia a number "18" superimposed on a green cactus plant under which is written "Noli me Tangere" which is the Latin motto for "Touch me Not."[92] The use of the cactus alludes to the desert conditions at Camp Travis.

The most common of 18th Division insignia features the cactus and the division motto, "Touch me not." embroidered in Latin on felt.

Campaigns:
None.

Division Organization (1918-1919):[93]

35th Infantry Brigade:

19th Infantry Regiment
85th Infantry Regiment
53rd Machine Gun Battalion

A felt on felt version of the device with a highly stylized cactus under a crescent moon.

The combined units of the 18th Division form themselves into a facsimile of their division patch at Camp Travis, Texas, 1918. Courtesy National Archives.

Some soldiers from the "Soldier Players" company outside their barracks at Camp Travis, Texas, 1918. These soldiers produced and performed plays for the entertainment of the soldiers undergoing training at the camp as well as the local community. Courtesy National Archives.

36th Infantry Brigade:

35th Infantry Regiment
86th Infantry Regiment
54th Machine Gun Battalion

Division Troops:

52nd Machine Gun Battalion

18th Field Artillery Brigade:

52nd Field Artillery Regiment
53rd Field Artillery Regiment
54th Field Artillery Regiment
18th Trench Mortar Battery

Division Support:

218th Engineer Regiment
218th Field Signal Battalion
18th Train Headquarters and Military Police
18th Ammunition Train
18th Supply Train
218th Engineer Train
18th Sanitary Train (Ambulance Companies & Field Hospitals 269th, 270th, 271st, and 272nd)

Division Service Narrative:[94]
The division was in training until January, 1919, when demobilization began. This was completed by the middle of February, except for such units as belonged to the Regular Army.

The division had one commanding general: Brig. Gen. George H. Estes.

Reference Bibliography:

General Divisional Histories:
Camp Travis and Its Part in the World War. New York: E.B. Jones, 1919.

19th Infantry Regiment
A History and Photographic Record of the 19th Infantry, USA. San Antonio, Texas: San Antonio Printing, 1919.

85th Infantry Regiment
A History and Photographic Record of the 85th US Infantry, COL Joseph O. Cecil, Commanding, 1918. San Antonio, Texas: Hymans, 1918.

19th Infantry Division

The War Department organized the 19th Division at Camp Dodge, Iowa in September, 1918. The 19th Field Artillery Brigade was organized at Camp Bowie, Texas, proceeded to Camp Doniphan, Fort Sill, Oklahoma and stayed there until demobilized. The 219th Engineer Regiment was organized at Camp Humphries, Virginia and joined the division in November. The 2nd and 14th Infantry Regiments and the cadre of the division came from regular units; however, all of the organizations were made up from draftees.[95]

Above: Company E of the 87th Infantry Regiment, in formation at Camp Dodge, Iowa, 1918. Courtesy Military History Institute.

Below: Privates Alfred, and Ralph J. Funk of Iowa. Ralph was a member of Company E, 87th Infantry Regiment. Courtesy Military History Institute.

Insignia:
A white "G" on a black triangle with white tips placed upon a red disc. Divisional records required a "1" and "9" to flank the letter "G" however, this appears not to have been followed. A second insignia is attributed to the division consisting of a white crescent alongside a white five pointed star, upon a disc of olive drab.[96] Variants of the division insignia are composed of a blue or khaki disc with a yellow or white crescent and white star on a khaki background. This was intended to represent the division's nickname, the "Twilight Division." The "G", stands for "gloaming", another word for twilight.

Campaigns:
None.

Division Organization (1918-1919):[97]

37th Infantry Brigade:

14th Infantry Regiment
87th Infantry Regiment
56th Machine Gun Battalion

38th Infantry Brigade:

2nd Infantry Regiment
88th Infantry Regiment
57th Machine Gun Battalion

Division Troops:

55th Machine Gun Battalion

19th Field Artillery Brigade:

55th Field Artillery Regiment
56th Field Artillery Regiment
57th Field Artillery Regiment
19th Trench Mortar Battery

Division Support:

219th Engineer Regiment
219th Field Signal Battalion

Above
Left: Embroidered 19th Division insignia with a central "G" representing gloaming; the Old English word for twilight, the division's sobriquet.

Center: Another style of the division insignia using a star and crescent moon representative of twilight.

Right: A variation of the crescent moon insignia done in white felt on olive drab wool.

19th Train Headquarters and Military Police
19th Ammunition Train
19th Supply Train
219th Engineer Train
19th Sanitary Train (Ambulance Companies & Field Hospitals 273rd, 274th, 275th, and 276th)

Division Service Narrative:[98]
The division was in training until January, 1919, when demobilization began. This was completed by January 29th, except for such units as belonged to the Regular Army.

The division had one commanding general: Brigadier General Benjamin T. Simmons.

Reference Bibliography:

General Divisional Histories:
None.

14th Infantry Regiment
U.S. Army, 14th Infantry Regiment. *Souvenir History, 14th Infantry*. Lawton, WA: 1918.

20th Infantry Division

20th Division insignia with an embroidered skull and cross bones below the division's numeric designation.

The War Department organized the 20th Division at Camp Sevier, South Carolina in August, 1918. The 20th Field Artillery Brigade was organized at Camp Jackson, South Carolina. The 220th Engineer Regiment was organized at Camp Humphries, Virginia and joined the division in November. The 48th and 50th Infantry Regiments and the cadre of the division came from regular units; however, all of the organizations were made up from draftees.[99]

Insignia:
The division selected as its insignia a white skull and crossbones placed on a black shield. "20" in white above the skull and crossbones and "Div" also in white placed below. The insignia may represent the historical connection between South Carolina and the exploits of Edward Teach, known as Blackbeard, the pirate who operated on the waters of South Carolina during his final days or it may have a connection to the danger involved in moonshining, as this division chose the unofficial nickname of the "Moonshine Division."[100]

Campaigns:
None.

Division Organization (1918-1919):[101]

39th Infantry Brigade:

Soldiers of the Machine Gun Company, 48th Infantry Regiment train on the machine gun range at Camp Sevier, South Carolina, 1918. Courtesy Military History Institute.

A company of the 48th Infantry Regiment during a rest on a road march at Camp Sevier, South Carolina, 1918. Courtesy Military History Institute.

Private Matthew A. Rusnak, 50th Infantry Regiment (center) poses for the photographer with two unidentified friends. Courtesy Military History Institute.

48th Infantry Regiment
89th Infantry Regiment
59th Machine Gun Battalion

40th Infantry Brigade:

50th Infantry Regiment
90th Infantry Regiment
60th Machine Gun Battalion

Division Troops:

58th Machine Gun Battalion

20th Field Artillery Brigade:

58th Field Artillery Regiment
59th Field Artillery Regiment
60th Field Artillery Regiment
20th Trench Mortar Battery

Division Support:

220th Engineer Regiment
220th Field Signal Battalion
20th Train Headquarters and Military Police
20th Ammunition Train
20th Supply Train
220th Engineer Train
20th Sanitary Train (Ambulance Companies & Field Hospitals 277th, 278th, 279th, and 280th)

Division Service Narrative:[102]
The division was in training until January, 1919, when demobilization began. This was completed the middle on February 28, except for such units as belonged to the Regular Army.

The division had two commanding generals: Brigadier General E. Leroy Sweetser, and Major General Harry E. Hodges.

Reference Bibliography:

General Divisional Histories:
None.

THE NATIONAL GUARD DIVISIONS

26th Infantry Division

"Stubby" the Yankee Division Mascot. Stubby was a Boston Bullterrier who went overseas with the division. He was a veteran of six fronts and was wounded in action at Seicheprey on April 20, 1918. Courtesy Military History Institute.

The division was composed of National Guard troops from Connecticut, Maine, Massachusetts, New Hampshire, Rhode Island, and Vermont. This division was the former 5th National Guard Division and was renumbered to conform to the new configuration of division numbering under direction of the Army Staff.[1] The division formed at Camp Greene, North Carolina, August 5, 1917.

Insignia:
The division selected as its insignia a blue monogram of the letters "Y.D." for Yankee Division on a diamond khaki background. This alludes to the New England origin of the soldiers who were principally drawn from the six New England states. The shoulder sleeve insignia was approved October, 1918, and authorized in November, 1918.[2]

Campaigns:
Champagne-Marne Defensive, Aisne-Marne Offensive, St. Mihiel Offensive, Meuse-Argonne Offensive, Chemin des Dames Sector, Toul (Boucq) Sector, Troyon Sector.[3]

Division Organization (1917-1919):[4]

51st Infantry Brigade:

101st Infantry Regiment
102nd Infantry Regiment
102nd Machine Gun Battalion

52nd Infantry Brigade:

103rd Infantry Regiment
104th Infantry Regiment
103rd Machine Gun Battalion

Division Troops:

101st Machine Gun Battalion

51st Field Artillery Brigade:

Contemporary sketch by Robert Brown of the 102nd Field Artillery Regiment of the graves of Nils Frostholm, George A. Johnson, Carl J. Lindburg and Walter A. Rand killed in action at La Croix Blance Ferme on July 28, 1918. Courtesy Military History Institute.

Corporal Edgar Gabe Smith, Company C, 101st Field Signal Battalion strikes a pose. Note trench watch with shrapnel cover, cotton tunic and "YD" patch. Courtesy Jay Graybeal Collection.

Pursing the Germans in the Marne – view of field headquarters of the 26th Division in the Chateau-Thierry sector. Left to right: 1st Lieutenant Edwin Cooper, Major General Clarence Edwards, the Division Commander, and Colonel Duncan K. Major, the division's Chief of Staff. Courtesy National Archives.

Dr. Morton Price, Massachusetts Representative, talking with men of the 26th Division, August 1918. Courtesy National Archives.

101st Field Artillery Regiment
102nd Field Artillery Regiment
103rd Field Artillery Regiment
101st Trench Mortar Battery

Division Support:

101st Engineer Regiment
101st Field Signal Battalion
101st Train Headquarters and Military Police
101st Ammunition Train
101st Supply Train
101st Engineer Train
101st Sanitary Train (Ambulance Companies & Field Hospitals 101st, 102nd, 103rd, 104th)

The standard 26th Division insignia features a felt on wool "YD" monogram sewn on an Olive drab wool background.

A 26th Division variant embroidered on felt.

Another variant of the 26th Division insignia.

26th Infantry Division Combat Narrative:[5]
The first unit to go overseas arrived at St. Nazaire, France, on September 20, 1917. The last element arrived November 12, 1917.

The division (less, artillery, engineers and signal battalion) remained in the training area with headquarters at Neufchâteau until February 1918. For purposes of training the artillery was sent to Coetquidan. It, as well as all other elements, rejoined the division early in February and remained with during all activities in which the 26th Division participated.

The division proceeded to the vicinity of Soissons on February 6, 1918, where attached to the French 11th Corps, its units went into line in the Chemin des Dames sector on February 10th. It was withdrawn March 21, and moved to the La Reine and Boucq sector northwest of Toul, relieving the American 1st Division and the French 10th Colonial Division in line on April 3. From April 10th to 13th the division successfully repelled an attack by the enemy on the Bois Brulé sub-sector of Aperemont. This was the first engagement in which American troops took part in any number. On April 20th and 21st the division was involved in a defensive operation know as the "Seicheprey Raid". This was an enemy attack in force against the defenses of the town of Seicheprey. Although American casualties were heavy, the enemy was repulsed, and all the ground taken by him was recaptured by counter-attack. Minor operations of an offensive and defensive character kept this sector active during the remainder of the division's stay therein.

On June 28th the division was relieved and proceeded northwest of Château-Thierry, relieving the 2nd Division in the Château-Thierry sector, on July 10th. It was now in the 1st American Army Corps operating under the Sixth French Army. From July 15th to July 18th it was in the Champagne-Marne defense and from July 18th to 25th it participated in the Aisne-Marne offensive. Capturing Torcy, Belleau and Givry on July 18th, and advancing beyond the Château-Thierry-Soissons road to Oulchy, it reached the heights of Beuva-des-la Charmel. The division (less artillery and engineers) was withdrawn July 25th and on August 16th, proceeded to the Châtilion training area. The 101st Engineers remained in line under the 1st Corps until August 3rd, and the artillery brigade until August 4th, supporting the 4th and 42nd Divisions.

On August 26th the division moved north to Bar-le-Duc, and thence to the Rupt and Troyon sector north of St. Mihiel, where on September 8th it entered the line as part of the 5th Corps. It participated in the St. Mihiel offensive September 12th to 16th. Attacking eastward on a front south of Les Eparges, it drove the enemy from St. Remy and Dommartin, broke his last hold on the Côte de Muse, and reached Hattonchatel and Vigneulles, at the extreme southern point of the ridge. Meanwhile the 1st Division on the left flank of the 4th Corps, had been approaching the same place from the south, and by a junction of the two divisions the tip of the salient was finally cut off. On September 13th it turned eastward and occupied the line of heights about Hannonville and Taillot with advanced detachments near Doncourt. On September 26th the division participated in the general feint threatening Metz which was carried out by all front line units east of the Meuse to divert attention from the Meuse-Argonne offensive.

On October 7th the division was relieved in the Troyon Sector and moved to the vicinity of Verdun in Army reserve. It entered the line on the Meuse-Argone offensive north of Verdun on October 19th, relieving the 18th French Infantry Division. Operating successively under the 17th French Army Corps and the 2nd French Colonial Corps, it advanced slowly northeast and then east encountering stubborn resistance. When hostilities were suspended on November 11th, it held a line from Ville-devant-Chaumont south to a point near le Chaume.

Days in the Front Line: 42 (training) 118 (sector) 45 (battle) for a total of 205. During operations the division took 3148 prisoners and its casualties totaled 2281 soldiers killed in action or died of wounds, 11,383 wounded in action.[6]

On November 14, 1918, the division proceeded to the 8th Training Area, with headquarters at Montigny-le-Roi. In January it moved to the Le Mans Embarkation Center where it remained until its return to the United States.

Division headquarters sailed from Brest on March 27, 1919, and arrived in Boston April 4, 1919.

The Division commanders were as follows: Major General Clarence Edwards, Brigadier General C.H. Cole, Brigadier General Peter E. Traub, Brigadier General Frank E. Bamford, and Major General Harry C. Hale.

Reference Bibliography:

General Division Histories:

American Battle Monuments Commission, *26th Division: Summary of Operations in the World War.* Washington, DC: GPO, 1944.

Benwell, Harry A. *History of the Yankee Division*. Boston: Ornhill, 1919.

Cochrane, Rexmond C. *The 26th Division East of the Meuse, October, 1918.* Army Chemical Center, Maryland: Chemical Corps Historical Office, 1960.

Colby, Elbridge. "The March of the 26th ." Infantry Journal (Sep/Oct 1940): pp. 462-74.

Committee of Welcome. *Welcome Home: In Commemoration of the Foreign Service and Home-Coming of the 26th Division*. Official program. Boston: Everett, 1919.

Ford, Bert. *The Fighting Yankees Overseas*. Boston: McPhail, 1919.

George, Albert E. and Cooper, Edwin H. *Pictorial History of the Twenty-sixth Division, United States Army.* Boston: Ball, 1920.

Nelson, John. *A Brief History of the Fighting Yankee Division, A.E.F.: On the Battlefront. February 5, 1918- November 11, 1918.* Reprinted from *The Worchester Evening Gazette*, 1919.

Sibley, Frank P. *With the Yankee Division in France*. Boston: Little, Brown, 1919.

Taylor, Emerson G. *New England in France, 1917-1919: A History of the Twenty-sixth Division, U.S.A.* Boston: Houghton Mifflin, 1920.

26th Infantry Division *The Heroic 26th: Its Deeds and Valor Over There*. Boston: Ball, 1919.

—. *The Immortal Yankee Division, 1917-1919*. Boston: YMCA, 1919.

—. *The Welcome Home Book*. Lowell, Massachusetts: O'Connell, 1919.

101st Infantry Regiment

Duane, James T. *Dear Old «K»*. Boston: n.p., 1922.

102nd Infantry Regiment

Hill, Ratcliffe M. *The War History of the 102nd Regiment, United States Infantry*. n.p., 1924.

Markle, Clifford M. *Yankee Prisoner in Hunland*. New Haven, Connecticut: Yale University Press, 1920.

Strickland, Daniel W. *Connecticut Fights: The Story of the 102nd Regiment*. New Haven, Connecticut: Quinnipiack, 1930.

103rd Infantry Regiment

History of the 103rd Infantry, 1917-1919. Boston: Hymans, 1919.

McIntyre, Colby L. *The Old Man of the 103rd: The Biography of Frank M. Hume*. Houlton, Maine: Aroostook, 1940.

104th Infantry Regiment

Albertine, Connell. *The Yankee Doughboy*. Boston: Branden, 1968.

Fifield, James H. *The Regiment: A History of the 104th US Infantry, AEF, 1917-1919*.

Springfield, Massachusetts: 104th Infantry Association, 1946.

Westbrook, Stillman F. *Those Eighteen Months, October 9, 1917-April 8, 1919...From the Letters of Stillman F. Westbrook*. Hartford, Connecticut: Case, Lockwood & Brainard, 1934.

101st Field Artillery Regiment

Being a Narrative of Battery A of the 101st Field Artillery (Formerly Battery A of Boston) From the Time of Its Muster Into the Federal Service on July 25, 1917, Through Its 19 Months of Service in France, Nine Months of Which Were in Action at the Front, Until Its Demobilization at Camp Devens, Mass., on April 29, 1919. Cambridge, Massachusetts: Brattle Press, 1919.

Carter, Russell G. *The 101st Field Artillery, A.E.F., 1917-1919*. Boston: Houghton Mifflin, 1940.

A Short History & Photographic Record of the 101st U.S. Field Artillery, 1917: Col. John H. Sherburne Commanding Officer. Cambridge, Massachusetts: University Press, 1918.

Washburn, Slater. *One of the D "Yankee Division"*. Boston: Houghton Mifflin, 1919.

102nd Field Artillery Regiment

Embury, Aymar II. "Reminiscences of A Camouflage Officer." *Military Engineer* (May/Jun 1927): pp. 235-239.

LaBranche, Ernest E. *An American Battery in France*. Worcester, Massachusetts: Belisle, 1923.

Sirois, Edward D., & McGinnis, William. *Smashing Through "The World War" with Fighting Battery C, 102nd F.A. "Yankee Division", 1917-1918-1919*. [Ed by John Hogan] Salem, Massachusetts: Meek Press, 1919.

U.S. Army. 102nd Artillery Regiment. *History of the One Hundred Second Field Artillery, July 1917-April 1919*. Boston: Privately Printed, 1927.

103rd Field Artillery Regiment

Herzog, Stanley J. *The Fightin' Yanks: A Book of Plain Facts, Written with the Intent of Perpetuating the Deeds of the Boys of Battery F, 103rd Field Artillery, 26th or Yankee Division*. Stamford, Connecticut: Cunningham Print, 1922.

Kernan, William F., & Samson, Henry T. *History of the 103rd Field Artillery (Twenty-sixth Division, A.E.F.) World War, 1917-1919*. Providence, Rhode Island: Remington, 193-.

McKenna, Frederick A. *Battery A, 103rd Field Artillery in France*. Providence, Rhode Island: Livermore & Knight, 1919.

Russell, John W. *History of Battery B, One Hundred Third Field Artillery, Twenty-sixth Division*. Providence, Rhode Island: E. L. Freeman, 1922.

Samson, Henry T., & Hull, George C. *The War Story of C Battery, One Hundred and Third U.S. Field Artillery in France, 1917-1919*. Norwood, Massachusetts: Plimpton, 1920.

101st Engineer Regiment

Peck, E.D. "Army Engineer Operations: In the St. Mihiel & Meuse-Argonne Offensives." *Military Engineer* (Mar/Apr 1922).

Simmons, William S. *The "Little Peter" Papers*. Boston: n.p., 1921.

Swan, Carroll J. *My Company*. New York: Houghton Mifflin, 1918

U.S. Army. *Directory 101st Engineers: With Permanent Home Addresses at Time of Demobilization, April 28, 1919*. n.p: 1919.

—. *History of the 101st United States Engineers: American Expeditionary Forces, 1917-1918-1919*. Cambridge, Massachusetts: University Press, 1926.

—. *The 101st U.S. Engineers (1st Corps Cadets) in Foreign Service*. Boston: n.p., 1919.

—. Company E. *The Story of "E" Company, 101st Engineers, 26th Division: A*

Record of Their Service From May 1917 to April 1919. Boston: By the Company, 1919.

—. *The Story of F Company, 101st Regiment, U.S. Engineers: A Informal Narrative*. Boston: Metcalf, 1924.

Major General John F. O'Ryan, Commanding General, 27th Division. Courtesy National Archives

Opposite
Top: Major General John F. O'Ryan and King George V of England inspect troops of the 27th Division in France. Courtesy National Archives.

Bottom: Men of the 105th Machine Gun Battalion fall in after a nights rest at St. Souplet. Courtesy National Archives.

One of the Huns' locomotives taken by the boys of the 27th Division under the command of Major General John F. O'Ryan at the town of St. Souplet. October 19, 1918. Courtesy National Archives

27th Infantry Division

The division was composed of National Guard troops from New York. This division was the former 6th National Guard Division and was renumbered to conform to the new configuration of division numbering under direction of the Army Staff. The division formed at Camp Wadsworth, South Carolina July 18, 1917.

Insignia:
The division selected as its insignia a stylized monogram of the letters "N.Y." in red for New York on a black disk. Superimposed is the constellation Orion consisting of seven five-pointed stars. The constellation pattern was selected in tribute to the division's popular commander, Major General John F. O'Ryan. The shoulder sleeve insignia was approved by the AEF in October, 1918.[7]

Campaigns:
Somme Offensive, Ypers-Lys Offensive, Dickebush Lake and Scherpenberg Sectors.[8]

Division Organization (1917-1919):

53rd Infantry Brigade:

105th Infantry Regiment
106th Infantry Regiment
105th Machine Gun Battalion

54th Infantry Brigade:

107th Infantry Regiment
108th Infantry Regiment
106th Machine Gun Battalion

Division Troops:

104th Machine Gun Battalion

52nd Field Artillery Brigade:

104th Field Artillery Regiment
105th Field Artillery Regiment
106th Field Artillery Regiment
102nd Trench Mortar Battery

Division Support:

102nd Engineer Regiment
102nd Field Signal Battalion
102nd Train Headquarters and Military Police
102nd Ammunition Train
102nd Supply Train
102nd Engineer Train
102nd Sanitary Train (Ambulance Companies & Field Hospitals 105th, 106th, 107th, 108th)

27th Infantry Division Combat Narrative:[9]
The first unit of the division arrived in France May 7, 1918; the last element July 12, 1918.

For training purposes the division (less artillery) was attached to British units in the Department of the Somme until July 3, 1918. For the same purpose the artillery brigade

U.S.

U.S.

went to Camp de Souge where it remained until August 30, 1918. It never served with the 27th Division in France, but participated in the Meuse-Argonne Offensive, September 26, to November 11, 1918.

On July 3, 1918, the division proceeded to Belgium under the British 2nd Army, where for further training units were brigaded with troops of the British 19th Corps in the Dickebush Lake and Scherpenberg sectors southwest of Ypres from July 9 to August 23, 1918. On August 23, it relieved the British 6th Division in line southwest of Ypres, and participated in the Ypres-Lys Offensive from August 31 to September 2, 1918, in the battle before Mt. Kemmel. On September 3, it was withdrawn from the line, and proceeded to the Beauquesne Area near Beauval. From September 24 to October 20, 1918, the division participated in the Somme Offensive north of Saint Quentin in the 2nd American Corps, operating with the British 4th Army against the Hindenburg Line. The outstanding features of this operation were, the severe fighting in the vicinity of Guilllemont Ferme, Quennemont Ferme, and Gouy, September 27th and 28th, and the battle of La Selle River, October 17 to 20, 1918.

The division was withdrawn from the line October 21st, and proceeded to the Corbie Area with Headquarters at Corbie.

Days in the Front Line: 25 (training) 0 (sector) 32 (battle) for a total of 57. During operations the division took 2,357 prisoners and its casualties totaled 1,829 soldiers killed in action or died of wounds, 6,505 wounded in action.[10]

On November 23rd it moved to the Le Mans Embarkation Center preparatory to its return to the United States.

Division Headquarters sailed from Brest on February 26, and arrived at New York on March 6, 1919.

The division commanders were as follows: Major General James F. O'Ryan, Brigadier General Charles L. Phillips, and Brigadier General Robert L. Michie.

Opposite
Top: Private Starr A. Miller of the 102nd Field Signal Battalion poses on an ambulance "somewhere in France". Courtesy Military History Institute.

Bottom: Mail clerks of the 27th Division sort mail from home. In the field at Corbie, October, 1918. Courtesy National Archives.

27th Division insignia with soutache appliqué to felt.

This example of the 27th Division insignia is fully embroidered on felt.

Reference Bibliography:

General Division Histories:

American Battle Monuments Commission. *27th Division, Summary of Operations in the World War*. Washington, DC: Government Printing Office, 1944

Clarke, William F. *Over There With O'Ryan's Roughnecks*. Seattle: Superior Publications, 1968.

Mayor's Committee of Welcome to Home-Coming Troops. *Review and Parade of the 27th Division ,March 25, 1919*. n.p.: 1919.

O'Ryan, John F. *History of the 27th Division, New York's Own*. New York: Bennett & Churchill, 1919.

—. *The Story of the 27th Division*. New York: Wynkoop Hallenbeck Crawford, 1921.

Starlight, Alexander, comp. *The Pictorial Record of the 27th Division*. New York: Harper, 1919.

Swetland, Maurice J. *'These Men,' "For Conspicuous Bravery Above and Beyond the Call of Duty..."* Harrisburg, Pennsylvania: Military Service Publishing, 1940.

27th Division. *The 27th Division: The Story of Its Sacrifices and Achievements*. New York: John H. Eggers Co, 1919.

U.S. Army. 27th Infantry Division. *Records of the 27th Division of the American Expeditionary Forces (World War I), 1917-1919*. NARA microfilm publication, no.819, Washington, D.C.

105th Infantry Regiment

DeCastro, Vincent A., et. al. *"The Second New York Infantry at the Mexican Border."* Troy, New York: Troy Times, 1916.

Kolakwoski, Christopher L. "A Sister's Journey to the Western Front in 1920." *Military Collector & Historian* (Fall 2004): pp. 154-63.

105th Infantry. *A Short History and Illustrated Roster of the 105th Infantry, United States Army*. Philadelphia: Stern, 1918.

Sutliffe, Robert S. *Seventy-First New York in the World War*. New York: Little & Ives, 1922.

Turner, Charles B. *William Bradford Turner*. n.p.: New York: Country Life, 1920.

A much more refined version using dies to cut out the division monogram with embroidered stars.

Crude soutache construction no doubt made in France.

This "Iron Men" song sheet pays tribute to the deeds of the men of the 28th Division and prominently features the division Keystone insignia. Courtesy Military History Institute

106th Infantry Regiment

106th Infantry. *A Short History and Illustrated Roster of the 106th Infantry, United States Army*. Philadelphia: Stern, 1918.

107th Infantry Regiment

Gow, Kenneth. *Letters of a Soldier*. New York: Covert, 1920.

Harris, Stephen L. *Duty, Honor, Privilege: New York's Silk Stocking Regiment and the Breaking of the Hindenburg Line*. Washington, DC: Brassey's, 2001.

History of Company "E", 107th Infantry, 54th Brigade, 27th Division, USA. New York: War Vets' Association, 1920.

Holbrook, Richard G. *A Handbook of Company K, Seventh Regiment (107th Infantry, NYNG, 1860-1940)*. Binghamton, New York: Vail-Ballou, 1940.

Jacobson, Gerald. *History of the 107th Infantry, USA*. New York: DeVinne, 1920.

Leland, Claude G. *From Shell Hole to Chateau with Company I*. New York: Society of Ninth Co Vets, 7th Regt, NYNG, 1950

Mitchell, Harry T. *Company L, 107th Infantry, 54th Infantry Brigade, 27th Division*. n.p.: 1919.

Schoem, Elliott. *History of the 107th US Infantry, AEF, in the Battle of the Hindenburg Line, September 29, 1918, During World War I*. New York: Press Work, 1968.

The Seventh Regiment of New York, Organized in 1806. n.p.: 19--.

Todd, Frederick P., & Miller, Kenneth C. *Pro Patria et Gloria: The Illustrated Story of the One Hundred and Fifty Years of the Seventh Regiment of New York (107th Infantry Regiment N.Y.N.G.)*. Hartsdale, New York: Rampart House, 1956.

Veterans of the Seventh Regiment. *The Seventh Regiment of New York: On the Pages of This Book Are Recorded the Names of Those Who Once Stood in the Line of Grey*. New York: Veterans of the Seventh Regiment, 1956.

Vets of the 7th Regt. *The Seventh Regiment of New York*. New York: Veterans of the 7th Regiment, 1956.

108th Infantry Regiment

A Short History and Illustrated Roster of the 108th Infantry, United States Army. Philadelphia: Stern, 1918.

106th Field Artillery Regiment

The War Book of the One Hundred and Sixth Regiment Field Artillery, United States Army, 1917-1919. New York: Nation Press, 1919.

102nd Engineer Regiment

"Tablet to the Dead of 102nd Engineers." *Military Engineer* (Jul/Aug 1922).

28th Infantry Division

The division was composed of National Guard troops from Pennsylvania. This division was the former 7th National Guard Division and was renumbered to conform to the new configuration of division numbering under direction of the Army Staff. The division formed at Camp Hancock, Georgia on July 18, 1917.

Insignia:

The division selected as its insignia a red keystone to represent the "Keystone State" of Pennsylvania, as the state was known since the earliest days of the Republic. The color red was chosen at random by the commanding general.[11] The shoulder sleeve insignia was approved October 19, 1918, and authorized in November, 1918.[12]

Campaigns:

Champagne-Marne Defensive, Aisne-Marne Offensive, Oise-Aisne, Meuse-Argonne Offensive, Chateau-Thierry Sector, Fismes Sector, Thiaucourt Sector.[13]

Above: Captain Watson and Lieutenant Carlson of the 103rd Ammunition Train are visited by their wives and other family members during training at Camp Beauregard, Louisiana. Courtesy Military History Institute.

Right: Drivers from the Headquarters of the 107th Field Artillery pose in Proven Belgium, December, 1918. Courtesy Military History Institute.

Right: Major General Charles H. Muir, 28th Division commander confers with Colonel Frank Ely, commander of the 327th Infantry, La Forge France, October, 1918. Courtesy National Archives.

Below: First Sergeant W.H. Griffith, Bugler Tilbury, Sergeant P.F. Orr, and Corporal Ayers of the 28th Division after being decorated for bravery by the French. Courtesy National Archives.

Division Organization (1917-1919):[14]

55th Infantry Brigade:

109th Infantry Regiment
110th Infantry Regiment
108th Machine Gun Battalion

56th Infantry Brigade:

111th Infantry Regiment
112th Infantry Regiment
109th Machine Gun Battalion

Division Troops:

107th Machine Gun Battalion

53rd Field Artillery Brigade:

107th Field Artillery Regiment
108th Field Artillery Regiment
109th Field Artillery Regiment
103rd Trench Mortar Battery

Division Support:

103rd Engineer Regiment
103rd Field Signal Battalion
103rd Train Headquarters and Military Police
103rd Ammunition Train
103rd Supply Train
103rd Engineer Train
103rd Sanitary Train (Ambulance Companies & Field Hospitals 109th, 110th, 111th, 112th)

The common 28th Division insignia of die cut all wool construction.

28th Keystone Division insignia embroidered on wool.

Velvet variation of the 28th Division Keystone insignia.

28th Infantry Division Combat Narrative:[15]

The first unit of the division to go overseas arrived in France May 14, 1918; the last element; June 11, 1918.

For training purposes the division (less artillery) was attached to the 34th British Division south of Saint-Omer, where it remained until June 9th. The division proceeded to the vicinity of Paris June 13th, where it was attached to French troops for further training. For the same purpose the Artillery Brigade went to Camp Meucon. It rejoined the division in August, 1918, and remained with it until October, 1918, when it passed to the reserve of the First Army Artillery. It later participated with the 91st Division in the Ypres-Lys Offensive, October 29 to November 11, 1918.

On August 7th the division relieved the 32nd Division in the Fismes Sector and participated in the Oise-Aisne Offensive from August 18th to September 7th, during which operation severe fighting was encountered in the advance north of the Vesle River.

From September 8th until September 19th the division was moving to the Argonne, where it took over the sector extending across the Aire Valley, and in front of the Argonne Forest, on the morning of September 20th, excepting the outpost line which was held by the French until the night of September 25-26. In the Meuse-Argonne Offensive the division was heavily engaged from September 26th to October 9th, in which operation the capture of Varennes, Montblainville, Apremont, le Chêne Tondu, and Châtel-Chéhéry were the outstanding features. The division was relieved by the 82nd Division on October 9th, and proceeded to the Thiacourt Sector, Toul, which it held from October 16th to November 11, 1918.

An elaborate 28th Division insignia of felt on felt construction with "PA, 28, NG" embroidered in a chain stitch representing the Pennsylvania and National Guard connection.

After the Armistice, the division remained in the Thiacourt Sector until January 9, 1919, when it moved south of Toul with headquarters at Colombey-les-Belles, remaining there until the latter part of March, when it moved to the Le Mans Embarkation Center preparatory to returning to the United States.

Days in the Front Line: 14 (training) 44 (sector) 44 (battle) for a total of 102. During operations the division took 921 prisoners and its casualties totaled 2,874 soldiers killed in action or died of wounds, 11,265 wounded in action.[16]

Division Headquarters sailed from Saint Nazaire April 20, 1919, and arrived at Newport News, May 1, 1919.

The division had five commanding generals as follows: Major General Charles M. Clement, Brigadier General William G. Price, Brigadier General F.W. Stillwell, Major General Charles H. Muir, and Major General William H. Hay.

Reference Bibliography:

General Division Histories:

"An Early History of the 28th Division, U.S.A." *PA Guardsman* (Jul 1939): Pennsylvania Department of Military Affairs, Adjutant General's Office. *Histories and Records*. Pennsylvania: 1937.

—. *History of the 28th Infantry Division (Condensed)*. n.p.,19-.

Hendler, Charles J., [comp]. *Official History of the Militia and the National Guard of the State of Pennsylvania: Special Issue* Philadelphia: Hendler, 1939.

U.S. Army, 305th Military History Detachment. *History of the 28th Infantry Division (Condensed)*. n.p., 1968.

U.S. Army. 28th Infantry Division. *The First Century: A History of the 28th Infantry Division*. Harrisburg, Pennsylvania: 28th Infantry Division, 1979.

American Battle Monuments Commission. *The 28th Division Summary of Operations in the World War.* Washington, DC: Government Printing Office, 1944.

Gilbert, Eugene. *The 28th Division in France*. Nancy, France: Berger-Levrault, 1919.

Martin, Edward. *The Twenty-Eighth Division, Pennsylvania's Guard in the World War*. Pittsburgh, Pennsylvania: 28th Division Publishing Company, 1923.

Ohl, John Kennedy. "The Keystone Division in the Great War." *Prologue* (Summer 1978): pp. 82-99.

Pennsylvania in the World War: An Illustrated History of the Twenty-Eighth Division. Pittsburgh, Pennsylvania: States Publishing Society, 1921.

Proctor, H.G. *The Iron Division, National Guard of Pennsylvania in the World War*. Philadelphia: John C. Winston Co., 1919.

Warner, Frank A. *Journal of Operations, Twenty-Eighth Division, A.E.F., August 5, 1917 [to] November 30, 1918*. n.p., 1919.

Whitehorne, Joseph W.A. "The Survival of the Duquesne Grays, 1917." *Military Affairs* (Oct 1986): pp. 179-84.

109th Infantry Regiment

Hitchcock, Frederick L. *History, 13th Regiment, National Guard of Pennsylvania, and 109th Infantry: 108th Machine Gun Battalion, USAEF, and 109th Pennsylvania National Guard, 1877-1923*. Scranton: International Textbook, 1924.

A Short History and Photographic Record of the First Regiment. Pennsylvania Infantry, National Guard, United States. Philadelphia: Stern, 1917.

Keller, Joel W. *Company G in the World War (1917-19)*. n.p., 1919.

An American 28th Division soldier, just landed in France, cheerfully giving some cigarettes to wounded British, Calais, France, May 20, 1918. Courtesy National Archives

110th Infantry Regiment

History of the 110th Infantry (10th Pa.) of the 28th Division, U.S.A., 1917-1919: A Compilation of Orders, Citations, Maps, Records and Illustrations Relating to the 3rd PA. Inf, 10th PA. Inf., and 110th U.S. Inf. Pittsburgh, Pennsylvania: Pittsburgh Publishing Co, 1920

Kimball, Guy E. *One Soldier's Experience with the American Expeditionary Force in World War I, 2 October 1917 Through 1 October 1918*. n.p., n.d.

Lutz, Francis. *The 110th Infantry in the World War*. Haddonfield, New York: 1919.

A Short History and Illustrated Roster of the 110th Infantry (10th Pennsylvania Infantry), United States Army, 1917. Philadelphia: Stern, 1917.

Whitehorne, Joseph W.A. "The Survival of the Duquesne Grays, 1917." *Military Affairs* (Oct 1986): pp. 179-84.

111th Infantry Regiment

Cooper, George W. *Our Second Battalion: An Accurate and Authentic History of the Second Battalion, 111th Infantry*. Pittsburgh: Second Battalion Book, 1920.

A Short History and Illustrated Roster of the 111th Infantry, US, Formerly 18th Pennsylvania Infantry, N.G.U.S., Colonel Edward C. Shannon, Commanding Officer. Philadelphia: Stern, 1918.

112th Infantry Regiment

Baker, C. Earl. *Doughboy's Diary*. Shippensburg, Pennsylvania: Burd Street. Press, 1998.

Murrin, James A. *With the 112th in France: A Doughboy's Story of the War*. Philadelphia: Lippincott, 1919.

A Short History and Illustrated Roster of the 112th Infantry, Army of the United States. Philadelphia: Stern, 1918.

107th Field Artillery Regiment

Pennsylvania in the World War: An Illustrated History of the 28th Division. Vol. 2. Pittsburgh, Pennsylvania: States Publishing Society, 1921.

A Short History and Illustrated Roster of the 107th Field Artillery, U.S.N.G., Formerly First Pennsylvania Field Artillery. Philadelphia: Edward Stern, 1918.

108th Field Artillery Regiment

Pennsylvania in the World War: An Illustrated History of the 28th Division. Vol. 2. Pittsburgh, Pennsylvania: States Publishing Society, 1921.

A Short History and Illustrated Roster of the 107th Field Artillery, U.S.N.G., Formerly First Pennsylvania Field Artillery. Philadelphia: Edward Stern, 1918.

109th Field Artillery Regiment

Pennsylvania in the World War: An Illustrated History of the 28th Division. Pittsburgh, Pennsylvania: States Publishing Society, 1921.

A Short History and Illustrated Roster of the 109th Field Artillery, Third Penna. Field Artillery, 53rd Artillery Brigade, 28th Division, Armies of the United States. Philadelphia: Edward Stern, 1918.

Zierdt, William H. *Narrative History of the 109th Field Artillery, Pennsylvania National Guard, 1775-1930*. Wilkes-Barre, Pennsylvania: E.B. Tordy, n.d.

103rd Engineer Regiment

Crosson, W.H. "Training Employed by 103rd Engineers." *Military Engineer* (May/Jun 1928).

The 29th Division Commander, Major General Charles G. Morton who led the division throughout the war. Courtesy National Archives.

29th Infantry Division

The division was composed of National Guard troops from Maryland, Virginia, New Jersey, Delaware, and the District of Columbia. This division was the former 8th National Guard Division and was renumbered to conform to the new configuration of division numbering under direction of the Army Staff. The division formed at Camp McClellan, Alabama on August 25, 1917.

Captain Philip C. McIntyre, 115th Infantry Regiment poses proudly showing his division insignia. Courtesy Military History Institute.

Insignia:

"[As] the division was composed of men both from North and South, and partly from organizations formed in the Capital of the United States, as well as in the former Capital of the Confederacy - the designation "Blue and Gray" consequently was most appropriate. Major James A.

Private Teddy Raymond, Trainer (left) and Private Ritz Walters, Middle Weight Boxer, both men belonged to the 112th Field Artillery Regiment, taken in Paris, April 1919. Courtesy National Archives.

29th Division insignia constructed of felt on felt with no backing.

Variation 29th Division insignia hand embroidered on wool.

Ulio, Division Adjutant, then suggested the Korean Symbol of Life [the taeguk] composed half of blue color and the other half in gray, be selected as the Divisional Insignia."[17] The shoulder sleeve insignia was approved October 21, 1918, and authorized in November, 1918.[18]

Campaigns:
Champagne-Marne Defensive, Meuse-Argonne Offensive, Center Sector, Haute-Alsace.[19]

Division Organization (1917-1919):[20]

57th Infantry Brigade:

113th Infantry Regiment
114th Infantry Regiment
111th Machine Gun Battalion

58th Infantry Brigade:

115th Infantry Regiment
116th Infantry Regiment
112th Machine Gun Battalion

Division Troops:

110th Machine Gun Battalion

54th Field Artillery Brigade:

110th Field Artillery Regiment
111th Field Artillery Regiment
112th Field Artillery Regiment
104th Trench Mortar Battery

Division Support:

104th Engineer Regiment
104th Field Signal Battalion
104th Train Headquarters and Military Police
104th Ammunition Train
104th Supply Train
104th Engineer Train
104th Sanitary Train (Ambulance Companies & Field Hospitals 113th, 114th, 115th, 116th)

29th Division insignia embroidered on felt.

Fine cord appliqué 29th Division insignia on olive drab wool.

29th Infantry Division Combat Narrative:[21]
The first element of the division arrived in France June 8, 1918, and the last July 22, 1918. Many of the units landed in England before crossing the Channel.

Within a few days after its arrival the division proceeded to the 10th Training Area and established headquarters at Prauthoy (Haute Marne). After two weeks' training, orders were received to move to Upper Alsace for the purpose of taking over a quiet sector of the front. From the 17th to 25th of July the division was stationed near Belfort under command of the 40th French Corps.

The occupation of the Center sector, Upper Alsace, began on the 25th and was completed on August 7, at which time command of the sector passed from the French to the Americans.

On September 23rd the division was withdrawn to the vicinity of Belfort and ordered to the Robert Espagne Training Area. After leaving Belfort the division was assigned to the American First Army and ordered to the area in which the Meuse-Argonne Offensive was soon to be launched. Division Headquarters were established at Conde September 24th. From this point the division moved north with headquarters successively at St. Andre and Blercourt.

Members of Company A, 112th Machine Gun Battalion clown around with a Mademoiselle. Courtesy Military History Institute.

Private Milus F. Small, Jr. (in blackface) performs the opening number "Buttons" in the 29th Division show with some other "beauties" from the division. Bar sur Aube, France. March, 1919. Courtesy National Archives.

On October 1st it was placed in reserve of the 17th French Corps with headquarters at the Citadel of Verdun.

The American offensive west of the Meuse began on September 26th and soon progressed so far that its right was exposed to German fire from the heights on the east bank. To take these heights was the task of the 17th French Corps, then a part of the First American Army.

On October 7th division headquarters moved to Vacherauville, east of the Meuse and seven kilometers north of Verdun. The 58th Infantry Brigade was now attached to the 18th French Division, and on the 8th as a part of that division, attacked north from positions between Samogneux and Brabant. This attack penetrated the Bois de Consenvoye. Two days later, the 113th Infantry of the 57th Brigade having reinforced the line, the advance was resumed and the wood cleared.

On October 11 command of this section of the line passed from the French to the commanding general of the 29th Division; but parts of the division continued for some days to operate with the French units on the right.

By October 16 the line had been pushed forward on the north into the Bois de la Grande Montagne and on the north and east into the Bois d' Ormont. It was necessary to approach this latter wood by way of Etrayes Ridge and the Bois de Belleu; and on October 23rd the ridge was taken.

The line now ran from Hill 375 in the Bois de la Grande Montagne, around the head of Etrayes Ravine, and thence along the northern and eastern slopes of Etrayes Ridge. On this line the division was relieved by the 79th Division, October 30th.

During the division's occupation of the Center Section, Haute-Alsace, it was served by French artillery; during its participation in the Meuse-Argonne offensive it was supported by the 158th Field Artillery Brigade. Upon arrival in France the 54th Field Artillery Brigade was sent to Camp Meucon. It did not participate in active operations and joined the division after the Armistice in the 11th Training Area.

Days in the Front Line: 13 (training) 46 (sector) 23 (battle) for a total of 82. During operations the division took 2,187 prisoners and its casualties totaled 1,053 soldiers killed in action or died of wounds, 4,517 wounded in action.[22]

After the signing of the Armistice the division was removed to a rest area with division headquarters at Bourbonne-les-Bains. The movement to the embarkation center for return to this country began April 11, and on the 14th headquarters were established at Ballon, near Le Mans. Division headquarters sailed May 6th and arrived at Newport News, Virginia May 19.

Major General Charles G. Morton commanded the division from July 6th, 1917, until its demobilization.

Reference Bibliography:

General Division Histories:

American Battle Monuments Commission. *29th Division, Summary of Operations in the World War.* Washington, DC: Government Printing Office, 1944.

Cochrane, Rexmond C. *The 29th Division in the Cotes de Meuse, October 1918.* Army Chemical Center, US Army Chemical Corps, Historical Office, 1959.

Cutchins, John A., and Stewart, George S. *History of the Twenty-Ninth Division, "Blue and Gray," 1917-1919.* Philadelphia: Cutchins and Stewart, 1921.

Freeman, Douglas, and Foster, W.W. *Homecoming Celebration, Commemorating the Day When Virginia's Sons of the 29th and 80thDivision Returned from the World War.* Richmond, Virginia: National State & City Bank, 1919.

U.S. Army. 29th Infantry Division. *The Blue and the Gray Division: Historical Record of the Twenty-Ninth Division, Quartermaster Corps Activities, 1917-1918.* France, 1919.

—. *Operations of the 29th Division East of the Meuse River, October 8th to 30th, 1918.* Ft. Monroe, Virginia: Coast Artillery School, 1920.

—. *29th Division, Army of the United States.* n.p., 1918.

114th Infantry Regiment

Reddan, William J. *Other Men's Lives (Experiences of a "Doughboy"), 1917-1919.* Bloomfield, New York: By the Author, 1936.

115th Infantry Regiment

Reynolds, Frederick C. *115th Infantry, USA, in the World War.* Baltimore: Read-Taylor, 1920.

116th Infantry Regiment

Dinges, Harold R. *History of Company I in the World War: Part Played by [the] Old Winchester Militia Command From Time of Mustering in Till Return From France.* n.p., 1918.

Seal, Henry F., Jr. *"Ever Forward": World War I, 1917-1919. History of the 116th Infantry Regiment, 29th Infantry Division, Organized from the 1st and 4th Infantry Regiments, Virginia National Guard, at Camp McClellan, Anniston, Alabama, 4 October 1917.* Richmond, Virginia: Virginia National Guard, Adjutant General's Office, 1953.

110th Field Artillery Regiment

Jacobsen, A. Wilmot, & Mansfield, J. Carroll. *The Blue and Gray: A Story of Battery D 110th Field Artillery.* n.p., 1919.

U.S. Army. 110th Artillery Regiment. Battery E. *Battery E of the 110th Field Artillery: A Record of Service and Fellowship Here and "Over There".* n.p., 1919.

111th Field Artillery Regiment

"One Hundred Per Cent Regiments of the National Guard Field Artillery." *Field Artillery Journal* (Mar/Apr 1938): pp. 142-43.

Seal, Henry F. *Numquam non Paratus (Never Unprepared) World War I, 1917-1919: History of the 111th Field Artillery Regiment, 29th Infantry Division, Organized From the First Battalion, Field Artillery, Virginia National Guard, at Camp McClellan, Anniston, Alabama, 5 August 1917.* Richmond, Virginia: Virginia Department of Military Affairs, 1953.

104th Engineer Regiment

Engineers Club of Trenton. *Trenton's Own Company of Engineers: Its Experiences and Exploits With Some Facts About Its Organization and Personnel.* Trenton, New Jersey: SARCO, 1922.

Miller, John A., Jr. "Traffic Regulation in the Advanced Zone." *Military Engineer* (Sep/Oct 1922): pp. 297-99 & 339.

New Jersey National Guard. *History of 104th Engineers: A.E.F. October 1917-June 1919, N.J.N.G., July 1920-March 1927*. n.p., 1937.

Major General Edward M. Lewis showing off a captured German anti-tank gun following the battle at Bellicourt, October, 1918. Major General Lewis was the division's final commander. Courtesy National Archives.

Private Willard Newton, 105th Engineer Train, shows off his 30th Division insignia. Courtesy Military History Institute.

30th Infantry Division

The War Department directed the National Guard to form the 30th Division on July 18, 1917. Concentration of the division began at Camp Sevier, South Carolina on August 3, 1917. The division was composed of troops from North Carolina, South Carolina and Tennessee. This division was the former 9th National Guard Division and was renumbered to conform to the new configuration of division numbering under direction of the Army Staff. The division chose the sobriquet "Old Hickory" in tribute to Andrew Jackson and owing to its Tennessee roots.[23]

Insignia:
The insignia adopted by the division is a blue elliptically shaped letter "O" on its side, surrounding a blue letter "H" with blue Roman numerals XXX inside the cross bar of the "H," the "H" superimposed on a maroon field, "Andrew Jackson, "Old Hickory" will be always remembered for his amazing and glorious victory over the British at the Battle of New Orleans; his namesake, the "Old Hickory" Division added glory and perpetuation to his name as allies and comrade-in-arms to those who a century before were his adversaries."[24] It was approved October 23 1918. An unauthorized variant exists of a white "H" within a red "O" all placed on a blue disc.[25]

Campaigns:
Somme Offensive, Ypres-Lys Offensive, St. Mihiel Offensive, Meuse-Argonne Offensive, Canal Sector, Toul Sector, Woevre Sector.[26]

Division Organization (1917-1919):[27]

59th Infantry Brigade:

117th Infantry Regiment
118th Infantry Regiment
114th Machine Gun Battalion

60th Infantry Brigade:

119th Infantry Regiment
120th Infantry Regiment
115th Machine Gun Battalion

Division Troops:

113th Machine Gun Battalion

55th Field Artillery Brigade:

113th Field Artillery Regiment
114th Field Artillery Regiment
115th Field Artillery Regiment
105th Trench Mortar Battery

Division Support:

105th Engineer Regiment
105th Field Signal Battalion
105th Train Headquarters and Military Police

Soldiers of the 144th Field Artillery Regiment stand outside their headquarters in the Argonne Forest near Montfaucon. Courtesy Military History Institute.

Men of Company H 1st Infantry, North Carolina National Guard in training at Moorehead City, North Carolina. The North Carolina National Guard would become the 30th Division these men would form the 115th Machine Gun Battalion at the outset of the war. Courtesy Military History Institute.

30th Division insignia embroidered on wool showing the "OH" monogram representing "Old Hickory."

A twill on red wool version of the 30th Division insignia.

Variant pattern 30th Division insignia using the letter "H" and circular felt disc to represent "O" in "Old Hickory."

105th Ammunition Train
105th Supply Train
105th Engineer Train
105th Sanitary Train (Ambulance Companies & Field Hospitals 117th, 118th, 119th, 120th)

30th Infantry Division Combat Narrative:[28]
The first unit of the division to go overseas arrived in France May 14, 1918; the last element June 24, 1918.

For training purposes the division (less artillery) was attached to British units in the Eperlecques Area (Pas-de-Calais) where it remained until July 4, 1918. For the same purpose the artillery brigade went to Coctquidan. It never served with the 30th Division in France, but participated in the Saint Mihiel Offensive September 12 to 16, 1918, and in the Meuse-Argonne Offensive September 25 to October 28, 1918. It was also in line in the Toul Sector August 23 to September 11, 1918, and in the Woevre Sector October 11 to November 8, 1918.

On July 4, 1918, the division was ordered to Belgium under the Second British Army, where for further training units were brigaded with British divisions in the Canal Sector southwest of Ypres from July 16 to August 17. On August 18 the division took over the Canal Sector from the British holding this position until August 30, 1918. From August 31 to September 2 the division participated in the Ypres-Lys Offensive in the battle before Mt. Kemmel.

From September 24 to October 19, 1918, the division participated in the Somme Offensive in the 2nd American Corps, operating with the 4th British Army. The outstanding features of this operation were the breaking of the Hindenburg Line near Bellicourt, and the capture of Bellicourt and Nauroy, September 29, and 30, the attack from Montbrehain, October 6 to 12 in which Brancourt, Prémont, Busigny, Vaux-Andigny and Saint Souplet were captured, and the Battle of La Salle River, October 17 to 20, 1918.

The division was withdrawn October 20 and proceeded to the vicinity of Amiens, where it remained until November 24, when it was ordered to the Le Mans Embarkation Center preparatory to returning to the United States.

Days in the Front Line: 33 (training) 1 (sector) 35 (battle) for a total of 69. During operations the division took 3,848 prisoners and its casualties totaled 1,641 soldiers killed in action or died of wounds, 6,774 wounded in action.[29]

Division Headquarters sailed from Saint Nazaire March 18, 1919, arrived at Charleston, S.C., on April 2, 1919.

The division had six commanding generals as follows: Major General John F. Morrison, Brigadier General William T. Scott, Major General C.P. Townsley, Brigadier General Samson L. Faison, Major General George W. Read, and Major General Edward M. Lewis.

Reference Bibliography:

General Division Histories:

American Battle Monuments Commission. *30th Division, Summary of Operations in the World War.* Washington, DC: GPO, 1944.

Murphy, Elmer A., and Thomas, Robert S. *The Thirtieth Division in the World War*. Lepanto, Arkansas: Old Hickory, 1936.

U.S. Army. 30th Infantry Division. *Operations, Thirtieth Division, Old Hickory*. Booklet, 191-.

118th Infantry Regiment

U.S. Army. 118th Infantry Regiment. *Historical and Pictorial Review, 30th Infantry Division, Army of the United States, Fort Jackson, South Carolina, 1941*. Baton Rouge, Louisiana: Army & Navy Pub, 1941.

—. *Washington Light Infantry, 1807-1957, Sesquicentennial*. Charleston, South Carolina: Walker, Evans & Cogswell, 1957.

119th Infantry Regiment

Conway, Coleman B. *History 119th Infantry, 60th Brigade, 30th Division, USA*. Wilmington, North Carolina: Wilmington Printing, 1920.

Melvin, Edward G., Sr. *One Man's War: World War I From the Memories of a Tennessee Farmboy.* [Comp. by Ella M. Winsbro] Kingston, Tennessee: By the Compiler, 1996.

120th Infantry Regiment

Williams, John F., III. *Experiences in the Great War*. n.p., 1975.

113th Field Artillery Regiment

Badon, William J. *History of the Fifty-fifth Field Artillery Brigade...1917, 1918, 1919*. Nashville, Tennessee: Benson, 1920.

Fletcher, Arthur L. *History of the 113th Field Artillery, 30th Division*. Raleigh, North Carolina: Historical Commission of the Regiment, 1920.

114th Field Artillery Regiment

Badon, William J. *History of the Fifty-fifth Field Artillery Brigade...1917, 1918, 1919*. Nashville, Tenessee: Benson, 1920.

West, Ernest P. *History of Battery B, 114th Artillery, 55th Brigade, 30th Division: Some of the Trials and Tribulations of its Personnel as Observed by*.... n.p., 1967.

115th Field Artillery Regiment

Badon, William J. *History of the Fifty-fifth Field Artillery Brigade...1917, 1918, 1919*. Nashville, Tennessee: Benson, 1920.

105th Engineer Regiment

Sullivan, Willard P., & Tucker, Harry S., comps. *The History of the 105th Regiment of Engineers, Division Engineers of the "Old Hickory" (30th) Division*. New York: Doran, 1919.

Members of the 119th Infantry Regiment, 30th Division, helping a little Belgium boy carry his burden home. Watou area, Belgium, July 8, 1918. Courtesy National Archives

31st Infantry Division

The War Department directed the National Guard to form the 31st Division on July 18, 1917. Concentration of the division began at Camp Wheeler, Georgia on August 25, 1917. The division was composed of troops from Alabama, Florida, and Georgia. This division was the former 10th National Guard Division and was renumbered to conform to the new configuration of division numbering under direction of the Army Staff. The division took the name "Dixie" division owing to its composition of soldiers from the deep south.[30]

Insignia:

The unit selected a red monogram "D" "D" for Dixie Division upon a white disc bordered red. It was approved March 7, 1919. An alternate design of a white "D" "D" on a pennant, worn point down and divided vertically, right red and left blue.[31]

The original pennant shaped insignia of the 31st Division; this version is executed in felt on felt.

Campaigns:

None.

Division Organization (1917-1919):[32]

61st Infantry Brigade:

121st Infantry Regiment
122nd Infantry Regiment
117th Machine Gun Battalion

62nd Infantry Brigade:

123rd Infantry Regiment
124th Infantry Regiment
118th Machine Gun Battalion

GAS HOUSE

Opposite
Top: Major General LeRoy S. Lyon, Commander, 31st Division, and members of the division staff waiting for the division to arrive overseas. Major General Lyon would not command the division in combat; instead he would see the division units used as fillers for other divisions. Courtesy National Archives.
Bottom: Men of the 31st Division leave the "Gas House" after training with their gas masks. Camp Wheeler, Georgia. Courtesy National Archives.

Above: Men of the 106th Field Signal Battalion in formation at Bracieux, France. December 1918. Courtesy National Archives.
Below: Sergeant Cletus Swann and the crew of gun number 1, Battery C, 56th Artillery. Mareuil-en-Dole, France. August, 1918. Courtesy National Archives.

A die cut 31st Division insignia; red felt "DD" on olive drab background.

31st Division insignia with red embroidered monogram on white felt background.

Fully embroidered pennant shaped 31st Division insignia on felt.

Division Troops:

116th Machine Gun Battalion

56th Field Artillery Brigade:

116th Field Artillery Regiment
117th Field Artillery Regiment
118th Field Artillery Regiment
106th Trench Mortar Battery

Division Support:

106th Engineer Regiment
106th Field Signal Battalion
106th Train Headquarters and Military Police
106th Ammunition Train
106th Supply Train
106th Engineer Train
106th Sanitary Train (Ambulance Companies & Field Hospitals 121st, 122nd, 123rd, 124th)

31st Infantry Division Service Narrative:[33]
Units of the division sailed overseas in September and October, 1918, the last element arriving in France November 9, 1918.

Upon arrival it was designated as a replacement division. The personnel of most of the units were withdrawn and sent to other organizations, leaving the 31st Division skeletonized. It remained at Brest until it returned to the United States in December, 1918.

The division had four commanding generals as follows: Major General Francis J. Kernan, Brigadier General John L. Hayden, Brigadier General Francis H. French, and Major General LeRoy S. Lyon.

Reference Bibliography:

General Division Histories:

American Battle Monuments Commission. *31st Division, Summary of Operations in the World War.* Washington, DC: GPO, 1944.

117th Field Artillery Regiment

U.S. Army , 117th Artillery Regiment. *History and Roster of the 117th Field Artillery*. n.p., 1919.

32nd Infantry Division

The War Department directed the National Guard to form the 32nd Division on July 15, 1917. Concentration of the division began at Camp McArthur, Texas on August 4, 1917. The division was composed of troops from Michigan and Wisconsin. This division was the former 11th National Guard Division and was renumbered to conform to the new configuration of division numbering under direction of the Army Staff. The division took the name "Arrow."[34]

Insignia:
The unit selected a red arrow piercing a line to show that the division pierced every line the enemy threw up before them. It was not approved until November 11, 1918.[35]

Campaigns:
Aisne-Marne Offensive, Oise-Aisne, St. Mihiel Offensive, Meuse-Argonne Offensive, Haute-Alsace Sector.[36]

Division Organization (1917-1919):[37]

Major General William Lassiter commanded the 32nd Division in France. Courtesy National Archives.

63rd Infantry Brigade:

125th Infantry Regiment
126th Infantry Regiment
120th Machine Gun Battalion

64th Infantry Brigade:

127th Infantry Regiment
128th Infantry Regiment
121st Machine Gun Battalion

Division Troops:

119th Machine Gun Battalion

57th Field Artillery Brigade:

119th Field Artillery Regiment
120th Field Artillery Regiment
121st Field Artillery Regiment
107th Trench Mortar Battery

Division Support:

107th Engineer Regiment
107th Field Signal Battalion
107th Train Headquarters and Military Police
107th Ammunition Train
107th Supply Train
107th Engineer Train
107th Sanitary Train (Ambulance Companies & Field Hospitals 125th, 126th, 127th, 128th)

Edwin F. Meyer shot this photo of the mess of B Company, 107th Field Signal Battalion near Montfaucon in the Argonne Forest. Courtesy Military History Institute.

Photo taken by Walter Zukowski, Company C 107th Ammunition Train, of his unit learning to drive the new motorized tractors. Courtesy Military History Institute.

32nd Infantry Division Combat Narrative:[38]

The 147th Field Artillery of the 41st Division was attached to the 57th Field Artillery Brigade and served with it throughout its activities.

The first unit of the division arrived in France Feb 6, 1918, and the last March 14, 1918. The first casualties were suffered when the transport "Tuscania", carrying the 107th Sanitary Train, was torpedoed and sunk February 5th, fifteen men of this organization being lost.

Division headquarters were established at Prauthoy, Haute Marne, on February 24th. The 32nd was originally designated as a replacement division and as such sent many of its members to other organizations. However, the German offensive of March 21st and the resulting necessity for additional American Troops forced a change in these plans. Replacements were furnished and the division assembled in the 10th Training Area preparatory to taking the field as a combat unit. After four weeks spent in this area, the division was ordered to the quiet Haute Alsace sector. The movement to this sector began May 15th, and on the 16th headquarters were

32nd Division Military Police Rengsdorf, Germany, February, 1919. Note the Military Police Armbands and the wide variety of division shoulder sleeve insignia. Courtesy Military History Institute.

established at La Chapelle. On the 18th the French troops in the sector were relieved and the division for the first time took over front line trenches, which were held until July 21st.

On July 26th the division was assembled near Verberie, in the neighborhood of Soissons, as a reserve of the 10th French Army. From this point a move was immediately made to the region of Chateau Thierry, and upon arrival the division was placed in the 38th French Corps, 6th Army, and later, August 4th, in the 5th American Corps. The Aisne-Marne offensive was by this time in full swing and on July 29-30th the 32nd relieved the 3rd Division in the vicinity of Roncheres, northeast of Chateau Thierry. The Commanding General of the 32nd Division assumed command of battle zone at 11:00 A.M., July 30th and at 2:30 P.M. the same day an attack was launched in which the Bois des Grimpettes was taken and the edge of the Bois des Cierges gained. On the night of the 30-31st of July the 63rd Brigade of the 32nd Division relieved the 28th Division on the Ourcq River extending the zone of action to the left toward Sergy. The attack was renewed on the 31st and the village of Cierges captured. Here the advance was stopped by strong resistance from Reddy and Bellevue Farm. An attack on August 1st gained Bois de la Planchette and Hill 230, and forced the enemy to abandon Bellevue Farm. The German forces were now rapidly withdrawing, and on August 3rd the division pushed forward to the Vesle River captured the town of Fismes, at which point it was relieved August 7th.

The division was next assembled in a reserve position between the Ourcq and Vesle where it remained for a period of ten days, when it was again ordered to the vicinity of Soissons for duty with the 10th French Army, then engaged in the Oise-Aisne offensive.

The 127th French division was relieved August 27th north of Soissons and approximately 2 kilometers due west of Juvigny. In an attack which began on the 28th the railroad tracks west of Juvigny were reached and on August 30th the town itself captured. The advance continued, and on the day following, the division reached the Terny-Sorny-Bethancourt road. At this point the 32nd was relieved September 1-2nd by the 1st Moroccan Division.

It was next sent to a rest area near Joinville and remained at this place until September 20th when it again started north to join the 5th Corps for the coming Meuse-Argonne Offensive. The 32nd Division, from a position in Corps Reserve, south of Avocourt, moved up and relieved, on the night of the 29-30th and the morning of the 30th, the 37th Division south of Cierges in the vicinity of Montfaucon, and moved forward driving the enemy north. On the night of October 3-4th part of the Division relieved the 91st Division in the vicinity of Gesnes. The latter village was immediately entered, but no attempt was made to hold it as it was under constant shell fire. On October 5th the Bois de la Marine was taken and from this point the attack swung to the north and the Bois du Chene Sector was captured. Here the advance was temporarily halted by strong resistance from Hills 255 and 269. During the night of the 7-8th of October the Division side-slipped to the east, giving up 2 kilometers of front in the west to a brigade of the 91st Division, and taking over 1 kilometer from the 3rd Division on the right. On the 9th of October the Division attacked and reached the Kriemhilde-Stellung, Cote Dame Marie and Romagne, where it made preparations for a drive through. On October 14th the Kriemhilde-Stellung was penetrated, Cote Dame Marie and Romagne being captured and the Bois de Chauvignon entered, making an advance of 2 kilometers. The Division slowly and steadily advanced in the Bois de Bantheville until it was relieved by the 89th Division on the night of the 19-20th of October. The division followed in the wake of the 5th, 89th and 91st Divisions, as a reserve of the 3rd Army Corps, with headquarters successively at Romagne and Ainereville. The 128th Infantry Regiment reentered the line November 6th as a unit of the 5th Division operating east of the Meuse, in the vicinity of Dun-sur-Meuse. On the night of the 9-10th of November the remainder of the Division crossed the Meuse and entered the line attacking on the 10th in the vicinity of Brandeville and Peuvillers; on the morning of the 11th a continuation of the attack was halted by the signing of the Armistice.

Days in the Front Line: 25 (training) 37 (sector) 38 (battle) for a total of 100. During operations the division took 2,153 prisoners and its casualties totaled 3,028 soldiers killed in action or died of wounds, 10,233 wounded in action.[39]

On November 17th the Division began its march from Vilosnes-sur-Meuse and on December 1st crossed the Sauer River and entered Germany as a first line unit of the 3rd Army. It was assigned a sector in the Coblenz Bridgehead with a front of 30 kilometers. Here

32nd Division insignia sewn to a wool background.

32nd Division Insignia embroidered on an olive drab felt background.

it remained until April, when the various units began entraining for ports of embarkation. Division headquarters sailed from Brest, April 27, 1919, and arrived at New York May 5th.

The division had commanding generals as follows: Major General James Parker, Major General William G. Haan and Major General William Lassiter.

Reference Bibliography:

General Division Histories:

American Battle Monuments Commission. *32nd Division: Summary of Operations in the World War.* Washington, DC: Government Printing Office, 1944.

Barrington, Harold P. *The Great Adventure: A World War I Soldier's Diary*. Edina, Minnisota: Mori Studio, 2000.

—. *Tales of the Thirty-Second.* West Salem, Wisconsin: Badger, 1927.

Haan, W.G. "Story of Wisconsin's "Red Arrow": The Making and the Fighting of the Famous Thirty-Second Division in the World War." Magazine section of *Milwaukee Journal* (2 Sep 1923).

—. *Thirty-Second Division Exploits.* Milwaukee, Wisconsin: Broadway, 1919.

Richards, Robert E., ed. *Chronicles of a Soldier: The 1918 Diary and Letters of Pvt. Elmer Eugene Richards, Company E., 107th Ammunition Train, 32nd Division, American Expeditionary Force.* n.p., 1994.

U.S. Army, 32nd Infantry Division. "'Second Battle of the Marne': Report of the Thirty-Second Division, July 29- August 7, 1918, Inclusive." Typescript, 46 pps.

—. *The Thirty-Second Division American Expeditionary Forces.* Coblenz, Germany: Kindt & Meinardus, 1919.

—. "The Thirty-Second Division, 1917-1918." Mimeo, 1921-22. 60 p.

War History Commission of Michigan and Wisconsin. *The 32nd Division in the World War, 1917-1919.* Milwaukee, Wisconsin: Wisconsin Printing, 1920.

125th Infantry Regiment

Donnelly, Joseph M. *A History of Company "G", 125th Infantry, 32nd Division, World War I.* [typescript] Houghton, Michigan: Donnelly, 1973.

126th Infantry Regiment

Gansser, Emil B. *History of the 126th Infantry in the War with Germany.* Grand Rapids, Michigan: Hicks, 1920.

Jonker, Hartger. *The "Old Command": Service History of Company "L", 126th Infantry.* n.p., 1919.

127th Infantry Regiment

Schmidt, Paul W. *Co. C, 127th Infantry, in the World War: A Story of the 32nd Division, Complete History of the Part Taken by Co. C.* Sheboygan, Wisconsin: Press Publishing Company, 1919.

119th Field Artillery Regiment

Embury, Aymar II. "Reminiscences of A Camouflage Officer." *Military Engineer* (May/Jun 1927): pp. 235-239.

Jacks, Leo V. *Service Record, by an Artilleryman.* New York: Scribners, 1928.

120th Field Artillery Regiment

Penner, Carl *The 120th Field Artillery Diary, 1880-1919.* Milwaukee, Wisconsin: Hammersmith-Kortmeyer, 1928.

121st Field Artillery Regiment

Menne, Edward P. *Diary of a Doughboy.* n.p., 1919.

U.S. Army, 121st Artillery Regiment. *Reunion Souvenir.* Racine, Wisconsin: Western Printing & Lithography 1920.

107th Engineer Regiment

Fiske, Harold C. "A Division Engineer at the Front." *Military Engineer* (Sep/Oct 1928): pp. 408-12.

33rd Infantry Division

The War Department directed the National Guard troops of Illinois to form the 33rd Division on July 18, 1917. This division was the former 12th National Guard Division and was renumbered to conform to the new configuration of division numbering under direction of the Army Staff. Concentration of the division began at Camp Logan, Texas on August 3, 1917. The division took the name "Illinois" division in tribute to its' mother state.[40]

Sergeant Valdo Meie Mirales (left) and a friend pose for a photograph. Courtesy Military History Institute.

Insignia:

The Division chose as their insignia a yellow cross on a black disc. It was derived from a symbol used by an Illinois regiment during the War with Spain. They were used to mark property and to avoid theft by Philippine tribesmen who were superstitious of yellow crosses. It was approved October 21, 1918.[41]

Campaigns:

Somme Offensive, St. Mihiel Offensive, Meuse-Argonne Offensive, Amiens Sector, Troyon Sector, Verdun Sector.[42]

Division Organization (1917-1919):[43]

65th Infantry Brigade:

129th Infantry Regiment
130th Infantry Regiment
123rd Machine Gun Battalion

66th Infantry Brigade:

131st Infantry Regiment
132nd Infantry Regiment
124th Machine Gun Battalion

Major General George Bell, Jr., 33rd Division commander, inspects the Liaison Detachment with the Division Signal Officer, Major Charles S. Forbes. Trouville, France, September, 1918. Courtesy National Archives.

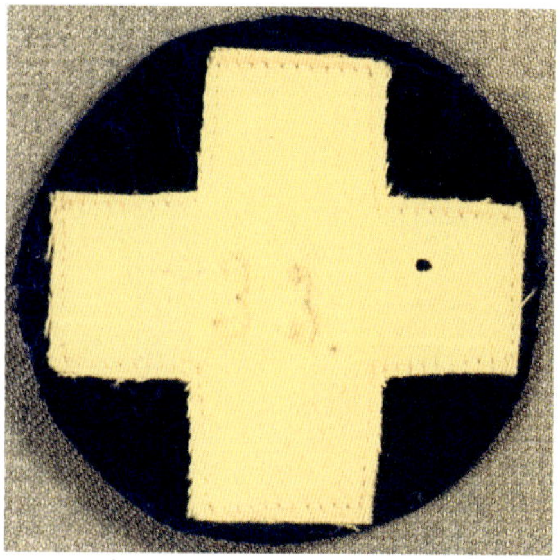

Crude felt on felt 33rd Division insignia.

Division Troops:

122nd Machine Gun Battalion

58th Field Artillery Brigade:

122nd Field Artillery Regiment
123rd Field Artillery Regiment
124th Field Artillery Regiment
108th Trench Mortar Battery

Division Support:

108th Engineer Regiment
108th Field Signal Battalion
108th Train Headquarters and Military Police
108th Ammunition Train
108th Supply Train
108th Engineer Train
108th Sanitary Train (Ambulance Companies & Field Hospitals 129th, 130th, 131st, 132nd)

33rd Infantry Division Combat Narrative:[44]

The first unit of the division arrived in France May 18, 1918; the last June 15, 1918.

For the purpose of training, the division (less artillery) was sent to the Huppy area near Abbeville where it began instruction with the British. On June 8th, it moved to the Eu area, and

Below: Field Headquarters 33rd Division, Tannois France; Major General Bell is second from right. September, 1918. Courtesy National Archives.

33rd Division officers observe the effects of American artillery fire on German lines near Les Epargas, France. Courtesy National Archives.

Writing Home – a snapshot of an artilleryman in the doorway of his splinter-proof shelter. March 7, 1918. Courtesy National Archives

on June 20th-21st advanced into the Amiens sector where certain units participated in several active operations. On July 4th two companies of the 131st Infantry and two companies of the 132nd Infantry took part in the attack of the Australians on Hamel. In the Somme offensive the 131st Infantry played a prominent part in the attack on Chipilly Ridge and Gressaire Wood.

On August 23rd, the division was transferred to the area of the First American Army in the Toul sector and was concentrated in the vicinity of Trenville-en-Barrois. On September 5th, it began its movement to the Verdun sector where it relieved the 120th French Division and the right regiment of the 57th French Division on the nights of September 7th, 8th and 9th.

At the opening of the Meuse-Argonne offensive, the 33rd Division formed the right of the Third American Army Corps. Its line ran from a point southwest of Forges, east to the Meuse River approximately 10 kilometers north of Verdun. From this position the division attacked on the morning of September 26th and captured Forges and the formidable Bois de Forges. In its position facing the Meuse, it continued for the next eleven days to act as the pivot of the American attack between that river and the Argonne Forest.

On October 6th, the division was transferred to the 17th French Army Corps operating east of the Meuse as part of the First American Army. In the general attack which occurred in that sector on October 8th, the 33rd Division was placed astride of the river. This necessitated the construction on the 8th, under constant shellfire, of two bridges; one at Brabant-sur-Meuse, the other at Consenvoye, and the forcing of the passage under direct observation and fire from the enemy on the heights east of the Meuse. This operation was successfully accomplished by three battalions of infantry and two machine gun companies from the 33rd Division which thereupon formed the left of the French attack and by nightfall reached their objective south of the Bois de Chaume. On the following day these units continued their advance to the road running from Sivry-sur-Meuse to the Villeneuve Farm, but at dusk a powerful attack delivered against their right flank forced a retirement to the Tranchée du Cable, just south of the Bois de Chaume. Reinforcements were immediately dispatched across the river and by an attack on the morning of October 10th regained all ground lost, which was subsequently held notwithstanding that the right flank remained exposed for four days.

Captain N.B. Clinch, Chaplain of the 129th Infantry Regiment and senior chaplain of the 33rd Division. Cousenvoye, Meuse, France, October 12, 1918. Courtesy National Archives

33rd Division insignia embroidered on felt.

Gold bullion on wool 33rd Division insignia.

The division was relieved in the Verdun sector by the 15th French Colonial division on the nights of October 20th, 21st and 22nd and proceeded to the Troyon-sur-Meuse sector in the quiet St. Mihiel salient relieving the 79th Division. A number of important raids were carried out and on November 10th Marchéville, the Bois d'Harville and other portions of the enemy defense system were captured.

Throughout its operations the division was never served by its own artillery. On the British front its operations were supported by British and Australian guns. On the Verdun front it had the cooperation of the 52nd Field Artillery Brigade from the 27th Division, in the St. Mihiel region the 55th Field Artillery Brigade of the 30th Division was attached to it, and so continued until relieved by the 58th Field Artillery Brigade, in January, 1919.

The latter organization was separated from the division at Camp Logan, Texas, and did not reach France until about the middle of June, 1918. It immediately went into training at Ornans and Valdahou. On August 20 it proceeded to the Toul sector in support of the 89th Division, and on the 28th was attached to the 1st Division and supported the attack at St. Mihiel.

During the Meuse-Argonne offensive it was first attached to the 91st Division, but, upon the relief of the latter on October 7, the Brigade remained in support of the 32nd Division. On the 11th it was withdrawn to the area of Ville-sur-Cousances for rest and refitting, but on the 24th went back into the line in the same sector and was again assigned to the 89th Division which it supported until active operations were terminated by the Armistice on November 11, 1918. On that date, the brigade was in the vicinity of Stenay, where it remained until January 4, 1919, when it began its march to rejoin the 33rd Division.

Days in the Front Line: 27 (training) 33 (sector) 38 (battle) for a total of 98. During operations the division took 3,987 prisoners and its casualties totaled 993 soldiers killed in action or died of wounds, 5,871 wounded in action.[45]

On December 8, 1918, the division commenced an advance which carried its leading brigade across the Moselle into Rhenish Germany. During this movement it was attached to the Army of Occupation, but upon the relocation of this disposition on December 15, it was withdrawn west of that river and established in the northern part of Luxembourg, with headquarters located at Diekirch. There it remained until the latter part of April, 1919, when the movement to Le Mans was begun preparatory to returning to the United States. Division Headquarters sailed from Brest on May 9, and arrived at Hoboken on May 17, 1919.

The division had one commanding general, Major General George Bell, Junior.

Reference Bibliography:

General Division Histories:

American Battle Monuments Commission. *33rd Division, Summary of Operations in the World War*. Washington, DC: GPO, 1944.

Cochrane, Rexmond C. *The 33rd Division Along the Meuse, October 1918*. Army Chemical Center, MD: USA Chemical Corps Historical Office, 1958.

Harris, Barnett W. *33rd Division: Across No Man's Land*. Kankakee, Illinois: Harris & Nelson, 1919.

Huidekoper, Frederic L. *The History of the 33rd Division, A.E.F.* Springfield, Illinois: Illinois State Historical Library, 1921.

—. *The Story of the Thirty-Third Division, "The Prairie Division."* n.p., 1919.

Illinois in the World War. Chicago, Illinois: State Publishing Society, 1920.

Illinois in the World War: An Illustrated History of the Thirty-Third Division. Chicago, Illinois: States Publishing Society, 1921.

U.S. Army, 33rd Infantry Division. *33rd Division, A.E.F.: From Its Arrival in France Until the Armistice With Germany, November 11, 1918*. Diekirch, Luxembourg: Gustave Soupert, 1919.

131st Infantry Regiment

Sanborn, Joseph B. *The 131st US Infantry (First Infantry, Illinois National Guard) in the World War.* Chicago: n.p., 1919.

132nd Infantry Regiment

Davis, Abel. *The Story of the 132nd Infantry, A.E.F.* Luxembourg, 1919.

108th Engineer Regiment

Guilfoil, Dwight D. "Crossing the Meuse at Consenvoye." *Military Engineer* (May/Jun 1924) pp. 204-205.

Richards, Robert P., & Beall, John R., eds. *History, Co. "F", 108th Engineers, 33rd Div.* n.p., 1920.

Private Wheelock Wilson of Iowa, 135th Infantry. This photograph shows him as the company clerk, Prisoner of War Enclosure Company 242, Dijon, France 1919. Note the unusual divisional insignia, which is a printed Olla and bull skull on a shield shaped, two color background. Courtesy Military History Institute.

34th Infantry Division

The War Department directed the National Guard to form the 34th Division on July 15, 1917. Concentration of the division began at Camp Cody, New Mexico on August 19, 1917. The division was composed of troops from Iowa, Minnesota, Nebraska, North Dakota, and South Dakota. This division was the former 13th National Guard Division and was renumbered to conform to the new configuration of division numbering under direction of the Army Staff. The division took the name "Sandstorm" in memory of the frequent sandstorms they experienced at Camp Cody during training.[46]

Insignia:

The unit selected a red bull skull on an olla (a Mexican water flask) in keeping with its training camp experiences in the southwest. The design was approved October 29, 1918.[47]

Campaigns:

None.

Division Organization (1917-1919):[48]

67th Infantry Brigade:

133rd Infantry Regiment

134th Infantry Regiment

126th Machine Gun Battalion

68th Infantry Brigade:

Brigadier General George S. Gibbs speaking to Lieutenant Cook of the 109th Field Signal Battalion, Chitenay, Loir et Cher, France, December, 1918. Courtesy National Archives.

135th Infantry Regiment
136th Infantry Regiment
127th Machine Gun Battalion

Division Troops:

125th Machine Gun Battalion

59th Field Artillery Brigade:

125th Field Artillery Regiment
126th Field Artillery Regiment
127th Field Artillery Regiment
109th Trench Mortar Battery

Division Support:

109th Engineer Regiment
109th Field Signal Battalion
109th Train Headquarters and Military Police
109th Ammunition Train
109th Supply Train
109th Engineer Train
109th Sanitary Train (Ambulance Companies & Field Hospitals 133rd, 134th, 135th, 136th)

34th Infantry Division Service Narrative:[49]
The first unit of the division to go overseas arrived in France September 29, 1918, the last element, October 24, 1918.

Upon arrival the division was sent to the La Brede Area (Gironde) with headquarters at Castres. Here it remained under instruction until November 14, 1918 when, having been designated as a replacement division, it was sent to Le Mans. Here it was skeletonized, most of its personnel being sent to other organizations. Headquarters and the division permanent cadre returned to the United States via Bordeaux in December, 1918.

The division had commanding generals as follows: Brigadier General Frank Mauldin, Major General Augustus P. Blocksom, Brigadier General John A. Johnston, and Major General Beaumount B. Buck.

Opposite
Top: Private John L. Boran (second from right under arrow), Company C, 34th Engineers, participates in some unknown ritual with his buddies. France, 1918. Courtesy Military History Institute.

Bottom: Private Harry F. Hines, Battery C, 126 Field Artillery took this photograph of his friends on the U.S.S. Powhatan during the trip home from France, December, 1918. Courtesy Military History Institute.

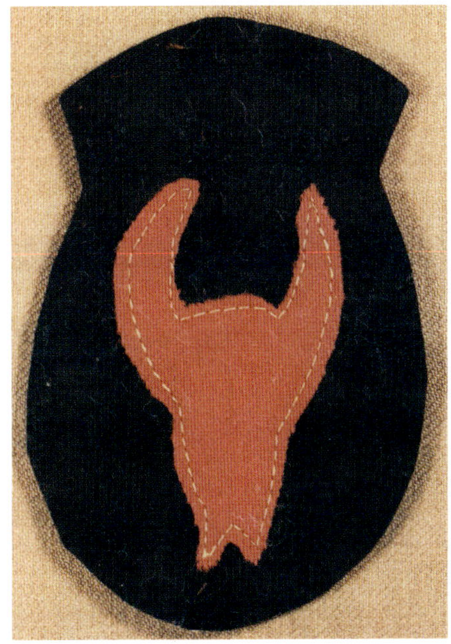

Crudely executed felt on felt 34th Division Insignia.

34th Division Insignia embroidered on felt with division nickname and number.

An unusual variation using a buffalo head in place of the skull; embroidered on wool and adding "SD" for Sandstorm Division and the divisional number.

34th Division Insignia felt on felt variation using chain stitch to spell out division nickname and number.

Another variation using the buffalo head; fully embroidered upon a rectangle in place of the olla.

Reference Bibliography:

General Division Histories:
None.

134th Infantry Regiment
C. LeRoy Meisinger [Ostergaard, Albert J., ed]. *A World War One Soldier's Diary, June 2, 1917 to July 26, 1919.* Ellisville, Missouri: By the Editor, 2001.

135th Infantry Regiment
Davies, Kenneth M. *To the Last Man: The Chronicle of the 135th Infantry Regiment of Minnesota.* St Paul, Minnesota: Ramsey County Historical Society, 1982.
Kreger, William G. *A Condensed History of the 135th Infantry from Gettysburg to the Po.* n.p., 1951.

136th Infantry Regiment
Waage, D.L. *History of the 136th Infantry „Bearcat" Regiment, 1861-1951.* n.p., 1991.

35th Infantry Division

The War Department directed the National Guard to form the 35th Division on July 18, 1917. The division was composed of troops from Kansas and Missouri.[50] This division was the former 14th National Guard Division and was renumbered to conform to the new configuration of division numbering under direction of the Army Staff. Concentration of the division began at Camp Doniphan, Fort Sill, Oklahoma on August 23, 1917.

Insignia:
The division chose a blue disc with green border, a white Santa Fe cross. The Santa Fe cross was originally a symbol used to mark the Santa Fe Trial. The insignia was approved March 27, 1918.[51] The subordinate elements of the division can be distinguished by variations in color in the quadrants of the divisional insignia. Division headquarters troop, area 1 yellow, all others blue; 70th Infantry Brigade, all numbered areas black; 139th Infantry Regiment, area 1, yellow, all others black; 140th Infantry Regiment, areas 2 & 4, yellow, all others black; 69th Infantry Brigade, all areas, yellow; 137th Infantry Regiment, area 1, blue, all other areas yellow; 138th Infantry Regiment, areas 2 & 4 blue, all other areas yellow; 60th Field Artillery

Milton B. Sweningsen of the 138th Infantry shares a laugh with a friend. Courtesy Military History Institute.

Major General Peter Traub, 35th Division Commander (left) speaks with Major S.C. Cordiner, 60th Coast Artillery Corps, at 35th Division Headquarters near Boureuilles, France. September 1918. Courtesy National Archives.

Brigade, all areas red; 110th Trench Mortar Battalion, area 1 green, all other areas red; 128th Field Artillery Regiment, area 1 blue, all other areas red; 129th Field Artillery Regiment, area 1, yellow, all other areas red; 130th Field Artillery Regiment, area 1, white, all other areas red; 128th Machine Gun Battalion, area 1, green, all other areas blue; 129th Machine Gun Battalion, areas 2 & 4, red, all other areas yellow; 130th Machine Gun Battalion, areas 1 & 2, yellow, all other areas, black; 110th Engineer Battalion, all white areas, or area 1, red, all other areas white; 110th Signal Battalion, all areas green; 110th Ammunition Train, area 1, white, areas 2,3 & 4 red, all outer quadrants, green; 110th Sanitary Train, areas 2, 3 & 4 maroon, area 1, green.[52]

Campaigns:
Meuse-Argonne Offensive, Gerardmer Sector, Vosges, Sommedieue Sector.[53]

Division Organization (1917-1919):[54]

69th Infantry Brigade:

137th Infantry Regiment
138th Infantry Regiment
129th Machine Gun Battalion

70th Infantry Brigade:

139th Infantry Regiment
140th Infantry Regiment
130th Machine Gun Battalion

Division Troops:

128th Machine Gun Battalion

60th Field Artillery Brigade:

128th Field Artillery Regiment
129th Field Artillery Regiment
130th Field Artillery Regiment
110th Trench Mortar Battery

Division Support:

110th Engineer Regiment
110th Field Signal Battalion
110th Train Headquarters and Military Police
110th Ammunition Train
110th Supply Train
110th Engineer Train
110th Sanitary Train (Ambulance Companies & Field Hospitals 137th, 138th, 139th, 140th)

35th Infantry Division Combat Narrative:[55]
The first unit of the division arrived in France May 11, 1918; the last element June 8, 1918.

For training purposes the division (less artillery) was sent to the vicinity of Eu (Somme) where it remained until June 8, 1918. It moved to the vicinity of Epinal June 11, and on June 30 it moved to the Vosges, where it was brigaded with the French in line in the Gerardmer

Below: Corporal Joseph N. Rizzi of Tarrytown, New York (boxer on right under arrow) takes part in a boxing match while a member of Company A, 110th Engineers in training at Camp Doniphan, Fort Sill Oklahoma in March, 1918. Courtesy Military History Institute.

Bottom right: Joseph N. Rizzi at age eighty-eight poses seventy years later in his old uniform, August 1983. Courtesy Military History Institute.

Sector. Command of the sector passed to the Commanding General, 35th Division, on July 27. The artillery brigade trained at Camp Coetquidan. It rejoined the division in the Vosges August 14.

On August 31 the division was relieved by units of the 6th American Division, and 131st French Division, and proceeded to the Foret de Haye west of Nancy for the concentration preparatory to the Saint Mihiel Offensive, in which operation it was in the reserve of the 1st Army.

On September 15, the division was placed under the tactical control of the Second French Army, and moved to the Naives-devant-Bar area with headquarters established at Passavant-en-Argonne on September 18. On September 19 it moved to the Vraincourt-Auzéville area with headquarters at Autrecourt. On September 23, it relieved the 73rd Division, French, in the line in the Grange-le-Comte sector.

In the Meuse-Argonne Offensive the division attacked from September 26 to October 1, capturing the towns of Vauquois, Verennes, Cheppy, Charpentry and Baulny. On October 1, it was relieved by the 1st Division, and proceeded to the Vavincourt Area arriving October 5.

On October 14, it relieved the 15th French Colonial Division in the Sommedieue Sector, where it remained until November 7, when it was relieved by the 81st Division. The artillery brigade remained in line supporting the 81st Division until the Armistice. It rejoined the division the latter part of January, 1919. The division proceeded to the Saint Mihiel Area with headquarters at Commercy. On March 9, 1919, it moved to Montfort (Sarthe) remaining until April 5 when it proceeded to Saint Nazaire preparatory to returning to the United States.

Days in the Front Line: 37 (training) 43 (sector) 30 (battle) for a total of 110. During operations the division took 781 prisoners and its casualties totaled 1,298 soldiers killed in action or died of wounds, 5,998 wounded in action.[56]

Division Headquarters sailed from Saint Nazaire on April 8, 1919, and arrived at Newport News, Va., April 20, 1919.

The division had six commanding generals as follows; Major General William M. Wright, Brigadier General Lucien G. Berry, Brigadier General Charles I. Martin, Brigadier General N.F. McClure, Major General Peter E. Traub, Brigadier General Thomas B. Dugan, and Major General William M. Wright.

This embroidered example is for the 110th Ammunition Train.

Wool on wool 60th Field Artillery Brigade.

Embroidered insignia of the 70th Infantry Brigade.

35th Division Insignia Colors

Division Headquarters: 1 yellow, 2-4 blue
69th Infantry Brigade: all yellow, 137th Infantry: 1 blue, 2-4 yellow, 138th Infantry: 2&4 blue, 1&3 yellow, 129th Machine Gun Battalion: 2&4 red, 1&3 yellow.
70th Infantry Brigade: 1-4 black, 139th Infantry: 1 yellow, 2-4 black, 140th Infantry: 2&4 yellow, 1&3 black, 130th Machine Gun Battalion: 1&2 yellow, 3&4 black.
60th Field Artillery Brigade: 1-4 red. 128th FA: 1 blue, 2-4 red, 129th FA: 1 yellow, 2-4 red, 130th FA: 1 white, 2-4 red, 110th Trench Mortar: 1 green, 2-4 red.
Division Troops:
128th Machine Gun Battalion: 1 green, 2-4 blue, 110th Engineer Regiment: 1-4 white or 1 red, 2-4 white, 110th Field Signal Battalion: 1-4 green, 110th Ammunition Train: 1 white, 2-4 red, 110th Sanitary Train: 2,3,4 maroon, 1 green.

Wedges of the 35th Division insignia were used to designate each of the subordinate units. This chart interprets the meaning of each 35th Division insignia variation.

An embroidered on wool insignia of the 110th Signal Battalion.

An embroidered on felt insignia of the 110th Engineer Regiment.

An embroidered insignia of the 110th Engineer Train.

Reference Bibliography:

General Division Histories:

American Battle Monuments Commission. *35th Division, Summary of Operations in the World War.* Washington, DC: Government Printing Office, 1944.

Carter, Robert L. *Pictorial History of the 35th Division.* St. Louis, Missouri: Carter, 1933.

Ferrell, Robert H. *Collapse at Meuse-Argonne: The Failure of the Missouri-Kansas Division.* Columbia, Missouri: University of Missouri, 2004.

Hoyt, Charles B. *Heroes of the Argonne: An Authentic History of the Thirty-fifth Division.* Kansas City, Missouri: Hudson, 1919.

Kenamore, Clair. *From Vauquois Hill to Exermont: A History of the Thirty-Fifth Division of the United States Army.* St. Louis, Missouri: Guard, 1919.

Rizzi, Joseph N. *Joe's War: Memoirs of a Doughboy.* Huntington, West Virginia: Der Angriff Publishing, 1983.

United States Army. "The Thirty-Fifth Division." Study, 1921-1922.

137th Infantry Regiment

Haterius, Carl E. *Reminiscences of the 137th US Infantry.* Topeka, Kansas: Crane, 1919.

Hudson, Ben S. *Company E, 137th Infantry, AEF, 1917-1919.* n.p., 1938.

Johnson, Thomas F. *Travels Over Here and Over There with "G" Company, 1915-1919: Being a Rambling and Somewhat Disconnected Homespun Tale of the Origin and History of Minneapolis' Own.* n.p., n.d.

138th Infantry Regiment

Fels, Daniel M. *History of "A" Company, 138th Infantry.* St. Louis: Woodward & Tierman, 1919.

History and Roster, Machine Gun Co., 138th Infantry. n.p., 1920.

139th Infantry Regiment

Kenamore, Clair *The Story of the 139th Infantry.* St. Louis, Missouri: Guard Publishing, 1920.

140th Infantry Regiment

Edwards, Evan A. *From Doniphan to Verdun: The Official History of the 140th Infantry.* Lawrence, Kansas: World, 1920.

Triplet, William S. *A Youth in the Meuse-Argonne: A Memoir, 1917-1918.* [Ed by Robert H. Ferrell] Columbia, Missouri: University of Missouri, 2000.

128th Field Artillery Regiment

Bucklew, Leslie. *The "Orphan Battery" and Operations, 128th U.S. Field Artillery (1st Missouri F.A.) with Notes on the Organization of Which Battery E Became a Part, and Various Commentary Extracts.* Cleveland, Ohio: H. M. White, 1921.

129th Field Artillery Regiment

Lee, Jay M. *The Artilleryman: The Experiences and Impressions of an American Artillery Regiment in the World War, 129th F.A., 1917-1919.* Kansas City, Missouri: Spencer, 1920.

130th Field Artillery Regiment

McLean, W.P. *My Story of the 130th F.A., A.E.F.* n.p., 1920.

110th Engineer Regiment

Gillette, George W. "The 110th Engineers 'Get It Done.'" *Military Engineer* (Sep/Oct 1926): pp. 424-25.

Rankin, E.P., Jr. "Combat Operations of 110th Engineers in the Meuse-Argonne Offensive." *Military Engineer* (Jul/Aug 1921): pp. 353-359.

—. *The Santa Fe Trail Leads to France: A Narrative of Battle Service of the 110th Engineers.* Kansas City, Missouri: Richardson, 1933.

The insignia of the 110th Sanitary Train.

Embroidered variety of the 129th Field Artillery Regiment insignia.

Felt on felt variety of the 130th Field Artillery Regiment insignia.

Felt on felt 128th Field Artillery Regiment.

Felt on felt 129th Machine Gun Battalion insignia.

Embroidered variety of the 130th Machine Gun Battalion insignia.

Embroidered 128th Machine Gun Battalion insignia.

Embroidered variety of the 130th Field Artillery Regiment insignia.

Felt on felt 137th Infantry Regiment insignia.

Felt on felt 138th Infantry Regiment insignia.

Embroidered 138th Infantry Regiment insignia.

Felt on wool 139th Infantry Regiment insignia.

German embroidered 140th Infantry Regiment insignia.

35th Division Headquarters felt on wool insignia.

35th Division Headquarters embroidered insignia.

Standard embroidered 35th Division insignia.

36th Infantry Division

The War Department directed the National Guard to form the 36th Division on July 18, 1917. This division was the former 15th National Guard Division and was renumbered to conform to the new configuration of division numbering under direction of the Army Staff. Concentration of the division began at Camp Bowie, Texas on August 17, 1917. The division was composed of troops from Oklahoma and Texas.[57]

Insignia:
The unit selected a light blue arrowhead point down, having an olive "T" upon it. The "T" representing the Texas troops and the arrowhead representing the Indian Territory, Oklahoma. It was approved November 12, 1918.[58] An alternate version exists with a blue star, representing the Lone Star State of Texas within a blue circle or letter "O" representing Oklahoma.

Campaigns:
Meuse-Argonne Offensive.[59]

Division Organization (1917-1919):[60]

71st Infantry Brigade:

36th Division Commander, Major General William R. Smith, Tronchow, France. December, 1918. Courtesy National Archives.

Sergeant Robert R. Cahal (standing second from left) Company C, 143rd Infantry Regiment, participates in machine gun training with the British Lewis Gun. Camp Bowie, Texas, 1918. Courtesy Military History Institute.

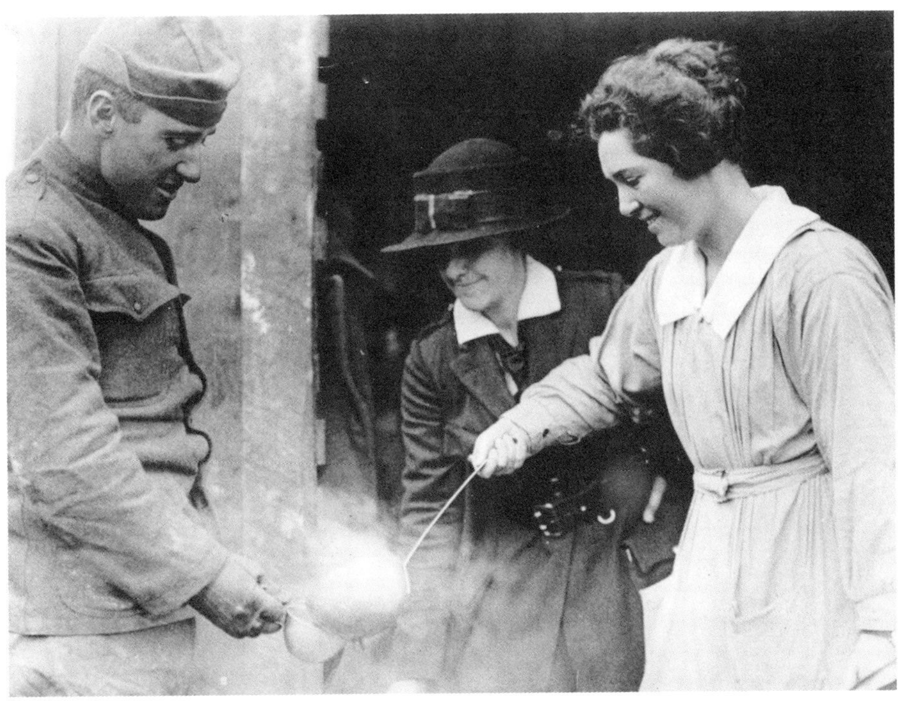

American Red Cross workers Adele Birdsall and Miss Thomas provide hot chocolate to a soldier of the 36th Division. Senoncourt, France, October, 1918. Courtesy National Archives.

Left: Private David Casanova. Courtesy Military History Institute.

A well executed all wool 36th Division insignia on a circular background.

141st Infantry Regiment
142nd Infantry Regiment
132nd Machine Gun Battalion

72nd Infantry Brigade:

143rd Infantry Regiment
144th Infantry Regiment
133rd Machine Gun Battalion

Division Troops:

131st Machine Gun Battalion

61st Field Artillery Brigade:

131st Field Artillery Regiment
132nd Field Artillery Regiment
133rd Field Artillery Regiment
111th Trench Mortar Battery

Embroidered 36th Division insignia on a square olive drab background.

Division Support:

111th Engineer Regiment
111th Field Signal Battalion
111th Train Headquarters and Military Police
111th Ammunition Train
111th Supply Train
111th Engineer Train
111th Sanitary Train (Ambulance Companies & Field Hospitals 141st, 142nd, 143rd, 144th)

36th Infantry Division Combat Narrative:[61]
The first units of the division arrived in France May 31st, 1918 and the last August 12, 1918.

Immediately upon arrival all units, with the exception of the artillery, were sent to the 13th Training Area in the vicinity of Bar-sur-Aube, where division headquarters were established on July 27. The 61st Field Artillery Brigade was detached and sent to Coetquidan, an artillery training camp in Brittany, where it remained throughout the period of hostilities.

The division was stationed at Bar-sur-Aube until September 26th at which time it moved by rail to the area between Epernay and Chalons and established headquarters at Pocancy, Department of the Marhe. Here it remained ten days, as a reserve of the French group of Armies of the Center, attached to the Fifth French Army for purposes of supply.

To the north, only a short distance, the Meuse-Argonne Offensive was under way. The American attack between the Argonne and the Meuse was being sided by the Fourth French Army in the Champagne just to the west. In the latter sector, the enemy stubbornly resisted every attack and on October 3rd the 36th was transferred to the Fourth French Army, with which the 2nd American Division was already serving.

On the night of October 4th units of the division began moving from the Pocancy Area to the vicinity of Suippes and Somme-Suippes.

The 71st Brigade began the relief of the 2nd Division on the night of October 6 on an irregular line about 4 kilometers long between St. Etienne and Medeah Farm facing generally north. Brigade headquarters were immediately established on Blanc Mont, approximately 5 kilometers northwest of Somme-Py.

The 71st Brigade attacked on the morning of October 8 with troops of the 2nd Division acting as reserves. The attack was a phase of an operation by the 2nd, 11th and 21st French Corps to extend the allied lines to Machault and Semide. The lines fluctuated, but the day's operation netted the brigade a substantial gain. Sixty-six officers and 1,227 men were lost during the day.

In the meanwhile, the remainder of the division moved from the Pocancy Area to the front and on the night of October 9, these units completed the relief of the infantry of the 2nd Division; the artillery of the latter division remaining in support of the 36th Division. The command of the sector passed to the 36th Division at 10 A.M., October 10. An attack of the 142nd Infantry north of St. Etienne failed that afternoon. However, the 141st succeeded in advancing its lines some 500 yards.

Between 5 and 6 o'clock P.M. the 72nd Brigade passed through the 71st and attacked in the direction of Machault and Cauroy. The attack resulted in a slight advance. The following morning, the enemy began his retreat to the north in the direction of Dricourt and Attigny. The 72nd Brigade took up the pursuit and lively rear guard actions followed between St. Etienne and Machault, which resulted in the encircling of the latter town and the establishment of lines to the north of it. The following day, the brigade pushed forward to Hill 167 northwest of Vaux Champagne, overlooking the valley of the Aisne from Attigny to Givry, from which positions patrols were pushed out to the canal.

A variation fully embroidered 36th Division insignia on a closely trimmed olive drab background.

The enemy was strongly entrenched on the northern bank of the Aisne and had taken every precaution to prevent a crossing. The 71st Brigade went into line on the 13th, taking over the front of the 73rd French Division to the east of the 72nd Brigade. The division's line at this time ran along the slope of Hill 167 approximately 4 kilometers from the Aisne. No further attempts to advance were made until the 27th when the strong Forest Farm was stormed and taken, the entire garrison being either killed or captured.

The relief of the 36th began on October 26 and was completed on October 28. The division was then assembled in the Suippes-Somme-Suippes area and from this point moved to the Triaucourt area and established headquarters at Condé-en-Barrois. Here it remained until the signing of the Armistice terms as a unit of the First American Army. In the Meuse-Argonne (Champagne) operation losses totaling 2513 were suffered.

The 111th Engineers was detached from the division September 10, 1917, and assigned as corps Engineers to the 1st American Army Corps. As such this organization participated in the St. Mihiel and Meuse-Argonne Offensives.

Shortly after the conclusion of hostilities the division moved to the 16th Training Area around Tonnerre and established headquarters at Cheney. Here it remained until April 26, 1919, when the first element started for a port of embarkation for return to this country.

Beautifully executed 36th Division insignia with a bullion embroidered "T" on wool arrowhead all on a circular wool background.

Days in the Front Line: 0 (training) 0 (sector) 19 (battle) for a total of 19. During operations the division took 549 prisoners and its casualties totaled 591 soldiers killed in action or died of wounds, 1,993 wounded in action.[62]

Division headquarters sailed from Brest May 23 and arrived at New York June 4.

The division had three different commanding Generals as follows: Brigadier General E. St. John Greble, Brigadier General George Blakely, and Major General William R. Smith.

Reference Bibliography:

General Division Histories:

American Battle Monuments Commission. *36th Division, Summary of Operations in the World War.* Washington, DC: Government Printing Office, 1944.

Chastaine, Ben H. *Story of the 36th: The Experiences of the 36th Division in the World War.* Oklahoma City: Harlow, 1920.

"Mann gegen masse." *Militar-Wochenblatt* (18 Jan 1931): p. 1039.

Maxfield, Bernice B. *Camp Bowie, Fort Worth, 1917-1918: An Illustrated History of the 36th Division In the First World War.* Fort Worth, Texas: Maxfield Foundation, 1975.

The Thirty-Sixth in the Great War. Paris: Arrowhead, Divisional Newspaper, A.E.F., 1919.

White, Lonnie J. *Forming the 36th Division in World War I.* Austin, Texas: Presidio Press, 1982.

—. *Panthers To Arrowheads: The 36th (Texas-Oklahoma) Division in World War I.* Austin, TX: Presidio Press, 1984.

142nd Infantry Regiment

Hart, Archibald. *Company K of Yesterday.* New York: Vantage, 1969.

37th Division Commander, Major General Charles S. Farnsworth in the Bois de Recicourt, France, September, 1918. Courtesy National Archives.

Sergeants Veda Thomas and Irl R. Lamport of the 145th Infantry Regiment pose for a studio portrait, April, 1919. Courtesy Military History Institute.

Opposite
Top: A Chauchat Gunner of Company F, 146th Infantry Regiment crosses a canal in Nedezwalem, Belguim. November, 13, 1918. Courtesy National Archives.

Bottom: 37th Division School, Second Class, Bayonet Fighting course. Note British Officer instructor in front row. Courtesy Military History Institute.

133rd Field Artillery Regiment

The Reconnaissance: 133rd Field Artillery, 2 der Kaiser. Camp Bowie, Texas: The Editors, 1919.

37th Infantry Division

The War Department directed the National Guard to form the 37th Division on July 18, 1917. This division was the former 16th National Guard Division and was renumbered to conform to the new configuration of division numbering under direction of the Army Staff. Concentration of the division began at Camp Sheridan, Alabama on August 3, 1917. The division was composed of troops from Ohio and West Virginia. The division took the name "Buckeye" division owing to the connection with the state of Ohio, the *Buckeye State*.[63]

Insignia:

The unit decided on a red disc bordered in white, the Buckeye symbol from the Ohio state flag. The design was approved November 5, 1918.[64]

Campaigns:

Ypres-Lys Offensive, Meuse-Argonne Offensive, Baccarat Sector, Pannes Sector, Thiaucourt and Troyon Sector, Troyon Sector.[65]

Division Organization (1917-1919):[66]

73rd Infantry Brigade:

145th Infantry Regiment
146th Infantry Regiment
135th Machine Gun Battalion

74th Infantry Brigade:

147th Infantry Regiment
148th Infantry Regiment
136th Machine Gun Battalion

Division Troops:

134rd Machine Gun Battalion

62nd Field Artillery Brigade:

134th Field Artillery Regiment
135th Field Artillery Regiment
136th Field Artillery Regiment
112th Trench Mortar Battery

Division Support:

112th Engineer Regiment
112th Field Signal Battalion
112th Train Headquarters and Military Police
112th Ammunition Train
112th Supply Train
112th Engineer Train
112th Sanitary Train (Ambulance Companies & Field Hospitals 145th, 146th, 147th, 148th)

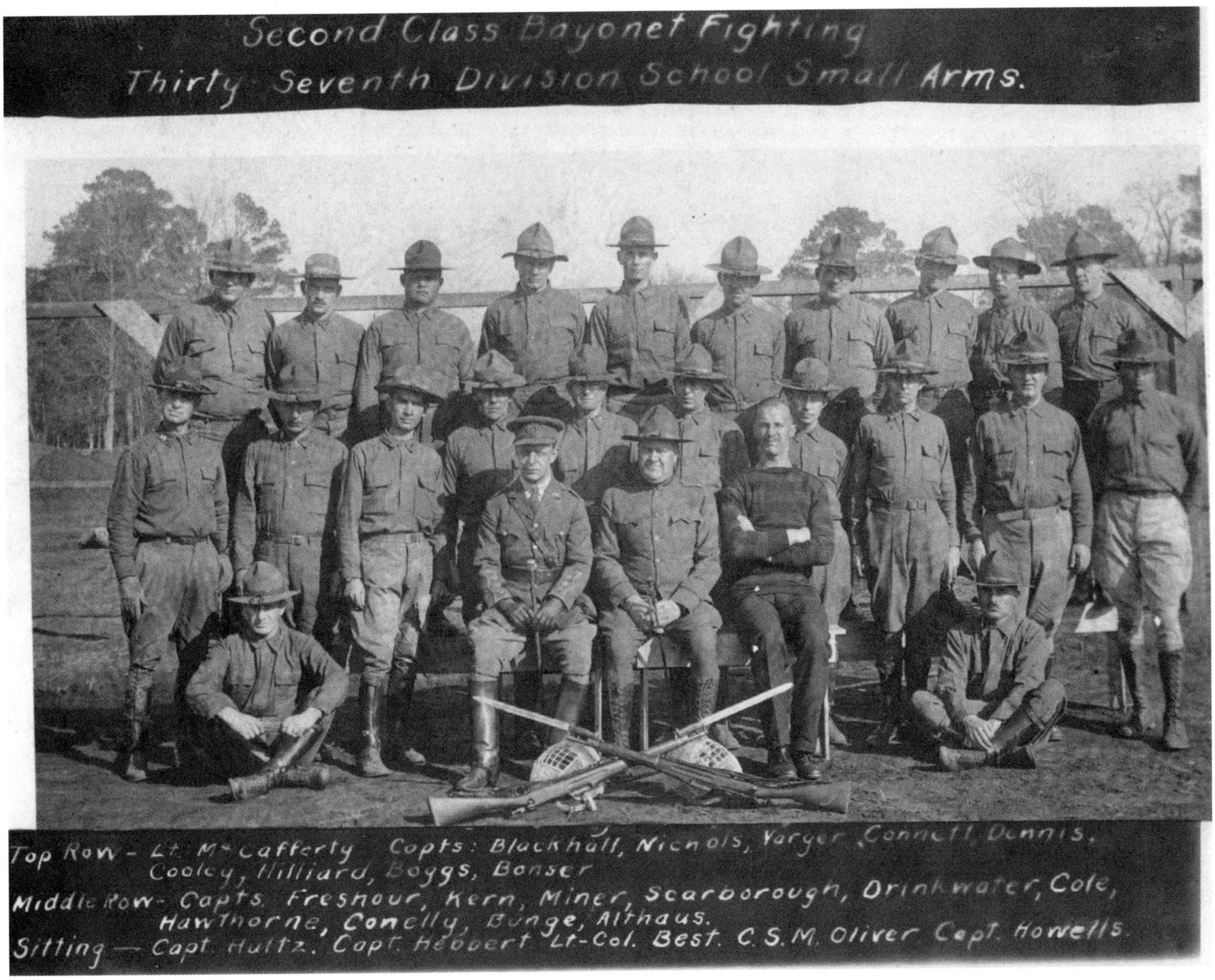
Second Class Bayonet Fighting
Thirty Seventh Division School Small Arms.
Top Row - Lt. McCafferty Capts: Blackhall, Nichols, Yarger, Connell, Dennis,
Cooley, Hilliard, Boggs, Bonser
Middle Row - Capts. Freshour, Kern, Miner, Scarborough, Drinkwater, Cole,
Hawthorne, Conelly, Bunge, Althaus.
Sitting — Capt. Hultz. Capt. Hebbert Lt-Col. Best. C.S.M. Oliver Capt. Howells.

Felt on felt 37th Division insignia.

Embroidered on felt insignia.

37th Infantry Division Combat Narrative:[67]

The first unit of the division arrived in France June 18, 1918 and the last July 21, 1918. All elements, with the exception of the artillery, were immediately dispatched to the Bourmont (Haute Marne) Area for preliminary training. For the same purpose the artillery was sent to Camp de Souge, near Bordeaux. It never rejoined the division during the period of hostilities, but participated in the Meuse-Argonne Offensive, serving successfully with the 4th American Corps, Second American Army, 2nd Colonial Army Corps (French) and the 17th French Army Corps.

The division remained in the Bourmont Area until the latter part of July at which time it entrained for the quiet Baccarat Sector in the Vosges. On August 4th front line trenches were occupied for the first time. The division was relieved in this Sector September 16th.

From Baccarat it moved to the area around the town of Robert-Espagne and after a rest of four days proceeded to Recicourt, department of the Meuse. Two days later the first elements of the division moved north to join in the Meuse-Argonne Offensive, soon to be launched. Division Headquarters were established at Verrieres-en-Hess Farm, four kilometers south of Avocourt.

The division was now a unit of the 5th Army Corps and on the night of September 24-25, took its position for the initial attack on a front of a little over three kilometers running east and west, and just north of Avocourt. From this line the division moved to the attack on the morning of September 26th, and rapidly advanced its lines during the first two days. The western edge of Montfaucon was entered by patrols of the 37th Division the night of September 26th. The town of Ivoiry was captured on the 27th, but on the 28th the resistance stiffened and the division was forced to extend itself to the utmost in its advance through Bois Emont, Bois de Beuge and to the Bois de Cierges. On October 1st it was relieved on a line just south of Cierges and retired to Pagny-sur-Meuse.

After a brief rest it was transported to the St. Mihiel Sector and headquarters were established at Euvezin. In this sector the division took over a line extending from the Bois de Hailbot, along the northern edge of the Bois de la Montagne and Bois de Charey to the southern edge of the Etang de Lachaussee. Although the sector was normally quiet the division was subjected to a heavy and continuous bombardment from the moment it entered. It was relieved in this sector on October 15th, and again moved to Pagny-sur-Meuse.

On the extreme left of the Allied front the Ypres-Lys Offensive was under way, and to this region the 37th was next sent. On October 22nd division headquarters were established at Hoogledge, Belgium, and the division was attached to the French Sixth Army, under command of General de Boissody, the group of armies being commanded by King Albert of Belgium. From Hoogledge successive moves were made to Lichtervelde, Meulebeke and to Denterghem. On the night of October 29-30 three kilometers of the front were taken over along the Courtrai-Ghent railroad, just across the Lys River, with Olsene approximately in front of the center. On October 31st an attack was launched from this position, and the enemy was forced back to Cruyshautem ridge, about half way between the Lys and Scheldt Rivers. Here he attempted to make a stand but failed, and was driven across the river on the same day. On November 2nd the crossing of the Scheldt was effected; on the 3rd a line was established on the east bank of the river and held against numerous counter-attacks.

The division was relieved on the 4th-5th and retired to Thielt front, and on November 9 headquarters were established at Chateau de Huysse. Another crossing of the river, this time between the villages of Asper and Heuvel, fifteen kilometers from Ghent, was the task assigned the 37th. The division came under a heavy fire as it approached the river; nevertheless a crossing was effected on the 10th and on the 11th the eastern bank was securely held by the Americans. The advance continued until 11 o'clock at with time the division's lines extended as far east as Dickele, Zwartenbrook Keerkem and Hundlegem.

Days in the Front Line: 7 (training) 57 (sector) 13 (battle) for a total of 77. During operations the division took 1,495 prisoners and its casualties totaled 1,066 soldiers killed in action or died of wounds, 4,321 wounded in action.[68]

After the signing of the Armistice the division started moving east; but just before reaching Brussels orders were received to turn back, and on December 7 headquarters were located at Hondschoote, France. Detachments of the division, however, participated in the entry of King Albert into Brussels.

From Hondschoote the 37th next moved to Wormhoudt and thence to Le Mans to embark for this country.

Division headquarters sailed March 15 and arrived at New York March 23.

The division had three commanding generals as follows: Brigadier General William R. Smith, Major General Charles G. Treat, and Major General Charles S. Farnsworth.

Fully chain stitched insignia with "37" and "AEF" designating the division number and the American Expeditionary Force.

Reference Bibliography:

General Division Histories:

American Battle Monuments Commission. *37th Division, Summary of Operations in the World War*. Washington, DC: Government Printing Office, 1944.

Belgium, Office Central D'Information. *The American Army in Belgium*. Brussels: Vromant, 1919.

Cole, Ralph D. *The Thirty-Seventh Division in the World War, 1919-1918*. Columbus, Ohio: Division Veterans Association, 1926.

The Thirty-Seventh's Bit in the World's War of 1914-1918: A Brief Story. n.p., 1918.

145th Infantry Regiment

Johnson, Ray N. *Heaven, Hell, or Hoboken*. Cleveland, Ohio: Hubbell, 1919.

148th Infantry Regiment

Cadwallader, William. *Major Conelly's Front Line Fighters, France, and Belgium: Glorious Record, First Battalion, 148th Infantry, 37th Division*. Cleveland, Ohio: Conelly, 1919.

134th Field Artillery Regiment

Battery D. Historical Committee. *Cease Firing: A History of Battery "D," 134th Field Artillery, U.S.N.G., A.E.F., Formerly Battery "D," 1st Ohio Field Artillery*. Dayton, Ohio: By the Committee, 1921.

135th Field Artillery Regiment

Mule Skinners: Supply Company, 135th Field Artillery, 62nd Brigade, 37th Division. Cleveland, Ohio: Evangelical Press, 1920.

U.S. Army, 135th Artillery Regiment, *Battery F, 135 F.A., A.E.F.*, n.p., 1919.

Witt, Fred R. *Riding to War with "A"; A History of Battery "A" of the 135th Field Artillery*. Cleveland, Ohio: C. Hauser, 1919.

136th Field Artillery Regiment

Coffin, Louis, & Sanders, Cameron H. *A History of the Third Field Artillery, Ohio National Guard, Which Served Through the World War, 1917, 1918, 1919 as the 136th F.A. Regiment, U.S.A., Including Chronicles and Composite Rosters of Its Individual Units with Certain Biographies*. Cincinnati, Ohio: Mounted Press, 1928.

112th Engineer Regiment

Brief History and Roster of Company "B", 112 Engineers, U.S.A., n.p., 1919.

Burdick, Roy. "Field Training of 112th Engineers." *Military Engineer* (Nov/Dec 1926): pp. 496-98.

Company A of the 112th U.S. Engineers with the American Expeditionary Forces in France and Belgium, 1918-1919. n.p., 1919.

Lieutenants E.G. Hamlin, and J.W. Brooks of the Machine Gun Company, 150th Infantry Regiment. St. Maurice, France, May, 1918. Courtesy National Archives.

38th Infantry Division

The War Department directed the National Guard to form the 38th Division on July 18, 1917. Concentration of the division began at Camp Shelby, Mississippi on August 3, 1917. The division was composed of troops from Indiana, Kentucky and West Virginia. This division was the former 17th National Guard Division and was renumbered to conform to the new configuration of division numbering under direction of the Army Staff. The division took the

name "Cyclone" owing to an incident during training. The winter of 1917 was one of the coldest on record for Mississippi, and in April, a cyclone whipped through Camp Shelby, killing Private Vaughn B. Beekman. Additionally, the monogram also represented the World War I era greeting of "Howdy, Cy."[69]

Opposite
Top: Soldiers of the Machine Gun Company of the 151st Infantry Regiment line up for inspection in France. Courtesy Military History Institute.

Bottom: Soldiers of the 151st Infantry Regiment, France. Courtesy Military History Institute.

Insignia:
The division chose a spade shaped shield, the left half blue, the right half red with a monogram of the letters "C" and "Y" for Cyclone in white. The insignia was approved October 31, 1918.[70]

Nicely executed fine wool 38th Division insignia.

Campaigns:
None.

Division Organization (1917-1919):[71]

75th Infantry Brigade:

149th Infantry Regiment
150th Infantry Regiment
138th Machine Gun Battalion

76th Infantry Brigade:

151st Infantry Regiment
152nd Infantry Regiment
139th Machine Gun Battalion

Division Troops:

137th Machine Gun Battalion

Embroidered 38th Division insignia.

63rd Field Artillery Brigade:

137th Field Artillery Regiment
138th Field Artillery Regiment
139th Field Artillery Regiment
113th Trench Mortar Battery

Division Support:

113th Engineer Regiment
113th Field Signal Battalion
113th Train Headquarters and Military Police
113th Ammunition Train
113th Supply Train
113th Engineer Train
113th Sanitary Train (Ambulance Companies & Field Hospitals 149th, 150th, 151st, 152nd)

A variation of a fully embroidered 38th Division insignia.

38th Infantry Division Service Narrative:[72]
The first unit of the division to go overseas arrived in France September 28, 1918; the last element October 25, 1918.

Upon arrival, the division (less artillery and engineers) was sent to a training area southeast of Nantes with headquarters at Reze. The 63rd Field Artillery Brigade and Ammunition Train went to the training center at Meucon, and the 113th Engineers to construction work in the Advance Section, Services of Supply, with headquarters at La Trecy near Langres. Early in November the division, having been designated a replacement organization was ordered skeletonized. All the infantry and machine gun units and the Supply Train were ordered to Le

Bullion on wool 38th Division insignia.

Mans where the personnel were used as replacements and distributed to various divisions. The permanent cadre of the division returned to the United States in December.

The division had commanding generals as follows: Major General William H. Sage, Brigadier General Edward M. Lewis, Brigadier General Henry H. Whitney, Brigadier General W. V. Judson, Brigadier General Frank M. Caldwell, and Major General Robert L. Howze.

Reference Bibliography:

General Division Histories:
None

139th Field Artillery Regiment
Moorhead, Robert L . *The Story of the 139th Field Artillery, American Expeditionary Forces.* Indianapolis, Indiana: Bobbs-Merrill, 1920.

113th Engineer Regiment
Souvenir Castle, 113th Engineers: Camp Shelby, Mississippi, August 1918. Hattiesburg, Mississippi: Dever, 1918.

39th Infantry Division

The War Department directed the National Guard to form the 39th Division on July 18, 1917. Concentration of the division began at Camp Beauregard, Louisiana on August 5, 1917. The division was composed of troops from Arkansas, Louisiana, and Mississippi. This division was the former 18th National Guard Division and was renumbered to conform to the new configuration of division numbering under direction of the Army Staff. The division took the name "Delta" division owing to its geographical proximity to the Mississippi River delta.[73]

Private Earl S. Hanix stands behind a tripod mounted Lewis Gun at Camp Beauregard, Louisiana, July 1918. Courtesy Military History Institute.

Insignia:
The division chose a blue triangular delta symbol representing the infantry inset with three smaller deltas representing the states of Arkansas, Louisiana, and Mississippi in red, white and blue. Another description of the patch states, "a white delta upon a black disc bordered red and placed upon a black square. Within the delta is a black delta, and in the center of the delta are four triangles, white, red, light blue and black. The whole design upon a black square." The insignia appears to have never been officially approved.[74]

Campaigns:
None. 114th Engineer Regiment and 114th Engineer Train - Meuse-Argonne Offensive.[75]

The 39th Division concentrated and conducted its initial training at Camp Beauregard, Louisiana. This scene shows the camp during that period. Courtesy Military History Institute.

Above: Brigadier General Ira A. Haynes and his staff of the 64th Field Artillery Brigade. Le Valdahon, France, February, 1919. Courtesy National Archives.

Below: Cadillac artillery tractor of Battery B, 140th Field Artillery Regiment, towing a field gun in training at Le Valdahon, France, February, 1919. Courtesy National Archives.

An embroidered on felt 39th Division insignia.

Embroidered on wool 39th Division insignia.

Wool on wool with soutache 39th Division insignia on a wool backing.

Division Organization (1917-1919):[76]

77th Infantry Brigade:

153rd Infantry Regiment
154th Infantry Regiment
141st Machine Gun Battalion

78th Infantry Brigade:

155th Infantry Regiment
156th Infantry Regiment
142nd Machine Gun Battalion

Division Troops:

140th Machine Gun Battalion

64th Field Artillery Brigade:

140th Field Artillery Regiment
141st Field Artillery Regiment
142nd Field Artillery Regiment
114th Trench Mortar Battery

Division Support:

114th Engineer Regiment
114th Field Signal Battalion
114th Train Headquarters and Military Police
114th Ammunition Train
114th Supply Train
114th Engineer Train
114th Sanitary Train (Ambulance Companies & Field Hospitals 153rd, 154th, 155th, 156th)

39th Infantry Division Service Narrative:[77]

The first unit of the division to go overseas arrived in France August 12, 1918; the last element September 12, 1918.

Upon arrival the division was sent to the St. Florent Area southwest of Bourges where it was designated as a replacement division. In November it moved to St. Aignan, and the personnel of most of the units were withdrawn and sent to other organizations leaving the

Fully embroidered 39th Division insignia on wool.

A fully embroidered 39th Division insignia with division number at center.

39th division skeletonized. With one exception the units of the division did not participate in combat operations, although a large number of the personnel were transferred to combat divisions, and took part in operations. The 114th Engineers participated in the Meuse-Argonne Offensive from October 3 to November 11, 1918. The 39th Division permanent cadre returned to the United States in December, 1918.

Commanding generals of the division were as follows: Major General Henry C. Hodges Jr., and Brigadier General Ira A. Haynes.

Reference Bibliography:

General Division Histories:
None.

155th Infantry Regiment
Mulvihill, M.J. *First Mississippi Regiment: Its Foundation, Organization, and Record-155th United States Infantry*. Vicksburg, Mississippi: Van Norman, 1931.

114th Engineer Regiment
Regimental Roster, 114th Engineers, First Army Corps, American Expeditionary Forces, France 1918-1919. France: n.p., 1919.

40th Infantry Division

The War Department directed the National Guard to form the 40th Division on July 18, 1917. Concentration of the division began at Camp Kearny, California on August 3, 1917. The division was composed of troops from Arizona, California, Colorado, Nevada, New Mexico, and Utah. This division was the former 19th National Guard Division and was renumbered to conform to the new configuration of division numbering under direction of the Army Staff. The division dubbed itself the "Sunshine" division in tribute to the abundant sunshine present in California.[78]

Insignia:
The division chose a sun in splendor with 12 rays, in yellow, on a blue square. The square was worn point up. The design alludes to the California sun and the blue field alludes to both the blue sky and Pacific Ocean. It was approved for wear on November 23, 1918.[79]

Campaigns:
None. 115th Field Signal Battalion and 115th Engineer Regiment: Toul Sector.[80]

Bottom left: Actress Mary Pickford (left) visits with the officers of the 143rd Field Artillery at Puente, California, 1918. Courtesy Military History Institute.

Below: Soldiers of the 145th Field Artillery Regiment clean the mud and rust from shells before firing. France, October, 1918. Courtesy National Archives.

Men of the 145th Field Artillery Regiment board the S.S. Santa Theresa at Bordeaux, France for the return trip to America. December 23, 1918. Courtesy National Archives.

Embroidered 40th Division insignia.

A variant of a fully embroidered 40th Division insignia.

Machine embroidered bullion 40th Division insignia.

Division Organization (1917-1919):[81]

79th Infantry Brigade:

157th Infantry Regiment
158th Infantry Regiment
144th Machine Gun Battalion

80th Infantry Brigade:

159th Infantry Regiment
160th Infantry Regiment
145th Machine Gun Battalion

Division Troops:

143rd Machine Gun Battalion

65th Field Artillery Brigade:

143rd Field Artillery Regiment
144th Field Artillery Regiment
145th Field Artillery Regiment
115th Trench Mortar Battery

Division Support:

115th Engineer Regiment
115th Field Signal Battalion
115th Train Headquarters and Military Police
115th Ammunition Train
115th Supply Train

Above: 40th Division troops at Camp Kearny, California, visit a field canteen . Courtesy Military History Institute.

115th Engineer Train
115th Sanitary Train (Ambulance Companies & Field Hospitals 157th, 158th, 159th, 160th)

40th Infantry Division Service Narrative:[82]

The first unit of the division to go overseas arrived in France August 12, 1918; the last element August 31, 1918.

Upon arrival in France the division (less Artillery, Engineers and Field Signal Battalion) was ordered to La Guerche (Cher), and became a replacement division. The 65th Artillery Brigade was sent to the training area at Camp de Souge (Gironde). The 115th Field Signal Battalion, and the 115th Engineers were detached from the division and participated in the operations of the 2nd Army in the Toul sector during October and November, 1918. Early in November the division was transferred to the 1st Army as a Regional Replacement Depot, with headquarters established at Revigny (Meuse). Division headquarters returned to the United States in February 1919.

The division commanding generals were as follows: Major General Frederick S. Strong, Brigadier General George H. Cameron and Brigadier General LeRoy S. Lyon.

A fine bullion example of the division insignia.

Reference Bibliography:

General Division Histories:

U.S. Army, 40th Infantry Division. *The Complete Roster of the Fortieth Division, Camp Kearny, California, November 15, 1917.* Camp Kearny, California: Milledge & Tyler, 1917.

History of the Fortieth (Sunshine) Division. Los Angeles, California: Hutson, 1920.

144th Field Artillery Regiment

California's Grizzlies. San Francisco, California: n.p., 1918.

Pioneer platoon, Headquarters Company, 164th Infantry Regiment, 41st Division and some of their equipment for laying barbed wire entanglements. 1st Corps School, Gondrecourt, France, August 16, 1918. Courtesy National Archives

41st Infantry Division

The War Department directed the National Guard to form the 41st Division July 18, 1917. Concentration of the division began at Camp Greene, North Carolina on September 19, 1917. It was composed of troops from Washington, Oregon, Montana, Idaho, Wyoming, Colorado, North Dakota, South Dakota, New Mexico, and District of Columbia.[83] This division was the former 20th National Guard Division and was renumbered to conform to the new configuration of division numbering under direction of the Army Staff. The division chose the sobriquet "Sunset Division" as a result of its' primarily western composition.

Insignia:
The unit selected a setting sun on a half circle of red above a horizontal blue stripe. This design suggests the Northwest Area of the United States with the blue representing the Pacific Ocean coupled with a red sunset. The AEF approved the design December 28, 1918.[84]

Campaigns:
None. 66th Field Artillery Brigade (minus 147th Field Artillery Regiment) Champagne-Marne Defensive, Aisne-Marne Offensive, St. Mihiel Offensive, Meuse-Argonne Offensive.[85]

Division Organization (1917-1919):[86]

81st Infantry Brigade:

161st Infantry Regiment
162nd Infantry Regiment
147th Machine Gun Battalion

82nd Infantry Brigade:

163rd Infantry Regiment
164th Infantry Regiment
148th Machine Gun Battalion

Division Troops:

146th Machine Gun Battalion

66th Field Artillery Brigade:

Below: Private Dewey A. Teall snapped this photo of men of Battery C, 147th Field Artillery Regiment engaged in a "Cootie Hunt" in France, 1918. Courtesy Military History Institute.

Bottom right: Major General Peter E. Traub (left) prepares to take command of the 41st Division from Brigadier General Eli K. Cole, United States Marine Corps, who is receiving the review of the division. St. Romaine, France, January, 1919. Courtesy National Archives.

Above: The men of the 41st Division Football Team, all drawn from Company A, 162nd Infantry Regiment, pose at Camp Mills, New York, July, 1917. Courtesy Military History Institute.

Left: The Fire Department at St. Nazaire France, January, 1918. Composed of men drawn from Companies A, B, C, and D, 162nd Infantry Regiment. Courtesy Military History Institute.

146th Field Artillery Regiment
147th Field Artillery Regiment
148th Field Artillery Regiment
116th Trench Mortar Battery

Division Support:

116th Engineer Regiment
116th Field Signal Battalion
116th Train Headquarters and Military Police
116th Ammunition Train
116th Supply Train
116th Engineer Train
116th Sanitary Train (Ambulance Companies & Field Hospitals 161st, 162nd, 163rd, 164th)

41st Infantry Division Service Narrative:[87]
The first unit of the division to go overseas arrived in France, December 27, 1917; the last element February 6, 1918. Upon arrival the division was designated as the 1st Depot Division, and was ordered to the St. Aignan training area. The 66th Field Artillery Brigade (less 147th F.A.) was detached and after a period of training at Camp de Souge and Libourne it was attached to the 1st Corps July 1, 1918. The brigade performed duty as corps and army artillery throughout its service in France, and was actively engaged in the Champagne-Marne Defensive, Aisne-Marne Offensive, St. Mihiel Offensive, and the Meuse-Argonne Offensive. After the Armistice it was assigned to the Army of Occupation in Germany.

Days in the Front Line: 0 (training) 0 (sector) 0 (battle) for a total of 0. During operations its casualties totaled 93 soldiers killed in action or died of wounds, 315 wounded in action.[88]

The division (less 66th Artillery Brigade) remained in the St. Aignan area until February 1919 when it returned to the United States.

The commanding generals of the division were as follows: Major General Hunter Liggett, Brigadier General Henry Jervey, Brigadier General LeRoy Irwin, Brigadier General Richard Coulter, Jr., Brigadier General Robert Alexander, Brigadier General Edward Vollrath, Brigadier General William S. Scott, Major General John E. McMahon, Brigadier General Eli K. Cole (USMC) and Major General Peter E. Traub.

Nicely made wool on wool 41st Division insignia.

Hand embroidered 41st Division insignia on felt with a wool background.

Bullion 41st Division insignia on velvet with wool surround.

Reference Bibliography:

General Division Histories:
None.

147th Field Artillery Regiment:

South Dakota Adjutant General Office, *Record of Service of 147th Field Artillery in France to 11th November 1918*. Pierre, South Dakota: n.p., 1919.

148th Field Artillery Regiment:

Davis, Paul M., & Clay, Hubert K. *History of Battery "C," 148th Field Artillery, American Expeditionary Forces, Written in Germany*. Colorado Springs, Colorado: Out West, 1919.

116th Engineer Regiment:

Bachman, Harold. *The Million Dollar Band: The Story of the Band of the 116th Regiment of Engineers, 41st (Sunset) Division, American Expeditionary Forces; The Original Million Dollar Band in World War I and the Professional Concert Band Which Succeeded It Under the Title of Bachman's Million Dollar Band*. Chicago: Ed Music Bureau, 1962.

Hough, Chester C. "116th Engineers, Idaho National Guard." *Military Engineer* (Sep/Oct 1927).

42nd Division Commander Major General Charles T. Menoher (far right) watches practice maneuvers at Division Headquarters, Baccarat, France, May, 1918. Colonel Douglas MacArthur, Division Chief of Staff is in the foreground looking up. In November of 1918 as a Brigadier General, he would command the division. Courtesy National Archives.

42nd Infantry Division

The 42nd Division was a composite division activated on November 1, 1917 at Camp Mills, New York. The division was formed from National Guard units from twenty-six states (Alabama, California, Colorado, Georgia, Illinois, Indiana, Iowa, Kansas, Louisiana, Maryland, Michigan, Minnesota, Missouri, Nebraska, New Jersey, New York, North Carolina, Ohio, Oklahoma, Oregon, Pennsylvania, South Carolina, Tennessee, Texas, Virginia, Wisconsin) and the District of Columbia. This division formed the first composite National Guard Division; to clearly represent this, Division leadership chose "Rainbow Division" as the division nickname. Then Major Douglas MacArthur noted; "As I remember, one of the correspondents spoke up and said, 'Rainbow – there's the name for the division – I shall call it the Rainbow in my dispatch.' I believe a number of others adopted this idea. So that the first composite division was announced to the country as 'The Rainbow Division.' We promptly took up the name in the War Department as a convenient means of designating this as yet unnumbered division."[89]

Insignia:

The division chose the Rainbow, whose various colors symbolized the numerous states from the National Guard who made up the division. General Orders Number 34, Headquarters First Army, AEF dated November 14, 1918 specified, "1 inch quarter circle band of three colors, 1-3 inch wide each of blue, yellow and red."[90] The design was first approved October 29, 1918.[91]

Major General Clement A. F. Flagler poses with his staff as Division Commander in Ahrweiler, Germany, January, 1919. Courtesy National Archives.

Campaigns:

Champagne-Marne Defensive, Aisne-Marne Offensive, St. Mihiel Offensive, Meuse-Argonne Offensive, Esperance-Souain Sector, Essey and Pannes Sector, Luneville Sector

Division Organization (1917-1919):[92]

83rd Infantry Brigade:

165th Infantry Regiment
166th Infantry Regiment
150th Machine Gun Battalion

84th Infantry Brigade:

167th Infantry Regiment
168th Infantry Regiment
151th Machine Gun Battalion

Division Troops:

149th Machine Gun Battalion

67th Field Artillery Brigade:

149th Field Artillery Regiment
150th Field Artillery Regiment
151th Field Artillery Regiment
117th Trench Mortar Battery

Division Support:

117th Engineer Regiment
117th Field Signal Battalion
117th Train Headquarters and Military Police
117th Ammunition Train
117th Supply Train
117th Engineer Train
117th Sanitary Train (Ambulance Companies & Field Hospitals 165th, 166th, 167th, 168th)

42nd Infantry Division Combat Narrative:[93]
The first unit of the division to go overseas arrived in France November 1, 1917; the last element arrived December 3, 1917.

For training purposes the division (less artillery) was sent to the Vaucouleurs Area, and then to the Rimaucourt and Rolemoont Areas, successively. For the same purpose the artillery brigade went to Coetquidan rejoining the division in the Rolampont Area in the middle of February. With the exception of three short periods when it supported the 4th, 32nd, and 2nd Divisions, successively, the artillery brigade served continuously with the 42nd Division throughout operations.

To complete its training, the division was attached to the French 7th Army Corps in the Luneville sector, February 21, 1918, and its units participated in raids of major and minor importance and the routine of trench warfare. On March 31st, the division took over the Baccarat Sector relieving the 123rd Division (French) in line. On June 21st, the division was withdrawn and proceeded to the east of Reims, where it took part in the Champagne-Marne Defensive in the Fourth French Army under General Gouraud. The division occupied the support line, but the German attack of July 15th penetrated the front-line positions, enabling the division's artillery, and a part of its infantry to become actively engaged in the operation.

On July 17th, the division was withdrawn and proceeded to the vicinity of Château Thierry. From July 25th to August. 3rd 1918, the division participated in the Aisne-Marne Offensive as part of the 1st Army Corps, capturing Croix Rouge Farms and Sergy, and engaging in other severe fighting at the crossing Ourcq.

In the St. Mihiel Offensive, September 12 to 16, 1918, the division was in the attacking line of the 4th Army Corps. It remained in front line position in the Essey and Pannes Sector until September 30th, when it was withdrawn and moved to the region south of Verdun, and became part of the reserve of the First Army.

In the Meuse-Argonne Offensive, the division relieved the 1st Division, 5th Army Corps, in the front line, north of Exermont on October 13, 1918. October 14th and 15th the division attacked and captured Hill 288, Hill 242, Tuilerie Farm and the Cote de Chatillou, thereby breaking through that part of the Hindenburg Line known as the Siellung. On October 31st the division was relieved by the 2nd Division and passed to reserve of the 1st Army Corps. On November 5th the division again attacked from the line Verrieres-Brieulles-sur-Bar, and captured the heights dominating the Meuse and Sedan on November 7th. On November 10th the relief of the division by the 77th Division was completed.

Major General Flagler wearing his field uniform in Ahrweiler, Germany, January, 1919. Note his use of a French Artillery helmet with his two general's stars attached. Courtesy National Archives.

Colonel William J. Donovan, Commander of the 165th Infantry Regiment, poses with Chaplain Francis P. Duffy. Remagen, Germany, May, 1919. Courtesy National Archives.

Days in the Front Line: 31 (training), 100 (sector), 45 (battle) for a total of 176. During Operations the division took 1,317 prisoners and its causalities totaled 2,810 soldiers killed in action or died of their wounds, 11,873 were wounded in action.[94]

After the Armistice the division was assigned to the Army of Occupation and began its march on November 20th. The first troops of the division crossed into Germany on December 2nd. Headquarters were established at Ahrweiler and remained there until the division returned to the United States.

Division Headquarters sailed from Brest on April 17, 1919 and arrived at New York on April 26, 1919.

The Division Commanding Generals were: Major General William A. Mann, Major General Charles T. Menoher, Brigadier General Douglas MacArthur, Major General Clement A.F. Flagler, Brigadier General George G. Gatley, and Major General George W. Read.

Serving in this division was perhaps the single most famous National Guard Regiment – the 69th New York, "The Fighting 69th" which became the 165th Infantry Regiment. This included a number of noted individuals: Colonel William F. "Wild Bill" Donovan, Father Francis P. Duffy, and Sergeant Joyce Kilmer.

Private Hugh F. McGriskin, Company L, 165th Infantry hams it up with some lady friends at Camp Mills, New York. Courtesy Military History Institute.

Standard fully embroidered example of the division insignia.

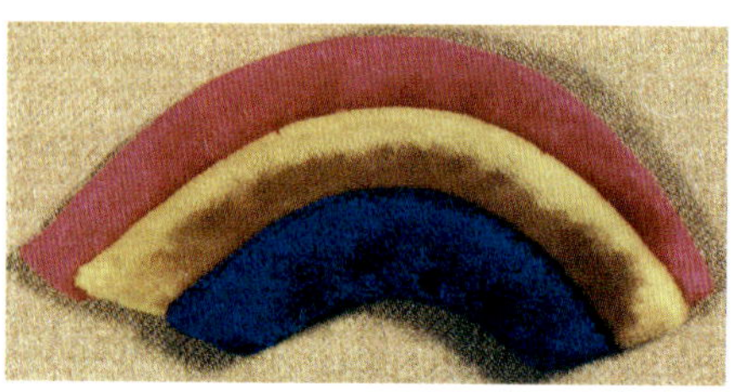

Velvet example of the 42nd Division rainbow.

Reference Bibliography:

General Division Histories:

American Battle Monuments Commission. *42nd Division Summary of Operations in the World War*. Washington, DC: The United States Government Printing Office, 1944.

Goode, J. Roy. *The American Rainbow*. The Straus Company "Economic" Printers and Stationers, 1918.

Johnson, Lieut. Harold Stanley. *Roster of the Rainbow Division (Forty-Second)* New York: Eaton & Gettinger, Inc., 1917.

Riley, Henry J. *Americans All: The Rainbow at War: Official History of the 42nd Rainbow Division in the World War*. Columbus, Ohio: The F.J. Heer Printing Company, 1936.

Sherwood, Elmer W. *Diary of a Rainbow Veteran*. Terre Haute, Indiana: Moore-Langen Company, 1929.

Tompkins, Raymond Sidney. *The Story of the Rainbow Division*. New York: Boni and Liveright, 1919.

Wolf, Walter B. *A Brief Story of the Rainbow Division*. New York: Rand, McNally & Co, 1919.

165th Infantry Regiment

Army Times. *The Daring Regiments: Adventures of the AEF in World War I*. New York: Dodd, Mead, 1967.

Bishop, Jim & Bishop, Virginia. *Fighting Father Duffy*. New York: Vision Books, 1956.

Duffy, Francis P., & Kilmer, Joyce. *Father Duffy's Story: A Tale of Humor and Heroism, of Life and Death with the Fighting Sixty-Ninth*. Garden City, New York: Garden City Publishing, 1919.

Ettinger, Albert M., & Ettinger, A. Churchill. *A Doughboy With the Fighting Sixty-Ninth: A Remembrance of World War I*. Shippensburg, Pennsylvania: White Mane, 1992.

Hogan, Martin J. *The Shamrock Battalion of the Rainbow: A Story of the "Fighting Sixty-Ninth"*. New York: Appleton, 1919.

Mahon, John. *New York's Fighting Sixty-Ninth: A Regimental History of Service in the Civil War's Irish Brigade and the Great War's Rainbow Division*. Jefferson, North Carolina: McFarland, 2004.

YMCA (NY). *The National War Work Council Y.M.C.A. Cordially Greets the Heroes of the 165th Infantry (the Old 69th N.Y.)*. New York: YMCA, 1919.

166th Infantry Regiment

Cheseldine, Raymond M. *Ohio in the Rainbow: Official Story of the 166th Infantry, 42nd Division, in the World War*. Columbus, Ohio: Heer, 1924.

Reppy, Alison. *Rainbow Memories: Character Sketches and History of the First Battalion, 166th Infantry, 42nd Division, American Expeditionary Forces*. New York: Carey, 1919.

167th Infantry Regiment

Amerine, William H. *Alabama's Own in France*. New York: Eaton & Gettinger, 1919.

42nd Division insignia embroidered on wool with a variant rainbow including many additional color bands.

168th Infantry Regiment

Rainbow Division Veterans Association. *Rainbow Division Veterans Association -Iowa, Twenty-Second Annual Reunion, Council Bluffs, Iowa, March 4-5, 1940*. Des Moines, Iowa: Skilling, 1940.

Robb, Winfred E. *The Price of Our Heritage: In Memory of the Heroic Dead of the 168th Infantry*. Des Moines, Iowa: American Litho, 1919.

Taber, John H. *The Story of the 168th Infantry*. Iowa City, Iowa: State Historical Society, 1925.

149th Field Artillery Regiment

Albert, Warren J. *Battery "A" in France, 1917-1918*. n.p., 19??.

Being the Story of a Light Field Artillery Battery From Illinois During the World War. Saint Louis: Gunthrop-Warren, 1930.

Johnson, Harold S. *Roster of the Rainbow Division (Forty-second) Major General Wm. A. Mann Commanding*. New York: Eaton & Gettinger, 1917. pp. 109-36.

Kilner, Frederic R. *Battery E in France: 149th Field Artillery, Rainbow (42nd) Division*. Chicago: n.p., 1919.

Langille, Leslie. *Men of the Rainbow*. Chicago: O'Sullivan Pub House, 1933.

This example features colored soutache sewn in bands to create the rainbow.

150th Field Artillery Regiment

Johnson, Harold S. *Roster of the Rainbow Division (Forty-second) Major General Wm. A. Mann Commanding*. New York: Eaton & Gettinger, 1917.

Straub, Elmer F. *A Sergeant's Diary in the World War: The Diary of an Enlisted Member of the 150th Field Artillery (Forty-second "Rainbow" Division) October 27, 1917, to August 7, 1919*. Indianapolis, Indiana: Indiana History Committee, 1923.

U.S. Army. 150th Artillery Regiment. Battery F. *Under the Rainbow: A History of Its Service in the War Against Germany, Battery F, 150th F.A.* Indianapolis, Indiana: By the Battery, 1919.

151st Field Artillery Regiment

Collins, Louis L. *History of the 151st Field Artillery, Rainbow Division*. [Ed by Wayne E. Stevens] St. Paul, Minnesota: McGill-Warner, 1924.

Johnson, Harold S. *Roster of the Rainbow Division (Forty-second) Major General Wm. A. Mann Commanding*. New York: Eaton & Gettinger, 1917.

Leach, George E. *War Diary*. Minneapolis, Minnesota: Pioneer Printers, 1923.

Peterson, Wilbur C. *Soldier WWI*. Las Vegas, Nevada: W.C. Peterson, 1988.

Weiler, Harold J. "Development of the National Guard." *Quartermaster Review* (Mar/Apr 1935).

Lieutenant Colonel Florence, 166th Infantry Regiment, Major R.C. Allen, 165th Infantry Regiment and staff leaving dugout for inspection of the front lines at Blemerey, France. Courtesy National Archives

117th Engineer Regiment

Sadler, E.J. *California Rainbow Memories: A Pictorial Review of the Activities of the 2nd Battalion, 117th Engineers During the World War*. n.p.,1925.

117th Trench Mortar Battery

Stansbury, Henry D. *Maryland's 117th Trench Mortar Battery in the World War, 1917-1919*. Baltimore, Maryland: Rainbow Division, 1942.

CHAPTER FIVE

THE NATIONAL ARMY DIVISIONS

Opposite
Top: The Band of the 303rd Infantry Regiment performs in front of the Palais des Fetes de Paris, Paris, France, November, 1918. Courtesy National Archives.

Bottom: Batteries A, B, C, and D of the 302nd Field Artillery Regiment pass in review, 1918. Courtesy National Archives.

Below: First Lieutenant John J. Maginnis poses with his "French Sweetheart" Jacqueline Punchon, at Biguy, France, July, 1918. Courtesy Military History Institute.

76th Infantry Division

The War Department established the division on August 5, 1917 at Camp Devens, Massachusetts. The division was composed of draftees from Connecticut, Maine, Massachusetts, New Hampshire, New York, Rhode Island and Vermont. The division was known as the "Liberty Bell" or "New England" Division.[1]

Insignia:
The division initially chose as its insignia a blue liberty bell superimposed on a khaki square; this was never officially approved. Later, the division selected a shield, bordered olive drab and divided by an olive drab or white bar into blue (upper) and red portions. A white "label" on the blue part heraldically denotes the "eldest son", significant of the fact that the 76th was the first numerically of the draft divisions; that is the eldest son of the Regular Army and National Guard Divisions. The design was approved March 14, 1919.[2] A variant exists with a sailing ship upon a five-pointed black star.

Campaigns:
None.

Division Organization (1917-1919):[3]

151st Infantry Brigade:

301st Infantry Regiment
302nd Infantry Regiment
302nd Machine Gun Battalion

152nd Infantry Brigade:

303rd Infantry Regiment
304th Infantry Regiment
303rd Machine Gun Battalion

Division Troops:

301st Machine Gun Battalion

LISTEN LESTER
Bond Bread

Company I, 301st Infantry Regiment pose at Versailles, France, June, 1918. Courtesy Military History Institute.

The standard 76th Division insignia of felt on felt construction.

151st Field Artillery Brigade:
301st Field Artillery Regiment
302nd Field Artillery Regiment
303rd Field Artillery Regiment
301st Trench Mortar Battery

Division Support:

301st Engineer Regiment
301st Field Signal Battalion
301st Train Headquarters and Military Police
301st Ammunition Train
301st Supply Train
301st Engineer Train
301st Sanitary Train (301st, 302nd, 303rd, 304th Ambulance Companies & Field Hospitals)

Division Service Narrative:[4]
The first unit of the division to go overseas arrived in France, July 10, 1918; the last element August 8, 1918. Upon arrival the division was designated as the 3rd Depot Division, and ordered to an area south of Bourges with headquarters at St. Amand-Mont-Rand, where it was broken up, training cadres were formed and the personnel were used as replacements for units at the front. The artillery brigade trained at Clermont-Ferrand (Puy-de-Dôme.). The 301st Engineer Regiment was detached from the division and assigned to duty with the 4th Corps under which it participated in the St. Mihiel offensive. The 301st Field Signal Battalion was detached and assigned to the 6th Corps under which command it participated in combat operations in the Marbache Sector until the Armistice. Upon completing its training the 151st Field Artillery Brigade (less 301st F.A.) was assigned to the 2nd Army. On arrival in the advanced zone it was attached to the French Second Colonial Corps in the Troyon Sector. On November 5th it passed to the French Seventeenth Army Corps and as corps artillery supported the action of the 33rd and 81st Divisions until the armistice. On November 13th it passed to the American 4th Corps.

Far left: An interesting variant of the insignia with silver numbers denoting the division attached in the field of the insignia.

Left: The alternate 76th division insignia featured a Liberty Bell; this example is embroidered on wool.

Below: Another design of the 76th Division insignia features a white ship placed upon a blue star all on a red circular field.

Days in the Front Line: 0 (training) 0 (sector) 0 (battle) for a total of 0. During operations the division took no prisoners and its casualties totaled 4 soldiers killed in action or died of wounds, 22 wounded in action.[5]

Headquarters and the division permanent cadre returned to the United States in December, 1918.

The division had two commanding generals: Major General Henry F. Hodges, and Brigadier General William Weigel.

Reference Bibliography:

General Division Histories:
None.

301st Field Artillery Regiment:
U.S. Army, 302nd Field Artillery Regiment. *The 302nd Field Artillery, United States Army*. Cambridge, Massachusetts: 302nd Field Artillery Association, 1919.

301st Engineer Regiment:
U.S. Army, 301st Engineer Regiment. *Company Book, D. Co., 301st Engineers, A.E.F.* n.p., 1919.
—. *"E" Company, 301st Engineers*. n.p., 1919.
—. *The Three Hundred and First Engineers: A History, 1917-1919*. New York: Houghton Mifflin, 1920.
—. *A Short History of the 301st Engineers: Being a Reprint of the History Appearing in the New Year's Edition of the "Topo Zeitung" With Slight Revisions and an Additional Chapter of Activities of the Regiment Since January 1st, 1919*. Germany: 301st Engineers Topographical Office, 1919.
—. Co. F. *Company F, Three Hundred and First Engineers*. n.p., 1919.
—. Co. G. *301 Engineers, Company D*. n.p., 1919.

Major Charles Whittlesey (right) Commander of the 308th Infantry Regiment, the "Lost Battalion", confers with Major Kenny of the 307th Infantry Regiment, whose 3rd Battalion was the first to relieve Whittlesley's men. Near Apremont, France, October 29, 1918. Courtesy National Archives.

77th Infantry Division

The War Department established the division on August 5, 1917 at Camp Upton, New York. The division drew its draftee soldiers from New York City and adjoining counties. The division took the name "Metropolitan" or "Liberty" Division as a result of its New York City roots.[6]

OFFICERS CO. I 305th INF. CAMP UPTON
622

Insignia:
The division selected as an insignia a patch with a flag blue background of truncated triangle shape, with a gold Statue of Liberty to denote that the division's personnel came from New York City.[7]

Campaigns:
Oisne-Aisne, Meuse-Argonne Offensive, Baccarat Sector, Vesle Sector.[8]

Division Organization (1917-1919):[9]

153rd Infantry Brigade:

305th Infantry Regiment
306th Infantry Regiment
305th Machine Gun Battalion

154th Infantry Brigade:

307th Infantry Regiment
308th Infantry Regiment
306th Machine Gun Battalion

Division Troops:

304th Machine Gun Battalion

152nd Field Artillery Brigade:

304th Field Artillery Regiment
305th Field Artillery Regiment
306th Field Artillery Regiment
302nd Trench Mortar Battery

Division Support:

302nd Engineer Regiment
302nd Field Signal Battalion
302nd Train Headquarters and Military Police
302nd Ammunition Train
302nd Supply Train
302nd Engineer Train
302nd Sanitary Train (305th, 306th, 307th, 308th Ambulance Companies & Field Hospitals)

Division Combat Narrative:[10]
The first unit of the division arrived in France April 12, 1918; the last, May 12, 1918.

For purposes of training the division (less artillery) was attached to the 39th British Division in the vicinity of Eperlecques (Pas-de-Calais). For the same purposes the artillery brigade was sent to Camp de Souge near Bordeaux. It rejoined the division in the Baccarat Sector July 12, and remained with it throughout combat operations. On June 11th the division proceeded by train to the Vosges, and on June 21st entered the line in the Baccarat Sector brigaded with the French. On August 4th it was relieved in the line by the 37th Division and marched to le Charme where it entrained August 6th for the Château-Thierry area.

On August 12th the division relieved the 62nd French and the 4th American Divisions in the Vesle Sector on a line south of and parallel to the Vesle River from Mont Notre Dame through St. Thibaut and Ville-Savoye in the direction of Fismes, a front of approximately five kilometers.

Opposite
Top: Major General Robert L. Alexander and the 77th Division staff pose in France, 1919. Courtesy Military History Institute.

Center: Survivors of the "Lost Battalion after their relief. Major Whittlesey is standing on the far left. Near Apremont, France, 1918. Courtesy National Archives.

Bottom: Officers of Company I, 305th Infantry Regiment in front of their barracks at Camp Upton, Long Island, New York, 1918. Courtesy Military History Institute.

The standard 77th Division insignia; this example is embroidered on wool.

77th Division insignia in Liberty Loan pattern; this style was issued as a premium for donors to the Third Liberty Loan, photographic evidence supports the use of Liberty Loan insignia by soldiers. The variant insignia incorporates a star atop Miss Liberty's hand.

Another version of the "Star in Hand" 77th Division insignia of embroidered on felt construction.

A nicely executed bullion example of the 77th Division insignia.

The Oise-Aisne Offensive commenced on August 18th, but it was not until the first days of September, when the enemy began to retire, that an advance was made by the division. On September 4th the Vesle was crossed and Bazoches, Fismes and Perles were taken. When the division was relieved on the night of September 15-16 by Italian troops the line ran from Vieil-Arcy through Villers-en-Prayères southeast to a point south of Glennes.

From the Vesle the division moved to the Argonne Sector, and on September 18th headquarters were established at Givry-en-Argonne. The 77th was assigned to the 1st Corps, which was the left flank corps of the 1st Army. In turn the 77th was assigned to the left flank of the corps sector. Its line ran from a point north of La Harazoe southeast and east for a distance of seven kilometers with the Argonne Forest directly in its front.

The plan of the Meuse-Argonne offensive called for an advance by the troops on the right and left of the 77th Division for the purpose of flanking the forest, thus permitting the 77th to advance. In the initial attack of September 26th it advanced rapidly, but opposition stiffened on the 27th, and even with the assistance offered on both flanks the problem of forcing the forest became increasingly difficult. The division fought its way through heavy woods, and dense underbrush which covered a terrain of hills and ravines that afforded the enemy many obstacles and natural defenses. On October 2nd, six companies of the 308th Infantry advanced farther than the flank units and became isolated from their command near Chârlevaux Mill. Although surrounded, these troops refused to surrender, but held out against every hardship until relieved on October 7th.

On the 9th, the division began to emerge from the forest, and on the 11th the Aire River was reached. St. Juvin on the right of the line was entered after severe fighting on October 14th, and Grand-Pré on the left was attacked and entered the morning of October 16th. The relief of the 77th Division the same day left the complete capture and consolidation of the town to the relieving unit, the 78th Division.

From October 16th to 30th the Division occupied a rest camp in the Argonne Forest between Grand-Pré and St. Juvin.

On the night of October 30-31 it relieved part of the 82nd Division on a line just south of Champigneulle preparatory to the general advance, which took place November 1st. Stubborn resistance was encountered in the vicinity of Champigneulle, but after this town fell on November 2nd, pursuit was rapid, and little resistance was met. After reaching Stonne, the advance turned to the northeast and on November 6th the Meuse River and the heights overlooking Sedan were reached. On November 9th the front occupied by the division extended from Pont-Maugis three and one-half kilometers south of Sedan to Meuzon, a distance of approximately eleven kilometers.

Days in the Front Line: 25 (training) 31 (sector) 63 (battle) for a total of 119. During operations the division took 750 prisoners and its casualties totaled 2,110 soldiers killed in action or died of wounds, 8,084 wounded in action.[11]

After the Armistice the division was sent to the 9th Training Area with headquarters established at Chateauvillain. Here it remained until it returned to the United States. Headquarters sailed from Brest on April 17th, and arrived at New York April 25, 1919.

The division commanders were: Major General J. Franklin Bell, Brigadier General Evan M. Johnson, Major General George B. Duncan, and Major General Robert Alexander.

Serving in this division was the well known "Lost Battalion" under the command of Major Charles Whittlesey. Although cut off for 5 days from the remainder of his division, Major Whittlesey maintained his position, which he had reached under orders received for an advance, and held the command, consisting originally of 46 officers and men of the 308th Infantry and of Company K of the 307th Infantry, together in the face of superior numbers of the enemy during the 5 days. Major Whittlesey and two other officers; Captain George McMurtry and Captain Nelson M. Holderman received the Medal of Honor for this action.

Reference Bibliography:

General Division Histories:

American Battle Monuments Commission. *77th Division, Summary of Operations in the World War.* Washington, DC: Government Printing Office, 1944.

Milhan, Charles G. *"Atta Boy!": The Story of New York's 77th Division, U.S.A.* New York: Brooklyn Daily Eagle, 26 January 1919.

Smith, Herbert E. "A.E.F. Divisional Insignia – The 77th Division." *Recruiting News* (1 May 1935): p. 3.

U.S. Army, 77th Infantry Division. *History of the Seventy Seventh Division, August 25th 1917 - November 11th 1918*. New York: 77th Division Association 1919.

—. *Roster of Officers, Seventy-seventh Division*. n.p., 1919.

305th Infantry Regiment:

Tiebout, Frank B. *A History of the 305th Infantry*. New York: 305th Infantry Auxiliary, 1919.

306th Infantry Regiment:

Adler, Julius O. *History of the 3 06th Infantry*. New York: 306th Infantry Association, 1935.

307th Infantry Regiment:

Eisenstein, Douglas R. *Whispers in the Wind: Based Upon the World War I Memoirs of Sergeant Jack L. Horn and Captain W. Kerr Rainsford, 307th Infantry, 77th Division, National Army, 1917*. Xlibris, 2000.

Rainsford, Walter K. *From Upton to the Meuse with the Three Hundred and Seventh Infantry*. New York: Appleton, 1920.

Through the War With Company D, 307th Infantry, 77th Division: A History of the Activities of Company D From the Time of Its Organization in September 1917 to the Time of Its Demobilization in May 1919. New York: n.p., 1919.

308th Infantry Regiment:

Beattie, Taylor V. "Ghosts of the Lost Battalion." *Military History* (Aug 2002): pp. 26-32.

—. "Whittlesey's 'Lost' Battalion." *Army History* (Winter 2002): pp. 21-30.

Demaree, Joseph P. *History of Company A (308th Infantry) of the Lost Battalion*. New York: Harvey, 1920.

Eager, Sherman W. "The Lost Battalion." *Scabbard and Blade* (April 1936): p.2.

Fuller, Hurley E. "Lost Battalion of the 77th Division." *Infantry Journal* (June 1926): pp. 597-608.

History of Company D, 308th US Infantry, 77th Division. New York: Harvey Press, 1919.

History of the 77th Div. New York: 77th Division Association, 1919.

Johnson, Thomas M., & Pratt, Fletcher. *The Lost Battalion*. Washington, DC: Infantry Journal Press, 1943.

Kennedy, Laurence S. *War Letters of...* New York: n.p., 1932.

McCollum, L.C. *History and Rhymes of the Lost Battalion*. New York: Bucklee Publications, 1929.

Nell, John W. *The Lost Battalion: A Private's Story*. San Antonio, Texas: History Publishing Network, 2001.

Perrett, Bryan. *Against All Odds! More Dramatic Last Stand Actions*. London: Arms & Armour, 1995.

Pratt, Fletcher & Johnson, Thomas M. "The Lost Battalion as the Germans Saw it." *American Legion* (April 1938): p. 22.

Ranlett, Louis F. *Let's Go: The Story of A.S. 2448602*. Boston: Houghton Mifflin, 1927.

Wardlaw, Miles L. *History of the 308th Infantry, 1917-1919*. New York: Putnam's, 1927.

Werstein, Irving. *The Lost Battalion*. New York: Norton, 1966.

302nd Engineer Regiment:

Crawford, Gilbert H., Ellett, Thomas H., & Hyland, John J. *The 302nd Engineers: A History*. New York: 1920.

78th Division Commander, Major General J.H. McRae poses with his son, Lieutenant Colonel D.M. McRae, the 78th Division G-2. Chatel Chehery, France, 1918. Courtesy National Archives.

Sergeant J.W. Killigrew of the 311th Ambulance Company entertains some children in Authe, France, November, 1918. Courtesy National Archives

78th Infantry Division

The War Department established the division on August 5, 1917 at Camp Dix, New Jersey. Draftees from Delaware, New Jersey, and New York State furnished the initial core of the division. From April through May, 1918, draftees from New York, New Jersey and Illinois arrived

The "Over There" Theater League members assigned to the 78th Division at their stage, Bourmont, France, August, 1918. Courtesy National Archives.

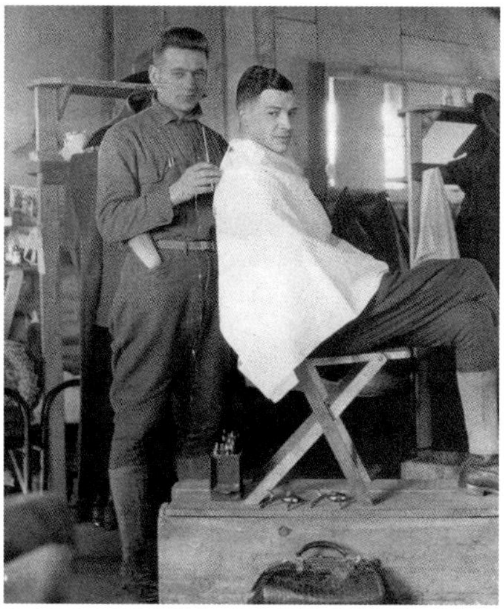

A member of the 303rd Engineer Regiment gets a haircut in France, 1918. Courtesy Military History Institute.

Private First Class George V. Reynolds, a baker in Battery B, 307th Field Artillery Regiment, posed for this portrait "Somewhere in France" August, 1918. Courtesy Military History Institute.

filling out the division. The division chose the nickname "Lightning Division" resultant of a French statement, which likened the action of the 78th Division on the battlefield to a bolt of lightning, which left the field red with enemy blood.[12]

Insignia:
The division used a red semi-circle bordered olive drab with a white bolt of lightning (the original insignia lacked the bolt). Alternate patterns are extant displaying three and five lightning bolts. The insignia was approved October 29, 1918.[13]

Campaigns:
St. Mihiel Offensive, Meuse-Argonne Offensive, Limey Sector, Toul Sector, Troyon Sector.[14]

Division Organization (1917-1919):[15]

155th Infantry Brigade:

309th Infantry Regiment
310th Infantry Regiment
308th Machine Gun Battalion

156th Infantry Brigade:

311th Infantry Regiment
312th Infantry Regiment
309th Machine Gun Battalion

Division Troops:

307th Machine Gun Battalion

153rd Field Artillery Brigade:

307th Field Artillery Regiment
308th Field Artillery Regiment
309th Field Artillery Regiment
303rd Trench Mortar Battery

Division Support:

303rd Engineer Regiment
303rd Field Signal Battalion
303rd Train Headquarters and Military Police
303rd Ammunition Train
303rd Supply Train
303rd Engineer Train
303rd Sanitary Train (309th, 310th, 311th, 312th Ambulance Companies & Field Hospitals)

Division Combat Narrative:[16]
The first unit of the division arrived in France May 18, 1918; the last June 12, 1918.

Upon arrival the division (less artillery) was assigned to the 2nd Army Corps, then operating with the British in Flanders. Training was begun in the area around Mielles-les-Bléquin, near the Ypres front. For the same purpose the artillery brigade was sent to Camp Meucon in Brittany. It left Camp Meucon on August 17th, and marched to the Toul Sector where it relieved the 1st Field Artillery Brigade on August 28-29. It supported the 90th Division in the St. Mihiel Offensive, and rejoined the 78th Division October 4th.

On July 18th the division moved to the Arras Area with headquarters established at Roëllecourt. On August 20th it left the British sector and moved to the 11th Training Area with headquarters at Bourbonne-les-Bains (Haute-Marne). While here the division was placed in the reserve of the 1st Army Corps, and the march north preparatory to the concentration for the St. Mihiel Offensive began.

Headquarters was established at Rosièces-en-Haye, on September 11th, and troops were moved into positions supporting the 2nd Division. The division remained in reserve until the night of September 15th, when it relieved the 2nd Division, and on the following night the 5th Division, in the Limey Sector. The organization of this sector just taken from the enemy, and the frequent raids carried out to divert the attention of the enemy from the approaching Meuse-Argonne Offensive, made its occupancy a particularly active one, and the division suffered 2,107 casualties.

On the nights of October 3-4, and 4-5, the division was relieved and moved to the Forêt de la Reine, and thence to the Clermont-en-Argonne Area. On October 10th it moved to the eastern border of the Argonne Forest with headquarters at Varennes. It was at this time a unit of the 1st Army Corps, operating as the left flank corps of the First Army.

The 78th Division entered the line on the night of October 15th, relieving the 77th Division on the line Petit Talma-Grand-Pré-Chevières-St. Juvin. From this position an attack was launched on October 16th with the Bois des Loges, and Grand-Pré as objectives. The town had previously been entered by the 77th Division, but it was not until October 23rd, after days of severe fighting, that the entire town including the so-called "Citadel", a commanding point in the northern part, was cleared of the enemy. On the same day Talma Hill, northwest of Grand-Pré, was captured, and the southern part of the Bois de Bourgogne was entered. The Bois des Loges was penetrated in the initial attack, but artillery fire from the northeast, and from the Bois de Bourgogne, and flanking machine gun fire from Champigneulle and Bellejoyeuse Farm caused such heavy casualties that on the night of October 20th, pursuant to orders from Corps headquarters, the line was withdrawn to the Grand-Pré-St. Juvin road.

The Bois de Bourgogne extending from Grand-Pré north to Boult-aux-Bois formed a most serious obstacle to the American forces in the advance planned for the first of November. The division was charged with the task of clearing the forest of the enemy. This was accomplished on October 29 by exploding 40,000 shells distributed over a strip one kilometer wide along its eastern edge, except for one kilometer in the southern edge next to the position of our troops. On November 1st Hill 180 in the southeastern part of Bois de Bourgogne was taken. The capture of this position rendered the Bois des Loges untenable, and on November 2 these

The standard 78th Division insignia; embroidered on felt.

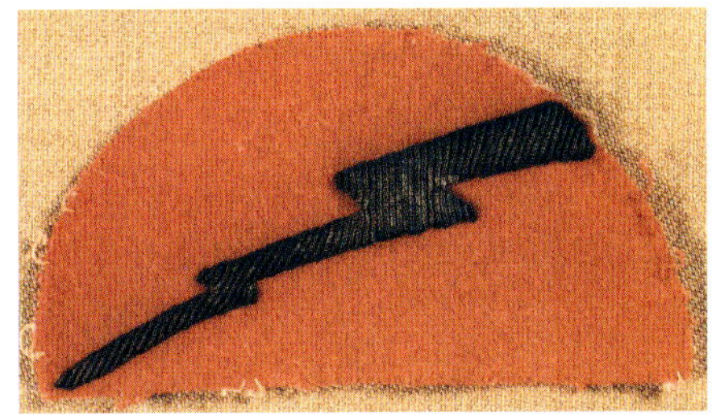

This variant substitutes the embroidered lightning bolt with bullion work.

The alternate design of the 78th Division features multiple lightning bolts.

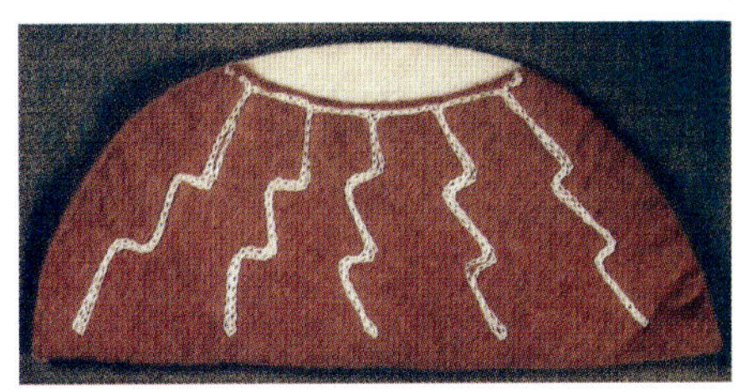

A variant of the alternative design includes a stylized cloud.

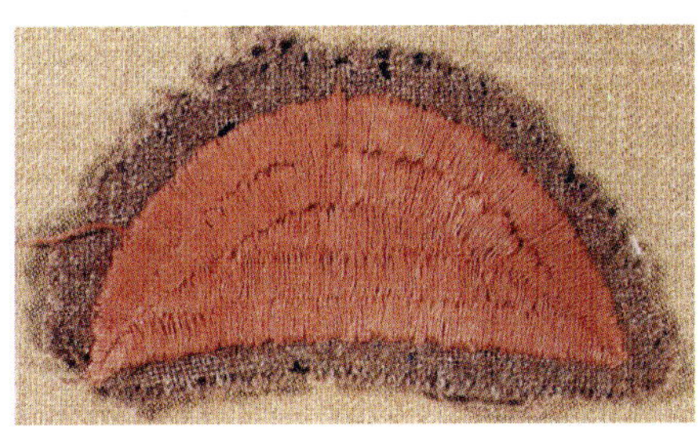

Another 78th Division insignia which omits the lightning bolt; this pattern is often described as the original design for the division.

woods were completely cleared of the enemy, and the division pushed on capturing the town of Briquenay, advance elements entering the town of Boult-aux-Bois. On the 3rd Germont, Belleville-sur-Bar, Authe, Chatillon-sur-Bar, Brieulles-sur-Bar, and Verrières were reached, and on the 4th les Petites Armoises was occupied, and a slight resistance offered at the Bois de Sy overcome. On the morning of the 5th the town of Tannary was occupied.

The division, less the artillery and ammunition train, was relieved by the 42nd Division on November 5, and moved south to the area near St. Menehould. The artillery brigade supported the 42nd Division on the 5th, then the 6th Division until the 9th.

Days in the Front Line: 0 (training) 18 (sector) 22 (battle) for a total of 40. During operations the division took 432 prisoners and its casualties totaled 1,530 soldiers killed in action or died of wounds, 5,614 wounded in action.[17]

The latter part of November the division moved to an area in the Cote d'or with headquarters at Semur-en-Auxois. It moved to ports of embarkation the latter part of April. Headquarters sailed from Bordeaux May 24, and arrived at New York June 6, 1919.

The division commanders were: Major General Chase W. Kennedy, Major General Hugh L. Scott, Brigadier General James T. Dean, and Major General James H. McRae.

Reference Bibliography:

General Division Histories

American Battle Monuments Commission. *78th Division: Summary of Operations in the World War.* Washington, DC: Government Printing Office, 1944.

Camp Dix Pictorial Review. *The Lightning (78th) Division in France*. Special edition, 1919.

Cochrane, Rexmond C. *The 78th Division at the Kriemhilde Stellung, October 1918*. Army Chemical Center, Maryland: USA Chemical Corps Historical Office, 1957.

Marcone, Rock. "At Bois des loges, Italian Immigrants in the U.S. Army's 78th Infantry Division Proved Their Mettle." *Military History* (June 2005): pp. 18 & 20-22.

Meehan, Thomas F. *History of the Seventy-Eighth Division the World War, 1917-18-19*. New York: Dodd, Mead & Co, 1921.

Searcy, Earl B. *Looking Back*. Springfield, Illinois: Journal Press, 1921.

310th Infantry Regiment:

Headquarters Company, 310th Infantry, USA, August 29, 1917-June 6, 1919. n.p., 1919.

A History of the Three Hundred Tenth Infantry, Seventy-Eighth Division, USA, 1917-1919. New York: Association of the 310th Infantry, 1919.

Sommers, W.A. *The Engagements of Company "G", Second Battalion, 310th Infantry, 78th Division, A.E.F.* Courcelles Les Semur, France: n.p., 1919.

311th Infantry Regiment:

Colonna, Benjamin A., ed. *The History of Company B, 311th Infantry in the World War.* Freehold, New Jersey: Transcript Printing, 1922.

Eberlin, Barnard. *History of the 311th Infantry (78th Division)*. Flavigny-sur-Ozerain, France: 1919.

U.S. Army. 311th Infantry Regiment *Daily Situation Reports, 311th Infantry, 12 Sep to 5 Nov 1918*. France, 2 April 1919.

—. *War Diaries of the 311th Infantry Regiment, 12 Sep to 15 Nov 1918*. Typescript, France,1918.

312th Infantry Regiment:

A History of the Three Hundred and Twelfth Infantry in France. New York: 312th Infantry Association, 1919.

307th Field Artillery Regiment:

History of the 307th Field Artillery, September 6, 1917-May 16, 1919. n.p., 1919.

308th Field Artillery Regiment:

Binder, Raymond S. *A History of Battery "C", 308th Field Artillery, 78th Division, American Expeditionary Forces*. n.p., 1919.

309th Field Artillery Regiment:

McCarthy, William E. *Memories of the 309th Field Artillery*. Rochester, New York: Henry Conolly, 1920.

303rd Engineer Regiment:

Kelly, J.E. *This and That About Co. F, 303rd Engineers, U.S.A.* n.p., 1919.

Roth, Joseph P.C., & Wheeler, Robert L., comps. *History of Company "E," 303rd Engineers of the 78th Division, 1917-1919*. Rochester, New York: John P. Smith, 1919.

79th Infantry Division

The War Department established the division on August 5, 1917 at Camp Meade, Maryland. The division was composed of draftees initially drawn from eastern Maryland, Pennsylvania, and the District of Columbia. Later increments came from New York, Ohio, Rhode Island and West Virginia. The division took the name "Lorraine Division."[18]

Insignia:

The division selected a white Cross of Lorraine, a symbol of triumph, within a white border all on a blue shield-shaped field. This design was approved November 16, 1918.[19]

Campaigns:

Meuse-Argonne Offensive, Troyon Sector.[20]

Division Organization (1917-1919):[21]

157th Infantry Brigade:

313th Infantry Regiment
314th Infantry Regiment
311th Machine Gun Battalion

Major General Joseph E. Kuhn, commander of the 79th Division confers with French officers, Vacherauville, France, October, 1918. Courtesy National Archives.

WS

158th Infantry Brigade:

315th Infantry Regiment
316th Infantry Regiment
312th Machine Gun Battalion

Division Troops:

310th Machine Gun Battalion

154th Field Artillery Brigade:

310th Field Artillery Regiment
311th Field Artillery Regiment
312th Field Artillery Regiment
304th Trench Mortar Battery

Division Support:

304th Engineer Regiment
304th Field Signal Battalion
304th Train Headquarters and Military Police
304th Ammunition Train
304th Supply Train
304th Engineer Train
304th Sanitary Train (313th, 314th, 315th, 316th Ambulance Companies & Field Hospitals)

Division Combat Narrative:[22]
The first unit of the division arrived in France July 12, 1918, and the last, August 3, 1918.

The division, less the artillery, immediately went into training in the 10th Training Area with headquarters at Prauthoy, Haute-Marne. The artillery upon landing in France was sent to La Courtine (Creuse), where it remained in training until after the Armistice and rejoined the division in January, 1919, in the Souilly Area, south of Verdun.

The work in the training area continued until September 8, when the movement to the front started. Moving by rail to an area around Robert Espagne and Bar-le-Duc, the division detrained and proceeded by trucks and marching; on September 16, it took over the Montfaucon or 304th Sector (about 16 kilometers northwest of Verdun), relieving the 157th French Division. This sector was approximately five kilometers in width, but on September 22, in anticipation of the Meuse-Argonne Offensive, was contracted to about two and a half kilometers. While in this sector two enemy raids were repulsed.

On September 26, the division as a part of the 5th Corps participated in the general attack, capturing the towns of Haucourt and Malancourt on this date. The following day the stronghold of Montfaucon was taken. The advance was continued through the Bois de Beuge and the town of Nantillois. Three assaults against Madeleine Farm, a strong position on the southern edge of the Bois de Cunel, failed to dislodge the enemy. After advancing ten kilometers during four days of severe fighting, on September 30, the division was relieved by the 3rd Division.

Upon being thus relieved, the division marched to the Troyon Sector (8 kilometers north of St. Mihiel) where it relieved the 26th Division on October 8. This sector extended from Fresnes-en-Woevre on the north to a point one kilometer south of Doncourt-aux-Templiers, a distance of eleven kilometers. At this time the division was under the 2nd Colonial Corps (French). Operations in this sector were limited to patrolling and severe artillery activity, no offensive action being undertaken. On October 26 the 33rd Division relieved the 79th Division in this sector, when it proceeded by marching to the Grande-Montagne Sector, seventeen kilometers north of Verdun, where it relieved the 29th Division and a part of the 26th Division on October 30th. The front of this sector was about seven kilometers wide and in the form of a quadrant, the left flank facing north and the right flank facing east. In this sector the division was under the command of the 17th Corps (French).

Opposite
Top: Three-ton Packard trucks of Water Service Train Number 2, attached to the 79th Division take a break near Brabant-sur-Meuse, France, November 3, 1918. Courtesy National Archives.

Bottom: Private First Class William Schellberg (standing fourth from right) poses with his buddies from the Machine Gun Company of the 313th Infantry Regiment Courtesy Military History Institute.

Private Casper W. Swartz of Company C, 314th Infantry Regiment. Courtesy Military History Institute.

The standard insignia for the 79th Division features a fully embroidered Cross of Lorraine upon a blue fully embroidered field.

Another example; embroidered on felt.

This 79th Division insignia of felt on felt uses soutache for the border.

On November 2, the division opened the final offensive by an attack to the north with its left flank. On November 6 after severe hand-to-hand fighting Borne-de-Cornouiller (Hill 378) was captured. The attack was continued, changing on November 8 to an easterly direction, and by that night the heights from Ecurey to Crepion had been captured. On the night of November 8th, the division sector limits were changed to include Etraye on the north and Moirey on the south. This found elements of the division at Ecurey, and it was necessary to execute a flank march of four and a half kilometers at night, through thick underbrush and woods in order to be in position for the attack at six o'clock the following morning.

On November 9th the towns of Crepion, Wavrille, Gibercy, Etraye and Moirey were captured. By the night of November 10th, Hill 328, the town of Chaumont-devant-Damvillers and Hill 319 had been taken. Ville-devant-Chaumont was taken on November 11th, and at the hour of the Armistice the troops were advancing up the western slope of the Côte de Romagne, with the enemy falling back along the entire front.

Days in the Front Line: 0 (training) 29 (sector) 18 (battle) for a total of 47. During operations the division took 1,077 prisoners and its casualties totaled 1,517 soldiers killed in action or died of wounds, 5,357 wounded in action.[23]

From November 11th to December 26th the division remained on the battle front, taking over a front extending from Damvillers on the north to Fresnes-en-Woevre on the south, for patrol and police. On December 10th, the headquarters, Headquarters Company and 3rd Battalion, 314th Infantry proceeded to an area around Montmedy, Stenay and Virton (Belgium) for the purpose of guarding property, listing material and maintaining order. On February 1, 1919, this detachment rejoined the division in the Souilly area.

Moving to the Souilly area south of Verdun on December 27th the division found itself completely assembled for the first time in France, when it was joined in January by the artillery brigade.

The division moved from the Souilly Area during the last days of March to the Fourth Training Area northeast of Chaumont around Andelot and Rimaucourt, where it was reviewed on April 12th by General Pershing. The movement from this area to Nantes and St. Nazaire began on April 19th, the artillery going to St. Nazaire and the infantry to the vicinity of Nantes and Cholet.

Division Headquarters sailed from St. Nazaire on May 18th, 1919 and arrived at New York City on May 27th, 1919.

The division commanders were: Major General Joseph E. Kuhn, Brigadier General William Nicholson, and Brigadier General Evan M. Johnson.

Reference Bibliography:

General Division Histories

American Battle Monuments Commission. *79th Division: Summary of Operations in the World War*. Washington, DC: Government Printing Office. 1944.

Clark, William B. *War History of the 79th Division National Army*. n.p.: Clark, 1918.

Cochrane, Rexmond C. *The 79th Division at Montfaucon, October 1918*. Army Chemical Center, Maryland: USA Chemical Corps Historical Office, 1960.

Fitzpatrick, Vincent deP. *"Over Here" Affectionately Dedicated to the Officers and Men Preparing for "Over There," Camp Meade, Md.* Baltimore: Horn-Shafer, 1919.

Historical Committee 79th Division Association. *History of the Seventy-ninth Division, A.E.F. During the World War: 1917-1919*. Lancaster, Pennsylvania: Steinman & Steinman, 1922.

U.S. Army, 79th Infantry Division. Headquarters Troop. *79th Division, Headquarters Troop: A Record*. Booklet, n.p., 1920.

313th Infantry Regiment:

Harlowe, Jerry. *Your Brother Will: The Great War Letters & Diary of William Schellberg, Machine Gun Company, 313th Infantry "Baltimore's Own"*. Ellicott City, Maryland: Patapsco Falls Press, 1992.

Muller, E. Lester. *The 313th of the 79th in the World War*. Baltimore, Maryland: Meyer & Thalheimer, 1919.

Thorn, Henry C., Jr. *History of 313th US Infantry, Baltimore's Own*. New York: Wynkoop Hallenbeck, Crawford, 1920.

A beautiful bullion French made 79th Division insignia

314th Infantry Regiment:

Joel, Arthur H. *Under the Lorraine Cross: An Account of the Experiences of Infantrymen Who Fought With the Lorraine Cross Division in France During the World War*. n.p., 1921.
Kress, John W. *The Great Adventure*. n.p., 1962.
Labrum, Joseph T. *History of Company G 314th Infantry*.n.p. n.d.

316th Infantry Regiment:

Glock, Carl E. *History of the 316th Regiment of Infantry in the World War, 1918*. Pittsburgh, Pennsylvania, 1919.
—., & Lisle, Clifton. *History of the 316th Regiment of Infantry*. 3 vols. Philadelphia, Pennsylvania, 1930-51.
U.S. Army. 316th Infantry Regiment. Co. F. *History of Company F, 316th Infantry, 79th Division,1917-18-19*. Philadelphia: Company F Association, 316th Infantry, 1930.

311th Field Artillery Regiment:

Bachman, William E. *The Delta of the Triple Elevens: The History of Battery D, 311th Field Artillery, United States Army, American Expeditionary Forces*. Hazelton, Pennsylvania: Standard Sentinel, 1920.
MacArthur, C.P. *A History of the Three Hundred and Eleventh Field Artillery, United States Army*. Nantes, France: Commerce, 1919.

304th Engineer Regiment:

Barber, J. Frank. "Destruction of Enemy Traps and Mines." *Military Engineer* (Sep/Oct 1924): pp. 374-77.
Colby, Elbridge. "The Traffic Jam at Avocourt." *Military Engineer* (Sep 1942): pp. 434-41.
Directory, Officers and Men 304th Engineers and Engineer Train, 79th Division, A.E.F., France, 1919. France: Topographical Office, 1919.
U.S. Army. 304th Engineer Regiment. *The Official History of the Three Hundred and Fourth Engineer Regiment, Seventy-ninth Division, U.S.A., During the World War*. Lancaster, Pennsylvania: Steinman & Foltz, 1920.

1st Lieutenant George F. Jonaitis, Catholic, chaplain of the 313th Infantry Regiment, 79th Division at the Regimental Command Post, Bois de L'Hospital, St. Hippolyte, Tryon, Meuse, France. October 14, 1918. Courtesy National Archives

80th Infantry Division

The War Department established the division on August 5, 1917 at Camp Lee, Virginia. The division was composed of draftees from Pennsylvania, Virginia and West Virginia. The division selected the sobriquet "Blue Ridge Division" acknowledging the large number of residents of the Blue Ridge Mountain area.[24]

Insignia:

The division selected as an insignia a khaki shield with white border, on which are three blue mountains, one for each state which furnished personnel for the division, resting upon a white bar. Variants exist in the coloring of the mountain, the shape of the patch (square and arc background exist), with the motto, "Vis Montium" in a ribbon beneath the patch and with the figure "80" alone on the shield. Approved on October 20, 1918.[25]

Campaigns:

St. Mihiel Offensive, Meuse-Argonne Offensive, Picardy Sector.[26]

Division Organization (1917-1919):[27]

159th Infantry Brigade:

U.S.
OFFICIAL

Above: The "Blue Ridge Entertainers" of the 320th Infantry Regiment pose in France with a young uniformed mascot. Courtesy Military History Institute.

317th Infantry Regiment
318th Infantry Regiment
313th Machine Gun Battalion

160th Infantry Brigade:

319th Infantry Regiment
320th Infantry Regiment
315th Machine Gun Battalion

Division Troops:

314th Machine Gun Battalion

155th Field Artillery Brigade:

313th Field Artillery Regiment
314th Field Artillery Regiment
315th Field Artillery Regiment
305th Trench Mortar Battery

Division Support:

305th Engineer Regiment
305th Field Signal Battalion
305th Train Headquarters and Military Police
305th Ammunition Train
305th Supply Train
305th Engineer Train
305th Sanitary Train (317th, 318th, 319th, 320th Ambulance Companies & Field Hospitals)

Opposite
Top: Major General S.D. Sturgis,(fourth from left) Commanding General of the 80th Division reviews the 80th Division Horse Show, Ancy le Franc, France, February 1919. Courtesy National Archives.

Bottom: Advanced Dressing Station of the 319th Ambulance Company at Gercourt, France, September 1918. Courtesy National Archives.

Division Combat Narrative:[28]
The first unit of the division arrived in France May 23, 1918, and the last June 18th.

The division, less the artillery, immediately went into training with the British in the Samer Training Area a few kilometers east of Boulogne. The artillery was first sent to Redon,

I.J. Cossel (right) and a fellow member of the 313th Field Artillery Regiment practice with Signal Corps buzzers. Courtesy Military History Institute.

The standard 80th Division insignia; embroidered on wool.

A variant of the 80th Division design; embroidered on felt.

near St. Nazaire, but completed its training at Camps de Coetquidan and Meucon. The brigade did not rejoin the division until September, 1918.

After a short period of training at Samer the division moved to the Third British Army Sector, with headquarters at Beauval. Second line trenches between Albert and Arras were occupied. During this period front line trenches were also occupied by battalion units. One battalion participated in an attack in conjunction with New Zealand troops, and one with the 38th Welsh Division.

The division was relieved in this sector on August 20th and moved south to the 14th Training Area lying between Chaumont and Çatillon-sur-Seine. Here it remained until August 31st. On September 1st the 80th moved by rail to the Stainville area, and later marched to the Tronville area. While in the latter the division composed the reserve of the First Army during the St. Mihiel Offensive. The 320th Infantry and 315th Machine Gun Battalion were attached to the 2nd French Colonial Corps and actively participated in the operation. The 155th Artillery Brigade rejoined the division while in this sector.

On September 14th the 80th was transported to the vicinity of Ippacourt and placed in the 3rd American Corps. On the night of the 20th it moved forward preparatory to entering the Meuse-Argonne Offensive.

In this operation the 3rd Corps, with right resting on the Meuse River, operated as the right flank corps of the First Army. The 80th Division was assigned to the center of the corps front. The division line on the morning of September 26th ran east and west directly south of the town of Bethincourt. Using its position on the river as a pivot the corps was to swing its center and left to the north and east so that its line would parallel the river.

The 80th Division moved to the attack on the morning of the 26th and immediately captured Bethincourt and by noon had overcome resistance in the Bois de Forges and the Bois Jure. The enemy's resistance stiffened from the east bank of the Meuse River. During the evening the Army objective near Dannevoux was reached and the right of the division rested on the Meuse, the left extending along the north edge of the Bois de la Côte Lemont.

The 318th Infantry had been dispatched to the support of the 4th Division on the left of the 80th. The 155th Artillery Brigade was also placed at the disposal of the same division while French artillery served the 80th.

On October 3rd the 3rd and 4th Divisions were drawn apart for the purpose of creating a new sector for the 80th. The new line ran through Nantillois with the strongly fortified Bois des Ogons directly in its front. Two battalions of the 318th Infantry were returned to the division to assist in the coming attack.

The offensive was resumed on October 4 and the Bois des Ogons entered, but it was not until October 6 that this formidable position was finally overcome. The advance continued and by nightfall the line extended to Ville aux Bois Farm. On the 9th the town of Cunel was entered. Another attack was launched on the 10th but the left of the division was unable to advance, while the right made only slight gains.

The 80th was relieved on the night of October 11 and moved south to the Foret de Hesse and thence on the 14th to the Triaucourt Area where it was placed in Army reserve.

On October 13 the division was transferred to the 1st Corps and on the 23rd moved to the vicinity of Les Islettes where it remained until the 30th. On this date it marched through the Argonne Forest and relieved the 82nd Division as the right of the 1st Corps on a line running between St. Georges and St. Juvin.

In the attack of November 1 the right of the division reached the Buzancy-Bayonville road but the left could get no further than Alliépont. The artillery of the 82nd Division was now serving the 80th, its own artillery having been left with the 3rd Corps.

A flank attack to the west on the morning of the 2nd permitted the left to advance to Verpel and Thenorgues. On the same day Buzancy was attacked and a line established to the north of the town.

The enemy was now rapidly withdrawing, and a vigorous pursuit ensued. On the 5th the Stonne-Beaumont road was reached and the slight resistance encountered at Warniforet was quickly overcome. The 80th now held the Stonne-Beaumont road from a point 1 kilometer west of Warniforet to Beaumont inclusive. During the afternoon of the 5th the town of Yoncq was taken.

On the following day the 1st Division passed through the 80th and the latter then retired to Sommauthe. On November 8 it marched to the Cornay-Apremont Area and on the 12th moved to the Les Islettes Area. Here it rested until the 18th, at which time the division moved by marching to the 15th Training Area southwest of Chatillon-sur-Seine.

The 155th Artillery Brigade rejoined December 5 after having served successively with the 80th, 4th, 5th and 90th Division, without relief, for a period of 48 days.

On March 30, 1919, the 80th started for the Le Mans area and upon arrival headquarters were established at Ecommoy. Here it remained until its return to this country.

Days in the Front Line: 16 (training) 0 (sector) 31 (battle) for a total of 47. During operations the division took 1,813 prisoners and its casualties totaled 1,241 soldiers killed in action or died of wounds, 4,788 wounded in action.[29]

Headquarters sailed from Brest, May 17, 1919, and arrived at Newport News May 26, 1919.

The division commanders were: Major General Adelbert Cronkhite, Brigadier General Lloyd M. Brett, Brigadier General Charles S. Farnsworth, and Major General S.D. Sturgis.

This 80th Division insignia uses soutache to highlight the mountains and border.

Another nicely executed 80th Division insignia using bullion soutache to highlight the design.

Reference Bibliography:

General Division Histories

American Battle Monuments Commission. *80th Division: Summary of Operations in the World War.* Washington, DC: Government Printing Office, 1944.

The Bayonet: Remembrance Book of Camp Lee, Virginia. Richmond, Virginia: Everett Waddey, 1918.

Stultz, Russell L., comp.; Anthony, Lee S., ed. *History of the Eightieth Division, A.E.F. in World War I*. Roanoke, Virginia: Jamont Communications, 2004.

Young, Rush S. *Over the Top With the 80th By a Buck Private, 1917-1919*. Washington, DC: By the Author, 1933.

317th Infantry Regiment:

Craighill, Edley. *History of the 317th Infantry*. n.p., 1919.

Eldred, Anson. *Overseas Diary of Company "G" 317th Infantry, France, June 1918-June 1919*. n.p., 1919.

Frantz, Frederick S. *A Resume of Experiences During the World War: Paper Read Before the Lebanon County Historical Society, December 16, 1935.* Lebanon, Pennsylvania: By the Society, 1935.

Shaw, Arthur F., comp. *Company "K" 317th Infantry: Being a History of Its Activities and a Record of Its Personnel, September 1917 to June 1919.* Grand Rapids, Michigan: White, 1919.

318th Infantry Regiment:

U.S. Army, 318th Infantry Regiment. *History of the 318th Infantry Regiment of the 80th Division, 1917-1919.* Richmond, Virginia: Byrd, 1919.

319th Infantry Regiment:

Herr, Charles. *Company F History, 319th Infantry: Published as a Matter of Record by the Officers and Men of the Company.* Somerville, New Jersey: Unionist-Gazette Association, 1920.

Peck, Josiah C. *The 319th Infantry A.E.F.* Paris: Clarke, 1919.

320th Infantry Regiment:

Lukens, Edward C. *A Blue Ridge Memoir.* Baltimore, Maryland: Sun Printing, 1922.

Stringfellow, John S. *Hell! No!: This and That, A Narrative of the Great War.* Boston: Meador, 1936.

U.S. Army, 320th Infantry Regiment. Company. I. *History of Company "I", 320th Infantry, 80th Division.* n.p.,1919.

War Diary of Company E, 320th Infantry, Compiled Upon the Occasion of the Eighth Annual Reunion, Commemorating the 10th Anniversary of the Company's Organization at Camp Lee, Virginia. n.p., 1927.

Westlake, Thomas H. *History of the 320th Infantry Abroad.* New York: McGraw Phillips, 1923.

Williams, Ashby. *Experiences of the Great War: Artois, St. Mihiel, Meuse, Argonne.* Roanoke, Virginia: Stone Printing, 1919.

313th Field Artillery Regiment:

Crowell, Thomas I. *A History of the 313th Field Artillery, U.S.A.* New York: Crowell, 1920.

314th Field Artillery Regiment:

History of the 314th Field Artillery. n.p., 1919.

Roberts, Rufus J., ed. *Our Answer to the Call.* Cambridge, Ohio: Callihan & Stottlemire, 1919.

305th Engineer Regiment:

Floyd, Frank T. *Company "F" Overseas.* Pittsburgh, Pennsylvania: Pittsburgh Print, 1921.

U.S. Army, 305th Engineer Regiment. *History and Roster of the 305th Engineers.* France: Regimental Headquarters, 1919.

Opposite
Top: Major General Charles J. Bailey, (left) Commander of the 81st Division, and the officer generally credited with the first use of division insignia with his primary staff, Epuneul, France, September, 1918. Courtesy National Archives.

Bottom: Soldiers of the 81st Division in "Wild Cat Square", Chaumont le Bois, France, April 1919. Note the street sign on the right for "Rue de North Carolina". Courtesy National Archives.

Below: Private Alonzo P. Saunders (left) of the Headquarters Company, 321st Infantry Regiment, 1919. Courtesy Military History Institute.

81st Infantry Division

The War Department established the division on August 5, 1917 at Camp Jackson, South Carolina. The division was made up of draftees from Florida, North Carolina and South Carolina. In May and June of 1918, the division was brought to full strength with additional men from Alabama and New York.[30] The division was known as the "Wildcat" division as the original members of the division came from the Carolinas where the wildcat was native.

Insignia:

The 81st Division is generally credited with the creation of divisional patches in the AEF. According to the December, 1919 *National Geographic Magazine*:

WILD-CAT
SQUARE

Wildcats taming some French dogs. France, summer 1919. Courtesy Military History Institute.

An embroidered example of the 81st Division insignia; the 81st Division used different color wildcats to designate subordinate units; black wildcats were used by the Division Headquarters, machine gun battalions and the 306th Engineer Regiment.

This die cut felt on felt insignia denotes the 161st Infantry Brigade.

An embroidered example of the 161st Infantry Brigade insignia.

> "In the summer of 1918 the War Department received a communication from the commanding general, Port of Embarkation, Hoboken, reporting that all members of the Eighty-first Division, at that time going through the port on their way to France, were wearing a "wildcat" in cloth on the arm, and requesting information regarding the authority for this device...On arrival of this division in France difficulties were at once encountered. The existence of the device was reported to General Headquarters and the Commanding General [Major General Charles J. Bailey] was directed to remove the insignia. He protested, saying that by its silence the War Department had tacitly authorized it; that it was most desirable, in order that the officers might readily know the men of the division; and, finally, that it was highly prized by the personnel and therefore was a great help toward maintaining and improving the morale of the command. It so happened that General Headquarters had been studying the question of identification of units in battle. Experience had shown that some method was necessary for quickly reassembling troops after an offensive. Organizations became confused, and after an advance they are almost inextricably mixed. To reassemble under their own officers rapidly is an important point ... The "wildcat" of the Eighty-first Division seemed to offer a solution of the problem, and as a result it was authorized and the commanding generals of all combat divisions in France were at once directed to select insignia for their divisions."[31]

The division selected a black silhouette of a wildcat on a khaki circle to represent the division. The insignia was approved October 18, 1918. Several variations of the patch exist where the color of the wildcat varies according to the different arms of the service. Examples are known with, a white cat and khaki surround for the 161st Infantry Brigade, white cat and orange surround or blue cat and khaki surround for 162nd Infantry Brigade, red cat with khaki surround for artillery/ammunition train, buff cat with khaki surround for the 306th Supply Train, yellow cat with blue surround for the 306th Signal Battalion, and green cat with khaki surround for the 306th Sanitary Train.[32]

Campaigns:

Meuse-Argonne Offensive, St. Die Sector.[33]

Division Organization (1917-1919):[34]

161st Infantry Brigade:

321st Infantry Regiment
322nd Infantry Regiment
317th Machine Gun Battalion

162nd Infantry Brigade:

323rd Infantry Regiment
324th Infantry Regiment
318th Machine Gun Battalion

Division Troops:

316th Machine Gun Battalion

156th Field Artillery Brigade:

316th Field Artillery Regiment
317th Field Artillery Regiment
318th Field Artillery Regiment
306th Trench Mortar Battery

Division Support:

306th Engineer Regiment
306th Field Signal Battalion
306th Train Headquarters and Military Police
306th Ammunition Train
306th Supply Train
306th Engineer Train
306th Sanitary Train (321st, 322nd, 323rd, 324th Ambulance Companies & Field Hospitals)

Die cut insignia of the 162nd Infantry Brigade.

This die cut example denotes the 156th Field Artillery Brigade of the Ammunition Train.

This insignia belongs to the 306th Signal Battalion.

Division Combat Narrative:[35]
The first unit of the division arrived in France August 15, 1918; the last element August 25, 1918.

For training purposes the division (less artillery) was sent to the 16th Training Area with Headquarters at Tonnerre, (Yonne). For the same purpose the artillery brigade was sent to Valdahon, (Doubs). It did not participate in operations, but rejoined the division in November 1918.

The division proceeded to the Vosges on September 14. Arriving September 20, it took over the St. Die Sector and remained in the front line from September 20 to October 10, 1918, as part of the French 33rd Corps, and later as part of the French 10th Corps. Command of the sector passed to the Commanding General, 81st Division on October 2. On October 19, it moved to the vicinity of Rambervillers (Vosges), and from there to the Sommedieue Sector southeast of Verdun where it was in the reserve of the French 72nd Colonial Corps. On November 7 it passed to the French 2nd Colonial Corps, and relieved the American 35th Division in line. From November 7 to November 11, it participated in the Meuse-Argonne Offensive, attacking in the Woevre plain east of Verdun from November 9 to 11, 1918, and capturing Moranville, Grimaucourt and Abaucourt.

Days in the Front Line: 14 (training) 18 (sector) 5 (battle) for a total of 37. During operations the division took 101 prisoners and its casualties totaled 248 soldiers killed in action or died of wounds, 856 wounded in action.[36]

On November 17, the division was relieved from Sommedieue Sector, and moved to the Chatillon-sur-Seine training area, with headquarters at Mussy-sur-Seine, where it remained

The 81st Division Sanitary Train used this die cut example.

until May 2d, when it was sent to the Le Mans Embarkation Center preparatory to returning to the United States.

Division Headquarters sailed from Brest June 1, 1919, and arrived at New York June 11, 1919.

The division had three commanding generals: Brigadier General Charles H. Barth, Major General Charles J. Bailey, and Brigadier General George W. Mcver.

Reference Bibliography:

General Division Histories

American Battle Monuments Commission. *81st Division, Summary of Operations in the World War.* Washington, DC: Government Printing Office, 1944.

Military Roster, Camp Jackson, Columbia, S.C.: Containing a List of Commissioned Officers of the U.S. Army, With Rank and Address, Alphabetically Arranged and Cross-Indexed by Units. Atlanta, Georgia: Southern Trade Publications, 1917.

321st Infantry Regiment:

Johnson, Clarence W. *The History of the 321st Infantry.* Columbia, South Carolina: Bryan, 1919.

324th Infantry Regiment:

Strange, John L. *History of Company "C" 324th Infantry, American Expeditionary Forces.* Paris: Clarke, 1920.

316th Field Artillery Regiment:

Stevens, Alexander C., ed. *The 316th Field Artillery: The Wildcat Record.* n.p., 1920.

306th Engineer Regiment:

U.S. Army, 306th Engineer Regiment. *Roster and History, 306th Regiment of Engineers and 306th Engineer Train.* Columbia, South Carolina: State Company, 1919.

Major General G.B. Duncan, Commander of the 82nd Division. Prauthey, France, November, 1918 Courtesy National Archives.

82nd Infantry Division

The War Department established the division on August 5, 1917 at Camp Gordon, Georgia. The division was composed of draftees from Alabama, Georgia, and Tennessee. Additional drafted men were sent from Camps Devens, Upton, Dix, Meade and Lee, to fill the division to full strength. As a result, men from every state of the Union were present in the division. When the division choose a nickname, "All American Division" seemed most appropriate.[37]

Insignia:

The division selected as its insignia a red square upon which was placed a blue disc with the white letters "AA" representing the division's nickname. A variant exists with yellow letters worn by officers.[38] A second variation exists where the letters "AA" are omitted.

Campaigns:

St. Mihiel Offensive, Meuse-Argonne Offensive, Marbache Sector, Toul Sector, Troyon Sector.[39]

Division Organization (1917-1919):[40]

163rd Infantry Brigade:

325th Infantry Regiment
326th Infantry Regiment
320th Machine Gun Battalion

164th Infantry Brigade:

327th Infantry Regiment
328th Infantry Regiment
321st Machine Gun Battalion

Division Troops:

319th Machine Gun Battalion

157th Field Artillery Brigade:

319th Field Artillery Regiment
320th Field Artillery Regiment
321st Field Artillery Regiment
307th Trench Mortar Battery

Division Support:

307th Engineer Regiment
307th Field Signal Battalion
307th Train Headquarters and Military Police
307th Ammunition Train
307th Supply Train
307th Engineer Train
307th Sanitary Train (325th, 326th, 327th, 328th Ambulance Companies & Field Hospitals)

Division Combat Narrative:[41]
The first unit of the division arrived in France May 8, 1918; the last element July 12, 1918.

For training purposes the division (less artillery) was sent to the Escarbotin Area west of Abbeville where it was attached to the 66th British Division. For the same purpose, the artillery brigade went to La Courtine (Creuse). It rejoined the division in August, 1918.

Sergeant Alvin C. York, 327th Infantry Regiment, poses near the spot in the Argonne Forrest where he with seventeen of his men captured 132 Germans. Cornay, France, February, 1919. Courtesy National Archives.

Above: Regimental Supply Sergeant Ernest Sherwin, 326th Infantry Regiment poses at Camp Gordon, Georgia in 1917, and at his home in Pittsburgh, Pennsylvania, October, 1976. Courtesy Military History Institute.

Right: Wagoner Stanley G. Pickett (standing) of Company A, 307th Engineer Battalion. France, 1918. Courtesy Military History Institute.

Above: The standard design for the 82nd Division; felt on felt construction using soutache for the "AA" monogram and to highlight the borders.

Top center: An embroidered on wool version of the standard 82nd Division design.

Top right: This wonderful example uses bullion soutache on wool.

A finely executed machine embroidered on felt example features a dark blue border.

82nd Division insignia with gold borders are usually described as officers insignia; however, photographic evidence suggests that they were worn by enlisted personnel as well.

The division left Escarbotin June 16, and on June 25 it relieved the 26th Division in the Toul Sector, where it was brigaded with the French until July 17, upon which date command passed to the Commanding General 82nd Division. On August 9, it was relieved by the 89th Division and proceeded to the vicinity of Toul with headquarters at Blenod-les-Toul. On August 17, it relieved the 2nd Division in the Marbache Sector astride the Moselle River and held this sector in the St. Mihiel Offensive September 12 to 16, 1918. While retaining contact with the French 125th Division on the right, it advanced the left of its line to maintain connection with the 90th Division which attacked on its left. It captured Norroy September 13th, and Vandieres September 15th. During these operations, the 328th Infantry suffered substantial losses from artillery fire from east of the Meuse.

The division was relieved in the Marbache Sector by the 69th French Division on September 21, and proceeded to the Triaucourt Area, southwest of Verdun, on September 24, where it was in the reserve of the 1st Army preparatory to taking part in the Meuse-Argonne Offensive. It passed to 1st Corps reserve on October 3 and moved northwest of Verdun where it entered the line between the 1st and 28th Divisions in line north of Varennes on the night of October 6. The impetus gained by the American Army had spent itself in ten days of hard fighting and the advance through the Argonne Forest and up the Aire Valley had come to a stop. The high command determined upon a bold and hazardous expedient. A surprise flank attack must be driven into the enemy flank west of the Aire River and north of Chatel Chehery. If the thrust accomplished its purpose, the Argonne Forest would be cleared and the way opened for a substantial American advance. The 82nd and 28th Divisions made the attack on October 7 against bitter resistance and on October 8, the success of the operation was assured. Enemy pressure in the Argonne Forest was relieved and a general advance by the American Army followed. On October 9, the 28th Division was relieved by elements of the 82nd Division and the attack up the Aire Valley was resumed. The outstanding features of this phase of the operation were the capture of Cornay October 9 and 10, Marcq, October 10, the piercing of the Kriemhilde-Stellung northwest of Sommerance October 14, and the capture of St. Juvin and its surrounding heights October 16. The division was relieved on October 31 by elements of the 77th and 80th Division, and moved by successive stages to the 10th Training Area with headquarters established at Prauthoy (Haute-Marne) on November 15, 1918. In March it moved to the vicinity of Bordeaux with headquarters at Castres preparatory to returning to the United States.

Days in the Front Line: 17 (training) 58 (sector) 30 (battle) for a total of 105. During operations the division took 845 prisoners and its casualties totaled 1,413 soldiers killed in action or died of wounds, 6,664 wounded in action.[42]

Division Headquarters sailed from Bordeaux on May 9, 1919, and arrived at New York, May 20, 1919.

The division commanders were: Major General Eben Swift, Brigadier General James D. Erwin, Brigadier General William P. Burnham, Brigadier General Marcus D. Cronin, and Major General George B. Duncan.

Serving in this division was perhaps the most famous soldier of World War I, Sergeant Alvin Cullom York, who during the battle of the Argonne Forrest, killed six and captured 132 Germans, earning him the Medal of Honor.

Reference Bibliography:

General Division Histories:

American Battle Monuments Commission. *82nd Division Summary of Operations in the World War*. Washington, DC: Government Printing Office, 1944.

Anzuoni, Robert P. *The All American: An Illustrated History of the 82nd Airborne Division, 1917-to the Present*. Atglen, Pennsylvania: Schiffer, 2001.

Cooke, James J. *The All Americans at War: The 82nd Division in the Great War, 1917-1918*. Westport, Connecticut: Praeger, 1999.

Mitchell, Gary A., ed. *82nd Division, AEF: WWI Battle Citation General Orders, 1918-1919*. US: Planchet Press, 1984.

Service Record: Home-Coming Souvenir Edition. Special issue periodical, Atlanta, Georgia, 5 June 1919.

U.S. Army, 82nd Division. *Official Camp Gordon Song Book*. Augusta, Georgia: 82nd Division, National Army, n.d.

—. *Official History of the 82nd Division, American Expeditionary Forces: "All American" Division*. Indianapolis, Indiana: Bobbs-Merrill, 1919.

325th Infantry Regiment:

Story of the 325th Bordeaux, France: Saugnac & Drouillard, 1919.

328th Infantry Regiment:

Holden, Frank A. *War Memories*. Athens, Georgia: Athens Book Co, 1923.

Jones, Herbert D.N. *History of Company "C", 328th Infantry*. Brooklyn, New York: Collins, 19??.

U.S. Army, 328th Infantry Regiment. *History of the Three Hundred and Twenty-Eighth Regiment of Infantry*. Atlanta, Georgia: Foote & Davies, 1922.

320th Field Artillery Regiment:

U.S. Army, AEF. 320th Field Artillery. *Report of Operations of 320th Field Artillery, N.A.*, Philadelphia: Smith-Edwards, 1919.

Another embroidered example of the 82nd Division "Officer Insignia."

A alternative design of the 82nd Division insignia; this embroidered on wool example omits the "AA" in the blue field.

83rd Infantry Division

The War Department established the division on August 5, 1917 at Camp Sherman, Ohio. The division was composed of draftees from Ohio and Pennsylvania. The division selected the nickname "Ohio" Division.[43]

Insignia:

The division insignia consisted of a black triangle with vortex down, the gold letters, "OHIO" forming a monogram within a gold circle. The insignia was approved December 26, 1918. The 332nd Infantry Regiment, detached from the division and assigned to Italy, selected as a symbol of their unique service the old Venetian emblem of the winged Lion of St. Mark, with one paw resting on an open bible inscribed in black "332." Several variants exist with different letters on the bible including; "AAS" for Army Ambulance Service, "MRC" for Motor Repair Company, "YMCA" for Young Man's Christian Association, "MTC" for Motor Transport Corps, "ARC" for American Red Cross, and blank with no numbers or letters. The 332nd Infantry Regiment was the only unit in the AEF that frequently wore three patches – the 332nd Regiment insignia, below this the 83rd Division insignia and below this the 3rd Army insignia.[44]

Campaigns:

Division none. 332nd Infantry Vittorio-Veneto (Italy).[45]

Division Organization (1917-1919):[46]

Major General E.F. Glenn, Commander of the 83rd Division, Montigney le Roi, June, 1918. Courtesy National Archives.

Private Jim Kay Wong of Cleveland, Ohio, on KP duty at 83rd Division Headquarters, Montigney le Roi, France, July, 1918. Courtesy National Archives.

Private George G. Dodge and his fiancée, Eva F. Gottschall, in 1918. Note the unusual "OHIO" collar disk. Courtesy Military History Institute.

165th Infantry Brigade:

329th Infantry Regiment
330th Infantry Regiment
323rd Machine Gun Battalion

166th Infantry Brigade:

331st Infantry Regiment
332nd Infantry Regiment
324th Machine Gun Battalion

Division Troops:

322nd Machine Gun Battalion

158th Field Artillery Brigade:

322nd Field Artillery Regiment
323rd Field Artillery Regiment
324th Field Artillery Regiment
308th Trench Mortar Battery

Division Support:

308th Engineer Regiment
308th Field Signal Battalion
308th Train Headquarters and Military Police
308th Ammunition Train
308th Supply Train
308th Engineer Train
308th Sanitary Train (329th, 330th, 331st, 332nd Ambulance Companies & Field Hospitals)

Division Combat Narrative:[47]
The first element of the division arrived in France, June 1, 1918; the last arrived June 28, 1918.

It was designated as a depot division and ordered to the Le Mans area. The 332nd Infantry, the 158th Field Artillery Brigade, and special units, such as the Engineer and Signal troops, were detached, and the remaining units provided replacements from their own personnel and trained additional personnel for replacements to combat divisions at the front. The 49th Infantry, upon its arrival in France the latter part of July, was sent to the Le Mans area where it took the place of the 332nd Infantry in the division.

Right: Private Norman J. Riegler and some buddies from Company G, 332nd Infantry Regiment pose with local residents in Brindisi, Italy, 1918. Courtesy Military History Institute.

Detached Units

332nd Infantry Regiment:
The 332nd Infantry was selected to represent the American forces with the Italian Army, and entrained for Italy via Marseilles July 25, 1918. With the idea of strengthening Italian morale and weakening that of the Austrians, battalions of the regiment visited different sections of the front daily, to create the impression that a vast body of American troops had arrived. The regiment was attached to the 31st Division, 14th British Army Corps, 10th Italian Army. From the 27th to 29th of October, it assisted in establishing bridgeheads across the Piave River, and from October 30 to November 4, it took part in the pursuit of the Austrians. On November 4, the regiment reached the Tagliamento River near Valvasone, crossed the river in the face of machine gun fire from front and flank, and pushed forward ten miles to Villaroba where it was when the Austrian Armistice went into effect. The regiment remained in Italy until March 29 when it returned to the United States, units sailing from Genoa March 29, and from Marseilles March 29 and April 4.

The standard 83rd Division insignia; embroidered on felt.

158th Field Artillery Brigade:
Upon arrival in France, the brigade was temporarily in a billeting area in Ille-et-Vilaine, but early in July it was sent to Camp Coetquidan. Having completed its training just prior to the beginning of the Meuse-Argonne offensive, the brigade was sent to the front. Brigade Headquarters, the 322nd Regiment, and the 308th Trench Mortar Battery arrived in time to take part in the initial stage of the offensive, September 26, as part of a provisional brigade supporting the 91st Division between Avecourt and Vauquois. On the night of October 3, the brigade marched to the Bois de Nixéville near Verdun. On the 6th and 7th it took positions behind Cote de Talou along the banks of the Meuse and from October 8 to 29 it supported the 29th American and the 18th French Divisions in their attacks east of the Meuse. On October 29 the brigade was relieved and assigned to the 32nd Division, then in reserve of the 3rd Corps, 1st Army. On the night of November 9-10, the division crossed the Meuse and entered the line, attacking in the vicinity of Brandeville and Peuvillera. During this operation the 158th Brigade furnished the artillery support. It remained with the 32nd Division during the march into Germany and served with this division in the Army of Occupation until it returned to the United States the latter part of April, 1919.

A chain stitch on felt 83rd Division insignia.

308th Engineers:
The regiment arrived at La Havre on June 17, 1918. On June 20 it was broken up, the several units being assigned to duty in the Service of Supply. On July 20, it was assembled at Changey (Haute-Marne), and on the 23rd was assigned as corps engineers, First Army Corps. From July 28 to August 6 it participated in the Aisne-Marne offensive, and from August 7 to September 9 operated in the Vesle sector. On August 13, the First Corps was withdrawn from the Vesle and the regiment passed to the Third Army Corps with which it remained during the remainder of its stay in the A.E.F. Early in September, the concentration of forces began for the contemplated Meuse-Argonne offensive, and on September 9th the regiment left the Vesle sector and proceeded to the area southwest of Verdun. On September 26, it advanced to Esnes. From this date until the Armistice, it participated in the Meuse-Argonne offensive advancing with the Third Corps and performing road work until November 6. From this date to November 11, the regiment was engaged in constructing a series of bridges across the Meuse River at Dun-sur-Meuse. After the Armistice, it became a part of the Army of Occupation where it remained until its return to the United States in June, 1919.

This example uses bullion soutache to form the Ohio monogram.

308th Field Signal Battalion:
The battalion was assigned as corps signal battalion of the Third Army Corps on July 7, 1918. It arrived at Chartèves (Aisne) in the 3rd Corps area on August 4, and performed active duty in the Aisne-Marne offensive until August 6. From August 7 to September 9 it operated in the Vesle sector, taking part in the Oise-Aisne offensive August 18-September 9. The battalion participated in the Meuse-Argonne offensive as corps signal battalion from September 26 to November 11, 1918, and after the Armistice continued duty with the Third Corps in the march into Germany, and in the Army of Occupation.

The 332nd Infantry Regiment adopted their own insignia; this beautiful bullion example is of the regiment's standard design.

A bullion variant of the 332nd insignia.

Another variant of the 332nd insignia.

The attached elements of the AEF Italy borrowed the 332nd design for their own use; this example substitutes the "332" on the bible with "AAS" denoting American Ambulance Service.

A variant of the "AAS" insignia.

This insignia with "ARC" in lieu of "332" was used by the American Red Cross.

This rare studio view shows an unknown soldier proudly displaying his 332nd, 83rd, and Army of Occupation insignia upon return to the United States. (Private Collection)

During operations its casualties totaled 67 soldiers killed in action or died of wounds, 257 wounded in action.[48]

The division's permanent cadres returned to the United States in January, 1919.

Major General Edwin F. Glenn commanded the division from the time of its organization until it was demobilized.

Reference Bibliography:

General Division Histories
None.

332nd Infantry Regiment:

Chronology of the Machine Gun Company, 332nd Infantry. n.p.,1919.

Lettau, Joseph L. *In Italy with the 332nd Infantry*. Youngstown, Ohio: By the Author, 1921.

U.S. Army War College, Historical Section. *332nd Regiment of Infantry (American) on the Italian Front*. Typescript, n.p. 1922.

U.S. Army, 332nd Infantry Regiment. Company. D. *The Company Log from September 7th, 1917 to May 2nd, 1919*. n.p., 1920.

—. Company. E. *History of Company E, 332nd Infantry, From Departure Overseas to Return and Discharge: An Active "Ring" in Wallace's "Circus" During the World War*. n.p.,1919.

—. Company. I. *Company "I", 332nd Infantry in the Great World War*. n.p., 1919.

322nd Field Artillery Regiment:

History of the 322nd Field Artillery. New Haven, Connecticut: Yale, 1920.

323rd Field Artillery Regiment:

Colyer, Charles M. *The History of the 323rd Regiment of Field Artillery, 158th F. A. Brigade, 83rd Division, 32nd Division*. Cleveland, Ohio: Britton, 1920.

Riggs, McDonald H., & Platt, Rutherford H. *A History of Battery F, 323rd Field Artillery*. Cleveland, Ohio: J. B. Dempsey, 1920.

324th Field Artillery Regiment:

Ashburn, Thomas Q. *History of the 324th Field Artillery, United States Army*. New York: George H. Doran, 1919.

308th Engineer Regiment:

Colby, Elbridge. "The Traffic Jam at Avocourt." *Military Engineer* (Sep 1942): pp. 434-41.

Davidson, W.F. "A 370-Foot Military Suspension Bridge." *Military Engineer* (Jul/Aug 1926): pp. 323-25.

Fiske, Harold C. "Bridging the Rhine." *Military Engineer* (Sep/Oct 1922): pp. 293-94.

Trippe, Harry M. "With the 308th Engineers in France." *Military Engineer* (Sep/Oct 1932): pp. 482-85.

U.S. Army, 308th Engineer Regiment. *With the 308th Engineers From Ohio to the Rhine and Back, 1917-1919*. Cleveland, Ohio: Veterans Association, 1923.

84th Infantry Division

The War Department established the division on August 5, 1917 at Camp Taylor, Kentucky. The division was composed of draftees from Illinois, Indiana and Kentucky. The unit was popularly known as the "Lincoln Division."[49]

Insignia:

The division insignia is a red disc bordered olive drab, with an ax splitting a rail, both in white. The design refers to Abraham Lincoln "the Rail Splitter" from whose home state many of the division's personnel were drawn. It was approved on February 16, 1924. World War I examples include an upright ax with the head faced left surrounded by a red circle, on which is superimposed "Lincoln 84" in blue, or a white disc bordered red with an axe with a red head and a blue handle, or finally, a red battle axe sewn directly on the uniform.[50]

Major General Harry C. Hale, (second from left) 84th Division commander, poses with 3rd Division officers in front of the headquarters of the German Crown Prince, Montfaucon, France, October, 1918. Courtesy National Archives.

Below: Soldiers of Company E, 336th Infantry Regiment board trains to the front as replacements, Monpont, France, October, 1918. Courtesy National Archives.

Campaigns:
None.

Division Organization (1917-1919):[51]

167th Infantry Brigade:

333rd Infantry Regiment
334th Infantry Regiment
326th Machine Gun Battalion

168th Infantry Brigade:

335th Infantry Regiment
336th Infantry Regiment
327th Machine Gun Battalion

Division Troops:

325th Machine Gun Battalion

159th Field Artillery Brigade:

325th Field Artillery Regiment
326th Field Artillery Regiment
327th Field Artillery Regiment
309th Trench Mortar Battery

Division Support:

309th Engineer Regiment
309th Field Signal Battalion
309th Train Headquarters and Military Police
309th Ammunition Train
309th Supply Train
309th Engineer Train
309th Sanitary Train (333rd, 334th, 335th, 336th Ambulance Companies & Field Hospitals)

Private Everett Godwin (standing) poses as a recruit in the 325th Field Artillery Regiment. Courtesy Military History Institute.

Division Service Narrative:[52]
The first element of the division arrived in France, September 21, 1918; the last October 25, 1918.

The division (less artillery) was sent to the West Perigeux Area (Dordogne) near Bordeaux with headquarters established at Neuvic on September 28, 1918. The artillery brigade was sent to Camp de Souge. In October the 309th Engineers were transferred to St. Nazaire for

Above: The standard 84th Division design; embroidered on felt.

Above center: An embroidered on wool version of the standard 84th Division design.

Above right: An 84th Division insignia with both the division nickname and numerical designation.

Right: This simplified embroidered on wool variant omits the 84th Division numerical designation and part of the inner design.

Far right: Another more simplified embroidered on wool variant simply uses the Lincoln Axe icon with border.

The most basic 84th Division design; an embroidered axe on wool.

construction work. The remainder of the division was broken up to provide replacements for combat units at the front and early in November, headquarters and the permanent cadres of organizations were transferred to Le Mans. They returned to the United States in January, 1919.

The division had two commanding generals, Brigadier General Wilber E. Wilder, and Major General Harry C. Hale.

Reference Bibliography:

General Division Histories
None.

335th Infantry Regiment:
U.S. Army, 335th Infantry Regiment. *History of Company E, 335th Infantry, A.E.F.* n.p.,1919.

325th Field Artillery Regiment:
Witherspoon, A.M. *A History of the 325th Field Artillery of the 84th Division, A.E.F., 1917-1919,* n.p.,1960.

309th Engineer Regiment:
Nelson, Thomas H., ed. *The Castle, Co. D, 1918, 309th Engineers*. n.p., 1919.
U.S. Army, 309th Engineer Regiment. *"B" Company, 309th Engineers: United States, August 15th, 1917 to September 9th, 1918, American Expeditionary Forces, September 21st, 1918 to June 12th, 1919.* Indianapolis, Indiana: Bookwalter-Ball, 1919.

85th Infantry Division

Private Carl M. Henricksen of Company F, 339th Infantry Regiment. Courtesy Military History Institute.

The War Department established the division on August 5, 1917 at Camp Custer, Michigan. The division was composed of draftees from Michigan and Wisconsin. The division was known as the "Custer Division" given George Custer's ties to the state of Michigan.[53]

Insignia:
The division shoulder sleeve insignia was an olive drab disc with red letters, "CD." The design denotes the division nickname in honor of General George A. Custer and also alludes to Camp Custer. The design was approved December 24, 1918. A variant of the shoulder sleeve insignia exists on an olive drab square.[54]

Campaigns:
None.

Division Organization (1917-1919):[55]

169th Infantry Brigade:

337th Infantry Regiment
338th Infantry Regiment
329th Machine Gun Battalion

170th Infantry Brigade:

339th Infantry Regiment
340th Infantry Regiment
330th Machine Gun Battalion

Four soldiers of Company D, 310th Engineer Battalion enjoy some R&R in Trier, Germany, Febuary 15, 1919. Courtesy Military History Institute.

Soldiers of Company B, 310th Field Signal Battalion practice with the heliograph, Germany, 1919. Courtesy Military History Institute.

The standard design 85th Division insignia of felt on felt construction.

An embroidered on felt version of the 85th Division insignia.

The 339th Infantry Regiment was detailed to the AEF North Russia; this printed version of the AEF North Russia is of the standard design featuring the Polar Bear walking on an iceberg.

Division Troops:

328th Machine Gun Battalion

160th Field Artillery Brigade:

328th Field Artillery Regiment
329th Field Artillery Regiment
330th Field Artillery Regiment
310th Trench Mortar Battery

Division Support:

310th Engineer Regiment
310th Field Signal Battalion
310th Train Headquarters and Military Police
310th Ammunition Train
310th Supply Train
310th Engineer Train
310th Sanitary Train (337th, 338th, 339th, 340th Ambulance Companies & Field Hospitals)

Division Service Narrative:[56]
The first unit of the division arrived in France July 26, 1918; the last August 12, 1918.

The 339th Infantry, the 1st Battalion, 310th Engineers, the 337th Field Hospital, and the 337th Ambulance Company were detached on arrival in England and were sent to North Russia as part of the allied force under British command which operated from Archangel as a base. The forward position occupied by the allies extended for a distance of approximately 450 miles. These, however, did not form a continuous line but were a series of occupied positions at vital points more or less fortified. The American troops occupied most of the front line defenses and bore the brunt of the fighting. They were engaged in hard active service extending beyond the Armistice.

The division (less artillery and the units detached in England) proceeded to an area in the Loire Valley with headquarters established at Pouilly (Nievre) on August 14th. It became the 4th Deport Division. The artillery brigade went to Coetquidan where it remained in training until October 22nd, when it moved to Rimaucourt (Haute-Marne). There it was split up, the 328th Field Artillery being attached to the 92nd Division, the 329th Field Artillery to the 4th Corps, and the 330th Field Artillery to the 2nd Corps. The 310th Engineer Regiment (less 1st Battalion.) was detached and assigned to the 5th Corps on September 9, 1918. On November 23rd it was transferred to the 7th Corps, Third Army. The 310th Field Signal Battalion was detached August 20th, and was assigned to the 4th Corps. Both engineers and signal battalion served in the Army of Occupation. The 3rd Battalion, 340th Infantry, was detached and assigned to duty at a tank school. Early in November the nucleus of the division was assigned to the Second Army. It was sent to the vicinity of Toul and designated as the 2nd Army Regional Replacement Division.

During operations its casualties totaled 145 soldiers killed in action or died of wounds, 281 wounded in action.[57]

Division Headquarters sailed from Brest March 22, 1919, and arrived at New York March 30, 1919.

The division had five commanding generals; Major General Joseph T. Dickman, Brigadier General S.W. Miller, Major General James Parker, Brigadier General B.C. Morse, and Major General Chase W. Kennedy.

Reference Bibliography:

General Division Histories

"The Custer Division in the World War." *Infantry Journal* (July 1926): pp. 25-29.

339th Infantry Regiment:

Doolen, Richard M. *Michigan's Polar Bears: The American Expedition to North Russia, 1918-1919*. Ann Arbor, Miiganch: University of Michigan, 1965.

Moore, Joel R. *"M" Company, 339th Infantry, in North Russia*. n.p.,1920.

—. et. al. *The History of the American Expedition Fighting the Bolsheviki: Campaigning in North Russia 1918-1919*. Detroit: Polar Bear, 1920.

York, Dorothea. *The Romance of Company "A", 339th Infantry, A.N.R.E.F. (American North Russia Expeditionary Force)*. Detroit: McIntyre, 1923.

328th Field Artillery Regiment:

Barry, Edward M., ed. *Doings of Battery F: Humorous Happenings and Striking Situations and Experiences of Its Members*. Grand Rapids, Michigan: Dean-Hicks, 1920.

U.S. Army, 328th Artillery Regiment. *The Red Guidon*. Milwaukee, Wisconsin: Hammersmith-Kortmeyer, 1919.

329th Field Artillery Regiment:

U.S. Army, 329th Artillery Regiment. *329th Barrage*. n.p., 1919.

310th Engineer Regiment:

Johnson, Robert C. "Mapping Northern Russia for the Archangel Expedition." *Military Engineer* (1920): pp. 437-46.

The alternate version of the AEF North Russia insignia used by the 339th Infantry Regiment; an embroidered on felt monogram "NR" denoting North Russia.

86th Infantry Division

The War Department established the division on August 5, 1917 at Camp Grant, Illinois. The division was composed of draftees from Illinois and Wisconsin.[58] This division was known as the "Black Hawk Division."

Insignia:

The division selected as its insignia a red shield with a black hawk upon which a small red shield appears on its breast emblazoned with the black monogram letters "BH." Variants are known where the hawk faces either left or right. The insignia was approved November 26, 1918.[59]

Theodore Roosevelt visits the 86th Division at Camp Grant, Illinois, accompanying him is Major General Thomas H. Barry, the division commander. September, 1917. Courtesy National Archives.

SIGNAL CORPS
OFFICIAL

Campaigns:
None.

Division Organization (1917-1919):[60]

171st Infantry Brigade:

341st Infantry Regiment
342nd Infantry Regiment
332nd Machine Gun Battalion

172nd Infantry Brigade:

343rd Infantry Regiment
344th Infantry Regiment
333rd Machine Gun Battalion

Division Troops:

331st Machine Gun Battalion

161st Field Artillery Brigade:

331st Field Artillery Regiment
332nd Field Artillery Regiment
333rd Field Artillery Regiment
311th Trench Mortar Battery

Division Support:

311th Engineer Regiment
311th Field Signal Battalion
311th Train Headquarters and Military Police
311th Ammunition Train
311th Supply Train
311th Engineer Train
311th Sanitary Train (341st, 342nd, 343rd, 344th Ambulance Companies & Field Hospitals)

Regimental Supply Sergeant John Earl Stewart, 344th Infantry Regiment. Courtesy Military History Institute.

Opposite
Top: Soldiers of the 342nd Infantry Regiment at Southampton, England, September, 1918. Courtesy National Archives.

Bottom: Soldiers of Company D, 311th Engineer Regiment unload crushed rock for roads from rail cars in France, 1918. Courtesy Military History Institute.

The standard design for the 86th Division insignia; an embroidered Blackhawk on felt with hand embroidered letters "BH."

An variant machine embroidered on felt 86th Division insignia.

Crude felt on felt version of the 86th Division insignia.

An unusual and crudely executed die cut example.

Division Service Narrative:[61]
The first unit of the division arrived in France on September 21st, 1918; the last on October 9th, 1918.

The division was sent to the vicinity of Bordeaux (Gironde) and headquarters were established in St. Andre de Cubzac. The infantry and machine gun organizations were greatly depleted to form replacements for combat units at the front and on November 8th what remained of them were ordered to the Le Mans area. The permanent cadre comprising the skeletonized division headquarters, infantry regiments and machine gun battalions returned to the United States in January, 1919. The 311th Field Signal Battalion returned in January and the 311th Engineers in June, 1919. Upon arrival in France, the 161st Field Artillery Brigade went to Le Courneau (Gironde) where it remained until its return to the United States in January and February, 1919.

The division had five Major General T.H. Barry, Brigadier General L.W.V. Kennon, Major General C.H. Martin, Brigadier General L.C. Andrews, and Major General C.H. Ballou.

Reference Bibliography:

General Division Histories
U.S. Army, 86th Infantry Division. *The Official History of the Eighty-Sixth Division*. Chicago, Illinois: State Publishing Society, 1921.

331st Field Artillery Regiment:
331st Field Artillery, United States Army, 1917-1919. Chicago: Rogers, 1919.

87th Infantry Division

Lieutenant Frank S. Hugill attempts to retrieve his cap from a small admirer, France, 1918. Courtesy Military History Institute.

The War Department established the division on August 5, 1917 at Camp Pike, Arkansas. This division was composed of draftees from Alabama, Arkansas, Louisiana, and Mississippi. A second draft of men from New Jersey, New York and Pennsylvania filled the division to full strength. It was popularly known as the "Acorn Division."[62]

Insignia:
The Division chose an insignia of a green disc on which is placed a gold acorn symbolizing strength and alluding to the oak trees common at Camp Pike. The design was approved on May 27, 1922. Variants exist with the acorn superimposed upon an oak leaf.[63]

Campaigns:
None.

Division Organization (1917-1919):[64]

173rd Infantry Brigade:

345th Infantry Regiment
346th Infantry Regiment
335th Machine Gun Battalion

174th Infantry Brigade:

347th Infantry Regiment
348th Infantry Regiment
336th Machine Gun Battalion

Division Troops:

334th Machine Gun Battalion

Above: Private Walter T. O'Malley (circled) of Company B, 336th Machine Gun Battalion poses with his company in France, January, 1919. Courtesy Military History Institute.

162nd Field Artillery Brigade:

334th Field Artillery Regiment
335th Field Artillery Regiment
336th Field Artillery Regiment
312th Trench Mortar Battery

Division Support:

312th Engineer Regiment
312th Field Signal Battalion
312th Train Headquarters and Military Police
312th Ammunition Train
312th Supply Train
312th Engineer Train
312th Sanitary Train (345th, 346th, 347th, 348th Ambulance Companies & Field Hospitals)

The standard 87th Division insignia of felt on felt construction.

Division Service Narrative:[65]
The first element of the division arrived in France August 28, 1918; the last September 16, 1918.

The division reported to the Commanding General, S.O.S., for duty in the latter part of September. Headquarters were established at Pons (Charente Inférieure) on September 12th. The organizations were distributed through the base and intermediate sections, S.O.S., but the division did not lose its identity as a combat unit, and when the Armistice was signed, it was under orders for service at the front and the headquarters and headquarters troops were actually in movement on November 11th.

Division headquarters sailed from St. Nazaire January 10, 1919, and arrived at New York January 22, 1919.

The division had three commanding generals: Major General Samuel D. Sturgis, Brigadier General Robert C. Van Vliet, and Brigadier General W.F. Martin.

Right: An embroidered on wool example of the 87th Division insignia.

Above: A very pleasing example of the 87th Division insignia using fancy stitching to form the acorn.

Above center: An alternative design for the 87th Division insignia adds an oak leaf as the background for the acorn; embroidered on felt construction.

Above right: A felt on felt version of the alternate 87th Division design.

Right: A bullion on wool 87th Division insignia.

Far right: An unusual variant of the 87th Division insignia. The crossed cannons above the acorn suggest usage by the Division Artillery Brigade or one of its subordinate units; beautifully executed with bullion embroidery on felt.

Brigadier General W.D. Beach, Commander of the 88th Division is shown here in Lucey, France in November, 1918 as commander of the 176th Infantry Brigade. Courtesy National Archives.

Reference Bibliography:

General Division Histories
None.

345th Infantry Regiment:
Richardson, Chalmer O. *Here Comes the Band! Unofficial History of the 345th Infantry Band in the Great War*. North Platte: Hemphill, 1928.

346th Infantry Regiment:
U.S. Army. *The 346th Infantry Historical Notes*. n.p.,1919.

88th Infantry Division

The War Department established the division on August 5, 1917 at Camp Dodge Iowa. The division was composed of draftees from Illinois, Iowa, Minnesota, and North Dakota. Additional troops were used from various states to bring the division up to full strength prior to deployment overseas.[66]

Insignia:
The division chose a royal blue cloverleaf. Two figure "8's" crossing each other at right angles forms the design of which alludes to the four states from which the division was drawn. It was approved November 12, 1918. Variants exist with the number "88" superimposed upon the cloverleaf and with red and black cloverleaves.[67]

Campaigns:
Center Sector, Haute-Alsace.[68]

Division Organization (1917-1919):[69]

175th Infantry Brigade:

349th Infantry Regiment
350th Infantry Regiment
338th Machine Gun Battalion

176th Infantry Brigade:

351st Infantry Regiment
352nd Infantry Regiment
339th Machine Gun Battalion

Privates Earl Winklepleck (left) and Ray D. Galvin of the 88th Division. Courtesy Military History Institute.

Left: The Larsen brothers pose for a post war photograph. Enger Larson,(seated) wears the divisional insignia for the 88th Division. Helmer, on the right wears the insignia of the 28th Division and Alvin, on the left wears an unidentified insignia. Courtesy Military History Institute.

The standard 88th Division insignia; die cut dark blue felt construction.

An embroidered on felt version of the 88th Division insignia.

Another variant of the standard design uses cording to highlight the design.

This die cut felt 88th Division insignia substitutes red for the usual dark blue of the design suggesting use by divisional artillery units and ammunition trains.

Division Troops:

337th Machine Gun Battalion

163rd Field Artillery Brigade:

337th Field Artillery Regiment
338th Field Artillery Regiment
339th Field Artillery Regiment
313th Trench Mortar Battery

Division Support:

313th Engineer Regiment
313th Field Signal Battalion
313th Train Headquarters and Military Police
313th Ammunition Train
313th Supply Train
313th Engineer Train
313th Sanitary Train (349th, 350th, 351st, 352nd Ambulance Companies & Field Hospitals)

Division Combat Narrative:[70]

The first units embarked for overseas on August 9, 1918; the last units arrived in France September 7, 1918.

Upon arrival, the division (less artillery) was ordered to the 21st Training Area with headquarters established at Semur (Cote d'Or). The artillery brigade was sent to the Artillery Training School at Clermont-Ferrand in the south of France. It never served in the division again and returned to the United States in January 1919.

On September 14th the division was placed under the command of the Seventh French Army and moved by rail to the Hericourt Training Areas (Haute-Saone) near Belfort. For administrative purposes alone the division was under the 7th American Corps with headquarters at Remiremont.

On September 23, 1918, the division relieved the 38th French Division in the Center Sector, Haute-Alsace, with Headquarters established at Montreux Chateau on October 7th. It held this sector until November 2, 1918, when it became a part of the 2nd American Army. One brigade was placed in reserve of the 4th Corps, the remainder of the division being in Army reserve with headquarters at Lagney.

Days in the Front Line: 22 (training) 21 (sector) 0 (battle) for a total of 43. During operations the division took 3 prisoners and its casualties totaled 20 soldiers killed in action or died of wounds, 58 wounded in action.[71]

On November 29th the division moved by marching to the First Training Area at Gondrecourt (Meuse). On April 15, 1919, the division was transferred to the 1st Army. On April 26th it passed to the command of the Commanding General, S.O.S., preparatory to its return to the United States. Division Headquarters sailed from St. Nazaire on May 21, 1919, and arrived at Newport News, Virginia on June 1, 1919.

The division had four commanders: Major General E.H. Plummer, Brigadier General R.N. Getty, Brigadier General William D. Beach, and Major General William Weigel.

Reference Bibliography:

General Division Histories

Larson, E.J.D. *Memoirs of France and the 88th Division*. Minneapolis-St. Paul, Minnesota: Webb, 1920.

U.S. Army, 88th Infantry Division. *The 88th Division in the World War of 1914-1918*. New York: Wynkoop Hallenbeck Crawford, 1919.

350th Infantry Regiment:

Fiske, Proctor M., ed. *History of the Three Hundred Fiftieth Regiment of US Infantry*. Cedar Rapids, Iowa: Laurence Press, 1919.

313th Engineer Regiment:

Parsons, G.C. "The 313 Engineer Regiment in France." *Military Engineer* (Nov/Dec 1926): pp. 453-57.

Major General Frank L. Winn, Commander of the 89th Division at Tailly, France, November, 1918. Courtesy Military History Institute.

89th Infantry Division

The War Department established the division on August 5, 1917 at Camp Funston, Kansas. The division was composed of draftees from Arizona, Colorado, Kansas, Missouri, New Mexico, Nebraska and South Dakota.[72] The division was known as the "Middle West" Division.

Insignia:

The division chose an olive drab disc with a black "W" in a black circle denoting both the "M" and "W" of the division nickname when the insignia is inverted. Early versions are an overlay monogram of "M" and "W." The design was approved on October 25, 1918. Different colors are placed in the lower part of the "W" according to the various branches of the service. Sky blue denotes 177th Infantry Brigade, cobalt blue 178th Infantry Brigade, cobalt with sunflower indicates the 353rd Infantry Regiment, red the 164th Field Artillery Brigade, half red/half khaki or silver the 341st Machine Gun Battalion, purple silk with buff border Supply Train, buff with red cross Sanitary Train. Division awards for best brigade, regiment and company were donated by white sections along the outer edge of the patch.[73]

Campaigns:

St. Mihiel Offensive, Meuse-Argonne Offensive, Euvezin Sector, Lucey Sector.[74]

Major Frank Wilbur Smith, G-2 for the 89th Division, taken in Kyllburg, Germany, December, 1918. Courtesy National Archives.

Division Organization (1917-1919):[75]

177th Infantry Brigade:

353rd Infantry Regiment
354th Infantry Regiment
341st Machine Gun Battalion

178th Infantry Brigade:

355th Infantry Regiment
356th Infantry Regiment
342nd Machine Gun Battalion

Division Troops:

340th Machine Gun Battalion

164th Field Artillery Brigade:

340th Field Artillery Regiment
341st Field Artillery Regiment
342nd Field Artillery Regiment
314th Trench Mortar Battery

Private Harold Wadleigh, Company H, 353rd Infantry Regiment. Of note is his Aero Service collar disk and the small sunflower centered in his divisional insignia. Courtesy Military History Institute.

Division Support:

314th Engineer Regiment
314th Field Signal Battalion
314th Train Headquarters and Military Police
314th Ammunition Train
314th Supply Train
314th Engineer Train
314th Sanitary Train (353rd, 354th, 355th, 356th Ambulance Companies & Field Hospitals)

Division Combat Narrative:[76]

The first unit of the division to go overseas arrived in France, June 11, 1918; the last element July 10, 1918.

For training purposes the division (less artillery) was sent to the 4th Training Area with Division Headquarters at Reynel. For the same purpose the artillery brigade went to Camp de Souge, near Bordeaux. It rejoined the division immediately after the Saint-Mihiel Offensive, operating with it until the relief of the division in the Euvezin sector on October 9, 1918, when it remained in support of the 37th and 28th Division, successively, until the Armistice. It rejoined the Eighty-ninth Division on the march into Germany.

On August 4, 1918, the division began the relief of the 82nd Division in the quiet Lucey sector north of Toul, completing the relief August 10th. The division operated under the 32nd Corps, 8th French Army until August 20th when it passed to the 4th Army Corps of the newly-organized First Army (American). In the Saint-Mihiel Offensive the division operated on the right flank of the 4th Corps, featuring in the capture of Bois de Mort-Ware, Bouillonville, Euvezin, Beney, and Zammes.

The Meuse-Argonne Offensive was initiated on September 26th. The division was relieved in the Lucey sector by the 37th Division on October 9th, and proceeded to the Recicourt area as part of the First Army Reserve. On October 20th the division relieved the 32nd Division in front line. Under the 5th Corps it participated in the operations until the Armistice, encountering and overcoming particularly stubborn resistance in the capture of Bois de Bantheville, the heights of Barricourt, and the crossing of the Meuse River the night of November 10th-11th.

Days in the Front Line: 0 (training) 54 (sector) 28 (battle) for a total of 82. During operations the division took 5,061 prisoners and its casualties totaled 1,466 soldiers killed in action or died of wounds, 5,625 wounded in action.[77]

After the Armistice the division was assigned to the Army of Occupation, and began its march on November 24th. The first troops of the division crossed into Germany on December 5th, at Echternach. Headquarters was established at Kyllburg, and remained there until the division returned to the United States.

Division Headquarters sailed from Brest on May 19, and arrived at New York on May 31, 1919.

Below: The men and guns of Battery E, 342nd Field Artillery Regiment, France, 1918. Courtesy Military History Institute.

This embroidered on wool example is the standard 89th Division insignia; the 89th Division used different color fills of the subsections of the design to designate subordinate units.

The light blue fill between the legs of the "W" indicates the 177th Infantry Brigade on this embroidered on wool 89th Division insignia.

A variant of the 177th Infantry brigade using the alternative design for the 89th Division.

Dark blue fill designates the 178th Infantry Brigade.

Red fill was reserved for the 164th Field Artillery Brigade; embroidered on wool construction.

This 340th Machine Gun Battalion insignia uses a divided gold and scarlet field to designate the unit and is accompanied by Best Company in the Battalion and Best Regiment in the Brigade Awards annotated by the white fill in the upper and lower sections.

The 341st Machine Gun Battalion insignia uses the blue and red color scheme, an embroidered on wool example.

The 89th Division Supply Train used a purple fill piped with white border.

The 314th Engineer Regiment used a red fill with white border as their insignia.

2nd Lieutenant Paul Weir Cloud, still operator, Photographic Unit, 89th Division, near Kyllburg, Germany, January 16, 1919. Courtesy National Archives

The division had three commanders; Major General Leonard Wood, Brigadier General Frank I. Winn, and Major General W.M. Wright.

Reference Bibliography:

General Division Histories

American Battle Monuments Commission. *89th Division, Summary of Operations in the World War.* Washington, DC: Government Printing Office, 1944.

Cochrane, Rexmond C. *The 89th Division Comes Into the Line.* Army Chemical Center, Maryland: USA Chemical Corps History Office, 1958.

—. *The 89th Division in the Bois de Bantheville, October 1918.* Army Chemical Center, Maryland: USA Chemical History Office, 1960.

English, George H., Jr. *History of the 89th Division, U.S.A.* Denver, Colorado: Smith-Books, 1920.

Masseck, C.J. *Official Brief History, 89th Division, U.S.A., 1917-1918-1919.* n.p., 1919.

U.S. Army, 89th Infantry Division. *Report on St. Mihiel Offensive, 89th Division, September 12-13, 1918.* Ft. Leavenworth, Kansas: Army Service Schools Press, 1919.

U.S. Army War College. Historical Section. "The Eighty-Ninth Division, 1917-1918." Analytical study, 1924.

353rd Infantry Regiment:

Dienst, Charles F., et. al. *History of the 353rd Infantry Regiment, 89th Division, National Army, September, 1917-June, 1919.* Wichita, Kansas: 353rd Infantry Society, 1921.

354th Infantry Regiment:

McGrath, John F. *War Diary of 354th Infantry (Missouri, Illinois), 89th Division.* Trier: J. Lintz, 1919.

356th Infantry Regiment:

U.S. Army, 356th Infantry Regiment. Co. M. *Company "M", 356th Infantry, 89th Division, Camp Funston, Kansas, to Schweich, Germany.* Trier: Kock, 1919.

341st Field Artillery Regiment:

U.S. Army, 341st Artillery Regiment. *Regimental History Three Hundred and Forty-first Field Artillery, Eighty-ninth Division of the National Army, Organized September Nineteen-seventeen; Demobilized June, Nineteen-nineteen.* n.p.,1920.

342nd Field Artillery Regiment:

U.S. Army, 342nd Artillery Regiment. *Regimental History, 342nd Field Artillery, 89th Division: Published by the Regimental Historian, 342nd Field Artillery.* n.p., 1921.

314th Engineer Regiment:

A.E.S. *Being a Brief Historical Sketch of Company "F" 314th Engineers.* Prum, Germany: n.p., 1919.

Haswell, William S., & Stevenson, Charles S. *A History of Company A, 314th Engineers, 89th Division.* n.p., 1919.

Hixson, Merrel E. *"E" Company, 314th Engineers, American Expeditionary Forces.* Germany: n.p.,1919.

Major General Joseph L. Hines (left) of the III Corps with Major General Henry T. Allen, commander of the 90th Division at Stenay, France, November, 1918. Courtesy National Archives.

90th Infantry Division

The War Department established the division on August 5, 1917 at Camp Travis, Texas. All of the first men in the division were from Texas and Oklahoma, those from Oklahoma being in the 179th Brigade and those from Texas in the 180th Brigade. These brigades were known as the Oklahoma and Texas Brigades respectively. Additional draftees from Illinois, Min-

Above: Private Henry W. Jordan (standing, far left) poses with the rest of the office staff of the 359th Infantry Regiment, 1918. Courtesy Military History Institute.

Below: Travis W. Brown, Bugler, Company A, 360th Infantry Regiment, 1918. Courtesy Military History Institute.

nesota, North Dakota and South Dakota filled out the division.[78] The division was known as the "Alamo Division."

Insignia:
The division shoulder sleeve insignia was an olive square with a letter "T" bisected by an oval letter "O" both red. The design follows from the initials of Texas and Oklahoma the native states of the first members of the division. Variants exist in the shape of the background including a shield and an oval and in the placement and design of the "TO" monogram.[79]

Campaigns:
St. Mihiel Offensive, Meuse-Argonne Offensive, Puvenelle Sector, Villers-en-Haye Sector.[80]

Division Organization (1917-1919):[81]

179th Infantry Brigade:

357th Infantry Regiment
358th Infantry Regiment
344th Machine Gun Battalion

180th Infantry Brigade:

359th Infantry Regiment
360th Infantry Regiment
345th Machine Gun Battalion

Division Troops:

343rd Machine Gun Battalion

165th Field Artillery Brigade:

343rd Field Artillery Regiment
344th Field Artillery Regiment

Musician Rudolph H. Hoefs of the 345th Field Artillery Regiment band strikes a martial pose at Berncastle, Germany, April 14, 1919. Courtesy Military History Institute.

345th Field Artillery Regiment
315th Trench Mortar Battery

Division Support:

315th Engineer Regiment
315th Field Signal Battalion
315th Train Headquarters and Military Police
315th Ammunition Train
315th Supply Train
315th Engineer Train
315th Sanitary Train (357th, 358th, 359th, 360th Ambulance Companies & Field Hospitals)

Division Combat Narrative:[82]
The first unit of the division to go overseas arrived in France June 23, 1918; the last element July 17, 1918.

For training purposes the division (less artillery) was sent to the Department of Cote d'Or, with headquarters at Aignay-le-Duc. For the same purpose the artillery brigade went to Camp Hunt at Le Courneau (Gironde). It did not participate in operations but rejoined the division after the Armistice on the march into Germany.

On August 19, 1918, the division moved to the vicinity of Toul with headquarters established at Gondreville. This move was scarcely completed when the division was ordered to relieve the 1st Division in the line in the Villers-en-Haye Sector north of Toul, which relief it completed on August 24, 1918.

The division participated in the Saint Mihiel Offensive September 12-16, 1918, occupying the extreme right of the attacking force in the 1st Army Corps, and forming the pivot upon which the advance was made south of the Saint Mihiel salient with the 82nd Division on the right holding its front astride the Moselle River.

The division remained in line in the Puvenollo Sector until October 10th, during which period it engaged in raids of major and minor importance, and participated in demonstration conducted against the enemy simultaneously with the initial attack in the Meuse-Argonne Offensive, September 26, 1918. On October 10th it was relieved by the 7th Division, and proceeded to the Blercourt area west of Verdun in the reserve of the 1st Army.

On October 17th it passed to the reserve of the 3rd Army Corps and on October 22nd relieved the 5th Division in line near Romágne-sous-Montfaucon. It remained in front line attacking until the Armistice, November 11, 1918. The outstanding features of this operation were the piercing of that part of the Hindenburg Line known as the Freya Stellung, and the crossing of the Meuse River, in which 14 villages were captured in an advance of 22 kilometers against organized defense.

Days in the Front Line: 0 (training) 43 (sector) 26 (battle) for a total of 69. During operations the division took 1,876 prisoners and its casualties totaled 1,496 soldiers killed in action or died of wounds, 6,053 wounded in action.[83]

After the Armistice the division was assigned to the Army of Occupation and began its march on November 24th. The first troops of the division crossed into Germany on December 6th. Headquarters were established at Berncastel December 21st, and remained there until the division returned to the United States.

Division Headquarters sailed from Saint Nazaire on May 28, 1919, and arrived at Boston on June 7, 1919.

The division had 5 commanding generals; Major General Henry T. Allen, Brigadier General J.A. Gaston, Brigadier General William H. Johnston, Brigadier General J.B. O'Neil, and Major General C.H. Martin.

Reference Bibliography:

General Division Histories

American Battle Monuments Commission. *90th Division, Summary of Operations in the World War.* Washington, DC: Government Printing Office, 1944.

Cochrane, Rexmond C. *The Use of Gas at Saint Mihiel: The 90th Division, September 1918.* Army Chemical Center, Maryland: USA Chemical Corps History Office, 1957.
U.S. Army, 90th Infantry Division. "Operations 90th Division, A.E.F., 18 August-11 November 1918." Report, 1918.
—. *Operations 90th Division, November 11th, 1918-May 6th, 1919.* Report, 1919.
Wythe, George. *A History of the 90th Division.* New York: 90th Division Association, 1920.

357th Infantry Regiment:
Marshall, Conrad H. *History of "M" Company, 357th Infantry, 1917-1919.* Carnegie, Oklahoma: *Carnegie Herald*, 1919.
U.S. Army, 357th Infantry Regiment. *357th Infantry: It's History from Organization Until Part of Army of Occupation, 1917-1919.* Trier, Germany: Lintz, 1919.

358th Infantry Regiment:
U.S. Army, 358th Infantry Regiment. *History and Statistics of the 358th Infantry, Ninetieth Division, US Army.* Gerolstein, 1919.
—. Co. E. *358th Inf., 90th Div., Company E, Sept. 1917, June 1919: American Expeditionary Forces, June 1918, June 1919.* Daun, Germany: A. Schneider, 1919.
—. Co. F. *Company F's Part, 358th Infantry, 1918-1919.* Daun, Germany: F. Werner, 1919.

359th Infantry Regiment:
Emmett, Chris. *Give "Way to the Right": Serving with the AEF in France during the World War.* San Antonio, Texas: Naylor, 1934.

360th Infantry Regiment:
Barnett, Victor F. *A History of the Activities and Operations of the 360th United States Infantry Regiment in the World War, 1914-1918: Army of Occupation, American Expeditionary Forces.* Zeltigen, Germany: 1919.
Hymans, H.I. *A Short History and Photographic Record of the 360th Infantry, Texas Brigade.* San Antonio, Texas: San Antonio Printing, 1918.

343rd Field Artillery Regiment:
Scott, Charles M. *Activities of the 343rd Field Artillery, 90th Division, United States Army.* Longkamp, Germany: 1919.

344th Field Artillery Regiment:
Regimental History and Roster 344th Field Artillery, September 1917-May 1919. Morbach, Germany: n.p., 1919.

The standard design of the 90th Division insignia; embroidered on felt.

A 90th Division insignia of wool on wool construction.

91st Infantry Division

The War Department established the division on August 5, 1917 at Camp Lewis, Washington. The division was composed of draftees from California, Idaho, Montana, Nevada, Oregon, Utah, Washington, and Wyoming. The division is known as the "Far West Division."[84]

Insignia:
The green fir tree with olive border emblematic of the Far West and representing readiness. The insignia was approved December 8, 1918.[85]

Campaigns:
Ypres-Lys Offensive, Meuse-Argonne Offensive.[86]

Division Organization (1917-1919):[87]

181st Infantry Brigade:

Major General William H. Johnston, commander of the 91st Division with his predecessor, Brigadier General Frederick S. Foltz, at Montigny le Roi, France, August, 1918. Courtesy National Archives.

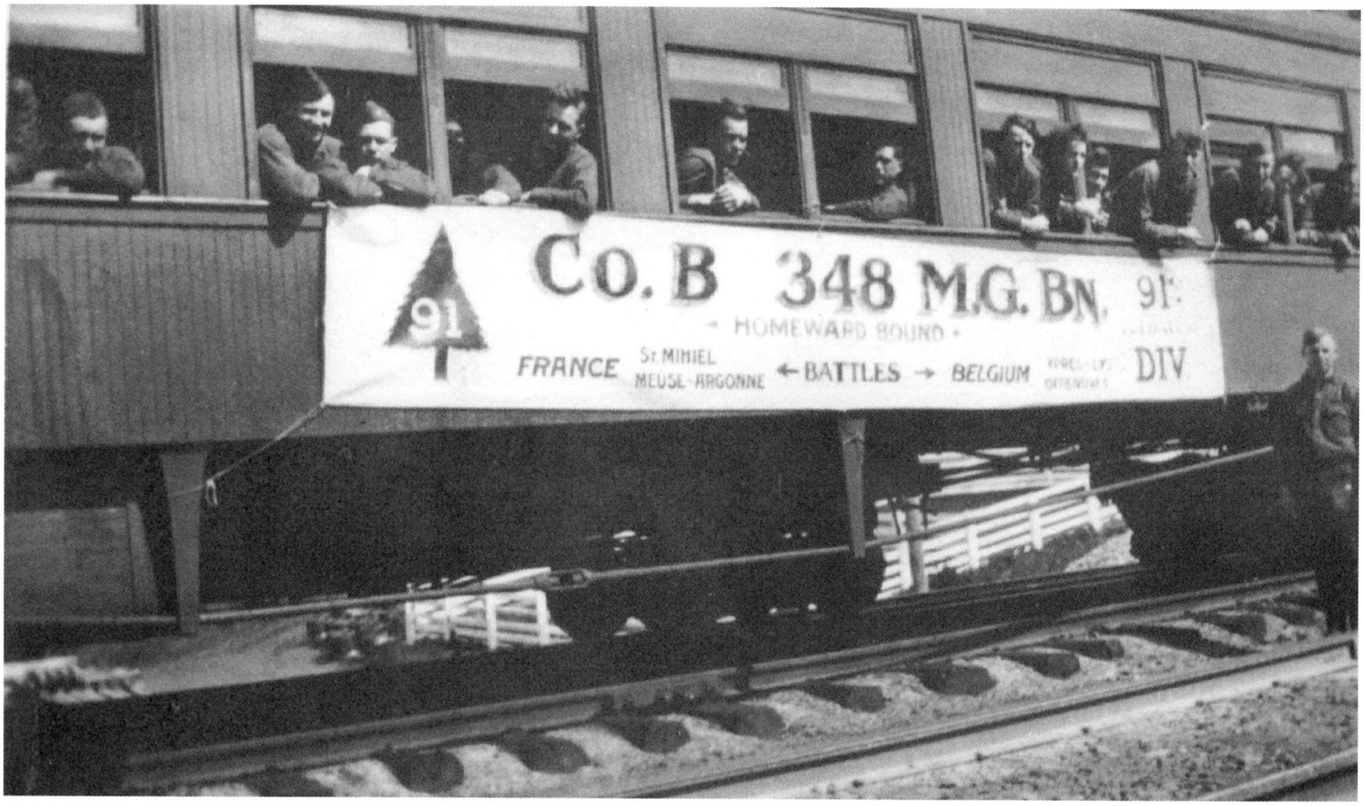

Homeward Bound. The men of Company B, 348th Machine Gun Battalion on the way home. Courtesy Military History Institute.

Officers and men of Company A, 348th Machine Gun Battalion pose with their Vickers machine guns in France, 1918. Courtesy Military History Institute.

361st Infantry Regiment
362nd Infantry Regiment
347th Machine Gun Battalion

182nd Infantry Brigade:

363rd Infantry Regiment
364th Infantry Regiment
348th Machine Gun Battalion

Division Troops:

346th Machine Gun Battalion

166th Field Artillery Brigade:

346th Field Artillery Regiment
347th Field Artillery Regiment
348th Field Artillery Regiment
316th Trench Mortar Battery

Division Support:

316th Engineer Regiment
316th Field Signal Battalion
316th Train Headquarters and Military Police
316th Ammunition Train
316th Supply Train
316th Engineer Train
316th Sanitary Train (361st, 362nd, 363rd, 364th Ambulance Companies & Field Hospitals)

Division Combat Narrative:[88]
The first unit of the division arrived in France July 20, 1918; the last element July 29, 1918.

For training purposes the division (less artillery) was sent to the 8th Training Area in the Department of Haute-Marne with headquarters at Montigny-le-Ron.

For the same purpose the artillery brigade went to Camp de Souge (Gironde), and Clermont Farrand (Puy-de-Dóms). It never rejoined the division nor did it participate in combat operations.

September 7th the division left the training area and moved to the vicinity of Gondrecourt with headquarters at that place. It was assigned to the reserve of the 1st American Army during the St. Mihiel Offensive and headquarters were established at Sorcy, September 21, 1918.

The success of the St. Mihiel Offensive being assured the concentration of troops preparatory to the Meuse-Argonne Offensive began during the stabilization of the lines in the St. Mihiel Salient. The division moved to the Vavincourt area September 14th, to the vicinity of Autrecourt September 17, and on September 20, it was concentrated in the Foret de Hesse. On September 26, it attacked on a front extending from Vauquois to a point about three kilometers east thereof. Passing through the Bois de Cheppy it made an advance of about eight kilometers capturing the towns of Very, Epinonville, Eclistontaine and Gesnes. The troops were withdrawn from the last-named place, a new and shorter line having been established by the corps; the rest of the ground gained was held against strong counter-attacks and on October 4 the division was relieved by the 32nd Division and went to the vicinity of Contrisson. On October 6 the 181st Brigade was attached successively to the 1st and 32nd Divisions and participated in the attack until relieved on October 12 when it rejoined the division.

On October 16 the division entrained for Belgium. Arriving October 18 it was placed at the disposal of His Majesty the King of Belgium commanding the Group of Armies in Flanders, and was assigned to the French 7th Corps. The division relieved the French 164th Division in line October 30 and participated in the Ypres-Lys Offensive October 31-November 4, 1918.

The standard die cut felt design insignia of the 91st Division.

An embroidered on wool version of the standard 91st Division design.

A variant of the standard 91st Division insignia with more elaborately embroidered fir tree.

This beautiful 91st Division insignia adds branches to the fir tree; embroidered on felt.

The alternate 91st Division design with the division numerical designation over the monogram "WW" for Wild West – another nickname for the division.

During this operation it attacked and held Spitaals Boschen a strongly fortified wood, captured the town of Audenande and drove the enemy east of the Scheldt River. On November 4th the division was relieved in line and withdrew to the area east of Vive St. Eloi with headquarters at Ocstroosebeke. On November 8 it passed from the French 7th Corps to the French 30th Corps and entered the front line again November 10 preparatory to the resumption of the attack and the crossing of the Scheldt River.

Days in the Front Line: 0 (training) 6 (sector) 17 (battle) for a total of 23. During operations the division took 2,412 prisoners and its casualties totaled 1,454 soldiers killed in action or died of wounds, 4,654 wounded in action.[89]

After the Armistice, November 11, 1918, the division remained in Belgium until January when it moved to the Le Mans Embarkation Center preparatory to its return to the United States.

Division headquarters sailed from St. Nazaire April 6, 1919, and arrived at New York April 16, 1919.

The division had four commanders; Major General Henry A. Green, Brigadier General James A. Irons, Brigadier General F. S. Foltz, and Major General William H. Johnston.

Reference Bibliography:

General Division Histories:

American Battle Monuments Commission. *91st Division, Summary of Operations in the World War.* Washington, DC: Government Printing Office, 1944.

Henderson, Alice Palmer. *The Ninety-First: The First at Camp Lewis.* Tacoma, Washington: John C. Barr, 1918.

Pages of Glory and History: The 91st Division in Argonne and Flanders. n.p., 1919.

The Story of the 91st Division. San Mateo, California: 91st Division Publishing Committee, 1919.

361st Infantry Regiment:

Tibbals, Mirton L., & Solve, Melvin T. *Nine Months Overseas, Being the History of "H" Company, 361st Infantry, 91st Division.* n.p.,1919.

U.S. Army, 361st Infantry Regiment. *History of Headquarters Company, 361st Infantry, 91st Division.* n.p., 1919.

Burton, Harold H. *600 Days Service: A History of the 361st Infantry Regiment of the United States Army.* Portland, Oregon: James, Kerns, & Abbott, 1921.

363rd Infantry Regiment:

U.S. Army, 363rd Infantry Regiment. Co. K. *Facts and Figures of "K" Company, 363rd Infantry.* San Francisco. California: Hartman, 1919.

364th Infantry Regiment:

Graupner, Adolphus E., ed. *War Book of "E" Company, 364th Infantry.* n.p., 1920.

1921 Regtimental Reunion Committee. *Journal of Operations of the 364th Infantry, A.E.F., 91.* Los Angeles, California: By the Committee, 1921.

Wilson, Bryant, & Tooze, Lamar. *With the 364th Infantry in America, France and Belgium.* New York: Knickerbocker, 1919.

316th Engineer Regiment:

Canfield, George H. "Work of the 316th Engineers in Belgium." *Military Engineer* (Nov/Dec 1928): pp. 479-86.

U.S. Army, 316th Engineer Regiment. *The History of the 316th Engineers: A Record of Military Operations from August, 1917 to April 1919*

92nd Infantry Division (Colored)

First Lieutenant Robert L. Campbell, Company I, 368th Infantry shown here just after his discharge from the hospital for wounds suffered in the Argonne. He was the first member of the 92nd Division to receive the Distinguished Service Cross. Courtesy National Archives.

The War Department established the division on October 24, 1917 at Camps Grant, Upton, Dix, Meade, Dodge, Sherman, and Funston. The division was to be made up of African-American selected service men from all parts of the United States. Headquarters, 183rd Infantry Brigade, 165th Infantry Regiment and the 350th Machine Gun Battalion mustered at Camp Grant, Headquarters, 184th Infantry Brigade, 167th Infantry Regiment and the 351st Machine Gun Battalion mustered at Camp Upton, Headquarters, 167th Field Artillery Brigade, 349th and 350th Field Artillery mustered at Camp Dix, the 368th Infantry and 351st Field Artillery mustered at Camp Meade, the 366th Infantry mustered at Camp Dodge, the 317th Engineer Regiment and 325th Field Signal Battalion mustered at Camp Sherman, and the Division Headquarters, 349th Machine Gun Battalion, and trains mustered at Camp Funston.[90] The division was popularly known as the "Buffalo Division" calling upon the deeds of the famous Buffalo Soldiers of the Western Campaigns. Native Americans believed that Americans of African descent were part man and part buffalo due to their skin color, hair texture and ferocious fighting spirit.

Insignia:
The division insignia was a black buffalo on an olive drab disc bordered black. The design was approved December 6, 1918. Variants of the insignia exist with blue and red backgrounds, red purportedly representing the division artillery.[91] A separate insignia exists for the 349th Field Artillery which consists of a red swastika upon a diamond background with a white dot superimposed.[92]

Campaigns:
Meuse-Argonne Offensive, Marbache.[93]

Division Organization (1917-1919):[94]

183rd Infantry Brigade:

365th Infantry Regiment
366th Infantry Regiment
350th Machine Gun Battalion

184th Infantry Brigade:

367th Infantry Regiment
368th Infantry Regiment
351st Machine Gun Battalion

Division Troops:

349th Machine Gun Battalion

167th Field Artillery Brigade:

349th Field Artillery Regiment
350th Field Artillery Regiment
351st Field Artillery Regiment
317th Trench Mortar Battery

Division Support:

317th Engineer Regiment
325th Field Signal Battalion
317th Train Headquarters and Military Police

The standard insignia for the 92nd Division features felt on felt construction with stitching used to highlight the Buffalo.

Right: Non-commissioned Officers of the 92nd Division at bayonet training, I Corps School, Gondrecourt, France, August, 1918. Courtesy National Archives.

Below: Troops of the 92nd Division on the road near Binarville, France, October, 1918. Note the 77th Division insignia on the tailgate of the truck. Courtesy National Archives.

An embroidered on felt version of the 92nd Division insignia.

In this example, the Buffalo faces right; felt on felt with stitching used to highlight the design.

A blue embroidered buffalo on French Horizon Blue material suggests French manufacture and possible use by 92nd Division Artillery personnel.

317th Ammunition Train
317th Supply Train
317th Engineer Train
317th Sanitary Train (35th, 366th, 367th, 368th Ambulance Companies & Field Hospitals)

Division Combat Narrative:[95]
The first unit of the division arrived in France June 19, 1918; the last element July 18, 1918.

For training purposes the division (less artillery) was sent to the 11th Training Area, with headquarters at Bourbonne-les-Bains (Haute-Marne). For the same purpose the artillery brigade went to La Courtine (Creuse). It rejoined the division in the Marbache Sector (Lorraine) Oct. 21, 1918. On August 11 the division went to the Vosges with headquarters at Bruyères. On August 24, it commenced the relief of the 5th Division in the St. Dié Sector, completing the relief August 31. It remained in line until September 21, when it proceeded to the vicinity of Triaucourt (Meuse).

On September 25 the division, less the 368th Infantry and the artillery brigade constituted the reserve of the 1st Army Corps I the Meuse-Argonne Offensive, and was assembled in the woods northwest of Clermont. The 368th Infantry formed a part of the combat liaison between the French 4th Army and the American 1st Army September 26 to October 4, 1918. On September 29th the division, less one infantry brigade, the artillery and the engineers, was placed at the disposal of the 38th French Army Corps operating in the Argonne Forest where it formed the reserve of the French 1st Dismounted Cavalry Division. On October 3 it was relieved and placed at the disposal of the 1st American Army, and assigned as 1st Corps Reserve. On October 4 it was assigned to the 4th American Corps and proceeded to the vicinity of Toul where on October 9 it relieved the 69th French Division in the Marbache Sector. It passed from the 4th Corps to the 6th Corps on October 25. The division participated in the attack of the 2nd American Army November 10-11, 1918, operating west of the Seille River along the heights on both banks of the Moselle River in the direction of Corny.

Days in the Front Line: 7 (training) 56 (sector) 0 (battle) for a total of 63. During operations the division took 38 prisoners and its casualties totaled 182 soldiers killed in action or died of wounds, 1,465 wounded in action.[96]

After the Armistice the division remained in the occupied area until the middle of December when it proceeded to the Le Mans Embarkation Center preparatory to its return to the United States.

Division Headquarters sailed from Brest on February 7, 1919, and arrived at New York on February 17, 1919.

The division had three commanding generals; Major General Charles C. Ballou, Major General Charles H. Martin, and Brigadier General James B. Erwin.

Embroidered version of a 92nd Division Artillery insignia.

Felt on felt construction is used for this 92nd Division Artillery insignia.

Right: The 350th Field Artillery Regiment adopted their own insignia; this embroidered example features a white swastika with a blue dot at center upon a red background.

Far right: Their sister regiment, the 351st Field Artillery Regiment, also adopted the white swastika as their insignia substituting a red dot on a blue field.

Reference Bibliography:

General Division Histories:

American Battle Monuments Commission. *92nd Division, Summary of Operations in the World War.* Washington, DC: Government Printing Office, 1944.

Cochrane, Rexmond C. *The 92nd Division in the Marbache Sector, October 1918.* Army Chemical Center, Maryland: USA Chemical Corps History Office, 1959.

U.S. Army War College Historical Section. "The Ninety-Second Division, 1917-1918." Study, 1923.

351st Field Artillery Regiment:

Ross, William O., Slaughter, Duke L. *With the 351st in France (A Diary).* Baltimore: Afro-American Company, 1919.

93rd Infantry Division (Colored)

Colonel William Hayward, commander of the 369th Infantry Regiment playing baseball with his men, St. Nazaire, France, February, 1918. Of note is the National Guard designation of 15 NY on his overseas cap signifying the unit's original designation as the 15th Infantry Regiment, New York National Guard. Courtesy National Archives.

The War Department established the 185th and 186th Brigades (Colored) on November 23, 1918 at Camp Stuart, Virginia. The 185th Brigade was composed of the 369th Infantry Regiment, the former 15th Infantry Regiment, New York National Guard, and the 370th Infantry, the former 8th Infantry Regiment, Illinois National Guard. The 186th Brigade was composed of the 371st Infantry Regiment, formed from African-American selective service men, and the 372nd Infantry Regiment, made up National Guard Units from Connecticut (1st Separate Company Connecticut Infantry), District of Columbia (1st Separate Battalion), District of Columbia Infantry, Maryland (1st Separate Company Maryland Infantry), Massachusetts (1st Separate Company Massachusetts Infantry), Ohio (9th Separate Battalion Ohio Infantry), and Tennessee (1st Separate Company Tennessee Infantry). This division was never organized to its full strength, only the 185th and 186th Infantry Brigades being formed.[97]

Insignia:

Originally, the division selected a red hand, the insignia of the French 157th Division, the French unit they served with. This alluded to the bloody hands of its soldiers from hand to hand combat. As this insignia was considered too graphic, the division was ordered to choose another insignia.[98] Then the division selected an insignia of a French Adrian helmet in light blue, superimposed on a black disc. The helmet symboled the service of the regiments with the French Divisions. The insignia was approved December 30, 1917. The subordinate regiments in this division adopted individual distinctive insignia: The 369th Infantry Regiment: a white snake with black markings upon a black square. The 372nd Infantry Regiment: A red hand bordered in blue on a khaki square. A number of variants of both the division and the regimental insignia exist.[99]

Above: Men of the 93rd Division back from the front line enjoy hot coffee and a snack, France, 1918. Courtesy National Archives.

Right: Kid Ferguson, a star basketball player of the 369th Infantry Regiment at St. Nazaire, France, February, 1918. Note again the 15 designation on his overseas cap, and the NY 15 monogram on his singlet. Courtesy National Archives.

Far right: First Lieutenant Marc J. Logie of Company F, 372nd Infantry Regiment, Germany, 1919. Courtesy Military History Institute.

The "Harlem Hellfighters" band of the 369th Infantry Regiment, leads the way on a road march in France, 1918. Bandleader Lieutenant James Reese Europe, an officer in the Machine Gun company marches to the right front of the band (left in photo). Courtesy National Archives.

The standard insignia of the 93rd Division; a felt on felt French Helmet of horizon Blue material.

Campaigns:

Meuse-Argonne Offensive, 369th Infantry Regiment, Champagne Sector, Thur Sector, Vosges. 370th Infantry Regiment, Argonne Sector. 371st Infantry Regiment, Verdun Sector. 372nd Infantry Regiment, Argonne Sector.[100]

Division Organization (1917-1919):[101]

185th Infantry Brigade:

369th Infantry Regiment
370th Infantry Regiment

186th Infantry Brigade:

371st Infantry Regiment
372nd Infantry Regiment

Division Combat Narrative:[102]

In compliance with War Department instructions organization of the 93rd Division was begun at Camp Stuart, Newport News, Virginia., in December, 1917. The nucleus of the division was composed of men from Connecticut, the District of Columbia, Illinois, Maryland, Massachusetts, New York, Ohio, Tennessee, and South Carolina.

The division was never fully organized, only headquarters and the 185th and 186th Infantry Brigades being formed. The Commanding General assumed command of the division at Camp Stuart, Newport News, Va., in December, 1917, at which time the infantry regiments of the organization were stationed at various widely separated posts in the United States.

Upon arrival in France, headquarters was stationed at Bur-sur-Seine (Aube) pending the arrival and assembly of the units of the division. These units, however, consisting of the 369th, 370th, 371st and 372nd Infantry Regiments were brigaded with the French Army, and in May, 1918, the personnel of headquarters was attached to the 1st and 42nd Division pending the contemplated re-assembling of the 93rd Division. It was never re-assembled, although never formally dissolved, and its history therefore resolves itself into the histories of its four infantry regiments.

Left: This variant uses die cut felt with a well worn velvet inset to form the design.

369th Infantry Regiment, Harlem Hellfighters or Rattlesnake Regiment.
This regiment was organized in April, 1917, as the 15th New York Infantry, a National Guard unit, but upon arrival in France it was designated as the 369th Infantry. The regiment arrived at Brest, December 26, 1917. Thence it moved to Saint Nazaire, January 1, 1918, remaining there until March 13, 1918, when it proceeded to Givry-en-Argonne. Upon arrival March 15, 1918, it was attached to the 16th Division, 8th Army Corps, 4th French Army, for purposes of instruction and training. Beginning April 8, 1918, the battalions of the regiment were successively placed in front line sector with French troops north of Saints-Monehould, in the Champagne. The regiment held this sector until July 5, 1918. It participated in the Champagne-Marne Defensive, July 15 to 19, 1918, in the Aisne-Marne Offensive, July 18 to 20, 1918, and in the offensive operations of the 4th French Army on the Champagne front, September 26 to 30, 1918. On October 14, 1918, the regiment, as part of the 161st Division, French, to which it has been assigned on July 15th, proceeded to Alsace. The battalions of the 369th Infantry took over sections of front line in the Vosges which they held until November 11, 1918. After the Armistice the regiment became a part of the French Army of Occupation. On December 8, 1918, it was relieved from duty with the French Army, and proceeded to the Le Mans Embarkation Center preparatory to its return to the United States. The regiment sailed from Brest February 2, 1919, and arrived at New York February 12, 1919.

An embroidered on wool example of the 93rd Division insignia.

370th Infantry Regiment, the Black Devils.
This regiment was organized from the 8th Illinois (National Guard). It arrived in France in April, 1918, and trained with various French divisions until August 31, 1918, during which period detachments of the regiment were in front line positions. On September 15, 1918, the regiment as a part of the 59th Division, French, went into line in the Vauxaillon Area northeast of Soissons, and participated in the Oise-Aisne Offensive, September 17 to October 12, 1918, and October 24 to November 11, 1918. The regiment embarked for the United States at Brest, February 1, 1919, and arrived at New York February 9, 1919.

This felt on felt variant of the 93rd Division insignia adds a helmet strap to the division design.

371st Infantry Regiment, the Red Hand.
This regiment arrived in France in April, 1918, and as an independent unit of the 13th French Army Corps was in training from April 26 to June 6, 1918, in the vicinity of Bar-le-Duc. It joined the 68th Division, French, on June 13, 1918, in the vicinity of Verdun, remaining in support of this unit until June 22, 1918. From June 23 to September 14, 1918, the regiment was in line in the Verdun Sector. It participated in the offensive operations of the 4th French Army on the Champagne front September 27 to October 6, 1918, in the 157th Division, 9th French Army Corps. The 157th Division was withdrawn from the line October 6, 1918, and proceeded to the Alsace Sector, Vosges. The regiment was in line in this Sector from October 16 to November 11, 1918. It was withdrawn November 15, 1918, and proceeded to the Le Mans Embarkation Center preparatory to returning to the United States. The regiment sailed from Brest February 3, 1919, and arrived at New York February 11, 1919.

372nd Infantry Regiment, The Red Hand.
This regiment arrived at Saint Nazaire, in April, 1918, and proceeded to the training center in the vicinity of Givry-en-Argonne for duty with the French Army. From June 6 to July 14, 1918, and from July 26 to September 9, 1918, the regiment was in line in the Argonne Sector. It participated in the offensive operations of the 4th French Army on the Champagne front September 26 to October 7, 1918, in the 157th Division, 9th French Army Corps. The regiment proceeded to the Vosges on October 11th where it occupied a sector of front from October 13, to November 11th. It remained in the Vosges until January 1, 1919, when it proceeded to the Le Mans Embarkation Center preparatory to returning to the United States. The regiment sailed from Brest on February 3, 1919, and arrived at New York on February 12, 1919.

The casualties of the four infantry regiments, 93rd Division, totaled 591 soldiers killed in action or died of wounds, 2,943 wounded in action.[103]

The 369th Infantry Regiment, the Rattlesnake Regiment, adopted their own insignia; this embroidered white rattlesnake upon a back field is the standard pattern.

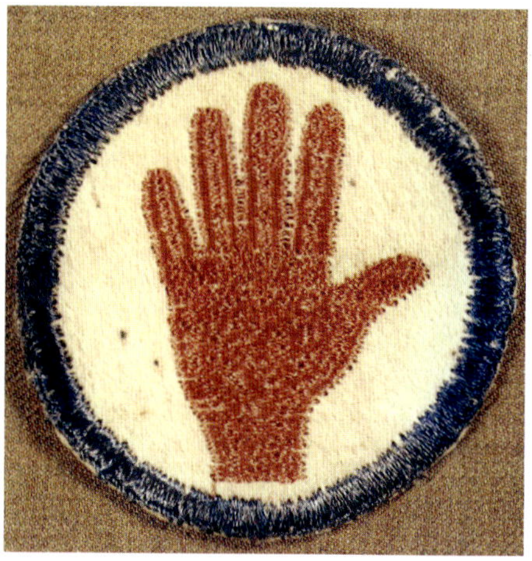

The 372nd Infantry Regiment adopted the original 93rd Division pattern, deemed too graphic by the AEF Headquarters, as their insignia; the embroidered Bloody Hand will forever be associated with the 372nd Infantry.

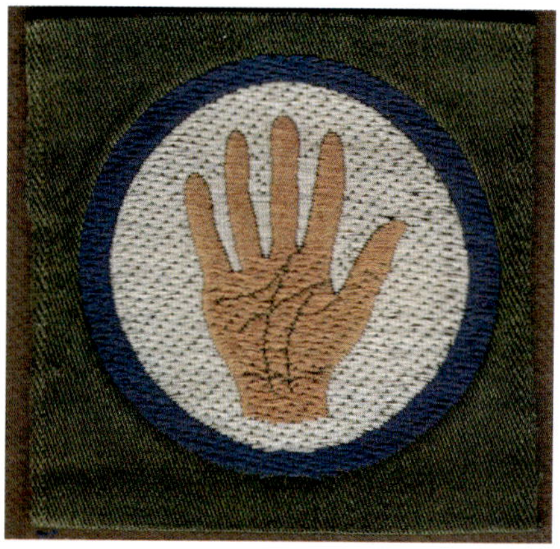

Liberty Loan style Bloody Hand pattern 93rd Division insignia.

Although never fighting as a complete division, the 93rd was assigned the famous 369th Infantry Regiment, the Harlem Hellfighters, or Rattlesnake Regiment - the single most storied African-American regiment of World War I. The regimental band formed from prominent musicians, was led by Lieutenant James Reese Europe, and Drum Major Noble Sissle, and was instrumental in introducing jazz music to France. During World War I, no Medal of Honor was bestowed upon an African-American soldier. Subsequent action by the Army to review the policy at the time found that although several had been recommended for the award, they had been downgraded to the Distinguished Service Cross, with the exception of one soldier whose file was never acted upon. In 1991, Corporal Freddie Stowers, Company C, 371st Infantry Regiment was awarded the Medal of Honor posthumously for his actions in combat in 1918.

Reference Bibliography:

General Division Histories

American Battle Monuments Commission. *93rd Division, Summary of Operations in the World War*. Washington, DC: Government Printing ,Office 1944.

Guttman, Jon. "Regiment's Pride." Military History (Oct 1991): pp. 35-41.

U.S. Congress, House of Representatives. *Erection of a Monument in France to Commemorate the Valiant Services of the Ninety-Third Division of the American Expeditionary Forces*. Hearings, 69th Congress, 1st session, Mar 1926.

—. Monument in France to Colored American Infantry Regiments Attached to the French Army. Report, 68th Congress, 2nd session, February 1925.

369th Infantry Regiment

Badger, Reid. *A Life in Ragtime: A Biography of James Reese Europe*. New York: Oxford, 1995.

Harris, Stephen L. *Harlem's Hell Fighters: The African-American 369th Infantry in World War I*. Washington, DC: Brassey's, 2003.

Harris, Bill. *The Hellfighters of Harlem: African-American Soldiers Who Fought for the Right to Fight for Their Country*. New York: Carroll & Graf, 2002.

Little, Arthur W. *From Harlem to the Rhine: The Story of New York's Colored Volunteers*. New York: Covici Friede, 1936.

Moore, William E., & Russell, James C. *U.S. Official Pictures of the World War: Showing America's Participation; Selected From the Official Files of the War Department*. 3 vols. n.p., Army & Navy Union, 1921.

371st Infantry Regiment

Beattie, Taylor V. "Corporal Freddie Stowers: An Appointment with Eternity on Hill 188." *Army History* (Winter 2003): pp. 14-20.

Beattie, Taylor V. "Seventy Three Years After his Bayonet Assault on Hill 188, Freddie Stowers Got His Medal of Honor." *Military History* (Aug 2004): pp. 74 & 76.

Deckard, Percy E. *List of Officers Who Served with the 371st Infantry and Headquarters, 186th Infantry Brigade during the World War*. Allegany, Pennsylvania: Allegany Citizen, 1929.

Heywood, Chester D. *List of Officers, 371st Infantry, World War I: A History*. n.p., nd.

—. *Negro Combat Troops in the World War: The Story of the 371st Infantry*. New York: 1928.

Scipio, L. Albert. *With the Red Hand Division*. Silver Springs, Maryland: Roman, 1985.

372nd Infantry Regiment

Mason, Monroe, & Furr, Arthur. *The American Negro Soldier with the Red Hand of France*. Boston: Cornhill, 1921.

94th Infantry Division

This division was not organized during the period of the war or during the occupation period.

Insignia:
Shortly after the war the War Department authorized as an insignia a gray disc, with a black silhouette of a pilgrim with flintlock fowling musket.[104]

95th Infantry Division

Organization of the division began at Camp Sherman, Ohio in September, 1918.

The standard 95th Division insignia originally featured an "OK" monogram; felt on felt construction.

Insignia:
The division selected an olive drab oval bordered red with a red "K" together representing "OK."[105]

Campaigns:
None.

Division Organization (1917-1919):[106]

189th Infantry Brigade:

377th Infantry Regiment
378th Infantry Regiment
359th Machine Gun Battalion

170th Field Artillery Brigade

Division Support:

320th Engineer Regiment
320th Field Signal Battalion
320th Train Headquarters and Military Police
320th Ammunition Train
320th Supply Train
320th Engineer Train
320th Sanitary Train

An unknown soldier and lady pose for the camera. Author's Collection

Division Service Narrative:[107]
Pursuant to letter of instructions from The Adjutant General of the Army, dated September 5, 1918, the organization of the 95th Division was begun at Camp Sherman, Ohio. The organization of the Division was to comply in every respect with Series "A", Tables of Organization, dated January 14, 1918.

One Infantry Brigade, the 189th, including the 359th Machine Gun Battalion was to be organized in France by the Commander in Chief, American Expeditionary Force. Subsequent instructions directed the organization of the 359th Machine Gun Battalion at Camp Sherman, Ohio.

The Artillery Brigade and the Ammunition Train were directed to be organized at Camp Taylor, Kentucky. The officers of the Division were in the main promptly assigned to the Division and reported at Camp Sherman, Ohio. The Artillery officers reported at Camp Taylor, Kentucky.

Five hundred and eighty-five (585) enlisted men, suitable for appointment as noncommissioned officers, were transferred to the 95th Division from Camp Lee, Va. These men had some training previous to transfer to the 95th Division.

The organization of the Engineer Regiment and Train were never definitely fixed as to location, and no part of the personnel for these units was ever designated.

The Division staff reported for duty during the first two weeks of October, the officers of the Division staff being graduates of the Staff Course organized at the War College during month of August.

Eleven hundred (1100) recruits were transferred to the Division from the 158th Depot Brigade at Camp Sherman during the latter part of October.

Under telegraphic instructions from the War Department 3000 Replacement Troops were turned over to the Division at Camp Sherman for training during the last week of October, 900 of these recruits being subsequently assigned to the 95th Division.

The organization of the Headquarters of all units of the Division at Camp Sherman was completed, and equipment as far as obtainable was furnished to all these organizations.

Brigadier General M. C. Smith was assigned to duty with the 95th Division, and reported October 24th, taking command of the Division.

The organization of the Artillery units at Camp Taylor was promptly affected, and training begun, the enlisted personnel for these units being about 75% complete when orders were received directing the demobilization of the Division.

Orders for the demobilization of the Division were received during the first week in December, and the demobilization of all units were completed December 21, 1918, the enlisted men being discharged or transferred, and all officers signifying desire to be discharged receiving their discharges, and all officers of the Regular Army and those desiring commissions in the same placed on duty with the 95th Division unassigned December 22, 1918.

Reference Bibliography:

General Division Histories
None.

96th Infantry Division

The division was organized at Camp Wadsworth, South Carolina, in the middle of September 1918.

Insignia:
None.

Campaigns:
None.

Division Organization (1917-1919):

191st Infantry Brigade:

381st Infantry Regiment
382nd Infantry Regiment
362nd Machine Gun Battalion

192nd Infantry Brigade:

383rd Infantry Regiment
384th Infantry Regiment
363rd Machine Gun Battalion

Division Troops:

361st Machine Gun Battalion

171st Field Artillery Brigade:

64th Field Artillery Regiment
65th Field Artillery Regiment
66th Field Artillery Regiment
22nd Trench Mortar Battery

Division Support:

321st Engineer Regiment
621st Field Signal Battalion
Train Headquarters and Military Police
Ammunition Train
Supply Train
Engineer Train
Sanitary Train (Ambulance Companies & Field Hospitals)

Division Service Narrative:[108]
The 191st Infantry Brigade was to have been organized in France and the 171st Field Artillery Brigade at Camp Kearney, California. The 192nd Infantry Brigade, the 621st Field Signal Battalion and the 321st Sanitary Train were partly organized at Camp Wadsworth, S.C., but upon the signing of the Armistice, November 11, 1918, further effort in this direction stopped and the division ceased to exist on January 7th, 1919.

Major General Guy Carleton was the commanding general of the division.

A soldier's individual equipment laid out on an Army bed for inspection. Author's Collection

Reference Bibliography:

General Division Histories
None.

97th Infantry Division

The division was organized at Camp Cody, Deming, New Mexico. The division was composed of National Army draftees mainly from Oklahoma and Minnesota. The organization of the division was never completed.

Insignia:
The division chose an insignia of a vertical trident on a blue shield with a white border. The trident represents the three states from which personnel were to be drawn. It also alludes to the New England maritime tradition. This design was approved October 18, 1922.[109]

An embroidered on wool example of the 97th Division insignia.

Campaigns:
None.

Division Organization (1917-1919):[110]

193rd Infantry Brigade:

385th Infantry Regiment
386th Infantry Regiment
365th Machine Gun Battalion

194th Infantry Brigade:

387th Infantry Regiment
388th Infantry Regiment
366th Machine Gun Battalion

A studio portrait of one of the "Sammies" going off to war; the reverse reads, "This is my soldier bud Oscar and his sister." Author's Collection

Division Troops:

Machine Gun Battalion

172nd Field Artillery Brigade:

61st Field Artillery Regiment
62nd Field Artillery Regiment
63rd Field Artillery Regiment
21st Trench Mortar Battery

Division Support:

322nd Engineer Regiment
622nd Field Signal Battalion
322nd Train Headquarters and Military Police
322nd Ammunition Train
322nd Supply Train
322nd Engineer Train
322nd Sanitary Train

Division Service Narrative:
The following units were assembled at Camp Cody: 387th Infantry, 388th Infantry, 366th Machine Gun Battalion and Trains.

The 172nd Field Artillery Brigade consisting of the 61st, 62nd and 63rd Field Artillery Regiments, and 21st Trench Mortar Battery, and the 322nd Ammunition Train were organized at Camp Jackson, South Carolina. The nucleus of the 322nd Engineer Regiment and train was organized at Camp Humphrey, Va., but never joined the division.

The several units of the division were demobilized in December, 1918. Their combat strength at the time of demobilization was 402 officers and 7889 men.

The division had two commanders; Colonel C. A. Martin, and Brigadier General James R. Lindsay.

Reference Bibliography:

General Division Histories
None.

Felt on felt example of the standard 98th Division insignia.

98th Infantry Division

The division was to have been organized in September, 1918, at Camp McClellan, Anniston, Alabama, but was never actually formed. The 52nd and 53rd Pioneer Regiments of Infantry were to have formed the nucleus for the Division; the designations of these regiments were to have been changed to the 389th and 390th Regiments of Infantry, respectively. Owing to the signing of the Armistice, the organization of this Division was never commenced and it existed in name only.[111]

Insignia:
The division selected a blue shield in the shape of the Great Seal of New York bordered orange and charged with the head of an Iroquois Indian chief in orange. The colors are those of the Dutch House of Nassau, responsible for the settlement of New York. The five feathers represent the five Iroquois Nations. The insignia was approved December 20, 1922.[112]

Campaigns:
None.

Division Organization:

None

Reference Bibliography:

General Division Histories:
None.

99th Infantry Division

The division was to have been organized in September, 1918, at Camp Wheeler, Macon, Georgia, but was never actually formed. The 54th and 55th Pioneer Infantry Regiments were to have furnished the nucleus for the division; the designations of these regiments were to have been changed to the 393rd and 394th Infantry Regiments, respectively. Owing to the signing of the Armistice the organization of the Division was never commenced and it existed in name only.[113]

Insignia:
None.

Campaigns:
None.

Division Organization:
None.

Reference Bibliography:

General Division Histories:
None.

100th Infantry Division

The division was never organized. Orders No. 246, War Department, October 19, 1918 assigned Brigadier General W.B. Cochran to command of the division at Camp Bowie, Texas and the officer personnel of a division staff were assigned by the War Department and reported for duty the latter part of October. With the signing of the Armistice, demobilization commenced and these staff officers were ordered elsewhere. On November 22nd General Cochran was ordered to command the 159th Depot Brigade at Camp Sherman, Ohio.[114]

Insignia:
None.

Campaigns:
None.

Division Organization:
None.

Reference Bibliography:

General Division Histories
None.

CHAPTER SIX

THE ARMY AIR SERVICE, AND THE SPECIALIST BRANCHES

Air Service

The War Department summarized operations as follows:

> "In April 1918 the Air Service had three squadrons at the front. This number increased rapidly until the Armistice, when 45 American Squadrons with 740 planes were operating. 12 of these squadrons had been equipped with American-built planes. In November 1918 the Air Service reached a total strength of 7,726 officers and 70,769 men; of these, 446 officers and 6,365 men constituted the balloon section. 23 American balloon companies served at the front. American aviators brought down 753 enemy planes and 71 balloons that were officially confirmed. American losses to enemy aviators were 357 planes and 35 balloons."[1]

Organizations:

The air service had a number of unique organizations specifically suited for its missions. The largest element of the air corps was the brigade consisting of three wings; a wing consisted of three groups, and a group of three squadrons. The squadron was the most basic element of the air corps and consisted of one flight of various air sections of one aircraft each. Organizations were arranged by mission areas as follows:

Monoplane Pursuit Brigade:
The brigade consisted of a headquarters, photo section, three wings and attached medical department, chaplains, ordnance and intelligence sections for a total of 691 aircraft.[2]

Multi-Engined Night Bombardment Brigade:
The brigade consisted of a headquarters, three wings and attached medical and ordnance department sections for a total of 270 aircraft.[3]

Army Observation Wing:
The mission of the wing was to manage the observation aspect of the air service including reconnaissance, photography, battle damage assessment and the effects of artillery fire upon the enemy. The wing consisted of a headquarters, one photo section, one Air Park, and eight observation groups with a total of 219 aircraft.[4]

Above: Second Lieutenant W. Brown of the 1st Aero Squadron crash landed his plane after an observation flight over German lines, Commune de la Saints, France, July 6, 1918. Note the squadron insignia prominently displayed on the side of the fuselage. Courtesy National Archives.

Right: Captain W.C. Schauffler, Jr. (standing) and Lieutenant Fred A. Tillman of the 90th Aero Squadron stand by their plane prior to a mission, Bethelainville, France, November 18, 1918. Courtesy National Archives.

Below: Breguet bomber of the 96th Aero Squadron piloted by First Lieutenant A.B. Alexander, with Second Lieutenant E. McLennon as observer prepare to take off, Amanty Field, Amanty, France, July 29, 1918. Courtesy National Archives.

Lieutenant G.R. Melin, Air Service of Esquadrille #3, Group 12 (French), 1st Division. Couves et Valsery, France, July 16, 1918. Note the French pilot wings worn on his right pocket. Courtesy National Archives

Balloon Wing:
Balloons were employed "principally for observation of artillery [fire]."[5] The wing consisted of a headquarters and three balloon groups.[6]

Bi-plane Pursuit Wing:
This was the fighter arm of the Army. The wing consisted of a headquarters, one photo section, one air park, three groups, with a total of 229 aircraft. Additionally, the group had an attached medical department, ordnance department, and intelligence sections.[7]

Day Bombardment Wing:
The wing consisted of a headquarters, one photo section, one air park, and three groups for a total of 229 aircraft.

Monoplane Pursuit Wing:
The wing consisted of a headquarters, one air park and three monoplane pursuit groups for a total of 229 aircraft with attached medical department, chaplains, ordnance and intelligence sections.[8]

Multi-Engined Night Bombardment Wing:
The wing consisted of a headquarters, one air park and three groups for a total of 90 aircraft with attached medical department, chaplains, and ordnance sections.[9]

Single-Engined Night Bombardment Wing:
The wing consisted of a headquarters, one air park and three groups for a total of 229 aircraft with attached medical department, chaplains, and ordnance sections.[10]

Balloon Group:
The Group consisted of a headquarters, five balloon companies, and an attached medical department for a total of five balloons.[11]

Bi-plane Pursuit Group:
The group consisted of a headquarters, supply and transportation section, engineering section, one photo section, three squadrons with a total of 76 aircraft. Additionally, the group had attached medical department, and ordnance department sections.[12]

Day Bombardment Group:
The mission of a bombardment group was to engage a variety of enemy targets through the use of bombers. The group consisted of a headquarters, supply and transportation section, an

An aerial observation camera being handed to Lieutenant J.H. Snyder of the 91st Aero Squadron before a reconnaissance mission. The pilot is Major J.N. Reynolds. Gondreville-sur-Moselle, August, 1918. Courtesy National Archives.

Basket of a captive observation balloon prior to launch. Of particular note are the telephone speaker and headphones worn by the observer, and the large map board suspended on the side of the basket. Brouville, France, April, 1918. Courtesy National Archives.

engineering section with attached medical department and ordnance department sections, and three squadrons with a total of 76 aircraft.[13]

An observation balloon being reeled to the ground after a spotting mission. Camp de Souge, France, April, 1918. Courtesy National Archives.

Multi-Engined Night Bombardment Group:
The group consisted of a headquarters, supply and transportation section, engineering section, three squadrons with a total of 30 aircraft. Additionally, the group had attached medical department and ordnance department sections.[14]

Observation Group:
The group consisted of a headquarters, supply and transportation section, engineering section, one photo section, one air park, and three squadrons with a total of 73 aircraft. Additionally, the group had attached medical department, ordnance department, artillery, infantry and intelligence sections.[15]

Pursuit Group:
The group consisted of a headquarters, supply and transportation section, engineering section, and three squadrons with a total of 76 aircraft. Additionally, the group had attached medical department and ordnance department sections.[16]

Single-Engined Night Bombardment Group:
The group consisted of a headquarters, supply and transportation section, engineering section, three squadrons with a total of 76 aircraft. Additionally, the group had attached medical department, and ordnance department sections.[17]

Day Bombardment Squadron:
The squadron had a headquarters, supply and transportation section, engineering section, one flight of six air sections, and an attached ordnance department for a total of 25 aircraft.[18]

Lieutenant Field E. Kindley, Coffeyville, Kansas, 148th Aero Squadron with his mascot Fokker, an English Bull Terrier, ready for a flight over German lines. Remainil, Somme, France. September 9, 1918. Courtesy National Archives

Multi-Engined Night Bombardment Squadron:
The squadron was composed of a headquarters, supply and transportation section, engineering section, two flights of five aero sections and a medical department with a total of ten aircraft.[19]

Observation Squadron:
The squadron consisted of a headquarters, supply and transportation section, engineering section, one flight of six air sections, and an attached ordnance department, with a total of 24 aircraft.[20]

Pursuit Squadron (bi-plane or monoplane):
The squadron consisted of a headquarters, supply and transportation section, engineering section, one flight of six air sections, and an attached ordnance department, with a total of 25 aircraft.[21]

Single-Engined Night Bombardment Squadron:
The squadron was composed of a headquarters, supply and transportation section, engineering section, three flights of six aero sections and a medical department with a total of 25 aircraft.[22]

Balloon Company:
The company consisted of one balloon and an attached medical department.[23]

Air Park:
The Air Park was the principal logistical element of the air corps. It consisted of a headquarters section, a supply and transport section, an engineering section and attached medical personnel.[24]

Photo Section:
The photo section was no more than a photo laboratory capable of developing the photographs taken by the observation squadron while on missions.

Insignia:

The standard Air Service roundel, fully embroidered on felt.

By the time of the entry of the United States into the war, roundels had become the standard marking for Allied Aircraft. The British used a three-color roundel of blue (outer band), white (center band), and red (inside circle), the French adopted a red (outer band), white (center band) and blue (inside circle). The AEF Air Service adopted this standard pattern with a red (outer band), blue (center band) and white (inside circle).[25] It was only natural that the Air Service adopted the same insignia for their uniforms. As such, the Air Corps roundel patch was commonly worn either alone or as part of other air corps devices.

Air Service Mechanic:
The members of an air park or squadron serving as mechanics wore a shoulder patch of the air corps roundel with a monogram above of an "A" (largest letter, in red), "S" (medium sized letter, in white) and "M" (smallest letter, in blue) representing air service mechanic.

Aerial Gunnery School:
The insignia consisted of an Air Corps Roundel with a sight post of black and cross hairs of white superimposed with a yellow bi-plane in the sight.

Numbered Patches:
Special Regulation #41, August 15, 1917 granted special insignia for enlisted soldiers without specialty ratings. They were to wear a white silk four bladed propeller with the aero squadron number embroidered above. Enlisted mechanics were to have the propeller enclosed in a circle of white silk.[26]

The addition of the "ASM" monogram to this roundel denotes an Air Service Mechanic in this fully embroidered example.

This example of the enlisted aviation insignia is for the 148th Aero Squadron.

The propeller in a circle of an enlisted mechanic.

A first lieutenant leans against an Army staff car adorned with the Air Service roundel. Courtesy Author's Collection.

First Army Aviation[27]

1st Army Observation Group:

9th Aero Squadron (Night):

The Ninth Aero Squadron was organized as a night observation squadron. It was assigned to the First Army Observation Group, August 26, 1918, and reached the Front at Amanty on August 28th. The Ninth was engaged in the operations at St. Mihiel, and the Argonne-Meuse first and second offensives. During this time it made 70 reconnaissances into the German lines, engaged in numerous combats but never received official confirmation for any victories. It received its demobilization orders on May 1, 1919. The squadron suffered six casualties, consisting of 1 killed, 4 wounded and 1 prisoner.

Insignia:

The squadron adopted a silhouette showing the beams of three search-lights pointing upward and forming the numeral IX.

Insignia of the Ninth Aero Squadron

91st Aero Squadron:

The Ninety-first Aero Squadron was an Army observation squadron. It was assigned to the First Army Corps on May 7, 1918, and on May 24th reached the Front at Condreville. It was engaged in the operations in the Toul Sector, at St. Mihiel and the Argonne-Meuse first and second offensives. The Ninety-first accomplished many war missions, fought 104 combats, and received credit for bringing down 21 German machines. It suffered 28 casualties, consisting of 10 killed, 8 wounded, 9 prisoners and 1 missing. The Ninety-first was ordered demobilized April 7, 1919.

Insignia:

The squadron insignia shows a mounted knight in pursuit of the winged devil whose blood he has already drawn by the lance.

Insignia of the 91st Aero Squadron

Insignia of the 24th Aero Squadron

24th Aero Squadron:

The Twenty-fourth Aero Squadron was an Army observation squadron. It was assigned to the first Army Observation Group on August 14, 1918, and reached the Front at Condreville on August 22nd to take part in the operations at St. Mihiel and the Argonne-Meuse first and second offensives. Before the Armistice it had carried out more that 80 reconnaissances, fought 54 combats and received official confirmation for 12 victories. The squadron suffered 7 casualties, consisting of 1 killed, 1 wounded, 3 prisoners and 2 missing. On April 10, 1919, it was assigned for further duty to the Army of Occupation.

Insignia:

The Twenty-fourth Aero Squadron is represented by an American eagle pouncing upon the German dachshund which is running away with its tail between its legs.

Insignia of the 186th Aero Squadron

186th Aero Squadron:

This squadron was an Army observation squadron. It was assigned to the First Army Observation Group, First Army, October 27, 1918, and reached the Front at Souilly two days later. It participated in the operation of the Argonne-Meuse two offensives. Up to the signing of the Armistice it had suffered no casualties and had never received confirmation for any victories. On April 10, 1919, it was assigned to the Army of Occupation.

Insignia:

Its insignia was a winged devil in flight peering at the enemy through binoculars.

1st Corps Observation Group:

Insignia of the 1st Aero Squadron

1st Aero Squadron:

The First Aero Squadron was organized and operated as a Corps Observation squadron. It arrived on the Front at Ourches, April 4, 1918, and was assigned to the First Corps April 8, 1918. The squadron was engaged in the operations in the Toul Sector, Chateau-Thierry, St. Mihiel and the Argonne-Meuse first and second offensives, and after the Armistice it was assigned to the Army of Occupation on November 20, 1918. This squadron suffered 26 casualties, consisting of 15 killed, 8 wounded, 2 prisoners and 1 missing. Having engaged in 94 combats it was officially accredited with having shot down thirteen enemy aircraft. The First Air Squadron was a continuation of the First Squadron in the United States Air Service beginning its service on the Mexican border.

Insignia:

The squadron insignia was a 48 star flag of the United States upon a pole fully extended in flight.

12th Aero Squadron:

The Twelfth Aero Squadron was a Corps Observation squadron. It was assigned to the First Corps on April 30, 1918, and three days later, May 3rd, reached the front at Ourches. This squadron was engaged in the operations in the Toul Sector, at Chateau-Thierry, St. Mihiel and the Argonne-Meuse first and second offensives. During its long period of activity it engaged in numerous reconnaissances, fought many combats and received confirmation for three victories. The Twelfth suffered heavy casualties, consisting of 8 killed, 9 wounded, and 4 prisoners. It received its demobilization orders April 1, 1919.

Insignia:

The squadron insignia was a screaming American Eagle in flight grasping a projectile in its talons.

Insignia of the 12th Aero Squadron

88th Aero Squadron:
The Eighty-eighth Aero Squadron was a Corps Observation squadron. It was assigned to the First Corps on May 29, 1918, and June 1 reached the Front at Toul. It was engaged in the operations in the Toul Sector, at Chateau-Thierry, St. Mihiel, and the Argonne-Meuse first and second offensives. This squadron accomplished many reconnaissances over the lines, taking many pictures, locating machine-gun nests and batteries and gathered military information of greatest value. It received official credit for four enemy planes brought down. The squadron suffered 14 casualties, consisting of 6 killed and 8 wounded.

Insignia:
The Eighty-eighth Aero Squadron insignia is a bucking bronco, ridden by a cowboy, all within a circle.

Insignia of the 88th Aero Squadron

3rd Corps Observation Group:

90th Aero Squadron:
The Ninetieth Aero Squadron was a Corps Observation squadron. It was assigned to the Third Corps Observation Group on June 11, 1918, and two days later reached the front at Ourches. It took part in the operations in the Toul Sector, St. Mihiel and the Argonne-Meuse first and second offensives. This squadron carried out many reconnaissances, fought 23 combats and received official confirmation for 7 victories. It suffered 3 casualties, consisting of 2 killed and 1 wounded. It was ordered demobilized on December 19, 1918.

Insignia:
Pair of dice; the lucky number, seven, is uppermost.

Insignia of the 90th Aero Squadron

Bibliography:
Carver, Leland M., *The Ninetieth Aero Squadron, American Expeditionary Forces; a history of its activities during the World War from its formation to its return to the United States.* Hinsdale, Illinois; n.p. 1920.

199th Aero Squadron (Air Park):
No information available.

5th Corps Observation Group:

50th Aero Squadron:
The Fiftieth Aero Squadron was a Corps Observation squadron. It was assigned to the Fifth Corps Observation Group, First Army, on August 14, 1918, and reached the Front at Bicqueley near Toul on September 8th. It engaged in the operations at St. Mihiel and the Argonne-Meuse first and second offensives. It ceased operations April 1, 1919. This squadron made many reconnaissance flights over the lines, taking many pictures and gathering much useful information, during the accomplishment of which it fought off many German attacks and was credited with one victory. It suffered nine casualties, consisting of 5 killed, 2 wounded, and 2 prisoners.

Insignia of the 50th Aero Squadron

Insignia:
The Fiftieth Aero Squadron insignia is a silhouette cartoon of a Dutch woman similar to the one in "Dutch Cleanser" advertisement.

Bibliography:
Morse, Daniel Parmelee. *The History of the 50th Aero Squadron: being the log and operations of the squadron while with the American Expeditionary Force in France, 1918-9, with other sundry items of interest to former members of the squadron and personal recollections by the author.* New York; The Blanchard Press, 1920.

This November, 1917 advertisement for Old Dutch Cleanser clearly illustrates the Dutch woman chasing away dirt.

99th Aero Squadron:

The Ninety-ninth Aero Squadron was a Corps Observation squadron. It was assigned to the Fifth Corps Observation Group June 12, 1918, having reached the Front on May 31, at Amanty. This squadron was engaged in the operations in the Toul Sector, at St. Mihiel and the Argonne-Meuse first and second offensives. The squadron performed many reconnaissance flights and war missions into German territory, fought 18 combats and received official confirmation for 3 victories. It suffered 13 casualties, consisting of 6 killed and 7 wounded. It ceased operations February 13, 1919.

Insignia:

A conventional American bison in silhouette is the insignia of the Ninety-ninth Aero Squadron.

Insignia of the 99th Aero Squadron

104th Aero Squadron:

The One Hundred Fourth Aero Squadron was a Corps Observation squadron. It was assigned to the Fifth Corps Observation Group, First Army, August 7, 1918, and reached the Front at Souilly on September 8, 1918. It was engaged in operations at St. Mihiel and the Argonne-Meuse first and second offensives. This squadron made many reconnaissance flights over the lines, fought 25 combats, was officially accredited with one victory and suffered four casualties, consisting of 2 killed, 1 wounded and 1 taken prisoner. The squadron ceased operations December 19, 1918.

Insignia:

A figure of winged sphinx, placed in a large circle.

Insignia of the 104th Aero Squadron

Bibliography:

Gilchrist, John W. Stuart. *The 104th Aero Squadron*. Richmond, Virginia; n.p. 1968.

1st Air Park:

No information available.

7th Corps Observation Group:

278th Aero Squadron:

The Two Hundred Seventy-eighth Aero Squadron was an Army observation squadron. It was assigned to the Seventh Corps Observation Group, Second Army, October 29, 1918. It reached the Front at Toul November 10; this squadron did not function on the Western Front and was finally ordered demobilized May 11, 1919.

Insignia of the 278th Aero Squadron

Insignia of the 248th Aero Squadron

Insignia:
The squadron insignia was a Flying Owl.

248th Aero Squadron:
The Two Hundred Forty-eighth Aero Squadron was a Crops Observation squadron. It was assigned to the Seventh Corps Observation Group, First Army, on September 10, 1918, and reached the Front at Luxeuil on September 19th. It was engaged in operations in the Vosges Sector.

Insignia:
A black cat wearing a broad grin and decorated with a large bow neck-tie made of an American flag.

258th Aero Squadron:
The Two Hundred Fifty-eighth Squadron was a Corps Observation squadron. It was assigned to the Seventh Corps Observation Group, September 10, 1918, and reached the Front at Luxeuil September 19th. This squadron was engaged in the operations in the Vosges Sector. It was finally assigned to the Army of Occupation on April 10, 1919. During its activity on the Western Front it did not suffer any casualties, nor gain any victories which received official confirmation.

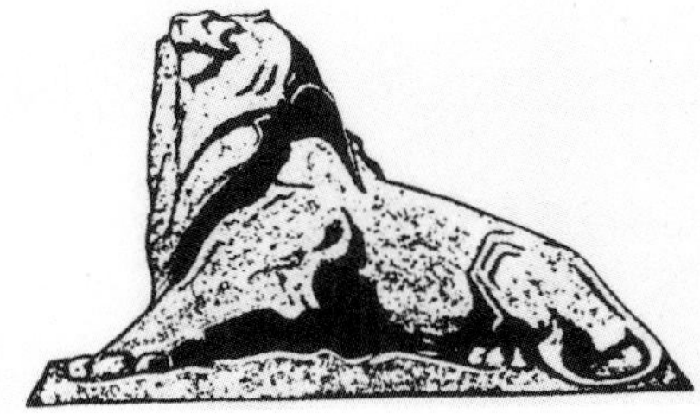

Insignia of the 258th Aero Squadron

Insignia:
A reproduction of a lion; apparently carved out of stone.

1st Day Bombardment Group:

Insignia of the 11th Aero Squadron

11th Aero Squadron:
The Eleventh Aero Squadron was a day bombardment squadron assigned to duty in the First Day Bombardment Group, First Army, on September 5, 1918. It had already reached the Front at Delouze on August 26th. The Eleventh was engaged in the operations at St. Mihiel and the Argonne-Meuse first and second offensives. It made 32 bombing raids, engaged in 17 combats and received official confirmation for 13 victories. It ceased operations December 11, 1918. The squadron suffered 20 casualties consisting of 10 killed, 1 wounded, 8 prisoners and 1 missing.

Insignia:
The squadron chose a cartoon of Mr. Jiggs carrying a bomb under his arm. Mr. Jiggs was a comedic character in a famous cartoon strip of the period named "Bringing up Father." Jiggs was an immigrant Irishman who struck it rich in the United States and was constantly running amuck of the members of high society with which he now could freely associate.

In this 1919 comic strip, Mr. Jiggs strides away from his barber, disconsolate.

Bibliography:
Thomas, Gerald C. *The First Team: Thornton Hooper and America's first bombing squadrons.* Dallas,Texas; League of World War I Aviation Historians, 1992.
United States Army Air Service, 11th Aero Squadron. *History of the 11th Aero Squadron, U.S.A.: a detailed account of the activities of the squadron from its formation in 1917 to demobilization in 1919.* n.p.; 1922.

20th Aero Squadron:
The Twentieth Aero Squadron was a day bombardment squadron. It was assigned to the First Day Bombardment Group, First Army, on September 5, 1918, and reached the Front at Amanty two days later. It was engaged in the operations at St. Mihiel and the Argonne-Meuse first and second offensives. It carried on numerous bombing raids into German territory, engaged in eleven combats and received confirmation for eleven victories. The Twentieth received demobilization orders on December 11, 1918. This squadron suffered 25 casualties, consisting of 13 killed, 3 wounded, 8 prisoners and 1 missing.

Insignia of the 20th Aero Squadron

Insignia:

Three legs in a circle arranged in pinwheel fashion comprise the insignia adopted by the squadron; this insignia was never official.

Bibliography:

Barth, Clarence G. *History of the Twentieth Aero Squadron American Expeditionary Forces compiled from official records, personal notes and recollections by C.G. Barth.* Winona, Minnesota; Winona Labor News, 19??.

96th Aero Squadron:

The Ninety-sixth Aero Squadron was a day bombardment squadron. It was assigned to the First Day Bombardment Group, First Army, on May 29, 1918, having reached the Front at Amanty on May 18th. It was engaged in the operations in the Toul Sector, at St. Mihiel, and the Argonne-Meuse first and second offensives. This squadron made many bombing raids into Germany, destroying a great amount of enemy property and gathering much valuable information. It fought 19 combats, and was officially accredited with 14 enemy airplanes. The squadron suffered 41 casualties, consisting of 12 killed, 12 wounded, 15 taken prisoners and 2 missing. It ceased operations December 11, 1918.

Insignia of the 96th Aero Squadron

Insignia:

The squadron is represented by the head and shoulders of a red devil, who prepares to launch an aerial bomb. This figure is placed on a white triangular-shaped background.

Bibliography:

Thomas, Gerald C. *The First Team: Thornton Hooper and America's first bombing squadrons.* Dallas, Texas; League of World War I Aviation Historians, 1992.

155th Aero Squadron:

The One Hundred Fifty-fifth Aero Squadron was a night bombardment squadron. It was assigned to the First Army on November 9, 1918, but, owing to the Armistice being signed two days later, it never functioned on the Front. It ceased operations December 4, 1918.

Insignia of the 155th Aero Squadron

Insignia:

The One Hundred Fifty-fifth Squadron had for its insignia the head of a large arrow, pointed upward.

166th Aero Squadron:

One Hundred Sixty-sixth Aero Squadron was a day bombardment squadron. It was assigned to the First Day Bombardment Group, First Army, September 20, 1918, and reached the Front at Maulan about September 25th. This squadron engaged in operations in the Argonne-Meuse, first and second offensives. It accomplished 11 war missions and bombing raids into German territory, fought off many German attacks and received official confirmation for 6 victories. It suffered 4 casualties, consisting of 1 killed and 3 wounded. It ceased operations April 7, 1919.

Insignia of the 166th Aero Squadron

Insignia:

The insignia includes the sun with a pair of wings made of the American flag. In the foreground is a map of Europe, with Germany distinctly marked, while a hand, armed with an aerial bomb, hovers over it, ready to drop the bomb.

1st Pursuit Group

Bibliography:

Frandsen, Herbert L. *The First Pursuit Group in the Great War: Leadership, technology, and the birth of American combat aviation.* Ann Arbor, Michigan; UMI Dissertation Services, 2003.

Hartney, Harold, Evans. *Up and at 'em, by Lieut. Col. Harold E. Hartney, D.S.C., Commander of the First Pursuit Group, United States Air Service, in the World War.* Harrisburg, Pennsylvania; Stackpole and Sons, 1940.

United States Army Air Corps, 1st Pursuit Group. *A chronological and narrative history of the 1st Pursuit Group, GHQ, Air Force, and associated units.* n.p., 1937.

Insignia of the 27th Aero Squadron

27th Aero Squadron:

The Twenty-seventh Aero Squadron was a pursuit squadron. It was assigned to the First Pursuit Group, First Army, on April 30, 1918, and reached the Front on June 1 at Toul. This squadron was engaged in the operations in the Toul Sector, at Chateau-Thierry, St. Mihiel, and the Argonne-Meuse first and second offensives. The Twenty-seventh carried out 314 patrols and war missions, engaged in 230 combats, and received official confirmation for 54 victories. In all it suffered 22 casualties, consisting of 8 killed, 4 wounded, 7 prisoners, and 3 missing. It ceased operations December 5, 1918.

Insignia:

The squadron insignia comprises another form of the American eagle, superimposed upon a large round spot.

Insignia of the 94th Aero Squadron

94th Aero Squadron:

The Ninety-fourth Aero Squadron was a pursuit squadron. It was assigned to the First Army Corps on April 9, 1918, having reached the Front at Epiez on April 1st. This squadron was engaged in the operations in the Toul Sector, at Chateau-Thierry, St. Mihiel, and the Argonne-Meuse first and second offensives. The squadron accomplished 304 patrols and war missions, fought 114 combats and brought down 64 enemy planes which were officially confirmed. It ceased operations on April 7, 1919. It had suffered 18 casualties, consisting of 10 killed, 4 wounded, and 4 taken prisoners.

Insignia:

The Ninety-fourth Aero Squadron insignia is the well-known "hat in the ring."

Bibliography:

Hartz, Robert Eugene. *The 94th Aero Squadron Scrapbook.* Annville, Pennsylvania; Hiester Printing Company, 1930.

Insignia of the 95th Aero Squadron

95th Aero Squadron:

The Ninety-fifth Aero Squadron was a pursuit squadron. It was assigned to the First Army Corps on May 29, 1918, having reached the Front at Amanty on May 18th. This squadron was engaged in the operations in the Toul Sector, at Chateau-Thierry, St. Mihiel, and the Argonne-Meuse, fought 230 combats, and was officially accredited with having brought down 47 enemy airplanes. It suffered 21 casualties, consisting of 6 killed, 4 wounded, 10 taken prisoners and 1 missing. It was ordered demobilized December 5, 1918.

Insignia:

The Ninety-fifth shows the familiar kicking mule, poised on its front feet, ready to deliver a blow, the history of this squadron indicates that the insignia was well chosen.

Bibliography:

Woolley, Charles. *First to the Front: the aerial adventures of 1st Lt. Waldo Heinrichs and the 95th Aero Squadron, 1917-1918.* Atglen, Pennsylvania; Schiffer Publishers, 1999.

147th Aero Squadron:

The One Hundred Forty-seventh Aero Squadron was a pursuit squadron. It was assigned to the First Army on May 29, 1918, and reached the Front at Toul on June 1st. The squadron was engaged in operations in the Toul Sector, at Chateau-Thierry, St. Mihiel and the Argonne-Meuse first and second offensives. This squadron accomplished many patrols and raids over German territory, fought 102 combats and received official confirmation for 31 victories. It suffered 8 casualties, consisting of 7 killed and 1 missing. It ceased operations on December 5, 1918.

Insignia of the 147th Aero Squadron

Insignia:
A cartoon of a rat terrier was used to represent the One Hundred Forty-seventh Aero Squadron.

Bibliography:
Clendenin, Kenneth W. *147th Aero Squadron excerpts, World War One, 1917-1918*. Parkersburg, West Virginia; K.W. Clendenin, 1964.

185th Aero Squadron:
The One Hundred Eighty-fifth Aero Squadron was a night pursuit squadron. It was assigned to the First Pursuit Group, First Army, October 5, 1918, and reached the Front at Rembercourt, three days later. It participated in the Argonne-Meuse first and second offensives. The squadron accomplished several night patrols into Germany, suffered only one casualty, one pilot being taken prisoner, and never received confirmation for any victories. It ceased operations on April 10, 1919.

Insignia of the 185th Aero Squadron

Insignia:
The squadron chose a silhouette of a bat within a circle.

Bibliography:
Gates, Percival T. *An American Pilot in the skies of France: the diaries and letters or Lt. Percival Gates, 1917-1918*. Dayton, Ohio; Wright State University Press, 1991.

4th Air Park:
No information available.

2nd Pursuit Group

This extremely rare insignia of the 13th Aero Squadron incorporates the squadron's skeleton figure and the number 13 superimposed on an "A" with an air service roundel to denote its affiliation with the First Army. It is embroidered on black wool.

13th Aero Squadron:
The Thirteenth Aero Squadron was a pursuit squadron. It was assigned to the Second Pursuit Group, First Army, on June 28, 1918, reaching the Front the same day. It engaged in the operations in the Toul Sector, at Chateau-Thierry, St. Mihiel, and the Argonne-Meuse first and second offensives. During this period it made 179 patrols and war missions, fought 89 combats and received official confirmation for 29 victories. It ceased operations on December 5, 1918. The Thirteenth suffered 13 casualties, consisting of 5 killed, 1 wounded and 7 prisoners.

Insignia:
The insignia for the Thirteenth Aero Squadron shows the figure of death depicted by a skeleton running at full speed with a bloody scythe in his hand.

Bibliography:
Biddle, Charles J. *The Way of the Eagle: A memoir of the 13th Aero Squadron and 4th Pursuit Group in France*. New York; Charles Scribner's Sons, 1919.

49th Aero Squadron:
The Forty-ninth Aero Squadron was a pursuit squadron. It was assigned to the First Army on August 14, 1918, having reached the Front at Toul Airdrome on August 2d. It was engaged in the operations in the Toul Sector, St. Mihiel, and the Argonne-Meuse first and second offensives. It accomplished 161 patrols and war missions, fought 53 combats and received official confirmation for 24 victories. It ceased operations on December 5, 1918. It suffered 6 casualties, consisting of 3 killed, 1 prisoner and 2 missing.

Insignia:
The Forty-ninth Aero Squadron is depicted by a snarling wolf's head within a circle.

Insignia of the 49th Aero Squadron

Another very rare insignia is that of the 139th Aero Squadron. This example also incorporates the "A" of the First Army and the Air Service roundel, executed in embroidery on wool, with interesting voids cut around the designs within the "A".

139th Aero Squadron:
The One Hundred Thirty-ninth Aero Squadron was a pursuit squadron. It was assigned to the First Army on June 12, 1918, and reached the Front at Toul on June 30 following. This squadron was engaged in operations in the Toul Sector, at St. Mihiel and the Argonne-Meuse first and second offensives. It accomplished 160 patrols and various other war missions, fought 80 combats and received confirmation for 34 victories. It suffered 8 casualties, consisting of 3 killed, 2 wounded, 1 taken prisoner and 2 missing. It ceased operations December 11, 1918.

Insignia:
The squadron was represented by an outline figure of flying Mercury.

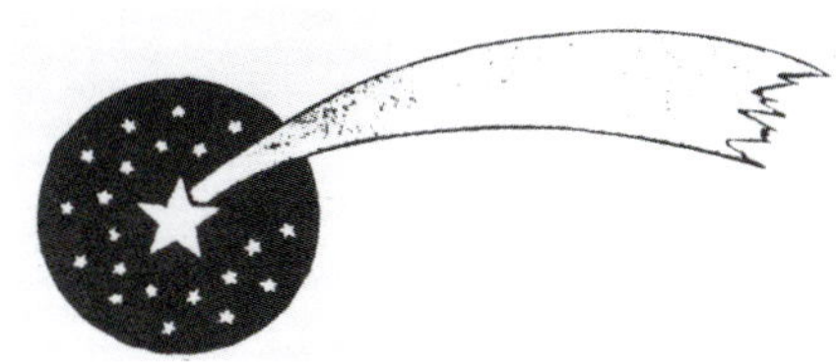

Insignia of the 22nd Aero Squadron

22nd Aero Squadron:
The Twenty-second Aero Squadron was a pursuit squadron. It reached the Front at Toul on August 16, 1918, and on August 22nd was assigned to the Second Pursuit Group, First Army. It was engaged in the operations in the Toul Sector, at St. Mihiel, and in the Argonne-Meuse first and second offensives. During its period of activity it performed 117 patrols and war missions, fought 90 engagements, and received official confirmation for 46 victories. It ceased operations April 4, 1919. It suffered 9 casualties, consisting of 6 killed, 2 prisoners and 1 wounded.

Insignia:
A number of stars in a ring with a large star with a tail, evidently a comet, superimposed, was the insignia that represented the 22nd Aero Squadron.

Insignia of the 5th Air Park executed in a felt on felt construction.

5th Air Park:
No information available.

Insignia
The composite letters "AP" above the number 5 in a stylized Air Service roundel.

3rd Pursuit Group

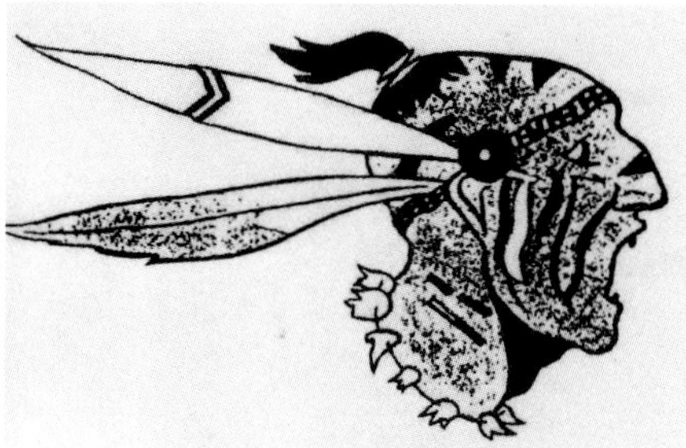

Insignia of the 93rd Aero Squadron.

93rd Aero Squadron:

The Ninety-third was a pursuit squadron. It was assigned to the Third Pursuit Group, First Pursuit Wing, First Army, and reached the Front at Vaucouleurs about July 28, 1918. It was engaged in the operations in the Toul Sector, at St. Mihiel, and the Argonne-Meuse first and second offensives. It took part in 157 war missions, fought 64 combats and received official confirmation for 32 enemy planes brought down. The Ninety-third suffered 8 casualties, consisting of 2 killed, 1 wounded, and 5 prisoners. This squadron ceased to function December 11, 1918.

Insignia:

The Ninety-third Aero Squadron is represented by an Indian head similar to that of the 28th Aero Squadron, but in the reverse direction and bearing two feathers instead of one.

Insignia of the 103rd Aero Squadron

103rd Aero Squadron:

The One Hundred Third Squadron was a pursuit squadron. It was assigned to the Second Pursuit Group, First Army, June 30, 1918. From February 18, 1918, until July 4, 1918, this squadron had served with the French Army as the Lafayette Escadrille. After joining the American Army it was engaged in the operations at St. Mihiel and the Argonne-Meuse first and second offensives. This squadron carried out many war missions, fought 327 combats and was officially accredited with 51 victories. It suffered 15 casualties, consisting of 6 killed, 3 wounded, 4 taken prisoners and 2 missing in action. It ceased operations December 11, 1918.

Insignia:

The One Hundred Third Squadron was represented by another Indian head with a large war bonnet decorated with a swastika.

Insignia of the 213th Aero Squadron

Bibliography:

Biddle, Charles J. *The Way of the Eagle: A memoir of the 13th Aero Squadron and 4th Pursuit Group in France*. New York; Charles Scribner's Sons, 1919.

Thenault, Georges. *The Story of the Lafayette Escadrille, Told by its commander, Georges Thenault, translated by Walter Duranty: with an introduction by Andre Tardieu*. Boston; Small, Maynard & Company, 1921.

213th Aero Squadron:

The Two Hundred Thirteenth Squadron was a pursuit squadron. It was assigned to the First Army on August 4, 1918, having reached the Front at Vaucouleurs July 26, preceding. It was engaged in operations in the Toul Sector, at St. Mihiel and in the Argonne first and second offensives. This squadron made 148 raids into German territory, fought 38 combats and received official confirmation for 16 victories. It suffered 10 casualties, consisting of 2 killed, 3 wounded, 4 taken prisoners and 1 missing. It ceased operations on April 10, 1919.

Insignia:

The squadron chose the head of an American Indian facing the right, with two feathers in his scalp lock.

28th Aero Squadron:

The Twenty-eighth Aero Squadron was a pursuit squadron. It was assigned to the Third Pursuit Group, First Army, on August 22, 1918, having reached the Front at Vaucouleurs July 15th. This squadron was engaged in the operations in the Toul Sector, St. Mihiel and the Argonne-Meuse first and second offensives. It ceased operations April 10, 1919. It made 128 patrols and bombing raids into Germany, fought 29 combats and received official confirmation for 15 victories. It suffered six casualties, consisting of 1 killed, 1 wounded, 2 prisoners and 2 missing.

Insignia of the 28th Aero Squadron

Insignia:
The Twenty-eighth Aero Squadron insignia is that of a painted American Indian looking to the left. Its headdress includes a single feather.

2nd Air Park:
No information available.

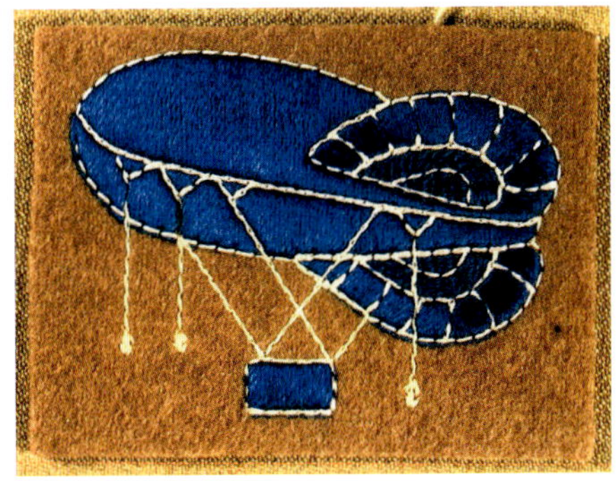

A finely embroidered example of the Balloon insignia, depicting a captive observation balloon on felt.

1st Corps Balloon Group

Insignia
The insignia for balloon units was a side view of an observation balloon and it's basket.

1st Balloon Company
2nd Balloon Company

Bibliography:
Herbert, Craig S. *Eyes of the Army: a story about the Observation Balloon Service of World War I.* Lafayette Hill, Pennsylvania; n.p. 1986.

5th Balloon Company

3rd Corps Balloon Group

3rd Balloon Company
9th Balloon Company
4th Balloon Company
42nd Balloon Company

5th Corps Balloon Group

6th Balloon Company
7th Balloon Company
8th Balloon Company
12th Balloon Company

First Army Balloons

1st Corps Balloon Group

11th Balloon Company
43rd Balloon Company

Second Army Aviation

4th Corps Observation Group:

8th Aero Squadron:
The Eighth Aero Squadron was of the Corps Observation type. It arrived on the Front at Ourches on July 31, 1918, and was assigned to the Fourth Corps, Observation Group, First Army, on August 14th. The Eighth was engaged in the operations in the Toul Sector, Chateau-Thierry, St. Mihiel, and the Argonne-Meuse first and second offensives, terminating its work on February 5, 1919. It suffered twelve casualties, consisting of 4 killed and 8 prisoners.

Insignia of the 8th Aero Squadron

Insignia:
The insignia for the Eighth Aero Squadron is a great American eagle, with the wings spread, holding the American Liberty Bell.

A wonderful example of the insignia of the 85th Aero Squadron uses a combination of wool on wool construction with hand embroidered details set within an olive drab wool border.

85th Aero Squadron:

The Eighty-fifth Aero Squadron was an Army observation squadron. It reached the front at the Toul Airdrome on October 24, 1918, and the next day was assigned to the Fourth Corps Observation Group. This squadron took part in the second Argonne-Meuse offensive. It accomplished several missions over the lines in the few remaining days before the Armistice, but was not accredited with any victories nor did it suffer any casualties. It was finally ordered to be demobilized May 11, 1919.

Insignia:

A winged Cupid with a campaign hat, sitting on the top of the world, was the insignia selected to represent the Eighty-fifth Squadron.

135th Aero Squadron:

The One Hundred Thirty-fifth Aero Squadron was a Corps Observation squadron. It was assigned to the Fourth Corps Observation Group July 28, 1918, and reached the Front at Ourches two days later. The squadron was engaged in the operations at the Toul Sector, at St. Mihiel and the Argonne-Meuse first and second offensives. This organization made many reconnaissance flights into German territory, gaining valuable information, fought many combats and was officially accredited with having brought down 8 enemy aircraft. It ceased operations February 5, 1919. The squadron suffered 7 casualties, consisting of 5 killed and 2 wounded.

Insignia of the 135th Aero Squadron

Insignia:

The squadron chose an insignia of the Statue of Liberty with the rising sun as a background.

Bibliography:

Hart, Percival Gray. *History of the 135th Aero Squadron from July 25 to November 11, 1918.* Chicago; n.p. 1939.

168th Aero Squadron:

The One Hundred Sixty-eighth Aero Squadron was a Corps Observation squadron. It was assigned to the Fourth Corps Observation Group, First Army, on September 30, 1918, and reached the Front at Toul October 5th. It was engaged in operations of the Argonne-Meuse, first and second offensives. It accomplished many war missions and reconnaissance flights over the German lines, gaining much valuable military information, fought several combats and received official confirmation for two victories. It suffered no casualties and ceased operations May 11, 1919.

Insignia:

The squadron insignia was a winged skull in a circle.

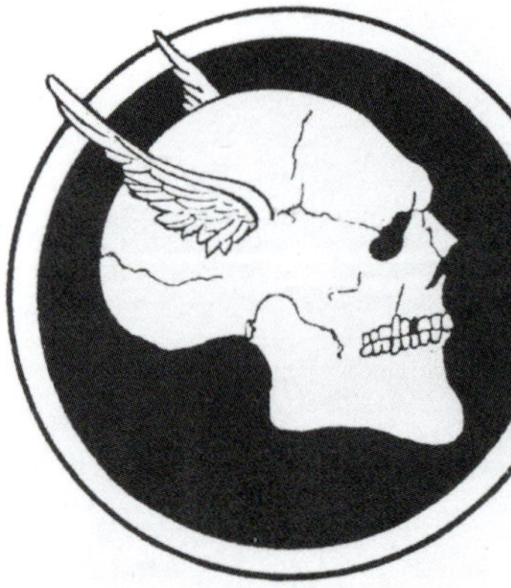

Insignia of the 168th Aero Squadron

6th Corps Observation Group

354th Aero Squadron:

The Three Hundred Fifty-fourth Aero Squadron was a Corps Observation squadron. It was assigned to the Sixth Corps Observation Group, Second Army, October 21, 1918, and reached the Front at Saizerais four days later. It was engaged in the Argonne-Meuse first and second offensives. This squadron made several reconnaissance flights over the German lines and gained a great deal of valuable military information. It neither gained any official victories nor suffered any casualties, and was finally ordered demobilized May 11, 1919.

Insignia:

A witch mounted on a broomstick supplied with model airplane equipment was the squadron insignia.

4th Pursuit Group

Bibliography:

Biddle, Charles J. *The Way of the Eagle: A memoir of the 13th Aero Squadron and 4th Pursuit Group in France*. New York; Charles Scribner's Sons, 1919.
Hartney, Harold, Evans. *Up and at 'em, by Lieut. Col. Harold E. Hartney, D.S.C., Commander of the First Pursuit Group, United States Air Service, in the World War.* Harrisburg, Pennsylvania; Stackpole and Sons, 1940.

Insignia of the 354th Aero Squadron

17th Aero Squadron:

The Seventeenth Aero Squadron was a pursuit squadron, assigned to the Second Army on November 4, 1918, and reached the American Front at Toul on the same day. This squadron had been assigned first to the Royal Air Force on July 15, 1918, and had operated with them until November. During its period of activity it had engaged in 110 combats, and received official confirmation for 54 victories. The Seventeenth ceased operations December 11, 1918. Since July it had suffered 24 casualties, consisting of 10 killed, 5 wounded, 7 prisoners and 2 missing.

Insignia:

The insignia for the squadron is the great snowy owl flying through the air ready to pounce upon the enemy.

Insignia of the 17th Aero Squadron

Bibliography:

Clapp, Frederick Mortimer. *A history of the 17th Aero Squadron, December, 1918*. Garden City, New York: Country Life Press, 1920.
Reed, Otis Lowell. *Camel Drivers: the 17th Aero Squadron in World War I*. Atglen, Pennsylvania: Schiffer Publishing, 1996.
Todd, Robert M. *Sopwith Camel Fighter Ace*. Falls Church, Virginia: Ajay Enterprises, 1978.

25th Aero Squadron:

The Twenty-fifth Aero Squadron was a pursuit squadron. It was assigned to the Fourth Pursuit Group, Second Army, on October 22, 1918, and reached the Front at Toul two days later. It was engaged in the operations of the Argonne-Meuse second offensive. It had been operating but a few days when the Armistice was declared, and had not received confirmation for any victories. Neither had it suffered any casualties.

Insignia:

A cartoon of a masked headsman with an ax was the insignia used by the Twenty-fifth Aero Squadron.

Insignia of the 25th Aero Squadron

148th Aero Squadron:

The One Hundred Forty-eighth Aero Squadron was a pursuit squadron. It was assigned to the Fourth Pursuit Group, Second Army, November 4, 1918. This squadron had previously been assigned with the Royal Air Force July 20, 1918, and had taken part in British operations up until it had been assigned to the Second Army. This squadron had accomplished many patrols over the enemy lines, fought 107 combats and received official confirmation for 71 victories. The squadron suffered 11 casualties, consisting of 3 killed, 3 wounded, 4 taken prisoner and 1 missing. It ceased operations on December 11, 1918.

Insignia:

The head of Liberty in a circle was the insignia of the One Hundred Forty-eighth Aero Squadron.

Insignia of the 148th Aero Squadron

Bibliography:

Taylor, William Parker. *Francis L. "Spike" Irvin's war diary and the history of the 148th Aero Squadron Aviation Section*. Manhattan, Kansas: Aerospace Historian, 1974.

—. *History of the 148th Aero Squadron, Aviation Section, U.S. Army Signal Corps, A.E.F.-B.E.F., 1917-1918.* Lancaster, South Carolina: Tri-County Publishing Company, 1957.

Insignia of the 141st Aero Squadron

141st Aero Squadron:

The One Hundred Forty-first Aero Squadron was a pursuit squadron. It was assigned to the Fourth Pursuit Group, Second Army, on October 18, 1918, and the next day reached the Front at Toul. This squadron was engaged in the Argonne-Meuse first and second offensives. It accomplished many patrols and war missions into German territory, gaining a great deal of valuable military information. It received official confirmation for bringing down two enemy aircraft. The squadron suffered no casualties before the Armistice and ceased operations May 11, 1919.

Insignia:

A Great Bengal tiger playing with a German helmet and iron cross was the insignia of the squadron.

6th Air Park:

Bibliography:

"Eye-Witness". *History of the squadron originally the 822nd (Repair), later the 6th Park Company, at present the 6th Air Park; written by an eye-witness.* Nancy, France: Berger-Levrault, Printers, 1918.

5th Pursuit Group:

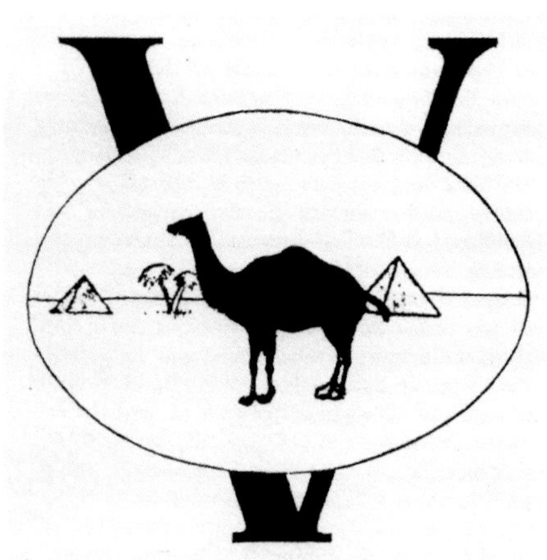

Insignia of the 41st Aero Squadron

41st Aero Squadron:

The Forty-first Aero Squadron was a pursuit squadron. It was assigned to the 5th Pursuit Group, Second Army, on October 29, 1918. It did not function on the Western Front before the Armistice. It was ordered demobilized on May 11, 1919.

Insignia:

The Forty-first Aero Squadron is represented by an oval inclosing a scene in an African desert, a camel appearing in the foreground. This is superimposed upon the numeral V, showing that the squadron was one of the Fifth Pursuit Group.

Insignia of the 138th Aero Squadron

138th Aero Squadron:

The One Hundred Thirty-eighth Aero Squadron was a pursuit squadron. It was assigned to the Fifth Pursuit Group, Second Army, on October 28, 1918, but due to the signing of the Armistice, a few days later, it did not function on the Front.

Insignia:

The squadron chose an insignia of a charging goat under full speed about to pass through the numeral V.

Bibliography:

United States Army, 138th Aero Squadron. *History of the One Three Eight Aero: 1917-1918-1919.* Lindsborg, Kansas: Bethany Printing Company, 1920.

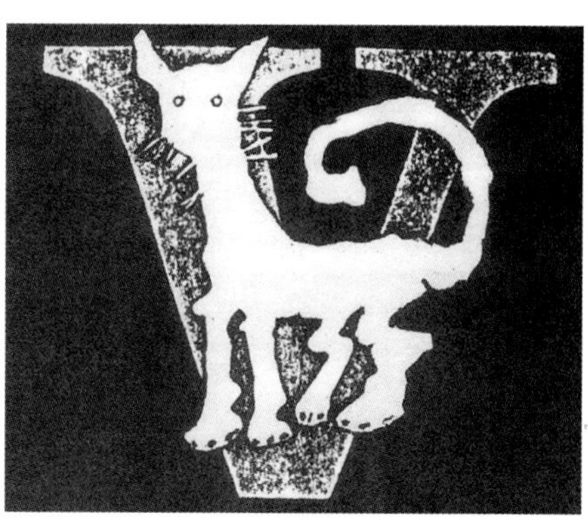

Insignia of the 638th Aero Squadron

638th Aero Squadron:

The Six Hundred Thirty-eighth Aero Squadron was a pursuit squadron, and was assigned to the Fifth Pursuit Group, Second Army, on October 28, 1918. It did not function on the Front before the Armistice and was finally ordered demobilized on May 11, 1919.

Insignia:

A half-starved cat superimposed on the numeral V, signifying the Fifth Pursuit Group was the squadron insignia.

2nd Day Bombardment Group

100th Aero Squadron:
The One Hundredth Aero Squadron was a day bombardment squadron. It was assigned to the Second Day Bombardment Group, Second Army, on October 26, 1918, having been on the Front since July 20, 1918, with the Royal Air Force. It was engaged in British operations. This squadron accomplished many raids into Germany without suffering any losses. It is not given official credit for any enemy planes brought down. It ceased operations on April 8, 1919.

Insignia:
The One Hundredth Aero Squadron insignia shows the devil riding on an aerial bomb in flight.

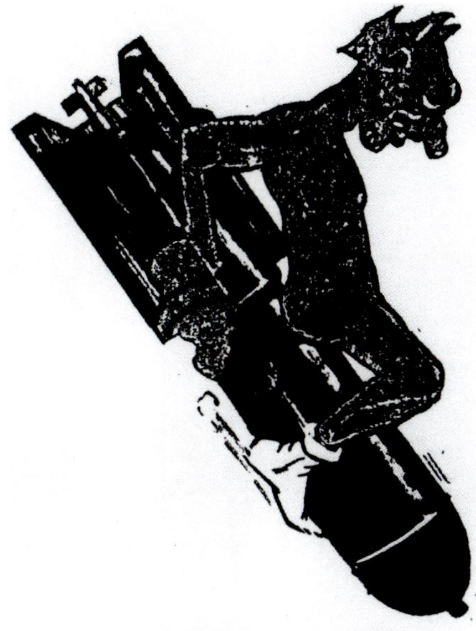

Insignia of the 100th Aero Squadron

163rd Aero Squadron:
The One Hundred Sixty-third Aero Squadron was a day bombardment squadron, and was assigned to the Second Day Bombardment Group, Second Army, October 27, 1918, reaching the Front three days later at Ourches. It engaged in the operations of the Argonne-Meuse first and second offensives. It accomplished several war missions during this period of activity, but never received official confirmation for any victories, neither did it suffer any casualties. It finally ceased operations April 8, 1919.

Insignia:
The squadron insignia is the silhouette of a cat with one eye closed, standing on a bomb.

Insignia of the 163rd Aero Squadron

4th Corps Balloon Group

15th Balloon Company
16th Balloon Company
69th Balloon Company

6th Corps Balloon Group

10th Balloon Company

3rd Air Park:

Insignia
An Air Service roundel with the number 3 in the center.

A wool on wool construction 3rd Air Park insignia.

Flight A attached to 2nd Pursuit Group, Flight B attached to First Army Observation Group, Flight C attached to IV Corps Observation Group.

Unassigned Squadrons

89th Aero Squadron:

Insignia:
The front view of an American eagle in full flight.

Insignia of the 89th Aero Squadron

Insignia of the 161st Aero Squadron

Insignia of the 162nd Aero Squadron

A felt on felt example of the insignia for the 169th Aero Squadron, whose meaning is unclear.

161st Aero Squadron:

Insignia:
A grinning clown with a cap and ruff.

162nd Aero Squadron:

Insignia:
The insignia of the One Hundred Sixty-second is a silhouette map of the United States.

169th Aero Squadron:

Insignia:
An unusual hieroglyphic, somewhat similar to the monogram CB.

174th Aero Squadron:

Insignia:
A black alley cat on a fence silhouetted against the moon.

370th Aero Squadron:

Insignia:
A triangle with a star in the centre.

486th Aero Squadron:

Insignia:
A large star or comet, with six smaller stars in its wake.

1105th Aero Squadron:

Insignia:
A winged elephant.

Insignia of the 174th Aero Squadron

Insignia of the 370th Aero Squadron

Left: Insignia of the 486th Aero Squadron

Below: Insignia of the 1105th Aero Squadron

A fine example of the Artillery School insignia.

Another example of the Artillery School insignia using gold bullion instead of red.

Artillery

Army Artillery School:

Insignia

The insignia of the Army Artillery School was a black disc bordered red with the head of Minerva the goddess of war facing left.

American and French officers at the Heavy Artillery School, St. Maur, France, May, 1918. Courtesy National Archives.

Above: Photo of a typical American Anti-Aircraft Artillery emplacement. The French 75mm gun was used in a modified form on an improvised mount to allow the extreme elevation needed for this type of fire mission. Courtesy National Archives.

Left: Coast Artillery Corps, Anti Aircraft Artillery Sound Locator, used to find incoming aircraft and relay this information to the firing batteries. France, 1918. Courtesy National Archives.

Embroidered on wool example of the Anti-Aircraft artillery insignia.

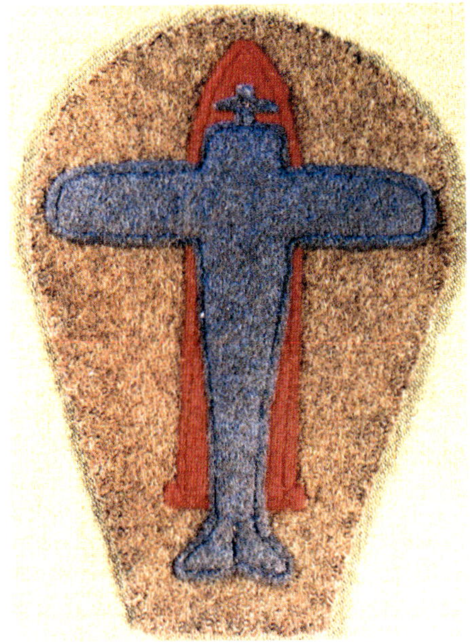

Another example of the Anti-Aircraft Artillery insignia in wool on wool construction.

An example of the 5th Anti-Aircraft Artillery insignia machine embroidered on felt.

Anti-Aircraft Artillery:

Insignia:
An Airplane superimposed upon an artillery shell.

5th Anti-Aircraft Artillery:

Insignia:
The red letters "AA" flanking an artillery shell.

71st Coast Artillery Regiment:
The regiment was originally assigned in the defense of Boston Harbor. They were then sent to England for training and onto France. They were still in training in France when the war ended. The regiment returned to the United States in 1919.

Insignia:
The regiment chose an insignia of a pair of playing cards; a "7" and an Ace of Diamonds in white with red suits, offset in a "V" shape with no background representative of the units numerical designation.

Organization:
The unit was assigned 8" Motorized Howitzers drawn by Artillery tractors in lieu of draft animals.

Commanding Officer:
Colonel Frank S. Long

Railway Artillery Reserve:
The Railway Artillery Reserve were heavy guns mounted used to support operations at the front.

Insignia
The insignia is a white hexagon bordered red with a green mythical bird, the Oozlefinch, standing on a section of rail with the letters "RAR" for Railway Artillery Reserve." Above

Men of Battery E, 60th Coast Artillery Corps Regiment man a French 155mm gun. On arrival in France the soldiers of all the CAC regiments found themselves manning much different guns than those of the coastal defenses of America. Chatel, France, October, 1918. Courtesy National Archives.

An excellent hand embroidered on wool example of the Railway Artillery Reserve insignia. Although the colors are not exactly the same as prescribed, it is instantly recognizable.

Another example of the Railway Artillery Reserve insignia hand embroidered on wool.

the Oozlefinch is an epi, a curved section of track, representative of the area from which the guns were fired.[28]

Bibliography:

Historical Report of the Railway Artillery Reserve, A.E.F., July 1917 to December 1918. France: A.E.F., Headquarters, Railway Artillery Reserve, 1918.

The crew of a camouflaged railway gun pause for a break. France, 1918. Courtesy Military History Institute.

This unique example of the Railway Artillery Reserve insignia is constructed of wool on wool construction with no embroidered details.

A simplified version of the Railway Artillery Reserve insignia embroidered on felt

Above: Trench Mortar troops practice firing a Stokes Mortar. France, 1918. Courtesy National Archives.

Trench Mortar:

Insignia

A red trench mortar shell with an olive drab border.

Bibliography:

Ottosen, Peter Hill. *Trench Artillery, A.E.F.; the Personal Experiences of Lieutenants and Captains of Artillery who served with Trench Mortars*. Boston: Lothrup, Lee and Shepard, 1931.

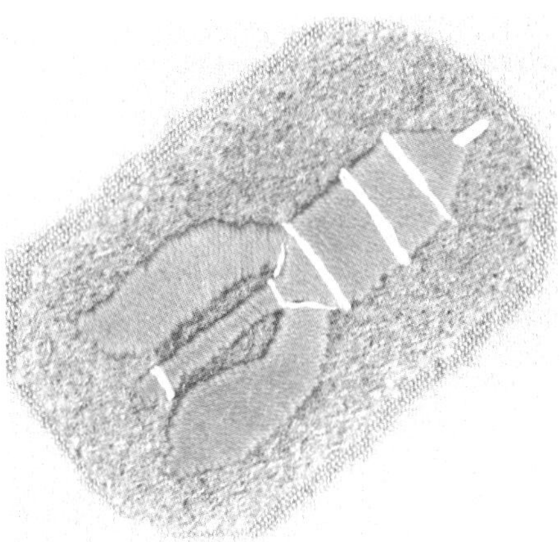

A hand embroidered on wool Trench Mortar insignia. This insignia was supposed to be worn with the tip of the shell pointing up and to the right at a forty-five degree angle.

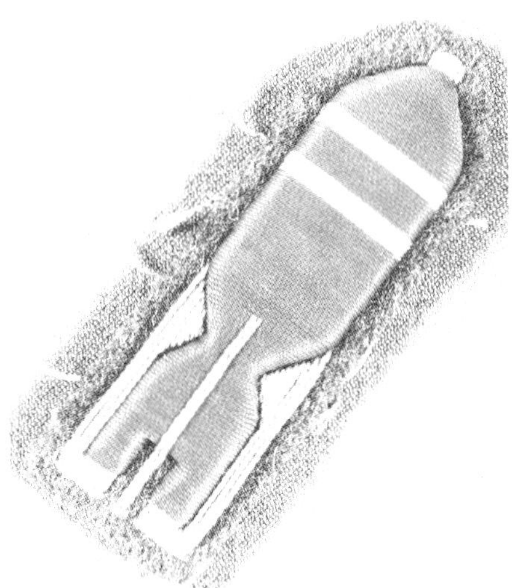

Another hand embroidered Trench Mortar insignia on wool shows a different bomb.

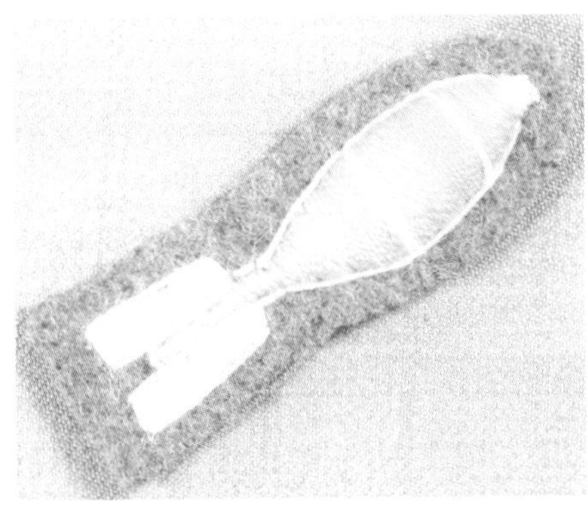

A German made hand embroidered example of the Trench Mortar insignia.

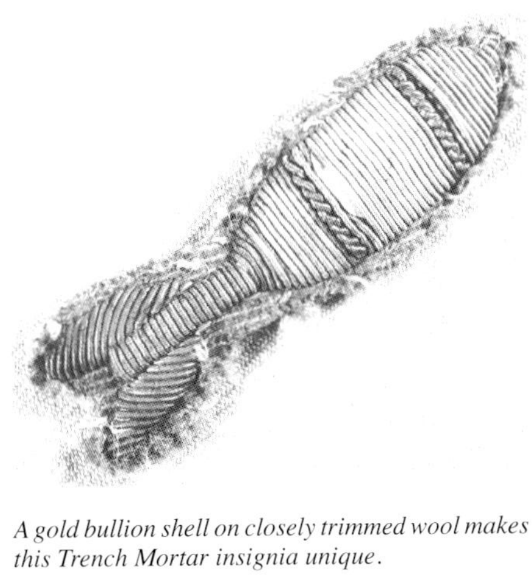

A gold bullion shell on closely trimmed wool makes this Trench Mortar insignia unique.

Above: Major General William L. Sibert, Commander of the Chemical Warfare Service at St. Nazaire, France, June, 1917. Courtesy National Archives.

Bottom: Colonel E.J. Atkissen, the commander of the 1st Gas Regiment poses with his staff at Chaumont, France, December, 1918. Courtesy National Archives.

Chemical Warfare Service

The mission of the Chemical Warfare Service was to provide instruction in defense against enemy use of chemical warfare agents and employ chemical weapons against the enemy.

Insignia:

The Chemical Warfare Service chose the insignia of a shield divided diagonally of cobalt blue (upper) and yellow (lower). These were the colors of the American Chemical Society. A variant of this insignia exists for the 1st Gas Regiment with a white numeral "1" superimposed upon the shield.

Organization:

The principal organization of the Chemical Warfare Service was the 1st Gas Regiment. The regiment was composed of a headquarters and six battalions (five combat and one replacement). Each battalion had a headquarters, a supply and workshop section and three companies. Each company had a headquarters section, one Stokes mortar platoon and three projector platoons.[29]

Commanding General:

Major General William L. Sibert.

Right: A standard Chemical Warfare Service insignia embroidered on felt

Far right: A wool example of the Chemical Warfare service shield with a hand embroidered "1"

Bibliography:

Addison, James Thayer. *The Story of the First Gas Regiment*. Boston: Houghton Mifflin Company, 1919.

Langer, William L. *With "E" of the First Gas*. Brooklyn, New York: Holton Printing Company, 1919.

United States Army, 1st Gas Regiment. *History of the First Gas Regiment*. By the Regiment, 1919.

Another Chemical Warfare Service insignia with a much larger "1"

This well worn felt on felt example of the Chemical Warfare Service insignia is somewhat crudely fashioned .

Education Corps

The Education Corps directed all schools in the AEF where, after the Armistice, Pershing established a vast school system to improve the lives of soldiers awaiting transport back to the United States. As an example, at Beaune, France, a university of advanced instruction was founded which at one point over 9,000 soldiers had registered for courses.[30]

Insignia:
The Education Corps selected as its insignia a torch in gold, with stylized wings on either side. Superimposed across the front of the torch was a ribbon in blue emblazoned with the words "Education Corps". The torch is symbolic of the pursuit of knowledge, and the subsequent enlightenment through knowledge.

Corps Schools:

2nd Corps School:
A white disc bordered red with the blue letters "C" and "S" flanking a large "2." The letters represent the words Corps School and the number that of the corps.

3rd Corps School:
A white disc bordered red with the blue letters "C" and "S" flanking a large "3." The letters represent the words Corps School and the number that of the corps.

Engineers

Branch Insignia:
The familiar three-turreted castle of the Engineer Corps is one of the most recognizable of the Army's branch insignia. It appeared originally in 1840 doubtless representing the major mission of the Corps of that time – construction of fortifications.[31]

Office of the Chief of Engineers:

Insignia:
A blue disk with a narrow white outer ring. In the center a red castle, the traditional symbol for the Corps of Engineers. This is surrounded with a large white letter "C" symbolic of Chief Engineer.

Construction Engineer:

Insignia:
Upon a dark blue shield, the letters in white "CE" for construction engineers with the upper part of the shield divided horizontally and containing three white stars.

13th Engineer Regiment (Standard Gauge Railway Operation):
This regiment operated the standard gauge railroads supplying the AEF.

A beautiful hand embroidered bouillon on wool insignia of the Education Corps.

Far left: An embroidered on felt Office of the Chief of Engineers.

Left: A variant of the Office of the Chief of Engineers embroidered on felt.

Private Thomas Fargher (standing, center) of the 13th Engineer Regiment poses with some friends in front of Engine 34, France, 1918. Courtesy Military History Institute.

The insignia of Construction Engineers; wool with hand embroidered details.

A variant Construction Engineer insignia of wool construction.

Below: Men of the 13th Engineer Regiment right derailed Engine 15 near Bugemont, France, February, 1918. Courtesy Military History Institute.

Insignia:
Their insignia consisted of a white Engineer Corps Castle upon a red square surrounded by thirteen white stars indicative of the regimental number.

Organization:
The regiment was composed of a headquarters and two battalions. The first battalion consisted of headquarters, three railway operating companies, and one advanced railway shop. The second battalion was assigned two railway maintenance right of way companies and a railway construction company.

Commanding Officer:
Colonel W.C. Langfitt

Bibliography:
History, Thirteenth Engineers (Railway) U.S. Army, 1917-1918-1919: With the American Expeditionary Forces in France. n.p., 19??.

Howard, N.L. "The Activities of the 13th Engineers." *Military Engineer* (Mar/Apr 1926): pp. 122-28.

A 13th Engineer insignia embroidered on felt.

A variant of the 13th Engineer insignia; embroidered on wool.

14th Engineer Regiment (Light Railway):
This regiment operated the narrow gauge railroads that carried the supplies to and from the standard gauge lines. Light rail often bridged the run from supply activities to the nearest railhead in the rear areas and ran from the railhead to the rear of the front line in combat areas.

Insignia:
The 14th Engineers insignia consisted of a red over green diamond divided vertically in the center by a winged train wheel in white.

Organization:
The regiment was composed of a headquarters and two battalions. The first battalion consisted of headquarters, three light railway operating companies, and one advanced light railway shop. The second battalion was assigned two light railway maintenance of way companies and a light railway construction company.

Commanding Officer:
Colonel William P. Wooten.

Below: Men of Company F, 14th Engineer Regiment lay wooden planks across the light rail tracks to allow wagons to pass over, Aubrecils, France, September, 1918. Courtesy National Archives.

This beautiful 14th Engineer Regiment insignia is hand embroidered on wool.

A Liberty Loan patch shows a variation of the 14th Engineer Regiment insignia.

Captain C.P. Hubbard of Company C, 11th Engineers. Note the First Army patch on his trench coat. Courtesy National Archives

Bibliography:

"Fourteenth Regiment of Engineers." *Military Engineer* (Jan/Feb 1923): p. 22.

Henderson, Robert G. *History of the Fourteenth Engineers U.S. Army, From May, 1917 to May 1919*. Boston: Privately Printed, 1923.

Irvine, V.R. "Light Railway Practice in the A.E.F." *Military Engineer* (Sep/Oct 1920): pp. 411-14.

Noce, Daniel. "Special Engineer Troops in Combat." *Military Engineer* (Nov/Dec 1923): pp. 536-37.

U.S. Army. Corps of Engineers, 14th Regiment. *Roster of Company D, 14th Engineers (Light Railway) April 24, 1919*. n.p., 1919.

30th Engineer Regiment (Forestry):

The 30th Engineers had the principal task of providing lumber to the AEF.

Insignia:

An Engineer Castle in white upon a circular field of blue bordered white.

Organization:

It was organized into a headquarters with four major staff sections: acquisition of timber, technical equipment and operation supplies, product shipment and fuelwood project. Additionally, the headquarters provided forestry officers to Base Section 2, and the Advance Section. The regiment was composed of fourteen battalions of forest and road engineer companies and service companies (the majority of the service companies were manned by African-Americans). By the end of the war, the 20th Engineers were operating 81 sawmills and producing two million feet of lumber every day including railroad ties, pilings, poles and fuelwood.[32]

Commanding Officer:

Colonel James A. Woodruff.

Bibliography:

Souvenir Edition for the 20th Engineers (Forestry), American Forestry, Vol 25, No. 306, June 1919.

32nd Engineer Regiment (Light Railway):

This regiment operated the narrow gauge railroads that carried the supplies to and from the standard gauge lines. Light rail often bridged the run from supply activities to the nearest railhead in the rear areas and ran from the railhead to the rear of the front line in combat areas.

Insignia:

The insignia of the regiment was a black diamond bordered (alluding to its mission at the railhead) imposed upon the diamond is a white engineer castle above which the white letters "RB" appear for Railway Battalion.

Organization:

The regiment was composed of a headquarters and two battalions. The first battalion consisted of headquarters, three light railway operating companies, and one advanced light railway shop. The second battalion was assigned two light railway maintenance of way companies and a light railway construction company.

Bibliography:

40th Engineer Regiment (Camouflage):

One camouflage battalion was to be allotted to each army. The mission was to provide camouflage to AEF fortifications and installations. The 40th was assigned to the First Army.

Above: Large rolls of wire mesh and fabric used to create camouflage netting, and the warehouses used to store them. 40th Engineer Regiment , Dijon France. Note the camouflage paint on the small building in the foreground. Courtesy Military History Institute.

Right: Soldiers of the 40th Engineer Regiment in their quarters, Dijon, France, 1918. Courtesy Military History Institute.

Below: A huge stockpile of materials dwarfs two men of the 40th Engineer Regiment, Dijon, France. Courtesy Military History Institute.

A machine embroidered 40th Engineers Insignia on wool.

An unusual wool on wool insignia for the 40th Engineers. The chameleon seldom is depicted with both eyes.

Insignia:
The regiment selected a gold chameleon, the chameleon as the symbol appropriately representing their mission, facing upward on an inverted and elongated black triangle.

Organization:
The battalion consisted of a headquarters and two companies of engineers.

Bibliography:
Embury, Aymar II. "Reminiscences of A Camouflage Officer." *Military Engineer* (May/Jun 1927): pp. 235-239.

56th Engineer Regiment (Searchlight):
Searchlight regiments provided illumination in support of artillery and anti-aircraft artillery against enemy airplanes and ships.

Insignia:
A red disk with the beam of a searchlight in white illuminating a red enemy aircraft. The colors are those of the Engineer Corps (red and white) with the insignia clearly delineating the mission.

Organization:
The regiment consisted of a headquarters, ten searchlight companies, and a medical department. Each company in the regiment had thirteen searchlight sets of two lights each for a total of 260 searchlights.

Commanding Officer:
Lieutenant Colonel John C. Gotwals.

Bibliography:
Macomber, Alexander, & Brunet, Meade, eds. *The 56th Engineers in the World War: Company Data Furnished by Company Commanders; Platoon Rosters by Platoon Commanders.* Albany, New York: Brandow, 1920.

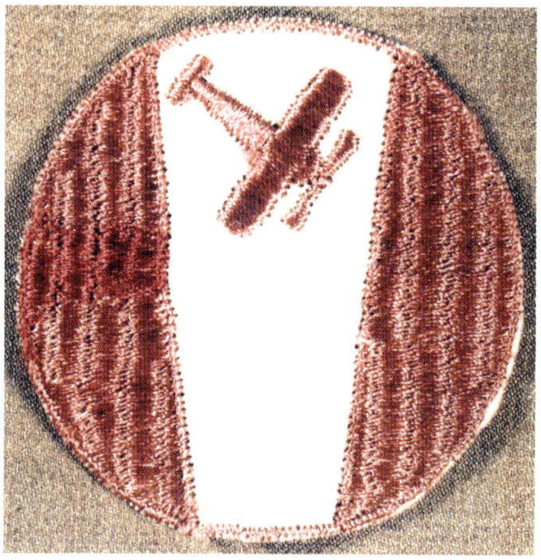

An example of the 56th Engineer Regiment insignia executed in machine embroidery on felt.

Another 56th Engineer Regiment insignia in felt on felt with a machine embroidered airplane.

Tank Corps

Insignia:

The insignia of the Tank Corps was a triangle divided into three sections of yellow (upper), blue (lower right) and red (lower left). These colors were representative of the new dimension of armor which combined the swift speed and shock of cavalry, represented by cavalry's branch color of yellow, the blue of infantry, representative of the combat power of an infantryman and the red of artillery representing the awesome firepower of that branch – the three together to form a new combined arm of devastating effect. Many variants exist with the basic colors reversed or inverted.

Commanding General:

Brigadier General Samuel D. Rockenbach.

Brigadier General Samuel D. Rockenback, Commanding General of the Tank Corps. Chaumont, France, September, 1918. Courtesy National Archives.

Bibliography:

Eisenhower, Dwight D. *Tanks with Infantry*. Typescript, Fort Leavenworth, Kansas: The Command and General Staff School, 1932.

Rockenbach, Samuel D. *Operations of the Tank Corps A.E.F. with the First American Army at St. Mihiel and in the Argonne Sept. 11th to Nov. 11th 1918 and with the British E.F. Sept. 18th to November 1918*. Typescript: 1932.

United States Army, 301st Tank Battalion, Company "A". *A Co. Tank, "Treated 'em Rough" 301st Bn., Tank Corps*. Philadelphia: E.A. Wright, 1919.

Wilson, Dale E. *Treat 'em Rough: the Birth of American Armor, 1917-20*. Novato, California: Presidio Press, 1989.

Right: Thirteen year old Lee Gerard, a French boy who was adopted as a mascot of the 1st Tank Brigade. He was in action with the unit at St. Mihiel and the Argonne Forrest. He was gassed twice in action at Exermont. Photographed with his tank at Varennes en Argonne, October, 1918. Courtesy National Archives.

American Renault tanks of the 321st Company at the 302nd Tank Center Varennes en Argonne, France, October, 1918. Courtesy National Archives.

Sergeant Paul Postal of the 321st Tank Company, and his mascot "Mustard" which attached itself to the unit when it first went into action. Halloween, 1918. Courtesy National Archives.

Standard Tank Corps insignia machine embroidered on wool.

Another Tank Corps insignia, this one is silk sewn on wool.

A Tank Corps insignia made from three pieces of silk.

This lovely Tank Corps insignia is hand embroidered on wool.

Rare insignia of the 330th Tank Battalion of wool on wool construction.

United States Marine Corps

Official Portrait of Major General John A. Lejeune as the 13th Commandant of the United States Marine Corps, 1920-1929. Courtesy Military History Institute.

The Commandant of the Marine Corps, Major General George Barnett, was determined to field an all Marine division as part of the AEF, however General Pershing opposed such an idea and prevailed. Ultimately, the U.S. Marine Corps contribution to the AEF amounted to two Marine Brigades. 4th Marine Brigade served intact in the Army's 2nd Infantry Division. 5th Marine Brigade was dispersed throughout the Services of Supply in general support to their missions. Additionally, marines from the 5th Brigade were used as replacements for troops in the 4th Marine Brigade.

Organization:

4th Marine Brigade (2nd Infantry Division):

5th Marine Regiment
6th Marine Regiment
6th Machine Gun Battalion

Insignia:
See the 2nd Infantry Division listing in Chapter 3.

Commanding Generals:
Brigadier Charles Doyen, USMC, Brigadier James G. Harbord, USA, Brigadier John A. Lejeune, USMC, and Brigadier Wendell C. Neville, USMC.

5th Marine Brigade

11th Marine Regiment
13th Marine Regiment
5th Machine Gun Battalion

Brigadier Smedley D. Butler (3rd from left) and his staff, Bordeaux, France, December, 1918. Courtesy Military History Institute.

Band of the 5th Regiment, United States Marines at Menancourt, France, 1918. Note how the censor has removed the regiment's designation from the drum. Courtesy National Archives.

"The Gang" Some Marines from Company C, 13th Regiment, United States Marines. Courtesy Military History Institute.

"Marines in Action at the K of C" Private Carl E. Jepson of Company C, 13th Regiment, United States Marine Corps has written on the back of this post card "This is a sketch drawn by one of our boys while at Casino Des Lalice, Bordeaux. But he surely made the girls better looking than any I ever saw at those dances." Courtesy Military History Institute.

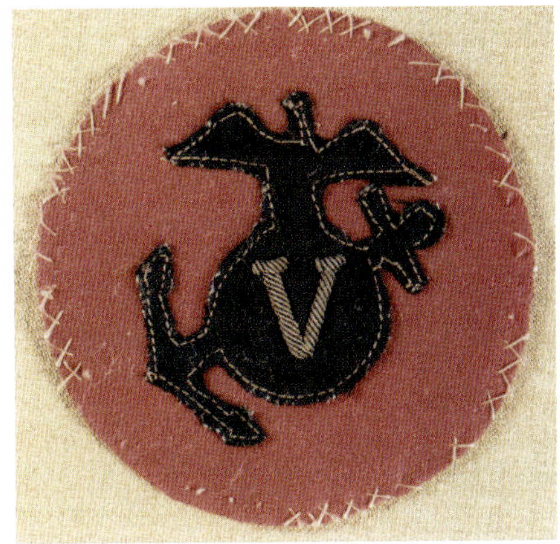

This insignia for the 5th Marine Brigade Headquarters uses wool on wool construction with gold bullion for the "V"

This insignia for the 5th Marine Brigade is on a shield shape not specified in the brigade insignia scheme.

Insignia:

The shoulder insignia of the 5th Marine Brigade was an eagle over globe and anchor, the traditional symbol of the United States Marine Corps, with a superimposed Roman numeral "V" alluding to the brigades numerical designation upon a background of red. The shape of the background indicated the unit and the color of the "V" further distinguished subordinate organizations within that element. Headquarters, 5th Marine Brigade, used a red circular background; the Brigade Headquarters used a gold "V" and the 5th Machine Gun Battalion a purple "V". The 11th Marine Regiment placed the insignia upon a square background with the Headquarters having a gold "V", 1st Battalion a red "V", 2nd Battalion a white "V", 3rd Battalion a blue "V", the Machine Gun Company a purple "V" and the Supply Company a green "V". The 13th Marine Regiment chose a diamond shape or "tipped" square background and used the same color scheme for their subordinate battalions and separate companies, as did the 11th Regiment.

Commanding Generals:

Brigadier General Eli K. Cole, Brigadier General Smedley D. Butler.[33]

Bibliography:

Brannen, Carl Andrew. *Over There: A Marine in the Great War.* College Station, Texas: Texas A & M University Press, 1996.

Butler, Smedley D. [Anne C. Venzon, Ed.] *General Smedley Darlington Butler: The letters of a Leatherneck, 1898-1931.* New York: Praeger, 1992.

Catlin, Albertus Wright. *With the Help of God and a few Marines.* Garden City, New York: Doubleday, Page & Company, 1919.

Clark, George B. *Devil Dogs: Fighting Marines of World War I.* Novato, California: Presidio Press, 1999.

Cowing, Kemper Frey. *"Dear Folks at Home" The glorious story of the United States Marines in France as told by their letters from the battlefield.* Boston: Houghton Mifflin Company, 1919.

Henry, Mark R. *U.S. Marine Corps in World War I, 1917-1918.* Oxford: Osprey, 1999.

Hewitt, Linda L. *Women Marines in World War I.* Washington, D.C.: United States Marine Corps, 1974.

History of the First Battalion, 5th Regiment, U.S. Marines, June 1917-August 1919, 2nd Division American Expeditionary Force. France: by the Battalion, 1919.

A felt on felt insignia for the 11th Marine Regiment Headquarters, denoted by the gold bullion "V".

History of the Third Battalion, Sixth Regiment, U.S. Marines, compiled from the official records kept by the battalion historian-and operations reports covering all of the engagements in which this battalion participated. Hillsdale, Michigan: Akers, Macritchie, and Hurlburt, 1919.

Bartlett, Merrill L. *Lejeune: A Marine's Life 1867-1942*. Columbia, South Carolina: University of South Carolina Press, 1991.

McClellan, Edwin North. *The United States Marine Corps in the World War*. Washington, D.C.: GPO, 1920.

Mackin, Elton E. *Suddenly we didn't want to die: Memoirs of a World War I Marine*. Novato, California: Presidio Press, 1993.

Stallings, Laurence. *The Doughboys: The story of the A.E.F. 1917-1918*. New York: Harper & Row, 1963.

Thomason, John W. *Fix Bayonets!* New York: Blue Ribbon Books, 1926.

Wise, Frederick May. *A Marine tells it to you, as told by Colonel Frederick May Wise to Meigs O. Frost*. New York: J.H. Sears & Company, Inc., 1929.

A time faded purple "V" denotes this felt on felt insignia as that of the 11th Marine Regiment Machine Gun Company.

This wool on wool insignia is for the 5th Machine Gun Battalion, denoted by the purple "V".

Another version of the 5th Machine Gun Battalion insignia. The purple die has faded to a very pale color in the "V" on this example.

This unusual insignia is for the 13th Marine Regiment. The use of gold bullion designates the Headquarters. In this example the "V" is bordered with blue which would denote the 3rd battalion. This may indicate Battalion Headquarters.

Colonel Neville, 5th Regiment of Marines at Damblain, France. Courtesy National Archives

Private Henry P. Levert of 16th Company, 5th Marines, 2nd Division who captured 78 privates and four German officers. Bois de Belleau, France, June 28, 1918. Courtesy National Archives

APPENDICES

Regular Army Division Composition
Major Subordinate Regiments

Division	Brigades	Infantry Regiment	MG Battalion	FA Regiment	Eng Regiment	APO
1	1, 2	16, 18, 26, 28	1, 2, 3	5, 6, 7	1	729
2	3, 4	9, 23, 5, 6	4, 5, 6	12, 15, 17	2	710
3	5, 6	4, 7, 30, 38	7, 8, 9	10, 18, 76	6	740
4	7, 8	39, 47, 58, 59	10, 11, 12	13, 16, 77	4	746
5	9, 10	60, 61, 6, 11	13, 14, 15	19, 20, 21	7	745
6	11, 12	51, 52, 53, 54	16, 17, 18	3, 11, 78	318	777
7	13, 14	34, 55, 56, 64	19, 20, 21	8, 79, 80	5	793
8	15, 16	8, 12, 13, 62	22, 23, 24	2, 81, 83	319	831
9	17, 18	45, 46, 67, 68	25, 26, 27	25, 26, 27	209	
10	19, 20	20, 41, 69, 70	28, 29, 30	28, 29, 30	210	
11	21, 22	17, 63, 71, 72	31, 32, 33	70, 71, 77	211	
12	23, 24	36, 42, 73, 74	34, 35, 36	34, 35, 36	212	
13	25, 26	1, 44, 75, 76	37, 38, 39	37, 38, 39	213	
14	27, 28	10, 40, 77, 78	40, 41, 42	40, 41, 42	214	
15	29, 30	43, 57, 79, 80	43, 44, 45	43, 44, 45	215	
16	31, 32	21, 32, 81, 82	46, 47, 48	46, 47, 48	216	
17	33, 34	5, 29, 83, 84	49, 50, 51	49, 50, 51	217	
18	35, 36	19, 35, 85, 86	52, 53, 54	52, 53, 54	218	
19	37, 38	2, 14, 87, 88	55, 56, 57	55, 56, 57	219	
20	39, 40	48, 50, 89, 90	58, 59, 60	58, 59, 60	220	

National Guard Division Composition

Major Subordinate Regiments

Division	Brigades	Infantry Regiment	MG Battalion	FA Regiment	Eng Regiment	APO
26	51, 52	101, 102, 103, 104	101, 102, 103	101, 102, 103	101	709
27	53, 54	105, 106, 107, 108	104, 105, 106	104, 105, 106	102	748
28	55, 56	109, 110, 111, 112	107, 108, 109	107, 108, 109	103	744
29	57, 58	113, 114, 115, 116	110, 111, 112	110, 111, 112	104	765
30	59, 69	117, 118, 119, 120	113, 114, 115	113, 114, 115	105	749
31	61, 62	121, 122, 123, 124	116, 117, 118	116, 117, 118	106	827
32	63, 64	125, 126, 127, 128	119, 120, 121	119, 120, 121	107	734
33	65, 66	129, 130, 131, 132	122, 123, 124	122, 123, 124	108	750
34	67, 68	133, 134, 135, 136	125, 126, 127	125, 126, 127	109	912
35	69, 70	137, 138, 139, 140	128, 129, 130	128, 129, 130	110	743
36	71, 72	141, 142, 143, 144	131, 132, 133	131, 132, 133	111	796
37	73, 74	145, 146, 147, 148	134, 135, 136	134, 135, 136	112	763
38	75, 76	149, 150, 151, 152	137, 138, 139	137, 138, 139	113	828
39	77, 78	153, 154, 155, 156	140, 141, 142	140, 141, 142	114	904
40	79, 80	157, 158, 159, 160	143, 144, 145	143, 144, 145	115	788
41	81, 82	161, 162, 163, 164	146, 147, 148	146, 147, 148	116	727
42	83, 84	165, 166, 167, 168	149, 150, 151	149, 150, 151	117	715

National Army Division Composition
Major Subordinate Regiments

Division	Brigades	Infantry Regiment	MG Battalion	FA Regiment	Eng Regiment	APO
76	151, 152	301, 302, 303, 304	301, 302, 303	301, 302, 303	301	773
77	153, 154	305, 306, 307, 308	304, 305, 306	304, 305, 306	302	739
78	155, 156	309, 310, 311, 312	307, 308, 309	307, 308, 309	303	755
79	157, 158	313, 314, 315, 316	310, 311, 312	310, 311, 312	304	771
80	159, 160	317, 318, 319, 320	313, 314, 315	313, 314, 315	305	756
81	161, 162	321, 322, 323, 324	316, 317, 318	316, 317, 318	306	791
82	163, 164	325, 326, 327, 328	319, 320, 321	319, 320, 321	307	742
83	165, 166	329, 330, 331, 332	322, 323, 324	322, 323, 324	308	762
84	167, 168	333, 334, 335, 336	325, 326, 327	325, 326, 327	309	905
85	169, 170	337, 338, 339, 340	328, 329, 330	328, 329, 330	310	789
86	171, 172	341, 342, 343, 344	331, 332, 333	331, 332, 333	311	916
87	173, 174	345, 346, 347, 348	334, 335, 336	334, 335, 336	312	906
88	175, 176	349, 350, 351, 352	337, 338, 339	337, 338, 339	313	795
89	177, 178	353, 354, 355, 356	340, 341, 342	340, 341, 342	314	761
90	179, 180	357, 358, 359, 360	343, 344, 345	343, 344, 345	315	770
91	181, 182	361, 362, 363, 364	346, 347, 348	346, 347, 348	316	776
92	183, 184	365, 366, 367, 368	349, 350, 351	349, 350, 351	317	766
93	185, 186	369, 370, 371, 372	None	None	None	
95	189	377, 378	359	None	320	
96	191, 192	381, 382, 383, 384	361, 362, 363	64, 65, 66	321	
97	193, 194	385, 386, 387, 388	365, 366	61, 62, 63	322	

Note: 94th Division and 98-100 Divisions were not allocated regiments prior to the end of the Occupation.

AEF Army Post Office Numbers

APO No.	Location/Unit
701	Sant-Nazaire, Loire-Inferieure Debarkation base, Base Section Number 1
702	Paris, Seine (29 Boulevard Bourdon)
703	Gondrecourt, Meuse (1st Army Infantry School), Services First Division
704	La Valdahon, Doubs (1st Army Artillery School) Services First Division
705	Bordeaux, Gironde, Debarkation Base, Base Section No. 2
705-A	Camp Genicart, Gironde, attached to 705
705-B	Paullac, Gironde, attached to 705
706	Chaumont, Haute-Marne, General Headquarters
707	Mailly, Aube
708	Nevers, Nievre (Intermediate Section Services of Supply)
709	26th Division
710	2nd Division (Via 712; Army of Occupation via 934)
711	Coetquidan, Morbihan, 26th Division instruction center
712	Is-sur- Tille, Cote d'Or, Major Distribution Center for Mobile Post Offices "Regulating Station"
713	Gievres, Loir-et-Cher, Main Depot war material, also Military Prison
713-A	Romorantin, Loir-et-Cher
714	Langres, Haute-Marne (Army Schools)
715	42nd Division (Via 712; Amy of Occupation via 934)
716	Brest, Finistere (Base Section No.5), Debarkation Base for Troops from Britain
717	Tours, Indre-et-Loir Headquarters (S.O.S.)
718	Saumur, Maine-et-Loire, (Cavalry School)
719	Haussimont, Marne
720	Bourbonne-Ies- Bains, Haute- Marne
721	Dijon, Cote d'Or
722	La Courtine, Creuse Instruction Center, Heavy Artillery
723	Clermont-Ferrand, Puyde-dome, Instruction Center Aviation
723-A	Chatel-Guyon, Puy-de-dome, Rehabilitation Center

AEF Army Post Office Numbers

APO No.	Location/Unit
724	Issoudon, Indre
725	Saint-Malxent, Deux-Sevres, Air Service facility
726	Blois, Loir-et-Cher
727	41st Division (St. Algnan, Loir-et-Cher)
729	1st Division (Used 703 and 704 at first. Via 712; Army of Occupation via 934)
730	Chatillon-sur-Seine, Cote d'Or
731	Neufchateau, Vosges
731-A	Colombey-les-Belles, Meurthe-et-Moselle, Air Service Facility
732	Vittel, Vosges
733	Angers, Maine-et-Loire
734	32nd Division (Via 712; Army of Occupation via 934)
734-A	Champlitte Haute-Saone
735	La Rochelle, Charente-Inferieure, Debarkation Base
735-A	Rochefort-Charente-Inferieure, Annex of 735
736	Aix-les-Bains, Savoie, Rehabilitation Center
736-A	Annecy, Haute-Savoie, Rehabilitation Center
736-B	Chamonix, Haute-Savoie, Rehabilitation Center
737	Cosne, Nievre
738	Chateauroux, Indre
739	77th Division (Via 712)
740	3rd Division (Via 712; Army of Occupation via 934)
741	Mehun, Cher
742	82nd Division (Via 712)
743	35th Division (Via 712)
744	28th Division (Via 712)
745	5th Division (Via 712; Army of Occupation via 936)
746	4th Division (Via 712; Army of Occupation via 936)
747	Sercy, Meuse; later at Commercy, Meuse, Mail transfer center to various points

AEF Army Post Office Numbers

APO No.	Location/Unit
748	27th Division (Via 702)
749	30th Division (Via 702)
750	33rd Division (Via 712)
751	Boulogne, Pas-de-Calais, Coal Supply Base
752	Marseille, Bouches-du-Rhone, Debarkation Base
752-A	Hyeres, Var, Rehabilitation Center
752-B	Cannes, Alpes Maritimes, Rehabilitation Center
752-C	Monte Carlo, Monaco, Rehabilitation Center
752-D	Menton, Alpes Maritimes, Rehabilitation Center
753	Limoges, Haute-Vienne
754	3rd Army Corps (via 712)
755	78th Division (Via 712; Army of Occupation via 934)
756	80th Division (Via 712; Army of Occupation via 934)
757	Nogent-en-Bassigny, Haute-Marne
758	Liffol-le-Grand, Vosges
759	1st Army Corps (Via 712)
760	Le Havre, Seine-Inferieure, Debarkation Base, Base Section No. 4
761	89th Division (Via 712; Army of Occupation via 920) (after the Armistice at Kylburg, Germany Via 930)
762	Le Mans, Sarthe (83rd Division Depot, Central Ammunition Depot and general staging area & depot staging area for Italy)
763	37th Division (Via 712)
764	Epinal, Vosges
765	29th Division (Via 712)
766	92nd Division (Via 712)
767	Nantes, Loire-Inferieure
768	Cherbourg, Manche, Coal Supply Base
769	5th Army Corps (Via 712)

AEF Army Post Office Numbers

APO No.	Location/Unit
770	90th Division (Via 712; Army of Occupation via 930)
771	79th Division (Via 712)
772	Verneuil, Nievre
772-A	Decize, Nievre
773	76th Division (St. Amand-Mt. Rond, Cher) (Depot Division)
774	1st Army Artillery Headquarters (Via 712)
775	4th Army Corps (Via 712) (After the Armistice at Kattenheim, Germany)
776	91st Division (Via 712)
777	6th Division (Via 712)
778	Le Courneau, Gironde
779	Meucon, Morbihan, Instruction Center Artillery
780	Mars-sur-Allier, Nievre
781	Vichy, Allier, Rehabilitation Center
782	Chateau- Thierry, Aisne
783	6th Army Corps (Via 712) (Army of Occupation via 936)
784	Toul, Meurthe-et-Moselle, Instruction Center
785	Allerey, Saone-et-Loire
786	Clamecy, Nievre
787	Azerailles, Meurthe-et-Moselle
788	40th Division (La Guerche, Cher)
789	85th Division (Pouilly, Nievre)
790	2nd Army Corps (Via 702)
791	81st Division (Via 712)
792	7th Army Corps (Via 712; Army of Occupation via 930)
793	7th Division (Via 712)
794	Perigueux, Dordogne
795	88th Division (Via 712)

AEF Army Post Office Numbers

APO No.	Location/Unit
796	36th Division (Via 712)
797	Orleans, Loiret
798	Meaves-sur-Loire, Nievre
799	Saint-Malo, Ille-et- Vilaine Coal Supply Base
800	Paris
827	31st Division (Loches) Merged with 762
828	38th Division (Reze) Merged with 762
831	8th Division, Did not arrive until after Armistice
901	Milano, Italy (Via 702)
902	Bourges, Cher. (Central Post Office)
903	Vitrey, Haute-Saone
904	39th Division (St. Florent)
905	84th Division (Neuvic, Dordogne) Merged with 762
906	87th Division (Pons, Charente-Infantry)
907	Bar-Ie-due, Meuse
908	Sougy, Nievre
909	Beaune, Cote-d'Or, Hospital and General Storage Depot
910	Chateau du Loir, Sarthe (Montrichard, Loire-et- Cher) (After the Armistice at Neuwied, Germany)
911	Libourne, Gironde
912	34th Division (Castres, Gironde) Merged with 762
913	Bar-sur-Aube, Aube, Instruction Center
914	Helppes, Meuse (Clermont-en-Argonne, Meuse)
915	Nancy, Meurthe-et-Moselle
916	86th Division, Merged with 762
917	Chatenay-sur-Seine, Seine-et-Marne
918	2nd Army Headquarters (Via 712)
919	Rimacourt, Haute-Marne
920	Chalons-sur-Marne, Marne

AEF Army Post Office Numbers

APO No.	Location/Unit
921	St.–Dizier, Haute-Marne
922	Angouleme, Charente
923	Grenoble, Isere, Rehabilitation Center
924	Le Blanc, Indre
925	Cour-Cheverny, Loir-et-Cher
926	Autun, Saone-et-Loire
	Army Post Offices set-up after the Armistice
927	3rd Army Headquarters (later at Coblenz, Germany)
928	La Valbonne, Alm
929	Joinville, Hayte-Marne (after the Armistice at Coblenz, Germany) Instruction Center
930	Treves, Germany
931	8th Army Corps
932	9th Army Corps
933	Nice, Alpes-Maritimes, Rehabilitation Center
934	Coblenz, Germany (General Headquarters)
935	Vannes, Morbihan
936	Thionville, Lorraine, Instruction Center
937	Pau, Basses-Pyenees, Rehabilitation Center
938	2nd Depot Division, 83rd Division
939	Savenay, Loire-Inferieure
940	Rennes, Ille-et-Vilaine
941	Nimes, Gard (Marseilles)
942	Vals-les-Bains, Ardeche (Marseilles) Rehabilitation Center
943	Lamadou-lesBains, Herault (Marseilles) Rehabilitation Center

AEF Army Post Office Numbers

APO No.	Location/Unit
944	Antwerp, Belgium, used as Base Center for supplying occupation troops
945	Conflans, Meurthe-et-Moselle, Instruction Center
946	Berlin, Germany
947	Le Fayet Saint Gervais Les Bains, Haute-Saone (Aix-les-Bains) Rehabilitation Center
948	Toulouse, Haute-Garonne, Rehabilitation Center
949	Montpellier, Herault, Rehabilitation Center
950	Rotterdam, Holland, used as Base Center for supplying occupation troops
951	Luxembourg, Luxembourg
952	Dun-sur-Meuse, Meuse, Instruction Center
953	Poitiers, Vienne, Rehabilitation Center
975	Peace Conference, Paris
	From: Theo. Van Dam, The Postal History of the AEF, 1917-1923

ENDNOTES

Chapter 1 Notes

1. Historical Section U.S. Army War College, *Order of Battle of the United States Land Forces in the World War: American Expeditionary Forces,* Washington, DC: United States Government Printing Office, 1931.pp. 1-26. This reference provides a complete listing of activities of and the directors of the staff.

2. *National Geographic*, Volume XXXVI, Number Six, p. 525.

3. Ibid, pp. 525-526.

4. OB pp. 27-80.

5. OB, p. 31.

6. *National Geographic*, p. 526.

7. Edward S. Farrow, *A Dictionary of Military Terms,* New York: Thomas Y. Crowell Company, 1918. p. 487.

8. Ibid, p. 503.

9. *National Geographic*, p. 526.

10. Major George S. Brady, History of the Ordnance Repair Shops, Mehun-sur-Yevre, France: Government Shop, 1919. pp. 3-5.

11. George O. Morgan and Mark Warren. *Shoulder Sleeve Insignia of the A.E.F. 1917-1919.* Keokuk, Iowa: Hill Printing Company, 1986., npn.

Chapter 2 Notes

1. John B. Wilson, *Armies, Corps, Divisions, and Separate Brigades*, Center or Military History: Washington, DC, 1993, p. 10.

2. Steve and Dave Johnson, *The Evolution of Shoulder Patches in the U.S. Army from 1918 to 2000*, a paper presented to members of the Association of American Insignia Collectors, 2000.

3. Ibid, p. 10.

4. OAEF, Vol II, pp. 82-84.

5. Wilson, p. 13.

6. Ibid, p. 13.

7. OAEF, Vol II, pp. 151-152.

8. Wilson, pp. 15-16.

9. OAEF, Vol II, p 171.

10. Wilson, 47.

11. Ibid, 48.

12. OAEF, Vol II, pp. 193-195.

13. Wilson, p. 51.

14. Ibid, p. 52.

15. OAEF, Vol II, pp. 220-221.

16. Wilson, p. 55.

17. Ibid, 56.

18. OAEF, Vol II, pp. 237-239.

19. Wilson, p. 59.

20. Ibid, p. 60.

21. OAEF, Vol II, pp. 268-269.

22. Wilson, p. 64.

23. Ibid, p. 64.

24. OAEF, Vol II, pp. 290-291.

25. Wilson, p. 67.

26. Ibid, p. 68.

27. OAEF, Vol II, pp. 316-317.

28. Wilson, p. 72.

29. Ibid, p. 72.

30. OAEF, Vol II, p. 329.

31. Wilson, p. 75.

32. OAEF, Vol II, p. 337.

33. Wilson, p. 78.

34. OAEF, Vol II, p. 341.

35. Ibid, pp. 381-384.

36. Ibid, pp. 385-389.

Chapter 3 Notes

1. Farrow. p. 20.

2. *Complete United States Infantry Guide*, Philadelphia, Pennsylvania: J.B. Lippincott Company, 1917. p 1658.

3. John B. Wilson, Maneuver and Firepower The Evolution of Divisions and Separate Brigades, Washington, DC: Center of Military History, 1998, p. 41.

4. Maurice de Castelbled, *History of the A.E.F.*, New York: Bookcraft, 1937, p. 61 and Wilson, p. 139.

5. Headquarters First Army General Orders 33, dtd November 9, 1918, paragraph I.

6. American Society of Military Insignia Collectors, *Cloth Patch of the U.S. Armed Forces*, American Society of Military Insignia Collectors: 1968, Divisions, pp 1., and George O. Morgan and Mark

Warren, *Shoulder Sleeve Insignia of the A.E.F. 1917-1919*, Hill Printing Company: Keokuk, 1986. No page number.

7. War Office United States of America, *Battle Participation of Organizations of the American Expeditionary Forces in France, Belgium and Italy 1917-1918,* Washington, DC: United States Government Printing Office, 1920, pp. 58-96.

8. OB, p. 2

9. Historical Branch of the War plans Division of the Army General Staff. *Brief Histories of Divisions, U.S. Army 1917-1918,* 1921.

10. AABE, pp. 515-517.

11. Castlebled, p. 64 and Wilson, p. 160.

12. World War I Veterans Survey Collection, number 93, Army Heritage Museum and U.S. Army Military History Institute, U.S. Army Heritage and Education Center, Carlisle, PA.

13. CP, pps 2-6.

14. 14,BPOAEF, 57-102.

15. OB, p. 22.

16. BHD, pp. 4-5.

17. AABE, p. 515-517.

18. Castlebled, p. 67 and Wilson, p. 178.

19. Wilson, p. 177 and National Geographic, Vol XXVI, Number 6, p.511. Hereafter, *National Geographic*.

20. Morgan, No page number.

21. BPOAEF, pp. 57-104.

22. OB, p. 44.

23. BHD, pp. 7-8.

24. AABE, pp. 515-517.

25. Castlebled, p. 69 and Wilson, p. 197.

26. Wilson, p. 195.

27. CP, pp. 7.

28. BPOAEF, pp. 61-105.

29. OB, p. 60.

30. BHD, pp. 10-11.

31. AABE, pp. 515-517.

32. Castlebled, p. 71 and Wilson, p. 210.

33. Wilson, p. 209, *National Geographic*, pp. 511, 514.

34. CP, pp. 8

35. BPOAEF, pp. 68-98.

36. OB, p. 76.

37. BHD, pp. 12-13

38. AABE, pp. 515-517.

39. Castlebled, p. 74 and Wilson, p. 220.

40. *National Geographic*, p. 514.

41. BPOAEF, pp. 74-92.

42. OB, p. 90.

43. BHD, p. 14.

44. AABE, pp. 515-517.

45. Castlebled, p. 76 and Wilson, p. 231.

46. Wilson, p. 228 and *National Geographic*, p. 514.

47. CP, pp. 9.

48. BPOAEF, p. 96.

49. OB, pp. 98-99.

50. BHD, p. 15.

51. AABE, pp. 515-517.

52. Castlebled, p. 78 and Wilson, p. 240.

53. Wilson, p. 239.

54. CP, pp. 10.

55. OB, p. 107.

56. BHD, pp. 16-17.

57. Ibid, p. 18.

58. CP, pp. 11.

59. BHD, p. 18.

60. Ibid, p. 18.

61. Ibid, p. 19.

62. Ibid, p. 19.

63. Ibid, p. 19.

64. Ibid, p. 20.

65. CP, pp. 12.

66. BHD, p. 20.

67. Ibid, p. 20.

68. Ibid, p. 21.

69. *National Geographic*, p. 514.

70. BHD, p. 21.

71. Ibid. p. 21.

72. Ibid, p. 22.

73. *National Geographic*, p. 514 and BHD, p. 22.

74. BHD, p. 22.

75. Ibid. 22.

76. Ibid, p. 23.

77. *National Geographic*, p. 514 and BHD, p. 23.

78. BHD, p. 23.

79. Ibid., p. 23.

80. JBW p. 64.

81. BHD, p. 24.

82. CP, pp. 14.

83. BHD, p. 24.

84. Ibid., p. 24.

85. Ibid, p. 25.

86. Ibid, p. 25.

87. Ibid., p. 25.

88. Ibid p. 26.

89. Ibid, p. 26.

90. Ibid., p. 26.

91. Ibid, p. 27.

92. *National Geographic*, p. 514 and BHD, p. 27.

93. BHD, p. 27.

94. Ibid., p. 27.

95. Ibid, p. 28.

96. CP, p. 15 and Morgan, No page number.

97. BHD, p. 28.

98. Ibid., p. 28.

99. Ibid, p. 29.

100. CP, p. 15

101. BHD, p. 29.

102. Ibid., p. 29.

Chapter 4 Notes

1. For details on the reorganization of the National Guard Divisions see JBW, Chapter 2.

2. CP; pp. 16-17 and Headquarters First Army, American Expeditionary Forces, France. General Orders No. 34, November 14, 1918, Paragraph I.

3. BPOAEF, pp. 58-103.

4. OB, pp. 114-115. Specific details of organization can be found in this reference.

5. BHD. pp. 30-31.
6. AABE, pp. 515-516.
7. CP, p. 17.
8. BPOAEF, pp. 63-90.
9. BHD, p. 32.
10. AABE, pp. 515-516.
11. Richard W. Smith, *Shoulder Sleeve Insignia of the U.S. Armed Forces 1941-1945*, np, 1981. pp. 34-35.
12. CP, pp. 17-18 and Headquarters First Army, American Expeditionary Forces, France. General Orders No. 33, November 14, 1918. paragraph I.
13. BPOAEF, pp. 59-98.
14. OB, pp. 140-141.
15. BHD, pp. 33-34.
16. AABE, pp. 515-516.
17. John A. Cutchins, *History of the Twenty-Ninth Division "Blue and Gray" 1917-1919*, Press of MacCalla & Co. Inc.: Philadelphia, 1921. p.16.
18. CP; p. 18 and GO34, Paragraph I.
19. BPOAEF, pp. 57-88.
20. OB, 153.
21. BHD, pp. 35-36.
22. AABE, pp. 515-516.
23. Castlebled, p.89.
24. Elmer A. Murphy, and Robert S. Thomas. *The Thirtieth Division in the World War*. Lepanto, AR: Old Hickory, 1936. p. 49. See also the General Order naming the division on pg. 48.
25. CP, pp. 18-19.
26. BPOAEF, pp. 57-106.
27. OB, p. 161.
28. BHD, pp. 37-38.
29. AABE, pp. 515-516.
30. Castlebled, p. 92.
31. CP, p. 19
32. OB, p. 171.
33. BHD, p. 39.
34. Castlebled, p 94.
35. CP, 20.
36. BPOAEF, p. 62-92.
37. OB, p. 176.
38. BHD, pp. 40-41.
39. AABE, pp. 515-516.
40. Castelbled. P.97
41. CP, 20-21
42. BPOAEF, p.63-104
43. OB, p. 193.
44. BHD, pp. 42-43.
45. AABE, pp. 515-516.
46. Castlebled. p.99.
47. CP, p. 21-22.
48. OB, p. 205.
49. BHD, p. 44.
50. Castlebled. p.101.
51. CP, p. 22-25; and Wilson, p. 339.
52. Morgan, npn.
53. BPOAEF, pp. 76-97.
54. OB, p. 211.
55. BHD, pp. 45-46.
56. AABE, pp. 515-516.
57. Clastlebled, p.103.
58. CP, pp. 25-26.
59. BPOAEF, p. 77.
60. OB, p. 223.
61. BHD, pp. 47-48.
62. AABE, pp. 515-516.
63. Castlebled, p.105.
64. CP, pp. 26-27..
65. BPOAEF, pp. 66-104.
66. OB, p. 231.
67. BHD, pp. 49-50
68. AABE, pp. 515-516.
69. Castlebled, p.107; William J. Watt, The Story of the 38th Infantry "Cyclone" Division, Indiana National Guard. Typescript, n.p., n.d.; and CP, 27-28.
70. Wilson, p. 343; and CP 27-28.
71. OB, p. 241.
72. BHD, p. 51.
73. Castlebled, p.109.
74. CP, p. 28..
75. BPOAEF, p. 82.
76. OB, p. 247.
77. BHD, p. 52.
78. Castlebled, p. 111.
79. Wilson, p. 351; and CP, p. 29.
80. BPOAEF, pp. 99-100.
81. OB, p. 255.
82. BHD, p. 53.
83. AABE, pp 515.
84. CP, pp. 29-31..
85. BPOAEF, pp. 59-81.
86. OB, p. 263.
87. BHD, p. 54.
88. AABE, pp. 515-516.
89. Henry J. Riley. *Americans All: The Rainbow at War: Official History of the 42nd Rainbow Division in the World War*. Columbus, Ohio: The F.J. Heer Printing Company, 1936. pp. 26-28.
90. GO34, Paragraph II.
91. CP, p. 31.
92. OB, pp. 276-287.
93. BHD, pp. 55-56.
94. AABE, pp.515.

Chapter 5 Notes

1. Castlebled, p. 118.
2. CP, p. 34.
3. OB, p. 289.
4. BHD, p. 57.
5. AABE, pp. 515-516.
6. Castlebled, p. 120.
7. CP, p. 35.
8. BPOAEF, pp. 64-105.
9. OB, p. 297.
10. BHD, pp. 58-59.
11. AABE, pp. 515-516.

12. Castlebled, p. 123.
13. CP, pp. 36-37.
14. BPOAEF, pp. 69-99.
15. OB, p. 309.
16. BHD, pp. 60-61.
17. AABE, pp. 515-517.
18. Castlebled, pp. 125.
19. CP, pp. 37.
20. BPOAEF, pp. 79-104.
21. OB, p. 319.
22. BHD, pp. 62-63
23. AABE, pp. 515-517.
24. Castlebled, p. 127.
25. CP, p. 38.
26. BPOAEF, pp. 69-95.
27. OB, p. 329.
28. BHD, pp. 64-65.
29. AABE, pp. 515-517.
30. Castlebled, p.130.
31. *National Geographic*, p. 501.
32. William Keller & Kurt Keller, *United States Shoulder Patches and Related Insignia World War I to Korea, 41st to 106th Division*, Schiffer: Atglen, Pennsylvania, 2002., p. 100 and CP p. 40.
33. BPOAEF, pp. 79-97.
34. OB, p. 339.
35. BHD, pp. 66-68.
36. AABE, pp. 515-517.
37. Castlebled, p. 132.
38. CP, 42.
39. BPOAEF pp. 69-99.
40. OB, p. 347.
41. BHD, pp. 67-69.
42. AABE, pp. 515-517.
43. Castlebled, p. 134.
44. Kevin Sindle, *The Lion of St. Mark*, Trading Post, American Society of Military Insignia Collectors, Volume LI, Number 4. , p. 2.
45. BPOAEF, p. 85.
46. OB, p. 359.
47. BHD, pp. 70-71.
48. AABE, pp. 515-517.
49. Castlebled, p. 137.
50. CP, pp. 44-45.
51. OB, p. 367.
52. BHD, p. 72.
53. Castlebled, p. 139.
54. CP, p. 46.
55. OB, p. 381.
56. BHD, p. 73.
57. AABE, p. 515.
58. Castlebled, p 141.
59. CP, p. 46.
60. OB, p. 359.
61. BHD, p. 74.
62. Castlebled, p. 143.
63. CP, p. 47.
64. OB, p. 387.
65. BHD, p. 75.
66. Castlebled, p. 145.
67. CP, p. 48.
68. BPOAEF, p. 88.
69. OB, p. 393.
70. BHD, p. 76.
71. AABE, pp. 515-517.
72. Castlebled, p. 147.
73. Keller & Keller, pp. 158-163.
74. BPOAEF, pp. 69-93.
75. OB, p. 401.
76. BHD, pp. 77-78.
77. AABE, pp. 515-517.
78. Castlebled, p. 149.
79. CP, pp. 52-53.
80. BPOAEF, pp. 69-106.
81. OB, p. 409.
82. BHD, pp. 79-80.
83. AABE, pp. 515-517.
84. Castlebled, p. 151.
85. CP, p. 53.
86. BPOAEF, pp. 66-81.
87. OB, p. 419.
88. BHD, pp. 81-82.
89. AABE, pp. 515-517.
90. Castlebled, p. 154.
91. CP, pp. 54-55.
92. African-Americans in the Great War, Military Images, Volume XXVII, Number 4., p. 9.
93. BPOAEF, pp. 81-95.
94. OB, p. 429.
95. BHD, pp. 83-84.
96. AABE, pp. 515-517.
97. Castlebled, p. 156.
98. *Military Images*, p. 18.
99. CP, pp. 56-57.
100. BPOAEF, pp. 81-104.
101. OB, p. 359.
102. BHD, pp. 95-97.
103. AABE, p. 515.
104. CP, p. 57.
105. Ibid, p. 58.
106. OB, p. 359.
107. BHD, p. 88.
108. Ibid, p. 89.
109. CP, p. 59.
110. BHD, p. 90.
111. Ibid, p. 91.
112. CP, p. 59.
113. BHD, p. 92.
114. Ibid, p. 93.

Chapter 6 Notes

1. AABE, p. 504.
2. OB Vol 1, p. 404.
3. Ibid, p. 414.
4. Ibid. p. 402.

5. Farrow, p. 54.
6. OB, p. 136.
7. Ibid, p. 408.
8. Ibid, p. 411.
9. Ibid, p. 415..
10. Ibid, p. 418.
11. Ibid, p. 328.
12. Ibid, p. 409.
13. Ibid, p. 412.
14. Ibid, p. 416.
15. Ibid, p. 326.
16. Ibid, p. 406.
17. Ibid, p. 419.
18. Ibid, p. 286.
19. Ibid, p. 417.
20. Ibid, p. 398.
21. Ibid, pp. 407, 410.
22. Ibid, p. 420.
23. Ibid, p. 228.
24. Ibid, p. 136.

25. Andrew Kershaw, editor, *The First War Planes*, London: BPC Publishing, Ltd., 1972, p. 41-44.

26. J. Duncan Campbell, *Aviation Badges and Insignia of the United States Army 1913-1946*, Harrisburg: The Triangle Press, 1977, pp. 41-42.

27. This succinct summary of operations of the Aero Squadrons in the war was compiled from a War Department summary provided for Insignia of the A.E.F. Aero Squadrons, *Daughters of the American Revolution Magazine*, Vol LIV, No 3, March, 1920. We have included these verbatim.

28. *National Geographic*, p. 526.

29. OB, p. 252.

30. AABE, p. 492.

31. William K. Emerson, *Encyclopedia of United States Army Insignia and Uniforms*, Norman and London: University of Oklahoma Press, 1996, p.p. 206-210.

32. Souvenir Edition for the 20th Engineers (Forestry), American Forestry, Vol 25, No. 306, June 1919, pp.1092-1110.

33. Anne C. Venzon, ed., *The United States in the First World War*, New York: Garland Publishing, Inc., 1995, p. 741.

BIBLIOGRAPHY

Primary Sources: First person Accounts, Manuscripts, Letters, Diaries, Speeches, Interviews and Other Material.

Brief Histories of Divisions, U.S. Army 1917-1918. A study prepared by the Historical Branch of the War Plans Division of the Army General Staff, 1921.

Johnson Steve and Dave. The Evolution of Shoulder Patches in the U.S. Army from 1918 to 2000, a paper presented to members of the Association of American Insignia Collectors, 2000.

Headquarters First Army, American Expeditionary Forces, France. General Orders Number 33, dated November 9, 1918.

Headquarters First Army, American Expeditionary Forces, France. General Orders Number 34, dated November 14, 1918.

Headquarters First Army, American Expeditionary Forces, France. General Orders Number 45, dated December 14, 1918.

World War I Veterans Survey Collection, Army Heritage Museum and US Army Military History Institute, US Army Heritage and Education Center, Carlisle, Pennsylvania.

Published Sources (Books).

American Battle Monuments Commission, *American Armies and Battlefields in Europe,* Washington, DC: U.S. Government Printing Office, 1938.

Brady, George S., Major. *History of the Ordnance Repair Shops, Mehun-sur-Yevre.* France: Government Shop, 1919.

Campbell, J. Duncan. *Aviation Badges and Insignia of the United States Army 1913-1946.* Harrisburg, PA: The Triangle Press, 1977.

Complete United States Infantry Guide. Philadelphia, Pennsylvania: J.B. Lippincott Company, 1917.

Cutchins, John A. *History of the Twenty-Ninth Division "Blue and Gray" 1917-1919.* Philadelphia: Press of MacCalla & Co. Inc., 1921.

Historical Section U.S. Army War College, *Order of Battle of the United States Land Forces in the World War: American Expeditionary Forces: Divisions,* Washington, DC: United States Government Printing Office, 1931.

Castelbled, Maurice de. *History of the A.E.F.* New York: Bookcraft, 1937.

Emerson, William K. *Encyclopedia of United States Army Insignia and Uniforms,* Norman and London: University of Oklahoma Press, 1996.

Farrow, Edward S. *A Dictionary of Military Terms.* New York: Thomas Y. Crowell Company, 1918.

Keller, William & Keller, Kurt. United States Shoulder Patches and Related Insignia World War I to Korea, 1st Division to 40th Division, Atglen, Pennsylvania: Schiffer:, 2002.

Keller, William & Keller, Kurt. *United States Shoulder Patches and Related Insignia World War I to Korea, Army Groups, Armies and Corps,* Atglen, Pennsylvania: Schiffer:, 2004.

Keller, William & Keller, Kurt. *United States Shoulder Patches and Related Insignia World War I to Korea, 41st to 106th Division,* Atglen, Pennsylvania: Schiffer:, 2002.

The Medical Department of the United States in the World War, 16 Volumes. Washington, DC: Government Printing Office, 1923.

Morgan, George O. and Warren, Mark. *Shoulder Sleeve Insignia of the A.E.F. 1917-1919.* Keokuk, Iowa: Hill Printing Company, 1986.

Murphy, Elmer A. and Thomas, Robert S. *The Thirtieth Division in the World War.* Lepanto, Arkansas Old Hickory, 1936.

Riley, Henry J. *Americans All: The Rainbow at War: Official History of the 42nd Rainbow Division in the World War.* Columbus, Ohio: The F.J. Heer Printing Company, 1936.

Schulz, Paul, Otoupalik, Hayes, and Gordon, Dennis, World War One Collectors Handbook, 2 Volumes. np., 1988.

Smith, Richard W. *Shoulder Sleeve Insignia of the U.S. Armed Forces 1941-1945,* np, 1981.

United States Army in the World War 1917-1919, 17 Volumes. Washington, DC: Center of Military History, 1988.

United States Army in the World War, 1917-1919, Organization of the American Expeditionary Forces, 3 Volumes, Washington, DC: Center of Military History, 1988.

Van Dam, Theo. *The Postal History of the AEF, 1917-1923,* State College, PA: American Philatelic Society, 1980.

Venzon, Anne C. editor, *The United States in the First World War,* New York: Garland Publishing, Inc., 1995.

War Office United States of America, *Battle Participation of Organizations of the American Expeditionary Forces in France, Belgium and Italy 1917-1918*. Washington, DC: United States Government Printing Office, 1920.

Watt, William J. *The Story of the 38th Infantry "Cyclone" Division, Indiana National Guard*. Typescript, n.p., n.d.

Wilson, John B. *Armies, Corps, Divisions, and Separate Brigades*, Washington, DC: Center or Military History, 1993.

Wilson, John B. *Maneuver and Firepower The Evolution of Divisions and Separate Brigades*, Washington, DC: Center or Military History, 1998.

Magazines, Periodicals, Pamphlets, and Miscellany

American Decorations and Insignia of Honor and Service, National Geographic, Volume XXXVI, Number Six.

American Society of Military Insignia Collectors, *Cloth Patch of the U.S. Armed Forces: Divisions*. American Society of Military Insignia Collectors: 1968.

Kershaw, Andrew, editor, *The First War Planes*, London: BPC Publishing, Ltd., 1972.

African-Americans in the Great War, Military Images, Volume XXVII, Number 4.

Shepard, Nelson M. Insignia of the A.E.F. Squadrons, Daughters of American Revolution Magazine, Volume LIV, Number 3.

Sindle, Kevin, The Lion of St. Mark, Trading Post, American Society of Military Insignia Collectors, Volume LI, Number 4.

Souvenir Edition for the 20th Engineers (Forestry), American Forestry, Vol 25, No. 306, June 1919

Victorious Doughboys march through the Arc de Triomphe in Paris following the Armistice. Courtesy National Archives

NOTES

NOTES

NOTES